W9-AGH-481

LOOK FOR!
— Books
— Booklets
— Cassettes
↓ Discs
— Videos
— Maps
— Patterns
— Charts
in back

Beginning Japanese

YOUR PATHWAY TO DYNAMIC LANGUAGE ACQUISITION

Michael L. Kluemper, Lisa Berkson, Nathan Patton, Nobuko Patton

TUTTLE PUBLISHING
Tokyo • Rutland, Vermont • Singapore

We would like to dedicate this book to the neverending support, inspiration, and patience of our families and friends, sensei and students—past and present.

Special thanks for the generous cooperation given by Heizaburou and Natsuko Ebata, and Hisaho Onodera in recording the audio. Special acknowledgement of Yuko Betsukawa, Rebecca Evans, Fumiko Kikuchi, Kaori Miyashita, John Sparks, Akiko and Calder Miyamoto, Manami Imaoka, Amy Noblitt, Paul Gatchell, friends in Omonogawa, and the many others who have assisted in so many ways in this endeavor.

Published by Tuttle Publishing, an imprint of Periplus Editions (HK) Ltd., with editorial offices at 364 Innovation Drive, North Clarendon, Vermont 05759 U.S.A. and at 61 Tai Seng Avenue #02-12, Singapore 534167.

Illustrations by Boya Sun and Keiko Murakami

Library of Congress Control Number: 2009933853

ISBN 978-0-8048-4056-9 (paperback edition)
ISBN 978-0-8048-4132-0 (hardcover edition)

Distributed by

North America, Latin America & Europe
Tuttle Publishing
364 Innovation Drive
North Clarendon, VT 05759-9436 U.S.A.
Tel: 1 (802) 773-8930
Fax: 1 (802) 773-6993
info@tuttlepublishing.com
www.tuttlepublishing.com

Japan
Tuttle Publishing
Yaekari Building, 3rd Floor
5-4-12 Osaki Shinagawa-ku Tokyo 141 0032
Tel: (81) 3 5437-0171
Fax: (81) 3 5437-0755
tuttle-sales@gol.com

Asia Pacific
Berkeley Books Pte. Ltd.
61 Tai Seng Avenue #02-12 Singapore 534167
Tel: (65) 6280-1330
Fax: (65) 6280-6290
inquiries@periplus.com.sg
www.periplus.com

First edition
12 11 10   5 4 3 2 1

Printed in Singapore

TUTTLE PUBLISHING® is a registered trademark of Tuttle Publishing, a division of Periplus Editions (HK) Ltd.

To the Learner

Welcome to *Beginning Japanese*. This first step on your journey to Japanese language proficiency will set you well on your way. This book will teach you how to:

- read and write all hiragana and katakana
- read and recognize 148 kanji
- use Japanese to describe basic details of your own life, including family, school, hobbies, likes and dislikes, and daily activities
- answer questions in Japanese about your daily life with low-level to mid-level fluency
- use Japanese to ask a friend about his/her family and daily life, and invite them to join you in an activity such as shopping
- describe a person or a situation using a variety of adjectives in Japanese
- skim and scan written Japanese passages for important content and meaning
- respond to short written communications, such as e-mail messages, in Japanese
- make a short oral presentation in Japanese about a hobby or a recent event
- talk at a basic level about Japanese geography, history, and culture

Be sure your seatbelt is on, and get ready to enjoy the journey of a lifetime as you learn this exciting language and experience the culture from which it comes!

The Authors

Contents

Goals and Guidelines

	Performance Goals	Language Points	Culture	Kanji
Chapter 1: Introductions and Getting Started	• pronounce Japanese vowels and syllabary • recognize the difference between Chinese characters and hiragana • introduce yourself politely • make simple statements and questions • use greetings appropriately • understand classroom commands	• particles は, か • は〜です statements • relative pronouns • じゃ ありません	• showing respect • name order	木 本 日 東 京 語 私 父 母 気 元 人 休
Chapter 2: Family and Friends in Tokyo	• describe your family and the families of others • count up to 100 and count objects • specify relative location of people and objects • make polite requests and offers	• particles の, と, を, and も • counters • verbs of existence: あります/います • use of ください/どうぞ	• lucky and unlucky numbers • Tokyo neighbor-hoods	何 家 兄 姉 弟 妹 一 二 三 四 五 六 七 八 九 十 百 犬
Chapter 3: The Ins and Outs of Schools in Japan	• talk about daily class schedules • tell time • make contrasting statements using DEMO • engage in small talk about the weather	• negative verb endings • particles を, に, and で (*by means of*), and the sentence ending particles よ, ね and ねえ • use of the conjunction でも (*but*)	• the Japanese school system and calendar • school club activities • Shinto shrine torii	高 小 中 大 学 校 年 先 生 山 英 国 音 楽 今 分 書 寺 時 門 間 下 暑 寒 神 社 風 友
Chapter 4: People and Places of Nagasaki	• inquire about nationality • discuss languages spoken in various countries • talk about eating and drinking • use the verbs for going, coming, and returning	• non-past and non-past negative of verbs • the て form of verbs • particle で for place of action • particles へ and に for place of direction	• Tokugawa period • geography of Kyushu • foreign trade and influence in early 17th-century Japan	言 外 話 食 飲 物 行 来 帰 見 聞
Chapter 5: Time in Nara	• make affirmative and negative past tense statements and questions • use a variety of time and date words to talk about past, present, and future schedules • state your birth date	• affirmative and negative past tense of verbs • particle に to indicate a specific time • the から - まで pattern	• Nara, its history, and historic sites • imperial reign periods and dating • Japanese festivals and holidays	午 後 良 月 火 水 金 土 曜 千 末 毎 電 達 週

Please visit TimeForJapanese.com for detail on how *Beginning Japanese* aligns with the standards set forth by organizations such as the Japanese National Standards Task Force, ACTFL (American Council on the Teaching of Foreign Languages), and others.

	Performance Goals	**Language Points**	**Culture**	**Kanji**
Chapter 6: Body Parts and Clothing in Hiraizumi	• name basic body parts and describe someone's physical features • inquire about someone's health • request, grant, and deny permission • talk about wearing clothes and accessories • ask what someone is doing and respond with a series of actions	• adverbs • the ~て form of verbs • particle で (*by means of*) • the ~て います (present progressive) form of verbs	• geography, history, and products of Hiraizumi, Iwate Prefecture, and Tohoku • Yoshitsune and his retainer Benkei • Chinese and Japanese medicine	体 目 口 耳 手 足 心 持 待 強 平 和 低 太 医 者 薬 着
Chapter 7: Hobbies in the Ancient City of Heian-kyou	• discuss your hobbies, and your likes and dislikes • state what you are good at and what you are poor at • point out different colors • state your opinion using "I think..."	• the particle が • dictionary form • negative adverbs • "...と 思います"	• Heian period culture • Murasaki Shikibu and *The Tale of Genji* • waka	花 池 趣 味 事 好 上 色 白 黒 赤 青 歌 思
Chapter 8: Adjectives in Amanohashidate	• describe objects and scenes using い and な adjectives in the present, past and negative conjugation	• adjective conjugation	• geography and history of Amanohashidate • Japanese folk tales, including *Urashima Tarou* • onomatopoeic words	美 長 短 海 安 悪 面 天 立 昔 々 有 広 島
Chapter 9: Purchasing and Giving Gifts in Edo	• go shopping, ask prices, and purchase goods • understand and use common shopping expressions • talk about what you gave someone, and what sort of present you received	• noun + SHIMASU expressions • もっと (comparative) • use of の to replace nouns • verbs of giving and receiving	• hanga and ukiyoe • Hokusai and other famous ukiyoe artists • Japanese bathing rituals • gift-giving practices	買 売 店 万 全 部 円 暗 明
Chapter 10: Meeting Basho in Kanazawa	• talk about and predict the weather • politely invite a friend to do something • accept, or decline, an invitation • say that you want, or don't want, to do something • note that something has not happened yet • talk about bringing someone, or taking something, somewhere	• DESHO • the ~たい form • まだ + negative verb	• history and attractions of Kanazawa • the poet Basho • hanami (cherry blossom viewing) • the song "Sakura"	春 夏 秋 冬 石 使 作 当 桜

Introduction

In *Beginning Japanese* some of the characters you meet are learning Japanese along with you. You will be able to interact with them, learn what they learn, and have a great time exploring Japanese language, history, and culture. The first person that you will meet is Kiara. She's about to arrive in Japan from the U.S. and will be attending a Japanese high school for the next year, maybe longer. That is, until a sudden change of plans occurs.

Many of you will be using this text to study a foreign language for the first time. Some of you already speak one or two other languages. Either way, as you go through this text, you will find some hints and techniques that will help the learning process. You might have heard people say that Japanese is a hard language to learn. The authors and characters of this textbook say that if you are interested in Japan and the Japanese language, Japanese will definitely be the easiest language for you to learn! It is going to take some time before you can consider yourself fluent, but the doors that are about to open for you will reveal fantastic treasures. Be ready for them!

This series is designed to help students take their language learning experience to the next level: *Beginning Japanese* will help you improve your understanding of the language and how this language, specific to this culture, developed and exists today. Historical aspects of Japan, its people, traditions, society, and culture are embedded into this series. This is done to give you, the learner, a clearer understanding of this unique language and the contexts in which it is used.

Using This Book

Anyone who experiences a new language can testify that you don't have to be fluent in a language to express yourself on a basic level or to understand general meaning. Conversations about when a train leaves, where the restroom is, or how much a t-shirt costs happen every day between people who do not share a common language. If the person speaking and the person listening are good communicators, information can be shared and understood. In fact, this sort of exchange often makes for a memorable experience. Skill with another language, however, allows you to delve much deeper into a culture and to more easily make new friends across cultures.

Beginning Japanese is the first step in a language learning series designed to give you a more natural experience in Japanese language acquisition. Aspects of this book and the accompanying web and audio resources include language beyond what is expected of you at any given point in your learning process. Through exposure to words, characters, sights, and sounds, you will come to have a deeper understanding not only of Japanese language, but also of its culture, sights, sounds, and history.

This series is different from other learning sources in that:

1. KANJI characters (non-phonetic) are taught from the first lessons. In traditional materials, often students are expected to master the two phonetic "alphabets," *hiragana* and *katakana*, prior to the introduction of kanji.

    The kanji characters include FURIGANA, phonetic guides below each kanji to help you read the new characters and to give assistance where needed. To challenge yourself, don't just rely on the furigana guides; rather, consciously cover up the furigana readings with your hand or a piece of paper while reading. This will help your reading skills improve enormously. Eventually, the furigana disappear from the text; if you have been weaning yourself off of them as you progress, you will not even miss them and will realize that it's much easier to read Japanese without this aid. For many, learning to read kanji and exploring ways to use them and learn vocabulary through them can be a very enjoyable part of the process.

2. Visuals are presented in a manga format and in photographs. The manga bring the characters in the story to life and help you interact with historical figures for a contextualized learning experience on a wide range of topics. The photographs provide authentic exposure to what Japan really "looks" like. They provide a source for conversation and contribute to your mastery of the vocabulary.

3. An engaging story is woven through the pages of the book and website. The story provides information about Japan's culture, history, and historical figures, and it offers a level of language learning that increases in difficulty as your language skills improve. This increase in difficulty challenges you and offers opportunities for practicing real-life skills.

Learning Strategies

For Western language speakers, the study of Japanese is generally a more abstract process than learning a European language. It may be difficult, at first, to make any intuitive leaps in your learning. Therefore, it is important to find constructive ways to organize the new information you will be learning. This organization process is useful not just for learning Japanese, but when studying any new language or content area.

Since new material, including language, can be learned in a variety of ways, it is crucial that you, the learner, find the most effective method for you to memorize vocabulary and other unfamiliar information. Try to use as many of your senses as you can. For example, writing down and saying out loud what you write lets you use more than one sense: you are moving your hand, you are seeing the words on paper, you are speaking, and you are hearing. Learning strategies like this will help you retain the information in a more intuitive way and speed up your learning so that you can naturally use new vocabulary and grammatical structures in your repertoire of linguistic tools. Here are some ideas for studying material effectively and producing it from memory when needed.

- Figure out what type of learner you are: visual, auditory, kinesthetic, or verbal. Then make your strengths work for you.
- Use flashcards. Visual/verbal flashcards for the vocabulary in this book can be downloaded on the TimeForJapanese.com website.
- Print out and use the kanji and vocabulary learning charts found on TimeForJapanese.com.
- Type your vocabulary words in Japanese, including their English meanings. Typing a word in Japanese helps you better understand unique Japanese language characteristics such as long and short vowels and double consonants.

Graphic Organizers

Use graphic organizers to organize your new Japanese vocabulary in different ways. When you place linguistic parts into different sorts of categories, it helps you remember vocabulary and sentence patterns.

Again, it is important for you as a beginning Japanese learner to find ways of organizing new material so that it is easier to incorporate into your mind, so that you can use words, kana, and kanji whenever you need them. A few graphic organizers you might try include grouping by:

- first, end, or overall sounds
- a-i-u-e-o order
- part of speech (verbs, adjectives, nouns, etc.)
- meaning (things that move, that you eat, that you drink, that are blue, etc.)
- mapping (making a story map on paper)
- making charts or graphs
- making up songs

Visit TimeForJapanese.com regularly for additional downloads, practice exercises, review games, and other activities. Be sure to send in ideas which you've found particularly helpful in your study, as well.

The Components

Beginning Japanese is made up of several component parts designed to assist you in gaining proficiency in the four aspects of language: speaking, listening, reading, and writing. Each chapter includes:

■ 漫画 Japanese Comics
MANGA

Each section begins with a manga. These manga generally include a dialogue or conversation between characters designed to help give context to the conversations through visual clues. The dialogue is designed to be adaptable to situations that you may experience in your own Japanese language learning.

■ 会話 Dialogue
KAI WA

The dialogue from the manga characters is presented in this component as straight text, allowing you to view the conversation from a more literary perspective.

■ 単語 New Words
TAN GO

Vocabulary words are largely introduced through images to help you associate a particular word with an image suggestive of that word's meaning. This way, you are not simply "translating" words as you say the Japanese words and sentences, but rather your brain is directly associating the Japanese word with the image. Using this technique, you are learning language in a more natural way and less as a "foreign" language.

■ 漢字 Written Characters from China
KAN JI

Beginning with Chapter 1, *Beginning Japanese* includes some of the kanji that you will see in authentic Japanese writing. For example, you will learn kanji such as these: 日本, the two kanji that mean "Japan."

Pronunciation sub-scripts (guides below) rather than super-scripts (guides above) are provided to help you develop your reading skills. Commonly used kanji characters, many of which originated as pictograms, are specifically taught to you from the first lesson. As you advance through this series, you will learn how and when it is appropriate to use kanji, and strategies to help you guess at their meaning from context. The way that written Japanese is used continually changes. As is the case with English and other languages today, much written Japanese is created with the aid of electronic devices, including computers and cell phones. *Beginning Japanese* takes these technological developments and changes into account as far as expectations for passive and active kanji knowledge and reading abilities are concerned. The degree to which you are required to use kanji increases gradually as you progress through the series. Written workbook exercises and tests where kanji are to be produced will include kanji banks where needed, allowing you to choose the necessary characters. Kanji that you see and write often will become very familiar to you, while you will probably refer to the kanji banks for those kanji less commonly used by you personally. Gradually, though, as you work your way through *Beginning Japanese*, you will be able to produce these kanji from memory.

Each kanji is introduced first by a large-sized example, with the stroke order numbered. In the box just to the right of this large example is a guide to common pronunciations. This includes the most common and useful pronunciations of kanji as well as others, which might prove to help you learn the kanji and vocabulary better. Kanji pronunciations can vary depending on the context in which the kanji is used. The first examples are written in katakana (ex.: ホン). These pronunciations are called ON-YOMI, or "Chinese readings." They are based on the original pronunciations of the kanji
HON

used in medieval China. The pronunciations following the on-yomi are written in hiragana and are known as the KUN-YOMI, or the pronunciations native to Japanese (ex.: もと).
MOTO

To the right of the pronunciation guides the kanji is shown stroke by stroke. Learning and using the proper stroke order when writing is very important as it later will help you more clearly understand new kanji and how to use a kanji dictionary when you achieve that level in your studies.

The box below the pronunciation offers some common usages of that kanji in vocabulary words. The most efficient way to study kanji is in the context of vocabulary words where they appear, as opposed to studying kanji independently of existing vocabulary.

The final portion of each kanji section is a short story or mnemonic device to help you remember the kanji. We encourage you to think of even better and more creative ways to help remember each kanji. Please share your ideas with others and on TimeForJapanese.com so learning kanji can become even more fun and creative.

The workbook pages contain writing practice exercises that will help you fix each kanji into your memory. Of course, you are welcome to do more kanji writing practice on your own—all over your notebook, for instance, or when you write notes to your friends!

■ 言葉の探索 Language Detection
KOTOBA NO TANSAKU

Unlike many other language books, this component is not limited to grammatical explanations. It also offers contextual, social, and cultural cues for how, when, and why the words and phrases being introduced are used. This component also includes several examples of each pattern.

■ 自習 Self Check
JI SHUU

This component is designed as a quick-check test for you to complete orally by yourself, to confirm your understanding of the patterns covered in the Language Detection section above. Doing this check orally allows you not only to read Japanese, but also to say and hear the words, helping you better learn the pattern being practiced. Examine the tasks and test yourself. If you are unsure of some point, reexamine the Language Detection section and ask your instructor for clarification. Do this section out loud by yourself to see if you can complete the task before moving on to the next component, which involves practice with a partner, in small groups, or as a class.

■ 練習の時間 Time for Practice
RENSHUU NO JIKAN

This practice area provides an opportunity to apply the material introduced in the Language Detection component with a partner, in a small group, or as a class. By the time you have completed this component, you should have a good understanding of the material covered in the Language Detection component and the new vocabulary in this section. If you are unclear about any aspect of the new material, do not hesitate to ask your instructor for clarification or additional examples and explanations.

■ 文化箱 Culture Chest
BUN KA BAKO

A comprehension of language cannot exist independently of an understanding of culture. This component explores everything from the intricacies of Japanese social interactions, history and geography, to the artistic and creative details of traditional and contemporary culture.

■ キアラのジャーナル Kiara's Journal
K I A R A N O J A - N A R U

In the first section of this text you meet Kiara, the main character of this text. She is an American student who has studied Japanese for less than a year and who is embarking on her journey, just as you are, to learn more about Japanese language and culture. Through her journals and the writings of other characters, you will learn, review, and be challenged to use a variety of language strategies to understand and, to some extent, participate in the experiences on this very atypical journey.

When you travel to Japan as a non-native speaker, you are bombarded with visual and auditory stimuli that must be decoded into something comprehensible to you. Essentially, this decoding happens through strengthening your translating and interpreting skills. Sifting through all of the authentic sights and sounds you experience to comprehend the core elements required to meet your needs is the process through which language is internalized and learned. As would happen in an actual experience in Japan, you will probably not understand everything you see and hear in this book or this series, but you will develop coping skills and learn to sort out the main points, ideas, and details that you need.

These journal entries and other writings are designed to simulate what you might experience in Japan as a non-native speaker of Japanese. Reading these, and searching for the "gist" of the passage, will develop and reinforce your interpretive skills. Kiara's story actually extends beyond the boundaries of this text. More details of her journey can be found at TimeForJapanese.com.

The manga images and journal entries found in this text are designed to provide insight into Japanese history, culture, and historical figures. The Japanese language, like all languages, has been constantly changing and evolving throughout its long history. Some liberties have been taken in order to present language as it's spoken in modern times, and to meld past and present to give you, the learner, an engaging story in which you can learn with the characters.

■ テクノの時間 Techno Time
T E K U N O N O J I K A N

This component of the series is designed to help you learn Japanese in a variety of ways that utilize technology. Computers, cell phones, and the Internet have made many aspects of Japan and the Japanese language easily accessible. Using technology also helps reinforce your Japanese learning in many fun and interesting ways.

Digital Dictionary

One of the greatest challenges for the new language learner is remembering vocabulary terms. Learning strategies such as making and using flash cards and repetition of writing (or typing) characters are ways to help make memorization of new vocabulary easier. As you progress through this series, you will be asked to keep a Digi-Dictionary, or digital dictionary. This dictionary will help you understand subtle differences in the meanings and pronunciations of words, especially words that contain elongated vowels or doubled consonants. It will also serve as your own personal reference tool and checkpoint. As you periodically review the vocabulary collected here, you will be able to see just how far you have come and just how much new vocabulary you have learned!

■ 単語チェックリスト New Word Checklist
T A N G O C H E K K U R I S U T O

Each chapter contains a comprehensive glossary where new words from that chapter are listed in the Japanese alphabetical (a-i-u-e-o) order by section. You will learn this alphabetical system in Chapter 1. If you have a question about the English meaning of a vocabulary word, you can quickly find a translation in this section of each chapter. A complete glossary for all the words in the New Word Checklists is also included in the back of the book.

Passport

Each chapter is finalized with a Passport component. The Passport challenges are included to provide a variety of tasks for you to demonstrate your ability to participate in interpersonal communications and use presentational skills. Once you have successfully completed each of these Passport components and received all ten of your Passport stamps, you will earn your "belt," or the certification needed to guarantee your successful completion of this book. Similar to the practice of martial arts or other aesthetic experiences in Japan, your "belt" is the recognition that you are ready to make the transition to the next level of study.

Workbook and Supplemental Materials

The workbook and CD-ROM material that accompany this book are designed to help check your understanding and to practice and apply previously learned and new material. Audio files for the text and activities can be found in the CD-ROM material.

TimeForJapanese.com

The web-based resource for this series, TimeForJapanese.com, contains additional learning content and practice tools. TimeForJapanese.com is continually being updated and enhanced. Bookmark or save it to your favorites list on your computer and visit it often.

Introductions and Getting Started

✔ Learning Goals

By the end of this chapter you will learn:

A) how to read and write Japanese words written in ROMAJI (roman letters) and pronounce them correctly

B) how to introduce yourself in Japanese

C) how to greet a person in Japanese appropriately

D) to respond correctly to your teacher when he or she gives you a common classroom command

E) a variety of learning strategies to facilitate your study of Japanese

F) how to read and write at least half of the hiragana and 13 kanji

✔ Performance Goals

By the end of this chapter you will be able to:

A) introduce yourself

B) introduce others

C) say things such as *This is sushi* or *That is a book.*

D) respond to and give basic classroom commands

E) read and write at least half of the hiragana and 13 kanji

Narita Airport, Tokyo's international airport

東京へ　いきます！
TOUKYOUe　IKIMASU
Going to Tokyo!

■ キアラのジャーナル Kiara's Journal
K I A R A no J A - N A R U

Dear Journal,

I've been thinking about some things that my Japanese teacher told me before I left. I was only in Japanese class for part of the semester before I had to leave, but I think that I got a pretty good start. She said that when learning Japanese, there are several things to think about. One of these is to be careful to practice good pronunciation. I really want to sound as much like a native Japanese speaker as possible, so I paid a lot of attention to this part. Japanese pronunciation didn't take me long to learn, because there are only five basic vowels and nearly every other sound uses the same vowels, but with a consonant or hard sound in front of them. The only sound that does not end in a vowel sound is the sound of the letter N. My teacher said that vowels should not be drawn out when pronounced, but instead should be "short and clear."

 Here is a pronunciation guide:

あ or **a** as in f<u>a</u>ther
い or **i** as in <u>ea</u>t
う or **u** as in b<u>oo</u>t
え or **e** as in g<u>e</u>t
お or **o** as in g<u>o</u>

Once you master these five vowel sounds, all of the remaining sounds (except for the "n" sound) are consonant/vowel combinations. The chart below shows the sounds of Japanese. It is written vertically starting on the right side, and reading from top to bottom. Japanese language can be written both horizontally like English (left to right) and vertically, as seen in the charts below, writing from the top down and starting on the right side and moving left. There are two charts because Japanese uses two writing styles: the hiragana is used for Japanese words, and the katakana is used for foreign and scientific words as well as onomatopoetic or mimetic words.

 ## 1A. Hiragana Chart

ん N	わ WA	ら RA	や YA	ま MA	は HA (part. WA)	な NA	た TA	さ SA	か KA	あ A
		り RI		み MI	ひ HI	に NI	ち CHI	し SHI	き KI	い I
		る RU	ゆ YU	む MU	ふ FU	ぬ NU	つ TSU	す SU	く KU	う U
		れ RE		め ME	へ HE (part. E)	ね NE	て TE	せ SE	け KE	え E
	を WO (part. O)	ろ RO	よ YO	も MO	ほ HO	の NO	と TO	そ SO	こ KO	お O

2. Katakana Chart

ン N	ワ WA	ラ RA	ヤ YA	マ MA	ハ HA	ナ NA	タ TA	サ SA	カ KA	ア A
		リ RI		ミ MI	ヒ HI	ニ NI	チ CHI	シ SHI	キ KI	イ I
		ル RU	ユ YU	ム MU	フ FU	ヌ NU	ツ TSU	ス SU	ク KU	ウ U
		レ RE		メ ME	ヘ HE	ネ NE	テ TE	セ SE	ケ KE	エ E
	ヲ WO	ロ RO	ヨ YO	モ MO	ホ HO	ノ NO	ト TO	ソ SO	コ KO	オ O

Many of my friends have the impression that Japanese is difficult, but the pronunciation is actually quite simple. This is one of the things that I really like about Japanese! Most sounds are pronounced just like they look. Here are a few sounds that you have to be a little careful with:

す (su) as in <u>soup</u>
ち (chi) as in <u>cheese</u>
つ (tsu) similar to the "ts" in ca<u>ts</u>
ふ (fu) is pronounced not with an "f," but like the sound you make when you blow out a candle.

The "ra" line, ら、り、る、れ、and ろ, is different from the "r" sound in English, but is close to the "r" sound in some other languages, such as Spanish. My sensei said that it was more like a combination of the letters R/L/D all rolled up into one. It really isn't difficult at all if you just concentrate on trying to sound just like your teacher or like the voice on the audio files.

There are a few other things you should know about Japanese pronunciation. When you add two marks (˝), called TEN TEN, or a small circle (˚), called MARU, to the top right of a character (for example, か → が or は → ぱ), the sound of the consonant changes.

1B. Hiragana: Other Syllables

ぱ PA	ば BA	だ DA	ざ ZA	が GA
ぴ PI	び BI	ぢ JI	じ JI	ぎ GI
ぷ PU	ぶ BU	づ ZU	ず ZU	ぐ GU
ぺ PE	べ BE	で DE	ぜ ZE	げ GE
ぽ PO	ぼ BO	ど DO	ぞ ZO	ご GO

The sounds above make up the building blocks of all sounds in Japanese. There are a few combinations that change them slightly, but they don't add to the length of the syllables at all when they are placed together. They merely change the sounds. For example the KI and YO sounds following each other would be き よ (KIYO), two syllables. When the second character is "half-sized" or smaller, though, the sounds are combined, turning it into the one-syllable き ょ (KYO).

1C. Hiragana: Combined Sounds

り や RYA	み や MYA	ぴ や PYA	び や BYA	ひ や HYA	に や NYA	ち や CHA	じ や JA	し や SHA	ぎ や GYA	き や KYA
り ゅ RYU	み ゅ MYU	ぴ ゅ PYU	び ゅ BYU	ひ ゅ HYU	に ゅ NYU	ち ゅ CHU	じ ゅ JU	し ゅ SHU	ぎ ゅ GYU	き ゅ KYU
り ょ RYO	み ょ MYO	ぴ ょ PYO	び ょ BYO	ひ ょ HYO	に ょ NYO	ち ょ CHO	じ ょ JO	し ょ SHO	ぎ ょ GYO	き ょ KYO

Other important pronunciation points:

Some vowels are elongated sounds, which means they are held for twice as long. The difference between the two is like this: いえ means *house* while いいえ, which has an elongated vowel, means *no*. With
I E   I I E
katakana words, the elongated vowel sound is shown by a straight line after the katakana character. For example, the first "A" sound in the word ジャーナル (*journal*) is pronounced twice as long as the second
JA-NARU
"A" sound.

One other type of sound found in Japanese is the "doubled consonant." To make this sound, you pause, or freeze your mouth, for just a brief extra second between the sounds just before and after the small TSU (っ). The small TSU (っ) is about half the size of the normal つ and does not have a specific sound
TSU
of its own. Here are a few words with doubled consonants: いっぱい (a lot) and きっさてん (coffee
I P P A I   K I S S A T E N
shop). This isn't hard to do. Just pay attention when your teacher explains how to pronounce the doubled consonant and listen carefully to the audio files that come with this book.

■ 単語 New Words
TAN GO

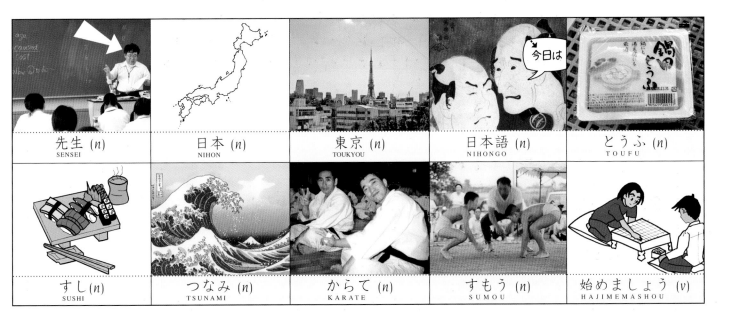

先生 (n) SENSEI	日本 (n) NIHON	東京 (n) TOUKYOU	日本語 (n) NIHONGO	とうふ (n) TOUFU
すし (n) SUSHI	つなみ (n) TSUNAMI	からて (n) KARATE	すもう (n) SUMOU	始めましょう (v) HAJIMEMASHOU

Vocabulary Learning Hints

There are several methods of learning vocabulary words. The trick is finding out which method works best for you. When learning anything new, the more of your senses that you use during the learning process the better, and the longer you will retain the information. An example of this is how we use flash cards. Flash cards are one of the best ways for the beginning learner to remember vocabulary. Many students make flashcards (you can also download flashcards from this book's website, TimeForJapanese.com) and think about the meanings in their heads. A more efficient way of using them is to say each word out loud as you review it. This method has you reading, speaking, AND hearing each vocabulary word. And if you've already written the word down, you have now used all four aspects of language learning and communication!

When learning vocabulary, cramming for a test might seem like a good way to learn the words quickly in the short term, but as with other things, it's easier and more efficient to learn words gradually and to build on them. Each word has to be memorized and incorporated into your long-term memory. Associating words with pictures or with other words that you already know is an excellent way to cement vocabulary into your knowledge base. This is the reason this book, when possible, gives interpretations of Japanese words in pictorial form rather than translating. Then, when you need that vocabulary word later, you can pull the picture out of your memory.

Finally, based on the "use it or lose it" concept, the more you use new words, the better you will remember them. Try to use new Japanese words with your teacher, classmates, family, Japanese speakers, and anybody else who will listen to you! If your goal is to memorize new vocabulary, do not worry whether your spoken Japanese is perfect or not, just try to use the new words as much as possible even if you have a hard time making complete sentences. Study partners are great for getting lots of focused practice as well. Find someone who wants to learn as much as you do!

■ キアラのジャーナル Kiara's Journal
KIARA no JA-NARU

Dear Journal,

I have been on this airplane for nearly 12 hours and am just about ready to land in 成田空港, Narita
NARITA KUUKOU
International Airport, the main international airport in 東京. I'm really excited about living in 日本 for
TOUKYOU   NIHON
the first time. I have wanted to go there for so long that I can't believe that it's really happening! My host
brother Jun and his parents are coming to the airport by train to take me back to their house in Tokyo. I
have a couple of days until I start school, which I am also a bit nervous about. But I'm excited, too, because
this is going to be such a cool adventure!

This airplane is huge. There are 10 seats from
side to side and it's full of people from all over the
world. The nice woman next to me is on her way to
Japan, too. She lives in Sendai, a city in northern
Japan, and the person on the other side of her is
going to the Philippines.

I always thought that the flight path to Japan
would cross the U.S. and then the Pacific, but instead
we flew north over Canada and then Alaska. When I
asked the flight attendant, he said that our path was
actually the shortest route. I also can't believe how
cold it is outside! The screen on the back of the seat in front of me shows that the outside temperature
at this altitude is REALLY cold. I can use the same screen to watch movies, or look at a map of where we
are, the current time at home and in Japan, how far we've come, and how far we have yet to go to our
destination. I think I've figured out which line on this screen tells the speed of the airplane. Which one do
you think it is?

I think that I've packed enough clothes for the entire year, but Jun told me not to worry about that
because there are some really good stores near his house. He says I'll be able to get what I need there
if I forgot something. Jun is going to take me shopping for school supplies before school starts, so I didn't
bring anything like that.

I did bring some candy, pencils and other things with my
school's name on them to give to the kids in my class, and
some Western food for my new host family. I've heard that it's
important to bring gifts called OMIYAGE, but I'm not sure if what
I brought is appropriate or not. My teacher gave me some good
recommendations, though. I know one of the most important
things is to welcome opportunities and enjoy new experiences. A
lot of my friends think I'm a bit crazy to do this, but I think it's
going to be the best experience of my life. Here goes. The captain
just said that we're landing in 20 minutes!!

日本
NIHON
Land of the Rising Sun

■ キアラのジャーナル Kiara's Journal
KIARA no JA-NARU

Dear Journal,

こんにちは！ I've got to practice writing what I've learned, so I don't forget. Writing Japanese is
KONNICHI wa
challenging, but I think it's very interesting. Japan had no written language of its own until the 4th century
C.E., when Japan began interacting with China. After that, manuscripts, mostly religious, began to arrive
in Japan, via Korea, and the Japanese adopted more and more Chinese institutions, including its writing
system. Japanese monks and scholars adopted these characters from Chinese writing to write down their
own Japanese language. Japanese call characters of Chinese origin 漢字. The process was difficult in the
KANJI
beginning, because the two languages don't sound at all alike, but it works for the Japanese today. Besides,
the writing system is a lot of fun to learn.

Some KANJI resemble pictures, so it is really easy to guess what they mean. Studying kanji is fun. I
already have a stack of flash cards that I look at regularly. The more kanji you learn, the easier it is to
learn more, because the characters build on each other. For example, the kanji for tree is 木. It looks a
KI
little like a tree with branches that stretch out and droop down. If you put two trees together, you have
the start of a small woods — 林; if you combine three trees, you get a forest 森. When a line is drawn
HAYASHI   MORI
across the bottom of the vertical stroke in 木, like this 本, the bottom part, or what's underground, that
KI   HON
is, the roots, is emphasized. 本 means *book* or *origin root/source* as in the "source" of knowledge.
HON

The kanji for *sun* is 日. The origin of this character is harder to guess. The character started out as a
NI
circle with a dot in it = ⊙ but the shape changed over time into something more square, like 日. Note that
modern kanji do not have circles in them. When you put together the
日 and 本, that is, the *origin* of the *sun*, or the place where the sun
NI   HON
rises, you get 日本, or Japan, the "land of the rising sun."
NI HON

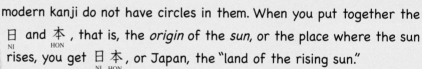

Although the origins of the writing system called HIRAGANA
are unclear, some believe hiragana were invented by a Buddhist
monk named Koubou Daishi (774-835), who had traveled to China.
Hiragana were created by simplifying some of the characters of
Chinese origin and creating a group of phonetic syllables, similar
to an alphabet. This was a system that could be used to write all
spoken Japanese. They were useful because nearly anyone could
learn to read them. It had taken years to learn to read all of the
characters of Chinese origin. During the Heian Period (794-1185 C.E.), women in the emperor's court wrote
with hiragana, and it came to be called "女手", or *women's hand*. There was a separate group of simplified
ONNA-DE
characters for the 46 basic Japanese sounds developed later called KATAKANA, which is currently used to
write foreign words and names in Japanese, such as ベースボール (*baseball*). Katakana is also used for
BE-SUBO-RU
scientific names of plants and animals, and the noises that they and other things make.

HIRAGANA and KATAKANA together are often called "KANA."

I would really like the chance to meet someone like Koubou Daishi, but of course he's been dead for
nearly 1,200 years, so that would be impossible … right?

■ 漢字 Kanji
KAN JI

Below are the kanji that you will have to learn for this section. When kanji are presented as they are below, you will need to learn how to read and write them. Be sure to pay attention to the numbers corresponding to the stroke order for each character. Stroke order is a very important aspect of kanji writing and is critical information when using kanji dictionaries. Learning correct stroke order might not seem that important at the beginning, but you will eventually understand why it is so crucial.

Notice that most kanji strokes start in the upper left corner and eventually end in the bottom right corner. The basic rule is to write strokes from left to right and from top to bottom. Make mental notes of exceptions to this rule when they come up, such as in the first stroke of the kanji 千 (1,000), which is written at a downward angle from right to left.
SEN

Soon you will notice that kanji are made up of parts called radicals. The more you can mentally break down a kanji into its parts, the easier it will be to memorize it. It will be easier to learn new kanji as well, since the new kanji contain some of the same parts (radicals). The kanji hints provided underneath each new kanji identify the parts that make up the new kanji while also offering mental images to help you learn that new kanji. For instance, it will be much easier down the road for you to memorize a potentially difficult new kanji such as "cherry tree." 桜 is made up of parts which easily help
SAKURA
explain the overall meaning of the kanji. The left side (木) is a tree; the right side has a woman (女) sitting with three
KI   ONNA
cherry petals floating down as she admires the spring display.

Here are your three KANJI for this section:

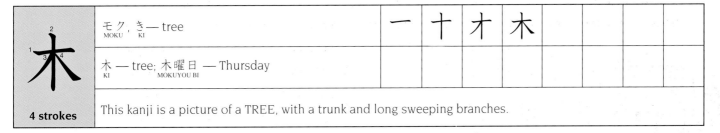

	モク, き — tree MOKU KI	一	十	才	木			
木 4 strokes	木 — tree; 木曜日 — Thursday KI MOKUYOU BI							
	This kanji is a picture of a TREE, with a trunk and long sweeping branches.							

	ニ, ひ, にち — day; sun NI HI NICHI	丨	冂	日	日			
日 4 strokes	日(本) — Japan; 日 — sun, day NI (HON) HI							
	This was originally a picture of the SUN that has been simplified over the years. It came to also mean DAY. This character appears as a part of many kanji related to time.							

	ホン — book, origin; もと — origin H O N MOTO	一	十	才	木	本		
本 5 strokes	本 — book; (日)本 — Japan; (日)本(語) — HON (NI) HON (NI) HON (GO) Japanese language; (松) 本 — family/place name (MATSU) MOTO							
	The origin of all BOOKS is one (一) piece of a tree (木). 本 is also a tree (木) where the roots or ORIGIN at the bottom is emphasized. The term for Japan (日本) means "origin of the sun."							

■ キアラのジャーナル Kiara's Journal
KIARA no JA-NARU

Dear Journal,

We just landed, but we're still sitting in the airplane. Taxiing toward the terminal seems to be taking forever. The plane trip from Chicago took about 12 hours. It was really cool to fly over Alaska. I could see snow-covered mountains and glaciers and then nothing but blue water, water, and more water, until the green rice fields of Japan appeared.

My host family should be at the airport waiting to pick me up. They said that I have to go through Immigration to get my passport stamped and then through Customs where they sometimes check your luggage. My sensei told me not to wrap any of my OMIYAGE because customs agents might open them.

I have got to practice introducing myself to my host family. I'm kind of nervous about meeting them. Besides Jun, there is his mother Mayumi, his father Tarou, his older brother Ichirou, and his little sister Aiko. We have been e-mailing messages back and forth, and we did one videoconference, but it was early in the morning at home and they were going to bed in Japan. We talked in both English and in Japanese. I'm just going to try to remember what my parents always say, about how good communication means being open to listening and not being afraid to respond. Well, we're at the gate and people are unbuckling their seat belts and getting up. HAJIMEMASHITE, HAJIMEMASHITE, HAJIMEMASHITE...

私は キアラ です。
WATASHI wa　KIARA　DESU
I am Kiara.

■ 会話 Dialogue
KAI WA

Male agent:	日本語が　わかりますか。
	NIHONGO ga WAKARIMASUKA.
Kiara:	はい、わかります。
	HAI. WAKARIMASU.
Female agent:	いい　ですね。 *Can you introduce yourself?*
	I I DESU ne.
Kiara:	初めまして。私は　キアラ　です。どうぞ　よろしく。
	HAJIMEMASHITE. WATASHI wa KIARA DESU. DOUZO YOROSHIKU.

■ 単語 New Words
TAN GO

はじめまして (v) HAJIMEMASHITE	私　(pron.) WATASHI	私達 (pron.) WATASHI TACHI	僕 (pron.) BOKU (note: used by males only)

よろしく　おねがいします –
YOROSHIKU   ONEGAISHIMASU

best regards, treat me favorably

どうぞよろしく　おねがいします –
DOUZO YOROSHIKU   ONEGAISHIMASU

polite for:

よろしく　おねがいします
YOROSHIKU   ONEGAISHIMASU

どうぞよろしく –
DOUZO YOROSHIKU

best regards, treat me favorably

(same meaning as:

よろしく　おねがいします)
YOROSHIKU   ONEGAISHIMASU

名前 (n) – name
NA MAE

〜先生 (n/suffix) – used immediately AFTER a teacher's or doctor's name
SEN SEI

〜さん (suffix) – used immediately AFTER a name (never use with your own name)
SAN

〜くん (suffix) – used immediately AFTER a boy's name (never use with your own name)
KUN

は (part.) – particle that denotes the sentence topic
wa

です (verb copula) – similar to "is" or "am"
DESU

Classroom Commands and Questions

The top row of each command below is a simple command form of the verb ("Stand!", for example), the second row is a polite request ("Please stand."), and the third row asks permission to do the action ("May I stand?").

たって
TATTE

たってください
TATTE KUDASAI

たっても いいですか。
TATTE mo I I DESU ka

すわって
SUWATTE

すわってください
SUWATTE KUDASAI

すわっても いいですか。
SUWATTE mo I I DESU ka

みて
MITE

みてください
MITE KUDASAI

みても いいですか。
MITE mo I I DESU ka

だして
DASHITE

だしてください
DASHITE KUDASAI

だしても いいですか。
DASHITE mo I I DESU ka

ひらいて
HIRA ITE

ひらいてください
HIRA ITEKUDASAI

ひらいても いいですか。
HIRA ITE mo I I DESU ka

とじて
TOJITE

とじてください
TOJITE KUDASAI

とじても いいですか。
TOJITE mo I I DESU ka

かいて
KAITE

かいてください
KAITE KUDASAI

かいても いいですか。
KAITE mo I I DESU ka

きいて
KIITE

きいてください
KIITE KUDASAI

きいても いいですか。
KIITE mo I I DESU ka

よんで
YONDE

よんでください
YONDE KUDASAI

よんでも いいですか。
YONDE mo I I DESU ka

■ 漢字 Kanji
KAN JI

When you get up in the morning and see the sun (日) behind a tree (木) like this (東), you are looking east at the sunrise. 東 means *east*.
HIGASHI

Historically, large walls surrounded cities in China, where kanji originated. Each of the four city walls had a large 門 or gate for people entering and leaving the city. This character for MON (門)
MON
looks like a gate, doesn't it? On either side of the gate stood large lanterns, often made of stone, similar to the one shown in the picture here. When you saw the large lanterns on either side of a gate, you knew you were approaching the capital. The kanji for *capital* is pronounced KYOU (京). Can you see the three legs and the small hole in the middle for candle light to shine through?

The second capital of Japan was the city of 京都. Later, the capital was moved to the east
KYOUTO
(東) where it is now. The present-day capital is written 東京, or *eastern capital*. Can you understand
TOUKYOU
the meaning by looking at these characters together?

Below you will find a list of kanji that you must learn for this section. Pay careful attention to the stroke order of each kanji. Following along with the examples in the next several chapters and paying close attention to the samples will help you understand exactly how to write other kanji. Be sure to use the kanji practice space in your workbook as instructed.

東 1⁶ 2 **8 strokes**	トウ；ひがし — east TOU　HIGASHI	一	一	一	一	一	車	東	東
	東(京)— (eastern) capital of Japan; TOU(KYOU) 東 — east (direction) HIGASHI								
	Think of the sun rising in the EAST behind a tree.								

京 ²¹ ³⁴ ⁵⁶ ⁷⁸ **8 strokes**	キョウ — capital K Y O U	'	一	广	亡	古	亨	京	京
	(東)京 — capital city of Japan (TOU) KYOU								
	Think of the picture of the lantern described above. You can also think of the top two strokes as a top hat, the next three strokes as a mouth (口), and the last three strokes as the kanji for small (小). Here is a person with a top hat talking loudly to politicians in the CAPITAL.								

語 ¹⁸⁹ ²³¹⁰ ⁴¹¹ ⁶¹³ ⁵⁷¹⁴ **14 strokes**	ゴ — language GO	、	二	三	言	言	言	言	言
	(日本)語 — the Japanese language (NIHON) GO	訂	訊	語	語	語	語		
	The left side is the kanji meaning *to say* (言); the right side includes the kanji for 5 (五), which is pronounced ゴ and the kanji for mouth (口). If at least five people can use their mouths to say something in common, it must be a LANGUAGE. GO								

■ 言葉の探索 Language Detection
KOTOBA no TANSAKU

1. Japanese grammar is relatively simple. Small parts of speech called "particles" show the "relationship" between the words they connect. Imagine that particles are like the hitches that hold train cars together: nearly every word (train car) has a particle (hitch) that connects it to the following word. You will see lowercase letters used for particles' furigana in this book. Particles are not written smaller in Japanese, but the case difference is there in the furigana to let you know that the characters above are particles. Check the appendix at the back of this book for a list of common particles and their uses.

2. The particle は and です
   - は is often called a "topic marker." The topic of a sentence is what is being spoken about. It is always followed by the particle は, pronounced WA).
   - です acts like the English verbs "is," "are," or "am." Verbs usually come at the end of the sentence in Japanese.
   DESU

When these two are together, the は usually connects two words (these words can be nouns, pronouns, adjectives or some combination) and gives the sentence an A = B meaning.

WATASHI wa KIARA DESU   = I am Kiara.

A   は   B   です。 = A is B.

山川さん は 先生 です。   = (Mr. *or* Ms.) Yamakawa is a teacher.
YAMAKAWASAN wa SENSEI DESU

ここは 日本 です。   = This place is Japan.
KOKO wa NIHON DESU

おすしは おいしい です。   = Sushi is delicious.
OSUSHI wa O I S H I I DESU

3. 〜たち
   TACHI
   For most nouns, Japanese does not distinguish between singular and plural. For instance, 名前 can mean *name* or *names*, depending on the context.
   NAMAE
   Certain terms used for people, however, can be pluralized by adding the suffix "〜たち".* Can you guess what these examples mean?
   TACHI

わたし   →   わたしたち
WATASHI   WATASHI TACHI

せんせい   →   せんせいたち
SENSEI   SENSEI TACHI

ぼく   →   ぼくたち
BOKU   BOKU TACHI

*The tilde (〜) is used from time to time to let you know that something precedes or follows the word.

■ 練習の時間 Time for Practice
RENSHUU no JIKAN

1. Pair Practice

Use the example dialogue below to take turns introducing yourself to a partner and letting them introduce themselves to you. When introducing yourself or when someone introduces himself or herself to you, it is proper to bow. With your arms at your sides, bow from the waist, letting your eyes move toward the ground with your head and shoulders. There are different degrees of bowing depending on the situation, but for beginners a good generic depth of your bow would be about 45 degrees. A good time to bow is when either of you says the word はじめまして.
HAJIMEMASHITE

A-SAN: はじめまして。 僕 は アダム (Adam) です。 どうぞ よろしく 。
       HAJIMEMASHITE. BOKU wa ADAMU   DESU.   DOUZO YOROSHIKU.

B-SAN: はじめまして。 私 は パメラ (Pamela) です。 どうぞ よろしく。
       HAJIMEMASHITE. WATASHI wa PAMERA   DESU.   DOUZO YOROSHIKU.

■ 文化箱 Culture Chest
BUN KA BAKO

I. Showing Respect

Japanese society is traditionally considered very polite and respectful. There are many ways that the Japanese people show respect to each other. One example of this is the tradition of bowing. When Japanese people first meet, they usually bow, rather than shaking hands. If a Japanese person is meeting a Westerner for the first time, the Japanese person may wait until the Westerner extends his or her hand before deciding whether to shake hands or to bow. Japanese teachers may nod their heads and make a slight bow when meeting their students in the hallway. Deep and extended bowing is an inherent part of other Japanese rituals such as the tea ceremony.

There are many different subtle and not so subtle ways that Japanese vary their bowing techniques depending on the social situation. Observing all the intricacies of the ways Japanese bow can be a fascinating spectator sport for foreigners in Japan. It is said that in a random mix of people from Asia, you can identify the Japanese from a distance because they are the ones bowing the most. Sometimes Japanese even bow when they are talking on the telephone!

Other ways to show respect are built into the language. You may have noticed that Kiara does not use the suffix さん after her own name. You should not use this or any other ending after your own name, either, when speaking SAN Japanese. However, when talking to others, it is polite to use their proper names (not the pronoun "you") followed by one of the following endings:

～さん
SAN
which is similar to *Mr.* or *Ms.* or *Mrs.* in English. It is the most common suffix attached to the end of a name.

～せんせい
SENSEI
can be used alone and means *teacher*. It is a respectful term used immediately *after* the names of teachers and some professionals such as doctors, lawyers and politicians.

～くん
KUN
is used after boys' names.

～ちゃん
CHAN
is used for babies, elementary school age children, girls who are younger than the speaker in informal situations, and sometimes with family members or close friends.

～さま
SAMA
is used when addressing someone in a letter or when showing extreme politeness as a service person would with a patron.

Can you tell which of the following people are older and which are younger? Notice the order of the family name and the given name in Japanese vs. English.

- 山 本　明先生　　Mr. Akira Yamamoto (Teacher)
  YAMAMOTO　AKIRA-SENSEI
- 山 田　道夫さん　　Mr. Michio Yamada
  YAMADA　MICHIO-SAN
- 高 橋　花子さん　　Mrs. Hanako Takahashi
  TAKAHASHI　HANAKO-SAN
- 山 口　愛子ちゃん　Aiko Yamaguchi
  YAMAGUCHI　AIKO-CHAN
- 中 山　けいた君　　Keita Nakayama
  NAKAYAMA　KEITA-KUN

2. Saying and Writing Your Name

East Asian names are usually written with KANJI; non-East Asian names, however, are written with KATAKANA. When saying and writing your name in Japanese, keep in mind that it won't necessarily sound the same as it does in English because not all English sounds are the same in Japanese (for instance, Rs and Ls) or even exist (for instance, the *th* sound and many English vowel sounds do not exist in Japanese). Can you guess what English names these are?

- キャシー
  KYASHI-
- ベン
  BEN
- レオナルド
  REONARUDO
- キム
  KIMU

- トム
  TOMU
- エミリー
  EMIRI-
- マイケル
  MAIKERU
- ジャック
  JAKKU

こちらは母　です。
KOCHIRA wa HAHA DESU
This is my mother.

■ 会話 Dialogue
KAI WA

(At the airport)

キアラ： はじめまして。私は キアラ です。よろしく おねがいします。じゅん君 ですか。
KIARA   HAJIMEMASHITE. WATASHI wa   KIARA   DESU. YOROSHIKU   ONEGAISHIMASU.   JUN-KUN   DESU ka.

じゅん： はい、そう です。僕は じゅん です。ようこそ！
JUN   HAI, SOU   DESU.   BOKU wa   JUN   DESU.   YOUKOSO!

よろしく おねがいします。こちらは 母 です。こちらは 父 です。
YOROSHIKU   ONEGAISHIMASU.   KOCHIRA wa   HAHA   DESU.   KOCHIRA wa   CHICHI   DESU.

まゆみ： はじめまして。
MAYUMI   HAJIMEMASHITE.

太郎： じゅんの父です。どうぞよろしくおねがいします。
JUN no CHICHI DESU.   DOUZO YOROSHIKU ONEGAISHIMASU.

■ 単語 New Words
TAN GO

| ようこそ (exp.) | こちら (pron.) | 母 (n) | 父 (n) |
| YOUKOSO | KOCHIRA | HAHA | CHICHI |

太郎 (n) –
TAROU
a male name

いいえ、ちがいます –
I I E,   CHIGAIMASU
No, it is not/different.

はい、そう です –
HAI, SOU DESU
Yes it is.

か (part.) –
KA
particle signifying
a question

■ 漢字 Kanji
KAN JI

私	わたくし — I, me (polite); わたし — I, me WATAKUSHI WATASHI	ノ	二	千	手	禾	私	私	
2⁴⁶⁷ **7 strokes**	私 — I, me (formal); 私 —I, me WATAKUSHI WATASHI								
	It's probably going to be easy to remember that this kanji means I or ME, since you'll be writing about yourself a lot! Just remember to keep the first stroke slanted and not straight across and note that it is written from right to left.								

父	フ;ちち;(お)とう(さん) — father FU CHICHI (O) TOU (SAN)	ノ	ハ	分	父				
1 2 **4 strokes**	父 — (my) father; (お)父(さん) — father; CHICHI (O) TOU (SAN) 祖父 grandfather SOFU								
	Here you see a picture of a FATHER's face with a mustache, mouth, and the top of a beard.								

母 5	ボ；はは；（お）かあ（さん）— mother BO HAHA (O) KAA (SAN)		L	口	口	母	母	
	母 — (my) mother；（お）母（さん）— mother HAHA (O) KAA (SAN) 祖母 — grandmother SOBO							
5 strokes	This is actually an ancient pictograph of a woman with two breasts, symbolizing a MOTHER. Be sure to give her two arms and two legs when you write MOTHER.							

■ 言葉の探索 Language Detection
KOTO BA no TANSAKU

1. AはB ではありません。 - Making a negative statement

   To change an affirmative ～です（日本　です。）statement to a negative statement, replace the です with ではありません or じゃありません. じゃありません is less formal.
   DESU NIHON DESU   DESU   dewaARIMASEN   jaARIMASEN   jaARIMASEN

   Affirmative: A   は   B   です。   = A is B.
                        wa   DESU
                   私   は   じゅん   です。   = I am Jun.
                   WATASHI wa   JUN   DESU

   Negative: A   は   B   では ありません。   = A is not B.
                      wa   dewa ARIMASEN
                 私   は   じゅん   では ありません。   = I am not Jun.
                 WATASHI wa   JUN   dewa ARIMASEN
                 私   は   じゅん   じゃ ありません。   = I am not Jun. (less formal)
                 WATASHI wa   JUN   JA   ARIMASEN

   田中 さんは   先生   ではありません。   = Mr./Ms. Tanaka is not a teacher.
   TANAKA SAN wa SENSEI dewa ARIMASEN
   ここ は   アメリカ   じゃありません。   = This (here) is not America.
   KOKO wa   AMERIKA   JA ARIMASEN
   日本語   ではありません。   = It is not Japanese.
   NIHONGO dewa ARIMASEN

2. ～か - Questions
   ka

   Forming a question in Japanese is easy. Simply add the particle か to the end of the sentence.
                                                                    ka

   1. すし   です。   = (This is sushi.)
      SUSHI   DESU
      すし   ですか。   = (Is this sushi?)
      SUSHI   DESU ka
   2. つなみ   です。   = (This is a tidal wave.)
      TSUNAMI   DESU
      つなみ   ですか。   = (Is this is a tidal wave?)
      TSUNAMI   DESU ka
   3. 日本人   です。   = (I am Japanese [person].)
      NIHONJIN   DESU
      日本人   ですか。   = (Are you Japanese?)
      NIHONJIN   DESU ka

3. Punctuation

   Japanese punctuation is not too complicated. Written Japanese uses periods (。), commas (、), and quotation marks (「 」). All sentences, whether statements or questions, end in periods in normal Japanese writing. Manga, signs, and advertising sometimes use English question marks, exclamation marks, and other symbols as well. Questions end with the particle か followed by the Japanese period (。). Commas may be used wherever writers feel a pause would be appropriate, or to convey meaning, however they are not regulated as much as they are in English.

■ 自習 Self Check
JI SHUU

1. First, cover up the "negative statement" column below; read the sentences and restate each as a negative statement by changing the です to ではありません or じゃありません.
DESU   dewa ARIMASEN   JA ARIMASEN

  Once you have correctly changed the sentences into negative statements, cover up the "question" column below and make each statement into a question by adding か to the end of each. Check your answers.
ka

Statement	Negative Statement	Question
こちらは 先生 です。 KOCHIRA wa SENSEI DESU	こちらは 先生 ではありません / KOCHIRA wa SENSEI DEWA ARIMASEN じゃありません。 JA ARIMASEN	こちらは 先生 ですか。 KOCHIRA wa SENSEI DESU ka
東京 です。 TOUKYOU DESU	東京 ではありません / じゃありません。 TOUKYOU DEWA ARIMASEN JA ARIMASEN	東京 ですか。 TOUKYOU DESU ka
なりたくうこう です。 NARITAKUUKOU, DESU	なりたくうこう ではありません / NARITAKUUKOU DEWA ARIMASEN じゃありません。 JA ARIMASEN	なりたくうこう ですか。 NARITAKUUKOU DESU ka
これは とうふ です。 KORE wa TOUFU DESU	これは とうふ ではありません / KORE wa TOUFU DEWA ARIMASEN じゃありません。 JA ARIMASEN	これは とうふ ですか。 KORE wa TOUFU DESU ka
けいこさん です。 KEIKOSAN DESU	けいこさん ではありません / KEIKOSAN DEWA ARIMASEN じゃありません。 JA ARIMASEN	けいこさん ですか。 KEIKOSAN DESU ka

■ 練習の時間 Time for Practice
RENSHUU no JIKAN

1. Small Group Practice (sets of pairs)

Use the dialogue below to ask your partner his/her name. Next, introduce your partner to another group of classmates. Take turns, each person introducing their partner to the others.

> 例 REI EXAMPLE
>
> A-SAN: お名前 は 何 ですか。
> ONAMAE wa NAN DESU ka
>
> (What is your name?)
>
> B-SAN: 私 は (*say your name with a Japanese pronunciation*) です。はじめまして。
> WATASHI wa DESU. HAJIMEMASHITE.
>
> (I am _____. How do you do?)
>
> (*with your same partner to new pair of students*)
>
> A-SAN: はじめまして。(*turns to C-SAN*) こちらは (B-SAN's name) です。
> HAJIMEMASHITE. KOCHIRA wa _____DESU.
>
> (This is _____.)

2. Class Activity

Your teacher will assign a Japanese name to you from Appendix 2 for this activity. Circulate among your classmates, introducing yourself with this name. When they introduce themselves to you, write down their English name next to their Japanese name. For example, if Todd's Japanese name is KEN'ICHI, write down "Todd" next to *Ken'ichi*. When you have written down the English names of everyone on your list, sit down. Your teacher may ask you to introduce one or more of your classmates to the class.

3. Pair Work

This is a good way to see if you know the English names of all your classmates and practice your 日本語 at the same time! First, look at the list of Japanese and English names from Class Activity #2, above. Select one of the English names there, then point to one of your classmates and ask your partner if that is (insert name).

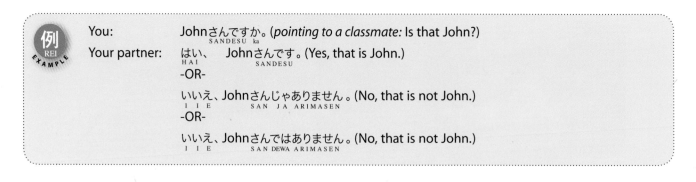

> 例 REI EXAMPLE
>
> You: Johnさんですか。(*pointing to a classmate:* Is that John?)
> SANDESU ka
>
> Your partner: はい、 Johnさんです。(Yes, that is John.)
> HAI SANDESU
>
> -OR-
>
> いいえ、Johnさんじゃありません。(No, that is not John.)
> IIE SAN JA ARIMASEN
>
> -OR-
>
> いいえ、Johnさんではありません。(No, that is not John.)
> IIE SAN DEWA ARIMASEN

■ 文化箱 Culture Chest
BUN KA BAKO

どうぞ よろしく おねがいします
DOUZO YOROSHIKU ONEGAISHIMASU

This phrase is often translated into English as "Pleased to meet you." It really has a broader implication and is useful in situations other than first meeting someone. よろしく おねがいします is used a great deal in everyday Japanese conversation. For instance, a high school baseball team will use this term when they bow in unison to their opponents before beginning a game. In this case you would translate よろしく おねがいします roughly as "please, take or keep me (in your) good favor." You are establishing a relationship with someone new and that relationship, in Japanese culture, is taken very seriously. You may or may not meet this person again, but when and if you do, you want them to remember you favorably just in case you might need to make a request of them at some point. Most classes in Japan begin with students standing up and everyone, including the teacher, saying this phrase in unison, to remind everyone of the importance of group cooperation. よろしく おねがいします！
YOROSHIKU ONEGAISHIMASU

こんばんは。
KONBAN wa
Good evening.

■ 会話 Dialogue
KAI WA

愛子 ： じゅん君、ただいま。キアラさんは どこ ですか。
AIKO　　JUN-KUN　TADAIMA.　KIARA-SAN wa　DOKO　DESU ka.

じゅん： おかえりなさい。キアラさんは へやに います。
JUN　　OKAERINASAI.　KIARA-SAN wa　HEYA ni　IMASU.

愛子 ： こんばんは。
AIKO　　KONBAN wa.

キアラ： こんばんは。
KIARA　　KONBAN wa.

愛子 ： はじめまして。愛子 です。
AIKO　　HAJIMEMASHITE.　AIKO　DESU

キアラ： はじめまして。キアラです。どうぞよろしく。
KIARA　　HAJIMEMASHITE.　KIARA DESU.　DOUZO YOROSHIKU.

まゆみ： これは おすし です。これは おはしです。どうぞ。
MAYUMI　　KORE wa　O-SUSHI　DESU.　KORE wa　O-HASHI DESU.　DOUZO.

キアラ： しょうゆは どれ ですか。
KIARA　　SHOUYU wa　DORE　DESU ka.

まゆみ： あれ です。それは わさび です。
MAYUMI　　ARE　DESU.　SORE wa　WASABI　DESU.

キアラ： たまごは それ ですか。
KIARA　　TAMAGO wa　SORE　DESU ka.

じゅん： はい、そう です。
JUN　　HAI.　SOU　DESU.

■ 単語 New Words
TAN GO

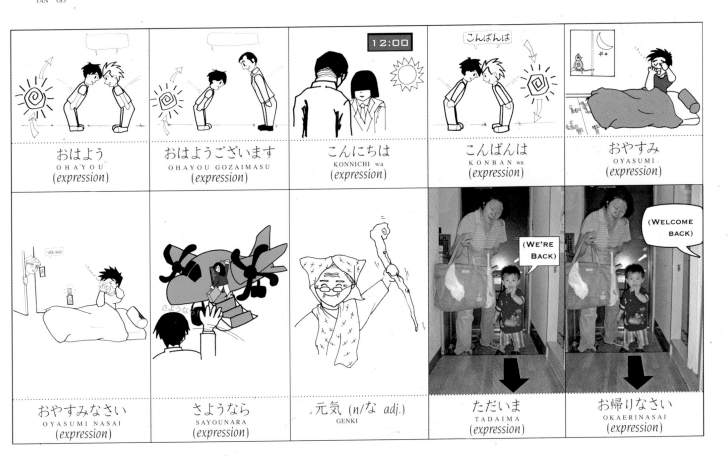

おはよう	おはようございます	こんにちは	こんばんは	おやすみ
OHAYOU	OHAYOU GOZAIMASU	KONNICHI wa	KONBAN wa	OYASUMI
(expression)	(expression)	(expression)	(expression)	(expression)
おやすみなさい	さようなら	元気 (n/な adj.)	ただいま	お帰りなさい
OYASUMI NASAI	SAYOUNARA	GENKI	TADAIMA	OKAERINASAI
(expression)	(expression)		(expression)	(expression)

| ごはん (n) GOHAN | (お) はし (n) (O) HASHI | これ KORE | それ SORE | あれ ARE |
| へや (n) HEYA | どれ (inter.) DORE | しょうゆ (n) SHOUYU | わさび (n) WASABI | たまご (n) TAMAGO |

じゃあ また – see you later
J A A   MATA
(*informal expression*)

では また – see you
dewa   MATA
(*expression*)

バイバイ – goodbye
B A I B A I
(*informal expression*)

に (*part.*) – particle after a location word denoting where someone/something exists

■ 漢字 Kanji
KAN JI

気 元 人 休

気 6 strokes	き — spirit; energy KI	ノ ヽ ⺊ 气 気 気
	気 — spirit; energy KI	
	A person's SPIRIT, marked with an "X," is kept between several layers that consist of flesh and bone. But there is always a key (the first stroke) to unbridling that SPIRIT.	

元 4 strokes	ゲン — an ancient currency; もと — origin GEN MOTO	一 二 テ 元
	元(気) — healthy, in good spirits GEN (KI)	
	The top two strokes make up the kanji for two (二), and the bottom two strokes can be thought of as legs. The ORIGIN of modern humans began when we started to walk on two legs.	

人 2 strokes	~ジン; ~ニン; ひと — person JIN NIN HITO	ノ 人
	人 person; (三)人 three (people) (counter for HITO (SAN) NIN people); (日本)人 (Japanese) person (NIHON) JIN	
	This is the shape of a PERSON standing up.	

休	やす (む) YASU (MU)	ノ	イ	仁	什	休	休		
	休 (む) — to rest, take a break, a vacation YASU (MU)								
6 strokes	The left side represents a person (人) and appears in many kanji that have something to do with people. The right side is a tree (木). This kanji represents a person RESTING against a tree.								

■ 言葉の探索 Language Detection
KOTOBA no TANSAKU

1. これ, それ, あれ, どれ
    KORE   SORE   ARE   DORE

これ   = this (one)
KORE
それ   = that (one) near the listener
SORE
あれ   = that (one over there) away from the speaker and listener
ARE
どれ   = which one?
DORE

The use of each of these pronouns depends on the location of an object and the relative locations of the speaker and the listener. これ is used for objects near you, the speaker. それ refers to object(s) near the listener and away from the speaker. あれ is used when the object is away from both the speaker and the listener. どれ is only used for questions.

2. お is placed in front of some nouns, especially words related to food or drink, to make them more polite. For example, people in the past were often lucky to get fresh water or rice so お was placed in front of those words to show gratitude. お is not used in front of proper names or words for other animate things. Some examples include:

おはし (chopsticks)   おすし (sushi)
OHASHI   OSUSHI
おみず (water)   おちゃ (green tea)
OMIZU   OCHA

■ 自習 Self Check
JI SHUU

Look at the two columns below. Say an appropriate time or greeting for each blank. The first one is done for you.

A	B
7 a.m.	おはよう　ございます OHAYOU GOZAIMASU
Noon	_____
_____ (Choose a time)	こんばんは KONBAN wa
11 p.m.	_____
10 a.m.	_____
_____ (Choose a time)	おはよう OHAYOU

2. Try saying the sentences below in Japanese using the pronouns これ, それ, あれ, and どれ. Test yourself to make
    KORE   SORE   ARE   DORE
    sure you know which pronoun to use in which situation.

This is a book.

That (near a partner) is a pencil.

This is an eraser (消しゴム)
KESHIGOMU

Which one is a notebook?

That one (over there) is a window. (まど)
MADO

That one (over there) is a car. (くるま)
KURUMA

That one (near a partner) is a cat. (ねこ)
NEKO

■ 練習の時間 Time for Practice
RENSHUU no JIKAN

---

1. Pair Practice

Place some of your hiragana or vocabulary flash cards (face up) near you, some near your partner, and some far away
from both of you. Take turns asking and answering questions about the location of each of the cards using the correct
pronoun. For example, if the flash card for あ is near you, you would say:

You:	これは "あ" ですか。 KORE wa "A" DESU ka. **Is this "A"?**
Your partner:	はい、それは "あ" です。 HAI, SORE wa "A" DESU. **Yes, that (near you) is "A."**

---

2. Pair Practice

Point to one of the items pictured below and ask your partner a question. If the object seems near you, use これ. If
KORE
the object seems near the speaker, use それ. If the object seems distant from both of you, use あれ.
SORE   ARE

You:	*(pointing to map of Japan)* これは KORE wa	日本ですか。 NIHON DESU ka	= Is this Japan?
Your partner:	*(if it is correct)* はい、そうです。 HAI, SOU DESU		= Yes, that is correct.
	-OR-		
	(if it is incorrect) いいえ、ちがいます。 IIE, CHIGAIMASU		= No, that is wrong.

Narita: なりた
NARITA

3. Pair Practice

Point to one of the pictures below. Your partner will say the appropriate greeting in 日本語。Take turns.

You: *(pointing to picture of the student greeting teacher early in the day)*

Your partner: おはよう ございます。
OHAYOU GOZAIMASU

よく できました。
YOKU DEKIMASHITA

Well done!

■ 単語 New Words
TAN GO

| Useful Classroom Commands and Expressions |

よく 出来ました。
YOKU DEKIMASHITA

ちょっとまって
ちょっと 待って 下さい。
CHOTTO MATTE KUDASAI

ゆっくり
おねがいします
ゆっくり おねがいします。
YUKKURI ONEGAISHIMASU

もういちど
いってください
もう一度 言って 下さい。
MOU ICHIDO ITTE KUDASAI

はい。わかります。
はい、分かります。
HAI WAKARIMASU

いいえ
わかりません
いいえ、分かりません。
IIE WAKARIMASEN

静かに して 下さい。
SHIZUKAni SHITE KUDASAI

えいごで
いって
ください
英語で 言って 下さい。
EIGO de ITTE KUDASAI

(えんぴつ)を
かしてください
X (object)を 貸して 下さい。
X o KASHITE KUDASAI

WHAT IS honey IN JAPANESE?
X は (英語/日本語)で
X wa (EIGO / NIHONGO) de
何と いいますか。
NANTO IIMASU ka

おてあらい へ
いっても
いい ですか。
(お)てあらいへ 行っても
(O) TEARAIe ITTE mo
いいですか。
IIDESUKA

MAY I GO TO MY LOCKER?
ロッカーへ 行っても
ROKKA-e ITTE mo
いいですか。
I I DESU ka

おみずを
のんでも
いいですか。
(お)水を 飲んでも
(O) MIZUo NONDE mo
いいですか。
I I DESU ka

きりつ
KIRITSU

れい
REI

ちゃくせき
CHAKUSEKI

■ 練習の時間 Time for Practice
RENSHUU no JIKAN

1. Pair Practice

Verbally order your partner to do one of the commands from the list of expressions in Chapter 1-3. Your partner will act it out. Switch roles and do it again until you have both gone through all the commands in that section. If your partner does a particularly good job, you can praise him or her by saying 良く出来ました。
YOKUDE KIMASHITA

2. Pair Practice

Look at the list of classroom objects in Appendix 4. Ask your partner to loan you one. Take turns.

A-さん:　けしゴムを　貸してください。　= Please lend me an eraser.
SAN　　KESHIGOMU o　KASHITEKUDASAI

B-さん:　(Handing, or pretending to hand over, object) はい、どうぞ。　= Here, please (take it).
SAN　　　　　　　　　　　　　　　　　　HAI　DOUZO

3. Class Practice

Play *Sensei Says* using the class-room commands you have learned. Students take turns being the "Sensei."

Caller says:　「Sensei says, たって ください。」
　　　　　　　　　　　TATTE KUDASAI

(all students stand up)

Caller says:　「すわって ください。」
　　　　　　　　SUWATTE KUDASAI

(no one should sit down)

Caller says:　「Sensei says, きょうかしょを 開いて ください。」
　　　　　　　　　　　　KYOUKASHO o HIRAITE KUDASAI

(everyone should open their textbooks)

It's time for your first passport stamp. An immigration officer will interview you. You will need to introduce yourself and demonstrate recognition of the words and kanji in this chapter in order to get your passport stamped or initialed. Each chapter in this text has a task to complete and a stamp to earn. Collect all ten stamps to show that you've completed the cycle and to earn your yellow-belt samurai status. Check the TimeforJapanese.com website for more rewards after collecting all the passport stamps!

■ 単語チェックリスト New Word Checklist
TANGO CHEKKURISUTO

Japanese	Location	English
1-1		
からて　空手 (n)	1-1	karate (martial art)
すし　寿司 (n)	1-1	raw fish on rice
すもう　相撲 (n)	1-1	Japanese sumo wrestling
せんせい　先生 (n)	1-1	teacher
つなみ　津波 (n)	1-1	tidal wave
とうきょう　東京 (n)	1-1	capital of Japan

Japanese	Location	English
とうふ　　豆腐 (n)	1-1	bean curd (tofu)
にほん　　日本 (n)	1-1	Japan
にほんご　　日本語 (n)	1-1	Japanese language
はじめましょう。　　始めましょう。(exp.)	1-1	Let's begin.
ぼく　　僕 (pron.)	1-1	I, me (used by males only)

1-3

Japanese	Location	English
かく/かきます　　書く/書きます(書いて) (v)	1-3	(to) write
きく/ききます　　聞く/聞きます (聞いて) (v)	1-3	(to) listen
〜くん　　〜君	1-3	used immediately AFTER a boy's name
〜さん	1-3	used immediately AFTER a name
すわる/すわります　　座る/座ります (座って) (v)	1-3	(to) sit
〜せんせい　　〜先生 (n)	1-3	used immediately AFTER a teacher's, lawyer's, or doctor's name
だす/だします　　出す/出します (出して) (v)	1-3	(to) take (it) out
たつ/たちます　　立つ/立ちます (立って) (v)	1-3	(to) stand
です (v)	1-3	helping verb/linking verb used similarly to "is" or "am"
どうぞ　よろしく (exp.)	1-3	best regards, please treat me favorably
どうぞ　よろしく　おねがいします　　どうぞ　よろしく　お願いします (exp.)	1-3	polite for よろしく　お願いします
とじる/とじます　　閉じる/閉じます (閉じて) (v)	1-3	(to) close; shut
なまえ　　名前 (n)	1-3	name
は (part.)	1-3	particle that denotes the sentence topic
はじめまして　　初めまして (exp.)	1-3	How do you do?
ひらく/ひらきます　　開く/開きます (開いて) (v)	1-3	(to) open (door/window)
みる/みます　　見る/見ます (見て) (v)	1-3	(to) look/see
よろしく　おねがいします　　よろしく　お願いします (exp.)	1-3	best regards, please treat me favorably (polite)
よむ/よみます　読む/読みます (読んで) (v)	1-3	read
わたし　私 (pron.)	1-3	I, me
わたしたち　私達 (pron.)	1-3	we, us

Classroom Commands and Questions

Japanese	Location	English
だして　　出して (v)	1-3	take (it) out
だしてください。　　出して下さい。	1-3	Take (it) out please.
だしても　いいですか。　　出しても　いいですか。	1-3	Is it OK to take out (it)?
かいて　　書いて (v)	1-3	write
かいてください。　　書いて下さい。	1-3	Write please.
かいても　いいですか。　　書いても　いいですか。	1-3	Is it OK to write?
きいて　　聞いて (v)	1-3	listen
きいてください。　　聞いて下さい。	1-3	Listen please.
きいても　いいですか。　　聞いても　いいですか。	1-3	Is it OK to listen?
みて　　見て (v)	1-3	look/watch
みてください　　見て下さい。	1-3	Look/watch please.
みても　いいですか。　　見ても　いいですか。	1-3	Is it OK to see/watch?
すわって　　座って (v)	1-3	sit

Japanese	Location	English
すってください　　座って下さい。	1-3	Sit please.
すわっても いいですか。　　座っても いいですか。	1-3	Is it OK to sit?
たって　　立って (v)	1-3	stand
たってください　　立って下さい。	1-3	Stand please.
たっても いいですか。　　立っても いいですか。	1-3	Is it OK to stand?
とじて　　閉じて (v)	1-3	close; shut
とじてください。　　閉じて下さい。	1-3	Close/shut (it) please.
とじても いいですか。　　閉じても いいですか。	1-3	Is it OK to close/shut (it)?
ひらいて　　開いて (v)	1-3	open (book)
ひらいてください。　　開いて下さい。	1-3	Open (book) please.
ひらいても いいですか。　　開いても いいですか。	1-3	Is it OK to open?
よんで　　読んで (v)	1-3	read
よんでください。　　読んで下さい。	1-3	Read please.
よんでも いいですか。　　読んでも いいですか。	1-3	Is it OK to read?

1-4

Japanese	Location	English
いいえ	1-4	no
か (part.)	1-4	particle signifying a question
こちら (pron.)	1-4	this person (polite)
たろう　　太郎 (n)	1-4	Taro (male name)
ちがう/ちがいます　　違う/違います (違って) (v)	1-4	is not right, incorrect
ちち　　父 (n)	1-4	father, dad
はい	1-4	yes, here (roll call)
はは　　母 (n)	1-4	mother, mom
ようこそ (exp.)	1-4	Welcome!, Nice to see you.

1-5

Japanese	Location	English
あれ (adj.)	1-5	that (over there)
おかえりなさい　　お帰りなさい (exp.)	1-5	welcome home
おはし　　お箸 (n)	1-5	chopsticks
おはよう (exp.)	1-5	good morning (informal)
おはようございます (exp.)	1-5	good morning (formal)
おやすみ　　お休み (exp.)	1-5	good night (informal)
おやすみ なさい　　お休み なさい (exp.)	1-5	good night (formal)
げんき　　元気 (n/な adj.)	1-5	healthy, energetic
ごはん　　ご飯 (n)	1-5	cooked rice, a meal
これ	1-5	this (one)
こんにちは　　今日は (exp.)	1-5	hello
こんばんは　　今晩は (exp.)	1-5	good evening
さようなら (exp.)	1-5	goodbye
じゃあ また (exp.)	1-5	see you later (informal)
しょうゆ　　醤油 (n)	1-5	soy sauce
それ	1-5	that (one)
ただいま (exp.)	1-5	I'm home
たまご　　卵 (n)	1-5	egg
では また (exp.)	1-5	see you later (formal)

Japanese	Location	English
どれ (*inter.*)	1-5	which (one)
に (*part.*)	1-5	used after a location or time word
ばいばい バイバイ (*exp.*)	1-5	bye-bye
へや 部屋 (*n*)	1-5	room (a)
わさび (*n*)	1-5	wasabi, Japanese horseradish

1-6

Useful Classroom Commands and Expressions

	Location	English
よく できました。 よく 出来ました。	1-6	Well done.
ちょっと まって ください。 ちょっと 待って 下さい。	1-6	Wait a minute please.
ゆっくり おねがいします。 ゆっくり お願いします。	1-6	Please say it more slowly.
もういちど いって ください。 もう一度 言って 下さい。	1-6	Say it again please.
はい、わかります。 はい、分かります。	1-6	Yes, I understand.
いいえ、わかりません。 いいえ、分かりません。	1-6	No, I don't understand.
しりません。 知りません。	1-6	I don't know.
しずかに して ください。 静かに して 下さい。	1-6	Please be quiet.
えいごで いって ください。 英語で 言って 下さい。	1-6	Please say it in English.
X (object)を かして ください。 X (object)を 貸して 下さい。	1-6	Please lend me X.
X (object)は (えいご/にほんご)で なんと いいますか。 X は (英語/日本語)で 何と 言いますか。	1-6	What is X in English/Japanese?
おてあらいへ いっても いいですか。 お手洗いへ 行っても いいですか。	1-6	May I go to the restroom/W.C.?
ロッカーへ いっても いいですか。 ロッカーへ 行っても いいですか。	1-6	May I go to my locker?
おみずを のんでも いいですか。 お水を 飲んでも いいですか。	1-6	May I drink (some) water?
きりつ 起立 (*n*)	1-6	standing up
れい 礼 (*n*)	1-6	bow
ちゃくせき 着席 (*n*)	1-6	sit down

Family and Friends in Tokyo

Learning Goals

By the end of this chapter you will learn:

A) vocabulary and kanji used for talking about family members
B) some ways to count, including general counting and counters for people and objects
C) vocabulary used for talking about basic locations of people and objects
D) several pronouns useful for differentiating basic locations of objects and people (i.e., this one or that one, here or there)
E) the rest of the hiragana if you haven't finished them and 18 additional kanji

Performance Goals

By the end of this chapter you will be able to:

A) read and write essential kanji for family member roles
B) talk about your family and the families of others in terms of numbers and relationships
C) count people and things from one to one hundred
D) talk in general about location of objects and people, and specifically about "which one"
E) read and write the rest of the hiragana if you haven't finished them and 18 additional kanji

それは　何　ですか。
SORE wa　NAN　DESU ka

第2課の1　**What is that?**

■ 会話 Dialogue
KAI WA

じゅん：　それは　何　ですか。
J U N 　　SORE wa　NAN　DESU ka

キアラ：　これは　私の　バッグ　です。　この　なかに　しゃしんが　あります。　これは　私の
KIARA 　　KORE wa　WATASHI no　BAGGU　DESU　KO NO　NAKA ni　SHASHIN ga　ARIMASU　KORE wa　WATASHI no

家族　です。
KAZOKU　DESU

家族は　六人　です。　こちらは　父と　母　です。　妹が　二人　います。　こちらの
KAZOKU wa　ROKUNIN　DESU　KOCHIRA wa　CHICHI to　HAHA　DESU.　IMOUTO ga　FUTARI　IMASU.　KOCHIRA no

二人が　妹　です。　こちらは　兄　です。　犬の　名前は　こま　です。
FUTARI ga　IMOUTO　DESU.　KOCHIRA wa　ANI　DESU　INU no　NAMAE wa　KOMA　DESU

■ 単語 New Words
TAN GO

家族 (n)
KAZOKU

何 (inter.)
NAN or NANI

だれ (inter.)
DARE

しゃしん (n)
SHASHIN

犬 (n)
INU

ねこ (n)
NEKO

電話 (n)
DENWA

ご家族 (n) – (someone else's family)
GOKAZOKU

姉 (n) – (my) older sister
ANE

兄 (n) – (my) older brother
ANI

弟 (n) – (my) younger brother
OTOUTO

妹 (n) – (my) younger sister
IMOUTO

兄弟 (n) – siblings
KYOUDAI

そ父 (n) – (my) grandfather
SOFU

そ母 (n) – (my) grandmother
SOBO

います (v) – to exist (animate beings)
IMASU

あります (v) – to exist (inanimate things)
ARIMASU

Other words you might like to know:

一番上の ICHIBANUE no~	兄/姉 ANI / ANE	my oldest brother/sister
二番目の NIBANMEN no~	兄/姉 ANI / ANE	my second oldest brother/sister
すぐ下の SUGUSHITA no	弟/妹 OTOUTO/IMOUTO	my next youngest brother/sister
一番下の ICHIBANSHITA no	弟/妹 OTOUTO/IMOUTO	my youngest brother/sister
ぎりの〜 GIRI no~		step-, or in-law, a non-"blood" relative*

Counting				Counting People			
一 ICHI	1	六 ROKU	6	一人 HITORI	1 person	七人 SHICHININ/ NANANIN	7 people
二 NI	2	七 SHICHI/NANA	7	二人 FUTARI	2 people	八人 HACHININ	8 people
三 SAN	3	八 HACHI	8	三人 SANNIN	3 people	九人 KYUUNIN	9 people
四 YON/SHI	4	九 KU/KYUU	9	四人 YONIN	4 people	十人 JUUNIN	10 people
五 GO	5	十 JUU	10	五人 GONIN	5 people	何人 NANNIN	how many people?
		いくつ IKUTSU	how many?	六人 ROKUNIN	6 people		

*Traditionally, Japanese families tended to be large, with three generations in one household. This is changing in Japan quite rapidly. Now one can find various types of non-traditional families. In the West, we often use "step-" or "half-" to refer to people in our families. In daily life in Japan however, these distinctions are rarely made; "step-" and "half-" relatives are often referred to simply as mother, father, brother, sister, etc.

■ 漢字 Kanji
KAN JI

何 7 strokes	なに; なん – what NANI NAN	ノ	イ	仁	仃	仃	伺	何
	何 – what; 何人 – how many people? NAN/NANI NANNIN							
	The first two strokes are a person. The 3rd and 7th strokes are a nail, and the center three strokes are a mouth. Imagine seeing a person striking a nail with his head; you will want to open your mouth and yell "WHAT?"							

家 10 strokes	カ, いえ – house; it is also sometimes KA IE pronounced as うち – house (home) UCHI	'	⼂	宀	宀	宁	字	家
	家 – house, home; 家(族) – family IE KA (ZOKU)	家	家					
	The first 3 strokes represent a roof; the remaining 7 strokes are the right side of pig 豚 (imagining these 7 strokes as pork ribs may help). Imagine the three little piggies hiding under the roof of their HOUSE.							

兄 5 strokes	キョウ; あに; (お)にい(さん) – older brother K Y O U A N I (O) N I I (SAN)	丶	口	口	尸	兄		
	兄 – (my) older brother; お兄さん – someone ANI O N I I S A N else's older brother							
	This kanji consists of a big mouth (口) with two long legs. Think of some tall big-mouthed OLDER BROTHER that you might know!							

 あね；（お）ねえ（さん）– older sister ANE (O) NEE (SAN)	く	夂	女	女`	女˧	女˧	妒	姉
姉 – older sister (informal)；（お）姉（さん）– older ANE (O) NEE (SAN) sister (polite term for someone else's older sister)								
8 strokes The left side of this kanji (女) is the kanji for female while the right side (市) means city and the combo could represent an OLDER SISTER who lives in the city.								

ダイ；おとうと– younger brother DAI OTOUTO	＼	＼＼	⺌	丷	当	弟	弟	
弟 – younger brother (informal)；弟（さん）– younger brother OTOUTO OTOUTO (SAN) (polite term for someone else's younger brother)；（兄）弟 – siblings (KYOU)DAI								
7 strokes Does this look like a YOUNGER BROTHER wearing a scary mask? If not, send your better idea to TimeForJapanese.com								

いもうと – younger sister IMOUTO	く	夂	女	女̆	女̄	姅	妹	妹
妹 – younger sister (informal)；妹（さん）– younger IMOUTO IMOUTO (SAN) sister (polite)								
8 strokes The left side of this kanji (女) again is the kanji for female, while the right side (未) is a tree with an extra horizontal line across representing the floor of a tree house the YOUNGER SISTER's father is making for her.								

■ 言葉の探索 Language Detection
KOTOBA no TANSAKU

1. います and あります "to exist"
   IMASU   ARIMASU

   Both of these verbs mean "to exist." The difference is that います is used for animate objects and あります is used
   IMASU   ARIMASU

   for inanimate objects. います and あります are often translated as "to have" or "there is."
   IMASU   ARIMASU

   The particle が is usually used in statements with います and あります. When います or あります are used in
   ga   IMASU   ARIMASU   IMASU   ARIMASU

   questions, you can use the particle は after the topic being asked about.
   wa

A) 兄が　います。 = I have an older brother./There is an older brother.
   ANI ga IMASU

B) 犬が　います。 = I have a dog./There is a dog.
   INU ga IMASU

C) 家族の　しゃしんが　あります。 = I have family pictures./There is a family picture.
   KAZOKU no SHASHIN ga ARIMASU

D) 私の　おはしが　あります。 = I have chopsticks./My chopsticks are (here).
   WATASHI no o HASHI ga ARIMASU

E) たまごは　ありますか。 = Do you have any eggs?/Are there eggs?
   TAMAGO wa ARIMASU ka

F) ご家族の　しゃしんは　ありますか。 = Do you have a picture of your family?
   GOKAZOKU no SHASHIN wa ARIMASU ka

2. **The particle の**

Two uses of the particle の are to show possession, and to show a relationship of one noun to another, one noun being "of" the kind/type of another.

To show possession, の is placed between two nouns with the first one "possessing" the second.

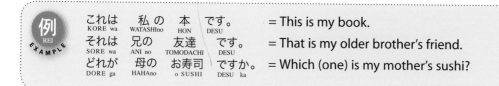

これは	私 の	本	です。	= This is my book.
KORE wa	WATASHI no	HON	DESU	
それは	兄の	友達	です。	= That is my older brother's friend.
SORE wa	ANI no	TOMODACHI	DESU	
どれが	母の	お寿司	ですか。	= Which (one) is my mother's sushi?
DORE ga	HAHA no	o SUSHI	DESU ka	

The particle の is used to show the relationship of one noun to another as in *Japanese book, Japanese sushi*, etc. The noun being described (*book* or *sushi* in these examples) is second and の comes after the first noun (the one doing the describing).

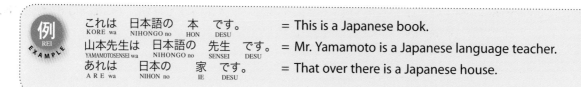

これは	日本語の	本	です。	= This is a Japanese book.
KORE wa	NIHONGO no	HON	DESU	
山本先生は	日本語の	先生	です。	= Mr. Yamamoto is a Japanese language teacher.
YAMAMOTOSENSEI wa	NIHONGO no	SENSEI	DESU	
あれは	日本の	家	です。	= That over there is a Japanese house.
ARE wa	NIHON no	IE	DESU	

■ 自習 Self Check
JI SHUU

1. Use the words from these two lists to make complete sentences. Use the particle の to say what belongs to whom. Follow the example, and say them out loud to yourself in Japanese. Then choose one word from List 1 to make a sentence using います and one word from List 2 to make a sentence using あります.
    IMASU   ARIMASU

A: 父 + 写真 → これは 父 の 写真 です。
    CHICHI   SHASHIN   KORE wa   CHICHI no   SHASHIN   DESU
    = This is my father's photo.

B: それは じゅんさんの バッグ です。
    SORE wa   JUN SAN no   BAGGU   DESU
    = That is Jun's bag.

List 1	List 2
父 CHICHI	バッグ BAGGU
僕 BOKU	姉 ANE
妹 IMOUTO	へや HEYA
英語 EI GO	先生 SENSEI
おとうと OTOUTO	ごはん GOHAN
じゅん JUN	はし HASHI
キアラ KIARA	(free choice)

2. How would you respond to the following?

    ⮑ ご家族は 何人 ですか。
       GOKAZOKU wa   NANNIN   DESU ka

    ⮑ ご家族を しょうかい (introduce) してください。
       GOKAZOKU o   SHOU KAI   SHITEKUDASAI

3. Look at a variety of objects around you. Practice saying whom they belong to. Refer to Appendix 4, Classroom Objects.

> A: これは 私 の えんぴつ です。　　　= This is my pencil.
> 　　KORE wa　WATASHIno　ENPITSU　DESU
> B: それは ジョンさん の バックパック です。　= That is John's backpack.
> 　　SORE wa　JON-SAN　no　BAKKUPAKKU　DESU

■ 練習の時間 Time for Practice
RENSHUU no JIKAN

1. Pair Practice

これは 私の えんぴつ です。
KORE wa WATASHIno ENPITSU DESU

Pretend you belong to Jun's family. Take turns giving each of his family members below possession of one of the objects. See how many combinations you and your partner can make. Make sure you use the correct word order, that is, X (person) の Y (possession). For instance, ベン君(person) の えんぴつ(possession) です。
　　　　　　　　　　　　　　　no　　　　　　　　　BEN-KUN　　　no　ENPITSU　　　DESU

> 例 REI EXAMPLE　これは 母の はし です。 = These are my mother's chopsticks.
> 　　　　　　　　KORE wa　HAHAno　HASHI　DESU

2. Pair Practice

Describing your family

Without letting your partner see your drawing, each of you should draw a quick picture of a family with 4 to 6 members and pets. Be sure to include the names of each in your drawing. Next, one of you (A-さん) needs to describe your family to your partner in Japanese. Make statements about the family you've drawn using です and います. The partner (B-さん) draws what he/she hears. Switch roles and repeat the exercise. After you have both finished, reveal the original drawing to your partner. Save your drawings for an activity in the second section of this chapter.

> 例 REI EXAMPLE　A-さん might say: 家族は 五人 です。 母と 父と 兄と 妹が います。 母の 名前は けいこ です。
> 　　　　　　　　　　　　　　　KAZOKUwa GONIN DESU HAHAto CHICHIto ANIto IMOUTOga IMASU HAHAno NAMAEwa KEIKO DESU
> = My family has five people. I have a mother, father, older brother, and younger sister. My mother's name is Keiko.

3. Pair Practice

Describing things in the room

Point out everything and everyone in the classroom that you know and say these in Japanese to your partner. Use the classroom objects appendix in the back of this book if needed.

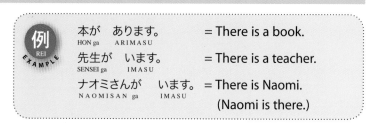

本が　あります。　= There is a book.
HON ga　ARIMASU

先生が　います。　= There is a teacher.
SENSEI ga　IMASU

ナオミさんが　います。= There is Naomi.
NAOMISAN ga　IMASU
(Naomi is there.)

4. Group Work

Each partner should take out 5 objects and place them on one of your desks. Take turns saying which objects belong to whom.

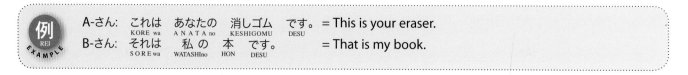

A-さん:　これは　あなたの　消しゴム　です。　= This is your eraser.
　　　　　KORE wa　ANATA no　KESHIGOMU　DESU

B-さん:　それは　私の　本　です。　= That is my book.
　　　　　SORE wa　WATASHI no　HON　DESU

■ 文化箱 Culture Chest
BUN KA BAKO

Humility

Outward signs of pride are frowned upon in Japan. Therefore, the use of humble terms when talking about yourself and your own family members is the rule. That is why Kiara uses the humble form of mother 母 when she talks about her own mother to others but the polite term お母さん when she speaks directly to her own mother. Polite family terms take the suffix　–さん　and sometimes the honorific お-, while the humble terms do not. The suffix　–さん　roughly means Mr. or Ms. and thus would be too polite when talking about one's own family (just as it would be strange to use Mr. and Ms. when talking about your own parents in English).

Since the Japanese people consider family members an extension of themselves, it is not uncommon for Japanese mothers to say rather negative things about their children or spouses as a natural way of being humble. For instance, some mothers may talk about how their children are unintelligent or lazy. It is wise NOT to agree with mothers when they say such things, as the opposite is quite often true!

■ キアラのジャーナル Kiara's Journal
KIARA no JA-NARU

Dear Journal,

I landed in Tokyo today. There were two nice people at the immigration desk at 成田空港 who were
NARITA KUUKOU
very helpful. After I showed them my passport, they asked me several questions about why I was coming to Japan, where I was staying, and how long I would be here. I was a bit nervous, but they smiled and welcomed me to 日本. Once I finished with Customs, I went out into the huge and noisy arrival lobby. Jun-kun stood among all the other greeters, with his お父さん and お母さん. Jun-san's お父さん、 holding up a sign with my name on it, was easy to spot. I'm so glad they are as friendly as I imagined. I was pretty nervous about whether or not we would like each other, but it looks like we'll get along fine.

じゅん君 is a little taller than I am and he is very thin. He's a really friendly guy but he does seem a little geeky. Once we left Narita Airport, we boarded the train for 東京. The train was amazing. By pushing a lever, you could turn the seats around 180° to adjust to the new direction of the train or to be able to face your friends or family members. There were even vending machines selling drinks, telephone cards, and disposable cameras in one of the cars. I've never seen anything like that. The train ride seemed long, about an hour. And that wasn't all: then we had to ride a bus for 15 minutes from 東京 Station to じゅん君 の家. じゅん君 brought along a manga and read almost the entire book before we reached his 家. I was excited, but exhausted too. I remember seeing rice fields and temples, then lots of cars and buildings.

I was a bit nervous about finally meeting the rest of じゅん君のご家族. Once we got to his house, his mother went out to get 天ぷら for dinner while I went to my room to unpack.

I almost forgot my おみやげ, but I grabbed it out of my bags at the last minute and brought it downstairs. They seemed to appreciate the gifts. After we ate the delicious 天ぷら, they gave me some green tea and cookies and let me take a bath and rest. I was more tired than I realized and nearly fell asleep in the bathtub.

■ テクノの時間 Techno Time

Though you've not been introduced to them all yet, type all of the vocabulary words from chapters 1 and 2 into a "digital dictionary." Your teacher will give you guidance on how to type in Japanese or you can find out more on TimeForJapanese.com. To help you organize your files, open a spreadsheet and title the document jishoXXXYYY. In place of the X's, use the first three letters of your family name. In place of the Y's, use the first three letters of your given name. For example, if your name is Tomo Tanuki you would title your dictionary *jishotantom.*

Be sure to type first the hiragana, then kanji, and then the English meaning, as the sample below shows.

とうきょう	東京	Tokyo, capital of Japan
です	です	is or am

こちらは　ベンくんの　お母さん　です。
KOCHIRA wa　BEN-KUN no　OKAASAN　DESU

This is Ben's mother.

1) ここは 友達の　家 です。　失礼 します。

2) はい　はい。

3) じゅん君、こんにちは。

4) こんにちは。こちらはベン君の お母さん です。

5) 私はキャシーです。

6) こんにちは。I'm Kiara. I'm staying with Jun's family. 日本語で 話してもいい ですか。

7) いい ですよ。日本 ですから。がんばって 下さい！どうぞ 上がって 下さい。

8) こちらは ベン君の お兄さん です。ジャックさん です。こちらは 妹さん達 です。ケーラさんと セーラさん です。

9) はじめまして。

（ジャック）

ケーラ and セーラ

■ 会話 Dialogue
KAI WA

じゅん　　：ここは　友達の　家　です。
　　　　　　KOKO wa　TOMODACHI no　IE　DESU

　　　　　　[knock knock] 失礼　します。
　　　　　　　　　　　　　SHITSUREI　SHIMASU

ベンの母　：はいはい。　じゅん君、　こんにちは。
　　　　　　HAIHAI　JU N-KUN,　KONNICHI wa

じゅん　　：こんにちは。　こちらは　ベン君の　お母さん　です。
　　　　　　KONNICHI wa　KOCHIRA wa　KE N-KUN no　OKAASAN　DESU

ベンの母　：私は　キャシー　です。
　　　　　　WATASHI wa　KYASHII　DESU

キアラ　　：こんにちは。I'm Kiara. I'm staying with Jun's family. 日本語で　話しても　いい　ですか。
　　　　　　KONNICHI wa　　　　　　　　　　　　　　　　　　　　　　　NIHON GO DE　HANASHITE MO　I I　DESU ka

ベンの母　：いい　ですよ。日本　です　から。　がんばって　下さい！どうぞ　上がって　下さい。
　　　　　　I I　DESU YO.　NIHON　DESU　KARA　GANBATTE　KUDASAI　DOUZO　AGATTE　KUDASAI

じゅん　　：こちらは　ベン君　の　お兄さん　です。ジャックさん　です。こちらは　妹さん達
　　　　　　KOCHIRA wa　BE N-KUN　no　ONIISAN　DESU　JAKKU-SAN　DESU　KOCHIRA wa　IMOUTOSAN-TACHI

　　　　　　です。*ケーラさんと　+セーラさん　です。
　　　　　　DESU　KEERA-SAN to　SEERA-SAN　DESU

キアラ　　：はじめまして。
　　　　　　HAJIMEMASHITE

*ケーラ - Kara (proper name in English)
　KEERA

+セーラ - Sarah (proper name in English)
　SEERA

■ 単語 New Words
TAN GO

お父さん (n) – (someone's) father
OTOUSAN

お母さん (n) – (someone's) mother
OKAASAN

お兄さん (n) – (someone's) older brother
ONIISAN

お姉さん (n) – (someone's) older sister
ONEESAN

弟さん (n) – (someone's) younger brother
OTOUTOSAN

妹さん (n) – (someone's) younger sister
IMOUTOSAN

おばあさん (n) – (someone's) grandmother
OBAASAN

おばさん (n) – aunt or woman (quite a bit older than you)
OBASAN

おじいさん (n) – (someone's) grandfather
OJIISAN

おじさん (n) – uncle or man (quite a bit older than you)
OJISAN

家 (n) – house/home
IE/UCHI

名前 (n) – name
NAMAE

人 (n) – person
HITO

と (part.) – particle used for "and"
TO

友達 (n)
TOMODACHI

十一 – 11 JUU ICHI	十六 – 16 JUU ROKU	二十一 – 21 NI JUU ICHI	七十 – 70 NANAJUU
十二 – 12 JUU NI	十七 – 17 JUUNANA, JUUSHICHI	三十 – 30 SAN JUU	八十 – 80 HACHIJUU
十三 – 13 JUU SAN	十八 – 18 JUUHACHI	四十 – 40 YON JUU	九十 – 90 KYUU JUU
十四 – 14 JUUYON, JUUSHI	十九 – 19 JUUKU, JUUKYUU	五十 – 50 GO JUU	百 – 100 HYAKU
十五 – 15 JUU GO	二十 – 20 NI JUU	六十 – 60 ROKU JUU	

For more on how to count by 100s up to 900, go to www.TimeForJapanese.com (Beginning Japanese, Ch. 2).

■ 漢字 Kanji
KAN JI

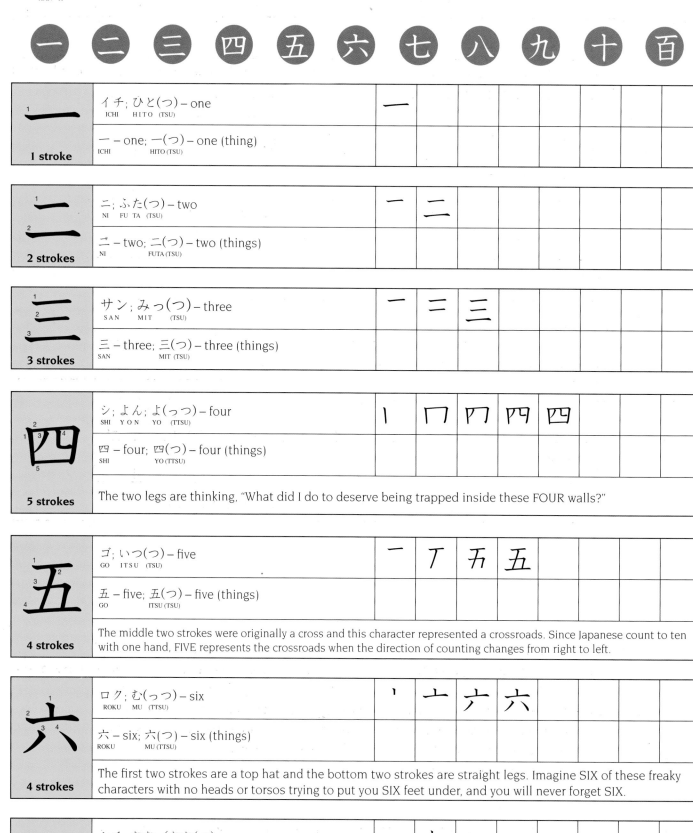

一　二　三　四　五　六　七　八　九　十　百

1 一 **1 stroke**	イチ; ひと(つ) – one ICHI HITO (TSU)	一						
	一 – one; 一(つ) – one (thing) ICHI HITO (TSU)							

1 **2** 二 **2 strokes**	ニ; ふた(つ) – two NI FU TA (TSU)	一	二					
	二 – two; 二(つ) – two (things) NI FUTA (TSU)							

1 **2** **3** 三 **3 strokes**	サン; みっ(つ) – three SAN MIT (TSU)	一	二	三				
	三 – three; 三(つ) – three (things) SAN MIT (TSU)							

1 **2 3 4** 四 **5** **5 strokes**	シ; よん; よ(っつ) – four SHI YON YO (TTSU)	丨	冂	冂	四	四		
	四 – four; 四(つ) – four (things) SHI YO (TTSU)							
	The two legs are thinking, "What did I do to deserve being trapped inside these FOUR walls?"							

1 **2** 五 **3** **4** **4 strokes**	ゴ; いつ(つ) – five GO ITSU (TSU)	一	丁	丆	五			
	五 – five; 五(つ) – five (things) GO ITSU (TSU)							
	The middle two strokes were originally a cross and this character represented a crossroads. Since Japanese count to ten with one hand, FIVE represents the crossroads when the direction of counting changes from right to left.							

2 1 **3 4** 六 **4 strokes**	ロク; む(っつ) – six ROKU MU (TTSU)	丶	亠	六	六			
	六 – six; 六(つ) – six (things) ROKU MU (TTSU)							
	The first two strokes are a top hat and the bottom two strokes are straight legs. Imagine SIX of these freaky characters with no heads or torsos trying to put you SIX feet under, and you will never forget SIX.							

2 **1** 七 **2 strokes**	シチ; なな／なな(つ) — seven SHICHI NANA / NANA (TSU)	一	七					
	七 – seven; 七(つ) – seven (things) NANA/SHICHI NANA(TSU)							
	Imagine a boy sitting down with outstretched hands to collect the money that falls from the sky. Talk about lucky SEVEN!							

八 2 strokes	ハチ — eight; や(っつ) – eight things HACHI YA (TTSU) ハ – eight; ハ(つ) – eight (things) HACHI YA (TTSU)	ノ	八						
	This kanji is made up of two strokes that look somewhat like a volcano. Volcanoes can reach at least a level EIGHT on a scale of hotness!								

九 2 strokes	キュウ; く; ここの(つ) – nine K Y U U K U KOKO no (TSU) 九 – nine; 九(つ) – nine (things) KU/KYUU KOKONO(TSU)	ノ	九						
	The two strokes of the kanji for NINE intersect at a NINEty degree angle with the second stroke starting at what would be NINE o'clock.								

十 2 strokes	ジュウ; とう – ten J U U T O U 十 – ten; 十 – ten (things) JUU TOU	一	十						
	This looks like a "T," the first letter of TEN and TOU (TEN things).								

百 6 strokes	ヒャク – hundred H Y A K U 百 – one hundred HYAKU	一	丆	丆	万	百	百		
	This character looks like a large tray holding 100 glasses of water on top of a hot sun.								

■ 言葉の探索 Language Detection
KOTOBA no TANSAKU

1. **Counters**

   In English, we have "counter" words such as *flocks*, *loaves*, *packs*, *slices*, *herds*, etc. to differentiate the numbers of various objects or animals. The Japanese language also uses different word endings (counters) to count various types of animate and inanimate objects. For example, one person is 一人, one tree is 一本, and one car is 一台 . When counting

HITORI   IPPON   ICHI DAI
   people, place the number in front of the kanji ~人 (person). The pronunciations for *one person* (一人) and *two people*

NIN   HITORI
   (二人) are based on an old Japanese counting system. Counting up from three people and higher is simple: use the

FUTARI
   numbers you have already learned and add the counter 人 after each number.

NIN

   For a list of other counters, see Appendix 1.

2. **と "and"**

to
   One use of と is as a particle that connects two or more nouns just like the word "and." Unlike English, however, と

to   to
   is used between every noun in a list, even if you are listing three or more things. Note that the particle と can only

                                                                                       to
   be used to connect nouns (people, places, and things) and not verbs, adverbs, and adjectives.

例 REI EXAMPLE

すしと わさびと しょうゆが あります。	= There is sushi and wasabi and soy sauce.
SUSHI to WASABI to SHOUYU ga ARIMASU	
お父さんと お母さんが います。	= He/she has a father and mother.
OTOUSAN to OKAASAN ga IMASU	
キアラと じゅんは いますか。	= Are Kiara and Jun (here)?
KIARA to JUN wa IMASU ka	

■ 自習 Self Check
JI SHUU

1. Column A contains family words for my own family. Column B contains words for a friend's family. See how well and quickly you can fill in the blanks, without using your book. Then check your answers. The first one is done for you.

A

1. いもうと
   IMOUTO

2. _____

3. _____

4. 母
   HAHA

5. おとうと
   OTOUTO

6. _____

7. あね
   ANE

8. そふ
   SOFU

B

いもうとさん
IMOTOUSAN

おにいさん
ONIISAN

おばあさん
OBAASAN

_____

_____

おとうさん
OTOUSAN

_____

_____

2. Count from one to ten, three times, as quickly as you can. Use hand motions. Then count backwards. Then take turns with your partner, each of you counting off one number.

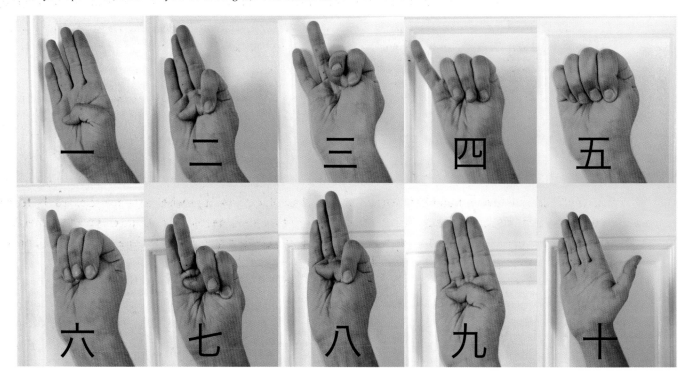

■ 練習の時間 Time for Practice
RENSHUU no JIKAN

---

1. Pair Practice

Introducing someone else's family

Look back at the 練習の時間 in Chapter 2-1 and use the drawing you created for that section, or find another online.
RENSHUU no JIKAN
Introduce that family to your partner (substitute your favorite Japanese name in place of 私 in the family tree).
WATASHI
Use the terms for someone else's family members. Take turns.

こちらは　いちろう君の　ご家族　です。　こちらは　お母さん　です。　お母さんの　名前は　けいこさん　です。
KOCHIRA wa　ICHIROU KUN no　GO-KAZOKU　DESU　KOCHIRA wa　OKAASAN　DESU　OKAASAN no　NAMAE wa　KEIKO -SAN　DESU

= This is Ichirou's family. This is his mother. His mother's name is Keiko.

---

2. Small Group Practice

Form groups of 4 students. In pairs, find out how many people are in your partner's family, and who they are. Share that information with your group. Take turns.

A-SAN:　ご家族は　何人　ですか。　　　　　　　　　= How many people are there in your family?
GO-KAZOKU wa　NANNIN　DESU ka

B-SAN:　四人　です。　父と　母と　妹　が　います。= Four people. My father, mother, and my younger sister.
YONIN　DESU　CHICHI to　HAHA to　IMOUTO ga　IMASU

A-SAN (to group):　B－さんの　ご家族は　四人　です。　お父さんと　お母さんと　妹さんと　B－さんの
B - S A N no　GOKAZOKU wa　YONIN　DESU　OTOUSAN to　OKAASAN to　IMOUTOSAN to　B - S A N no

四人　です。
YONIN　DESU

= _____ 's family has four people. His/her father, mother, younger sister, and
himself/herself equals four people.

Follow up by asking your partner the names of their family members and then sharing those names with the group.

A-SAN:　お母さんの　なまえは　何　ですか。　　= What is your mother's name?
OKAASAN no　NAMAE wa　NAN　DESU ka

B-SAN:　母の　名前は　さとみ　です。　　　　　= My mother's name is Satomi.
HAHA no　NAMAE wa　SATOMI　DESU

A-SAN (to other):　B-SAN の　お母さんの　なまえは　さとみさん　です。= B's mother's name is Satomi.
B - S A N no　OKAASAN no　NAMAE wa　SATOMI-SAN　DESU

---

3. Class Practice

Your sensei will hold up between 1 and 10 fingers. Quickly and silently form groups with as many people as the teacher holds up fingers. Upon the sensei's cue, call out the counter for that many people. For example, if your teacher holds up three fingers, you quickly form groups of three and, upon cue, call out 三人. Repeat, when your sensei holds up
SANNIN
another group of fingers.

■ 文化箱 Culture Chest
BUN KA BAKO

It's all in the numbers...

In Japan some numbers are considered unlucky. し, one of two pronunciations for *four* (四), is often considered the unluckiest number because し can also mean *death* (死). Hospitals in Japan rarely have a fourth floor (floors skip from three to five), and some hospitals intentionally omit the number four in room numbers. Many times the alternate pronunciation よん is used. Nine is also an unlucky number, since the sound KU can also mean *suffering* in both the words 苦 and 苦労.
_{KU} _{KUROU}
There are even unlucky ages. For men, it is well known in Japan that 42 is the unluckiest age, since the kanji 四二 can be pronounced SHI NI, which is close to 死に or "to the death." Less well known is that 33 is the unluckiest age for women because one way you can read the kanji 三三 is SANZAN, which can also mean "to have a terrible time."

■ キアラのジャーナル Kiara's Journal
KIARA no JA-NARU

Read these questions and then read Kiara's journal entry to answer them.

❶ How many people are in Jun's family?
❷ Compare Japanese naming traditions with how you received your name. Are there any similarities?
❸ How many people are in Ben's family?
❹ What is Ben's older brother studying?

My family
(Kiara's)

Dear Journal,

じゅん君の ご家族は 五人です。お父さんの 名前は 太郎さん です。お母さんの
JUN KUN no GO-KAZOKU wa GONIN DESU OTOUSAN no NAMAE wa TAROU SAN DESU OKAA SAN no
名前は まゆみ さん です。じゅん君の お兄 さんは 一郎 さん です。妹さんは
NAMAE wa MAYUMI SAN DESU JUN KUN no ONII SAN wa ICHIROU SAN DESU IMOUTOSAN wa
愛子ちゃんです。 I didn't know that all Japanese names have meaning. For instance, 愛 means love. So
AIKO-CHAN DESU AI
愛子 actually means "love child"! Can you guess what his older brother's name means? Parents put a lot of time and consideration into choosing names for their children. The meanings and even the stroke count are important and so parents often consult family members (especially grandparents) when naming a child.

Tonight I met Jun's 友達. 友達 の 名前は ベン です。ベン君の 家は広尾に あります。
TOMODACHI no NAMAE wa BEN DESU BEN-KUN no IE wa HIROO ni ARIMASU
広尾 is an upscale part of 東京. オーストラリア大使館は (Embassy) very close. ベン君は
O-SUTORARIA TAISHIKAN BEN-KUN wa
オーストラリア人 です。 ベン君の お母さん works at the オーストラリア 大使館 and his
O-SUTORARIAJIN DESU BEN-KUN no OKAA SAN O-SUTORARIA TAISHIKAN
お父さん works for a Japanese export company.
OTOUSAN
ベン君には お父さんと お母さんと お兄さん 一人と 双子の 妹さんが います。犬2匹と
BEN-KUN niwa OTOUSAN to OKAASAN to ONIISAN HITORI to FUTAGO IMOUTOSAN ga IMASU INU NIHIKI
ねこも一匹 います。お兄さんは studying 日本語 at 東京国際大学, Tokyo International
NEKO mo IPPIKI IMASU ONIISAN KOKUSAI DAIGAKU
University.

この　バッグに　おみやげが　あります。どうぞ。
KONO　BAGGU ni　OMIYAGE ga　ARIMASU. DOUZO.
The souvenirs are in this bag. Here you go.

■ 会話 Dialogue
KAI WA

キアラ：　　この　　バッグに　みなさんのおみやげが　あります。どうぞ。
KIARA　　　KONO　BAGGU ni　MI NA SAN no OMIYAGE ga　ARIMASU　DOUZO

まゆみ：　　あらっ…　どうも　ありがとう。
MAYUMI　　A RA　　DOU mo　ARIGATOU

キアラ：　　どう　いたしまして。その　本は　お母さんへの　おみやげ　です。その　ぼうしは　お父さん
KIARA　　　DOO　ITASHIMASHITE　SO no　HON wa　OKAASAN e no　OMIYAGE　DESU.　SO NO　BOUSHI wa　OTOUSAN

　　　　　のです。このTーシャツは　じゅん君の　です。この　キャンディは　お兄さんと　妹さんの
　　　　　no DESU　KONO T - SHATSU wa　J U N-KUN no　DESU　KO NO　KYANDII wa　ONIISAN to　IMOUTOSAN no

　　　　　です。
　　　　　DESU

じゅん：　　どうも　ありがとう。
J U N　　　DOUMO　ARIGATOU

キアラ：　　じゅん君、　クラスには　　何人　いますか。クラスの　皆にも　おみやげが　あります。
KIARA　　　J U N-KUN,　KURASU ni wa　NANNIN　IMASU ka　KURASU no　MINNA ni mo　OMIYAGE ga　ARIMASU

じゅん：　　四十人　です。
J U N　　　YONJUUNIN　DESU

■ 単語 New Words
TAN GO

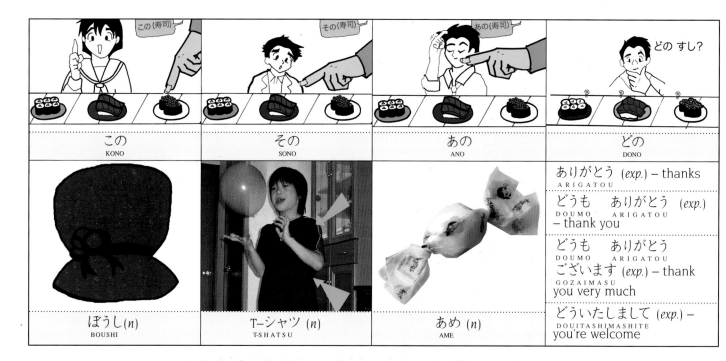

この	その	あの	どの
KONO	SONO	ANO	DONO

ぼうし(n)	Tーシャツ (n)	あめ (n)	ありがとう (exp.) – thanks
BOUSHI	T-SHATSU	AME	ARIGATOU

ありがとう (exp.) – thanks
ARIGATOU

どうも　ありがとう (exp.)
DOUMO　ARIGATOU
– thank you

どうも　ありがとう
DOUMO　ARIGATOU
ございます (exp.) – thank
GOZAIMASU
you very much

どういたしまして (exp.) –
DOUITASHIMASHITE
you're welcome

■ 漢字 Kanji
KAN JI

犬

犬	いぬ I N U	一	ナ	大	犬			
4 strokes								

This is the kanji for DOG. 大 means big, and if you can picture the top right corner of this as a big DOG's mouth and the last stroke as a bone being thrown into the DOG's mouth, you should be able to remember this kanji.

■ 言葉の探索 Language Detection
KOTOBA no TANSAKU

1. この 、その 、あの 、どの
    KONO   SONO   ANO   DONO

These words have similar meaning to これ、 それ、 あれ、 どれ. The only difference is that この 、 その 、 あの、
KORE SORE ARE DORE   KONO   SONO   ANO

どの come before a noun in ALL cases. これ、 それ、 あれ、 どれ are not attached to nouns since they are pro-
DONO   KORE SORE ARE DORE

nouns that replace nouns.

これ KORE	= this one	
この　すし KONO　SUSHI	= this sushi	
それ SORE	= that one (near the listener)	
その　わさび SONO　WASABI	= that wasabi (near the listener)	

あれ ARE	= that one (over there)
あの　しょうゆ ANO　SHOUYU	= that soy sauce (over there)
どれ DORE	= which one
どのへや DONO HEYA	= which room?

2. を
    o

The particle を follows the direct object of a sentence. The direct object is the noun that receives the action of the verb,
         o

that is, what is eaten, what is written, what is played, etc. This particle will be explained in more detail in Chapter 3.
Here are some English sentences that contain direct objects. The direct objects are bolded and underlined here.

I ate the **hamburger**.　　　　　Jose watches **TV**.

Please write the **report**.　　　　Timmy did not kick the **ball**.

A. Object を　下さい.　⇒　This phrase is used to ask someone to give you something.
          o　　KUDASAI

> 例 REI EXAMPLE
>
> しょうゆを　下さい。　　= Please give me the soy sauce.
> SHOUYU o　　KUDASAI
>
> 本を　下さい。　　　　= Please give me a/the book.
> HON o　　KUDASAI
>
> まんがを　下さい。　　= Please give me a/the manga.
> MANGA o　　KUDASAI

B. Object を　どうぞ.　⇒　This phrase is used to offer something to someone.
          o　　DOUZO

> 例 REI EXAMPLE
>
> お水を　どうぞ。　　= Have some water.
> OMIZU o　　DOUZO
>
> ケーキを　どうぞ。　　= Have some cake.
> KE-KI o　　DOUZO
>
> ティッシュを　どうぞ。　= Please have a tissue.
> TISSHU o　　DOUZO

The word どうぞ, when used by itself, can often be translated as "go ahead" or "here you are."
         DOUZO

■ 自習 Self Check
JI SHUU

1. Count the number of students in the classroom, using the proper counter words for people.

2. What words best fit in the blanks below?

    A) _____ すし = this sushi
       SUSHI

    B) _____ いぬ = that dog near you
       INU

    C) _____ ごはん = that bowl of rice over there
       GOHAN

    D) _____ たまご = which egg?
       TAMAGO

3. Translate the following into English, out loud, to yourself.

    A) その すしを　どうぞ。
       SONO SUSHI o DOUZO
    B) しゃしんを　下さい。
       SHASHIN o KUDASAI

4. Translate the following into Japanese, out loud, to yourself.

    A) Please give me the chopsticks.
    B) Here you are. (go ahead)

■ 練習の時間 Time for Practice
RENSHUU no JIKAN

1. **Pair Practice**

    Use the classroom objects in Appendix 4 for vocabulary. Ask your partner to give you as many different items as he or she can. Your partner responds.

    例   A-SAN: えんぴつ を 下さい。 = Please give me a pencil.
    REI   ENPITSU o KUDASAI
    EXAMPLE B-SAN: えんぴつ を どうぞ。 = Here is a pencil.
                 ENPITSU o DOUZO

2. **Pair Practice**

    Do the same pair practice as above, but this time, point and insert the words この 、 その、 あの、 どの into the
                                                                          KONO   SONO   ANO   DONO
    sentences. Remember, you will use a different word depending on where the object is located IN RELATION to the
    speaker.

    例   A-SAN: その 本を 下さい。 = Please give me that book.
    REI   SONO HONo KUDASAI
    EXAMPLE B-SAN: はい、この 本を どうぞ。 = Yes, please take this book.
                 HAI, KONO HONo DOUZO

3. Pair Practice

Point to something near you and make a statement. Your partner responds. Take turns.

A-さん: (*pointing to your backpack*) このバックパックは　私の　です。   = This backpack is mine.
SAN   KONO BAKKUPAKKU wa   WATASHI no   DESU

B-さん: そう　ですか。　この　本は　私の　です。   = Is that so? This book is mine.
SAN   SOU   DESUka   KONO   HONwa   WATASHI no   DESU

■ 文化箱 Culture Chest
BUN KA BAKO

おみやげ, Giving Gifts
OMIYAGE

Japan is a "gift giving" nation. Foreigners are sometimes unsure about what to bring for their hosts when visiting Japan for the first time. The following sorts of things might be good for a high school student to give to a Japanese host family:

- Picture books from home
- items with local place names or school/college names from your hometown
- items with your school logo on them
- T-shirts with English written on them
- famous products from your home region, handmade crafts or local foods

Items related to the interests and hobbies of your host family are good places to start.

Since giving very expensive presents might lead your Japanese hosts to feel obligated to buy an expensive gift for you in return, the best gift is something unique but not necessarily expensive.

Be sure to think ahead when making or purchasing things to take or send to Japan, since there are many things that cannot legally be taken into or out of countries and other things that cannot be taken onto airplanes.

In Japan, *omiyage* can be readily purchased at any tourist site.

その えんぴつと けしゴムを 二つ 下さい。
SONO ENPITSU to KESHIGOMU o FUTATSU KUDASAI
Please give me that pencil and two erasers.

■ 会話 Dialogue
KAI WA

じゅん　　：　ここは　おちゃのみず　です。*本屋が　たくさん　あります。
JUN　　　　KOKO wa　OCHA no MIZU　DESU　HONYA ga　TAKUSAN　ARIMASU

本屋の人　：　いらっしゃいませ。
HONYA no HITO　IRASSHAIMASE

じゅん　　：　キアラさん、ノートは　ここ　です。
JUN　　　　KIARA-SAN,　NO-TO wa　KOKO　DESU

キアラ　　：　ええと、その　えんぴつと　けしゴムを　二つ　下さい。
KIARA　　　E E TO　SONO　ENPITSU to　KESHIGOMU o　FUTATSU　KUDASAI

　　　　　　　それから、その　ノートと　あの　まんがも　下さい。
　　　　　　　SOREKARA　SONO　NO-TO to　ANO　MANGA mo　KUDASAI

*本屋 – bookstore
 HONYA

■ 単語 New Words
TAN GO

1. えんぴつ (n)
   ENPITSU
2. こくばん (n)
   KOKUBAN
3. ボールペン (n)
   BO-RUPEN
4. チョーク (n)
   CHO-KU
5. ペン (n)
   PEN
6. まんが (n)
   MANGA
7. けしゴム (n)
   KESHIGOMU
8. みず (n)
   MIZU
9. ノート (n)
   NO-TO
10. かばん (n)
    KABAN
11. バックパック (n)
    BAKKUPAKKU
12. したじき (n)
    SHITAJIKI
13. かみ (n)
    KAMI

ここ (pron.) – here
KOKO

そこ (pron.) – there
SOKO

あそこ (pron.) – over there
ASOKO

どこ (inter.) – where
DOKO

一つ – 1 thing/object
HITOTSU

二つ – 2 things/objects
FUTATSU

三つ – 3 things/objects
MITTSU

四つ – 4 things/objects
YOTTSU

五つ – 5 things/objects
ITSUTSU

六つ – 6 things/objects
MUTTSU

七つ – 7 things/objects
NANATSU

八つ – 8 things/objects
YATTSU

九つ – 9 things/objects
KOKONOTSU

十 – 10 things/objects
TOO

いくつ (inter.) – How many things/objects?
IKUTSU

To help you remember how to count objects, be sure to listen to and learn the counting song on the CD-ROM.

■ 言葉の探索 Language Detection
KOTOBA no TANSAKU

1.   General counters

一つ , 二つ , etc. are the counters for:
HITOTSU FUTATSU

a. objects that do not have a particular shape (like erasers and bags)
b. objects that do not fit into any of the categories for counters (see the chart of counters in Appendix 1).

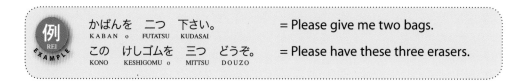

かばんを　二つ　下さい。   = Please give me two bags.
KABAN o FUTATSU KUDASAI

この　けしゴムを　三つ　どうぞ。   = Please have these three erasers.
KONO KESHIGOMU o MITTSU DOUZO

While it is more common for the counter to follow the noun and the particle, as in the above two examples, the following pattern is also acceptable:

四つの　りんごを　下さい   Please give me four apples.
YOTTSU no RINGO o KUDASAI

2.   ここ、そこ、あそこ、どこ
KOKO SOKO ASOKO DOKO

These words follow the same pattern as これ、それ、あれ、どれ but refer only to location (and not physical
KORE SORE ARE DORE

objects) and do not need to precede a noun.

ここ   = here
KOKO

そこ   = there near the listener
SOKO

あそこ   = over there
ASOKO

どこ   = Where?
DOKO

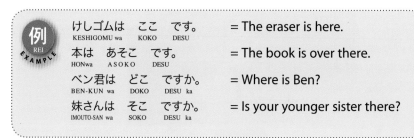

けしゴムは　ここ　です。   = The eraser is here.
KESHIGOMU wa KOKO DESU

本は　あそこ　です。   = The book is over there.
HON wa ASOKO DESU

ベン君は　どこ　ですか。   = Where is Ben?
BEN-KUN wa DOKO DESU ka

妹さんは　そこ　ですか。   = Is your younger sister there?
IMOUTO-SAN wa SOKO DESU ka

3.   も
mo

も is a particle that means "also" or "too."
mo

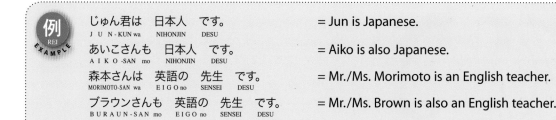

じゅん君は　日本人　です。   = Jun is Japanese.
JUN-KUN wa NIHONJIN DESU

あいこさんも　日本人　です。   = Aiko is also Japanese.
AIKO-SAN mo NIHONJIN DESU

森本さんは　英語の　先生　です。   = Mr./Ms. Morimoto is an English teacher.
MORIMOTO-SAN wa EIGO no SENSEI DESU

ブラウンさんも　英語の　先生　です。   = Mr./Ms. Brown is also an English teacher.
BURAUN-SAN mo EIGO no SENSEI DESU

While "too" and "also" can fit many different places in an English sentence, in Japanese sentences the も will always come after the person or thing that it is modifying. For instance, in the first example above, あいこ is being added
AIKO

from the first sentence to the second sentence, so the name あいこ is followed by the particle も. In the second
AIKO mo

example above, Ms. Brown is being added to the first sentence and consequently is followed by particle も. Particle
mo

も **replaces** the particles は , が , and を .
mo   wa ga   o

■ 自習 Self Check
JI SHUU

1. Fill in the blanks with Japanese according to the English translations.

えんぴつは＿＿＿＿＿＿＿＿＿＿＿＿ です。　　= The pencil is here.
ENPITSU wa   DESU

＿＿＿＿＿＿＿＿は＿＿＿＿＿＿＿＿＿ です。 = The eraser is near you.

＿＿＿＿＿＿＿＿＿＿＿＿＿＿＿＿＿＿＿ = The notebook is over there.

＿＿＿＿＿＿＿＿＿＿＿＿＿＿＿＿＿＿＿ = The book is also over there. (use も)

＿＿＿＿＿＿＿＿＿＿＿＿＿＿＿＿＿＿＿ = Where is Tokyo?

■ 練習の時間 Time for Practice
RENSHUU no JIKAN

1. Pair Practice

With a partner, count the number of backpacks in the classroom using 一つ, 二つ, etc. After you have done this, try
HITOTSU FUTATSU
to find other objects that do not have a particular shape and count them.

2. Pair Practice

Using the classroom object vocabulary in Appendix 4, ask your partner where objects or people are in the classroom.

A-SAN:	せんせいは どこ ですか。	= Where is the teacher?
	SENSEI wa DOKO DESU ka	
B-SAN:	(pointing) せんせいは あそこ です。	= The teacher is over there.
	SENSEI wa ASOKO DESU	

■ キアラのジャーナル Kiara's Journal
KIARA no JA-NARU

Read the journal entry below, and then answer these questions.

❶ What means of transportation did Kiara and Jun use to get to Ocha-no-mizu?
❷ Why were they going there?
❸ Why did Jun want Kiara to try an Indian restaurant for dinner?

Dear Journal,

I went to a part of 東京 called お茶の水 today. We took the 山手 line and then transferred to the
OCHA no MIZU   YAMAno TE
そうぶ line to get there. Through the train windows we could see how different the various parts of 東京
SOUBU
are. It was much better than riding the subway and only seeing those ads on the station walls. One thing
I realized is that 東京 is really crowded in some parts but not in others.

We headed to お茶の水 because Jun said there were lots of colleges and bookstores near there, and I needed to get supplies for school and a book about the history of 東京. I also wanted to get some まんが MANGA ☺.

Later, we met up with じゅん君の 友達 JUN-KUN no TOMODACHI Ben again for dinner in 六本木 ROPPONGI, an area of 東京 where many foreigners live. He and じゅん君 went to the same elementary school and he hopes to go to the same high school as じゅん君 next year. He seems like he's really smart and kind of cute too.

We went into an Indian restaurant where we each ordered a different kind of curry. It was really good but pretty spicy. I had to drink about five little glasses of 水 MIZU (water) to help cool my mouth down afterwards. For lunch, じゅん君 had taken me to a Japanese curry restaurant so that I could see the difference between the two types of curries.

■ 文化箱 Culture Chest
BUN KA BAKO

The Tokyo Subway

The map below shows the Yamanote train line that circles Tokyo. The closest station to Jun's house is Ueno (上野 UENO). How many stops did Kiara and Jun travel to get to Ochanomizu? Find the Shinjuku station on the map. It is one of the busiest stations in the world, with over 3 million people travelling through this station daily. It is a good place NOT to be during rush hour!

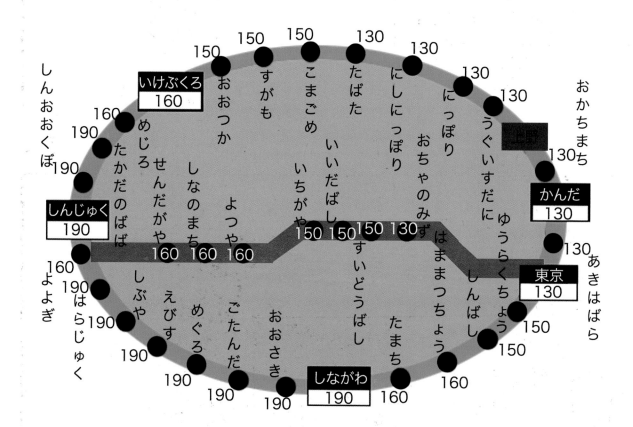

お母さん、晩ご飯は　何　ですか。
OKAASAN, BANGOHAN wa　NAN　DESU ka

Mom, what's for dinner?

■ 会話 Dialogue
KAI WA

キアラ　　　：ああ、私は　おなかが、ペコペコ　です。
KIARA　　　　A A　WATASHI wa　ONAKA　ga　PEKOPEKO　DESU

じゅん　　　：僕も　ペコペコ　です。お母さん、ばんごはんは　何　ですか。
JUN　　　　　BOKU mo　PEKOPEKO　DESU　OKAASAN　BANGOHAN wa　NAN　DESU ka

まゆみ　　　：たこ　ですよ。
MAYUMI　　　TAKO　DESU yo

キアラ　　　：たこ？！
KIARA　　　　TAKO

まゆみ　　　：あいちゃん、お父さん、ばんごはん　ですよ〜！
MAYUMI　　　AICHAN,　OTOUSAN,　BANGOHAN　DESU yo

愛子＆太郎：はい！
AIKO　TAROU　HAI

まゆみ　　　：はい，たこ　です。どうぞ。
MAYUMI　　　HAI　TAKO　DESU　DOUZO

キアラ　　　：これが　たこ？
KIARA　　　　KORE ga　TAKO

■ 単語 New Words
TAN GO

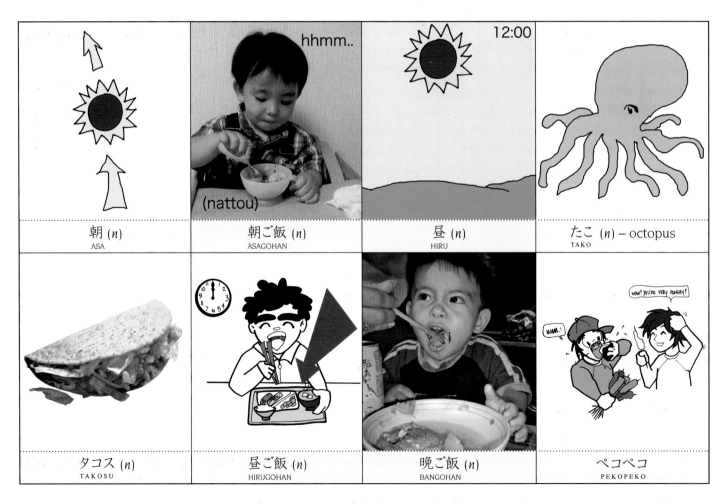

| 朝 (*n*) ASA | 朝ご飯 (*n*) ASAGOHAN | 昼 (*n*) HIRU | たこ (*n*) – octopus TAKO |
| タコス (*n*) TAKOSU | 昼ご飯 (*n*) HIRUGOHAN | 晩ご飯 (*n*) BANGOHAN | ペコペコ PEKOPEKO |

ああ (*inter.*) – Ah!, Oh!
A A

■ 言葉の探索 Language Detection
KOTOBA no TANSAKU

1. **Homonyms**

The Japanese language contains fewer sounds than English. This results in many more homonyms, words that sound the same but have different meanings. Some examples of English homonyms are *too–two–to*, *which–witch*, *read–red*, etc. Homonyms in Japanese may have the same pronunciation but will use different kanji. For example, 箕 - chopsticks, HASHI 橋 - bridge, and 端 - edge; another example is 紙 - paper, 髪 - hair, and 神 - gods. HASHI   HASHI   KAMI   KAMI   KAMI

Many Japanese homonyms have subtle differences in intonation such as raised or lowered pitch and therefore are not pure homonyms in the English sense. The best way to distinguish between homonyms in spoken Japanese is to pay attention to the context, both by listening to and watching the situation closely. In written Japanese, the different meanings for homonyms are made clear through the different kanji and/or context.

2. **Abbreviating names in Japanese**

Japanese people often shorten the names of small children, family members, and friends to indicate familiarity. The suffix ~ちゃん(~CHAN) can replace the more polite suffix ~さん(~SAN). ~ちゃん(~CHAN) is used often with females younger than the speaker and for very young boys, but it can be used with the name of anybody you are very close to.

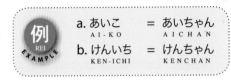

| 例 REI EXAMPLE | a. あいこ AI-KO | = | あいちゃん AICHAN |
| | b. けんいち KEN-ICHI | = | けんちゃん KENCHAN |

3. **Mimetic or onomatopoeic words - ぎたい語**
GITAIGO

Expressions or words that mimic sounds associated with a thing or action are called onomatopoeia. Japanese has many such expressions.

例 REI EXAMPLE	ペコペコ PEKO PEKO	=	your stomach growling
	ゴロゴロ GOROGORO	=	the sound of something rolling; This also refers to the action (or lack thereof) of being a "couch potato."
	ペラペラ PERA PERA	=	to speak fluently

■ 自習 Self Check
JI SHUU

1. **Homonyms**

Can you guess which of these two kanji for AME means *rain* and which means *candy*?

a. 飴   b. 雨

If at the beginning of your class your teacher says, 「かみを 出して ください。」, which of the three meanings of かみ is meant?
KAMI o   DASHITE   KUDASAI

KAMI

a. god   b. paper   c. hair

2. **Abbreviating names**

Pretend that the following are family members or close friends. Think of a pet name to show that you are close to them.

a. 真一   b. 祥子   c. 健一   d. 大輔   e. 祐介
SHINICHI   SHOU KO   KEN ICHI   DAI SUKE   YUUSUKE

3. Mimetic or onomatopoeic words - ぎたい語
    GITAIGO

    Can you match the ぎたい語 expression with its meaning?
    GITAIGO

    1. プンプン   a. shining
        PUNPUN
    2. ツルツル   b. being angry
        TSURUTSURU
    3. ピカピカ   c. smiling
        PIKA PIKA
    4. ニコニコ   d. slippery
        NIKONIKO

■ 練習の時間 Time for Practice
RENSHUU no JIKAN

1. Pair Practice

With a partner, shorten and add ちゃん to the names of the students in your class to come up with "cute" new names
CHAN
for everyone.

2. Small Group Practice

Practice asking who your partner's friends are. Take turns asking in Japanese. In your answers, try to shorten your
friends' names and add ちゃん .
CHAN

A-さん:	あなたの	友達は	だれ	です	か。	= Who are your friends?
	ANATA no	TOMODACHI wa	DARE	DESU	ka	
B-さん:	友達は	マーちゃんと	ジェイ君	です。		= My friends are Maa and Jei.
	TOMODACHI wa	MA - CHAN to	J E I KUN	DESU		

■ 文化箱 Culture Chest
BUN KA BAKO

Tokyo Neighborhoods

Tokyo is a city of neighborhoods. You have already read a little about Hiroo, Ochanomizu, and Roppongi. These are just
a few of the many neighborhoods in Tokyo. Each neighborhood has a different feel. Here are some other famous areas of
Tokyo:

⮑ Ginza is a trendy part of the city with top quality shops and the city's Kabuki theater.

⮑ Akihabara has a high concentration of electronic stores. One of the few places in Japan where it's OK to bargain
   for what you buy!

⮑ Harajuku is the place to watch crazy modern fashion trends of the young, especially on Sundays.

Many foreigners find Tokyo to be a comfortable city in which to live, despite its being one of the largest cities in the world.
Perhaps this is because with so many neighborhoods to choose from, most people can find something to their liking.

Dear お母さん、

I arrived in 東京 a few days ago in the late afternoon. I've had a fantastic time so far! じゅん君 is a really nice guy.
He's a year younger in school so he won't be in any of my classes when I start in two days, but he's introducing me to
a lot of other kids who will be. Last night we met an Australian named Ben. Ben's been living here since he was six.

His お母さん works for the Australian Embassy here and his お父さん works for an export company. His Japanese is amazing and he knows a lot about Japanese history. I haven't learned that much about Japanese history yet, but I want to. And I don't know if I'll be as fluent in Japanese as he is after my year here, but I'm going to try!

I went with my new 友達 to a part of the city called 六本木. There are a lot of international restaurants there. Ben
TOMODACHI   ROPPONGI
wanted to take us to his favorite Indian restaurant. I had Japanese curry for lunch and they wanted to take me to an Indian restaurant for dinner, so I could compare the two types of curry. Both were good, in very different ways. Have you had both? Which is your favorite?

Schools here in 日本 are getting ready to start their second trimester of the school year, which is why everyone already knows their classmates. My first day is coming up soon, so while we were out today, we stopped by a stationery shop. I bought 鉛筆、下敷き、ノート、消しゴム、and a 鞄. We also went to a clothing store so that I
ENPITSU   SHITAJIKI   NO-TO   KESHI GOMU   KABAN
could buy my school 制服. The 制服 that I have to wear is kind of cute, but I'm not sure how much I'll like wearing
SEIFUKU
a uniform all of the time. The good thing is that it is versatile: the girls' uniforms come with a light jacket, as well as athletic clothes for gym class and for wearing after school. And it's kind of nice not to have to worry about what to wear every day.

Well お母さん、I have to go. E-mail 下さい！Tell everyone else こんにちは！
KUDASAI

Love, or as they would say in Japan, 大好きです！
DAISUKI DESU

キアラ
KIARA

■ テクノの時間 Techno Time
TEKUNO no JIKAN

You will need to "call" your Japanese teacher's voice mail and leave a message (of at least four sentences) introducing your family. Alternative: you can make a "my little book" (your teacher will instruct you on what to do) about your family, labeling family members and writing an eight-sentence introduction of your family on the first page of the "my little book".

■ 単語チェックリスト New Word Checklist
TAN GO CHEKKURISUTO

Japanese	Location	English
2-1		
あに　兄 (n)	2-1	older brother (my)
あね　姉 (n)	2-1	older sister (my)
ある/あります (v)	2-1	(to) exist (inanimate things)
いち　一 (n)	2-1	one
いちばんうえの あに/あね　一番上の 兄/姉 (n)	2-1	my oldest brother/sister

Japanese	Location	English
いちばんしたの　あに/あね　　一番下の　弟/妹 (n)	2-1	my youngest brother/sister
いぬ　　犬 (n)	2-1	dog
いもうと　　　妹 (n)	2-1	younger sister (my)
いる/います (v)	2-1	(to) exist (animate beings)
おとうと　　　弟 (n)	2-1	younger brother (my)
かぞく　　　家族 (n)	2-1	family (my)
きゅうにん　　　九人 (n)	2-1	nine people
きょうだい　　　兄弟 (n)	2-1	siblings
ぎりの〜 (n)	2-1	step-
く/きゅう　　　九 (n)	2-1	nine
ご　　　五 (n)	2-1	five
ごかぞく　　　ご家族 (n)	2-1	someone else's family
ごにん　　　五人 (n)	2-1	five people
さん　　　三 (n)	2-1	three
さんにん　　　三人 (n)	2-1	three people
しち/なな　　　七 (n)	2-1	seven
しちにん/ななにん　　　七人 (n)	2-1	seven people
しゃしん　　　写真 (n)	2-1	photograph
じゅう　　　十 (n)	2-1	ten
じゅうにん　　　十人 (n)	2-1	ten people
そふ　　　祖父 (n)	2-1	grandfather (my)
そぼ　　　祖母 (n)	2-1	grandmother (my)
だれ (inter.)	2-1	who
でんわ　　　電話 (n)	2-1	telephone
なん/なに　　　何 (inter.)	2-1	what
なんにん　　　何人 (inter.)	2-1	how many people
に　　　二 (n)	2-1	two
ねこ　　　猫 (n)	2-1	cat
はち　　　八 (n)	2-1	eight
はちにん　　　八人 (n)	2-1	eight people
ひとり　　　一人 (n)	2-1	one person
ふたり　　　二人 (n)	2-1	two people
よにん　　　四人 (n)	2-1	four people
よん/し　　　四 (n)	2-1	four
ろく　　　六 (n)	2-1	six
ろくにん　　　六人 (n)	2-1	six people

Other words you might like to know

Japanese	Location	English
いちばんうえの　あに/あね　　一番上の　兄/姉 (n)	2-1	my oldest brother/sister
いちばんしたのおとうと/いもうと　　一番下の　弟/妹 (n)	2-1	my youngest brother/sister
ぎりの〜	2-1	step-
すぐしたの　おとうと/いもうと　　すぐ下の　弟/妹 (n)	2-1	my next youngest brother/sister
にばんめの　あに/あね　　二番目の　兄/姉 (n)	2-1	my second oldest brother/sister

Japanese	Location	English
2-2		
いえ/うち　家 (n)	2-2	house, home
いもうとさん　妹さん (n)	2-2	younger sister (someone else's)
おかあさん　お母さん (n)	2-2	mother (someone else's)
おじいさん (n)	2-2	grandfather (someone else's)
おじさん (n)	2-2	uncle or man quite a bit older than you
おとうさん　お父さん (n)	2-2	father (someone else's)
おとうとさん　弟さん (n)	2-2	younger brother (someone else's)
おにいさん　お兄さん (n)	2-2	older brother (someone else's)
おねえさん　お姉さん (n)	2-2	older sister (someone else's)
おばあさん (n)	2-2	grandmother (someone else's)
おばさん (n)	2-2	aunt or woman quite a bit older than you
きゅうじゅう　九十 (n)	2-2	ninety
ごじゅう　五十 (n)	2-2	fifty
さんじゅう　三十 (n)	2-2	thirty
じゅういち　十一 (n)	2-2	eleven
じゅうく/じゅうきゅう　十九 (n)	2-2	nineteen
じゅうご　十五 (n)	2-2	fifteen
じゅうさん　十三 (n)	2-2	thirteen
じゅうなな/じゅうしち　十七 (n)	2-2	seventeen
じゅうに　十二 (n)	2-2	twelve
じゅうはち　十八 (n)	2-2	eighteen
じゅうよん/じゅうし　十四 (n)	2-2	fourteen
じゅうろく　十六 (n)	2-2	sixteen
と (part.)	2-2	and
ともだち　友達 (n)	2-2	friend
ななじゅう　七十 (n)	2-2	seventy
にじゅう　二十 (n)	2-2	twenty
にじゅういち　二十一 (n)	2-2	twenty-one
はちじゅう　八十 (n)	2-2	eighty
ひと　人 (n)	2-2	person
ひゃく　百 (n)	2-2	one hundred
よんじゅう　四十 (n)	2-2	forty
ろくじゅう　六十 (n)	2-2	sixty
2-3		
あの	2-3	that (thing) over there
あめ (n)	2-3	candy, rain
ありがとう (exp.)	2-3	thanks
この	2-3	this (thing)
その	2-3	that (thing)
てぃーしゃつ　Tシャツ (n)	2-3	T-shirt
どういたしまして (exp.)	2-3	you're welcome
どうも　ありがとう (exp.)	2-3	thank you
どの (inter.)	2-3	which (thing)
ぼうし (n)	2-3	hat/cap

Japanese	Location	English
2-4		
あそこ (*pron.*)	2-4	over there
いくつ (*inter.*)	2-4	how many (things)?
いつつ　五つ (*n*)	2-4	five (things)
えんぴつ　鉛筆 (*n*)	2-4	pencil
かばん　鞄 (*n*)	2-4	bag, satchel
かみ　紙 (*n*)	2-4	paper
けしごむ　消しゴム (*n*)	2-4	eraser
こくばん　黒板 (*n*)	2-4	blackboard
ここ (*pron.*)	2-4	here
ここのつ　九つ (*n*)	2-4	nine (things)
したじき　下敷き (*n*)	2-4	writing pad, mat
そこ (*pron.*)	2-4	there
ちょーく　チョーク (*n*)	2-4	chalk
とお　十 (*n*)	2-4	ten (things)
どこ (*inter.*)	2-4	where?
ななつ　七つ (*n*)	2-4	seven (things)
のーと　ノート (*n*)	2-4	notebook
ばっくぱっく　バックパック (*n*)	2-4	backpack
ひとつ　一つ (*n*)	2-4	one (thing)
ふたつ　二つ (*n*)	2-4	two (things)
ぺん　ペン (*n*)	2-4	pen
ぼーるぺん　ボールペン (*n*)	2-4	(ballpoint) pen
まんが　漫画 (*n*)	2-4	Japanese comics
みず　水 (*n*)	2-4	water
みっつ　三つ (*n*)	2-4	three (things)
むっつ　六つ (*n*)	2-4	six (things)
やっつ　八つ (*n*)	2-4	eight (things)
よっつ　四つ (*n*)	2-4	four (things)
2-5		
ああ (*exp.*)	2-5	Ah! Oh!
あさ　朝 (*n*)	2-5	morning
あさごはん　朝ご飯 (*n*)	2-5	breakfast
たこ (*n*)	2-5	octopus
たこす　タコス (*n*)	2-5	Mexican taco(s)
ばん　晩 (*n*)	2-5	evening
ばんごはん　晩ご飯 (*n*)	2-5	dinner, evening meal
ひる　昼 (*n*)	2-5	daytime, noon
ひるごはん　昼ご飯 (*n*)	2-5	lunch
ぺこぺこ　ペコペコ	2-5	mimetic expression for hunger

The Ins and Outs of Schools in Japan

第 **3** 課

✎ Learning Goals

By the end of this chapter you will learn:

A) how schools and grades in Japan compare to your school system

B) what happens in a typical Japanese school day

C) about daily class schedules of students in Japan

D) how to compare two situations using "but"

E) how to engage in basic small talk about the weather

F) 28 additional kanji

✔ Performance Goals

By the end of this chapter you will be able to:

A) say that things do or do not exist and talk about things that you have or do not have

B) use direct objects appropriately in statements and questions

C) use time words to talk about the past, present, and future

D) talk about your school, grade level, and class schedule

E) talk to a Japanese person about his/her own school day and answer basic questions about your school day in Japanese

F) talk about which classes you are taking and which you are not taking

G) read and write 28 additional kanji

■ 会話 Dialogue
かいわ

じゅん：　中学校は　ここ　です。高校は　あそこ　です。
きあら
キアラ：　大学は　ありますか。
きあら
じゅん：　はい、私の　友達の　お兄さんの　大学が　あります。
きあら
キアラ：　小学校は　ありますか。
きあら
じゅん：　いいえ、小学校は　ありません。

じゅん：　キアラさんは　高校　二年生　ですね。僕は　一年生　です。じゃあ、学校に　はいり
ましょう*。
きあら
キアラ：　はい、はいりましょう。
きあら
じゅん：　あっ！くつは　だめ　です！
きあら
キアラ：　すみません。教室は　どこ　ですか。
きあら
じゅん：　1の3は　あそこ　です。先生も　あそこに　います。
　　　　こちらは　山本　先生　です。英語の　先生　です。
きあら　　　やまもと　せんせい　　　　えいご　　せんせい
キアラ：　初めまして。私は　キアラ　です。どうぞ　よろしく　おねがいします。
きあら　はじ
山本　：　ああ、キアラさん　ですか。初めまして。どうぞ　よろしく。
やまもと　　　きあら　　　　　　　　はじ
　　　　ここに　すわって　下さい。
　　　　　　　　　　　　くだ

*はいりましょう − let's enter/go into

■ 単語 New Words
たんご

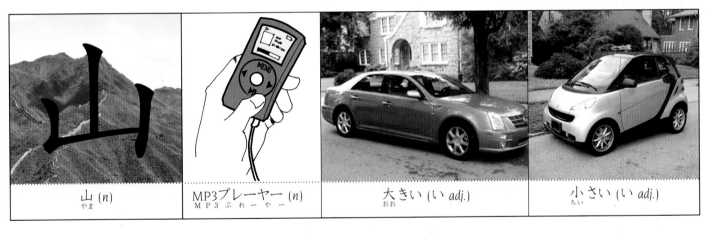

| 山 (n) | MP3プレーヤー (n) | 大きい (い adj.) | 小さい (い adj.) |
| やま | ＭＰ３ぷれーやー | おお | ちい |

携帯 (電話) (n) −
けいたい　でんわ
cellular telephone

山本 (n) −
やまもと
a family name

みんな (n) −
everyone

皆さん (n) −
みなさん
everyone
(polite)

とても (adv.) −
very

たくさん (n) −
many, a lot

少し (adv.) −
すこし
a little

あっ (interj.)
− oh

 学校 (n) school
がっこう

 生徒 (n) or 学生 (n)
せいと / がくせい

 高校 (n)
こうこう

 高校生 (n)
こうこうせい

 中学校 (n)
ちゅうがっこう

 中学生 (n)
ちゅうがくせい

小学校 (n)
しょうがっこう

小学生 (n)
しょうがくせい

大学 (n)
だいがく

大学生 (n)
だいがくせい

保育園 (n)
ほいくえん

幼稚園 (n)
ようちえん

小学 一年生 (n) – elementary school first grader
しょうがく いちねんせい

小学 二年生 (n) – elementary school second grader
しょうがく にねんせい

小学 三年生 (n) – elementary school third grader
しょうがく さんねんせい

小学 四年生 (n) – elementary school fourth grader
しょうがく よねんせい

小学 五年生 (n) – elementary school fifth grader
しょうがく ごねんせい

小学 六年生 (n) – elementary school sixth grader
しょうがく ろくねんせい

何年生 (inter.) – What year/grade?
なんねんせい

中学一年生 (n) – middle school, first year student (7th grader)
ちゅうがくいちねんせい

中学二年生 (n) – middle school, second year student (8th grader)
ちゅうがくにねんせい

中学三年生 (n) – middle school, third year student (9th grader)
ちゅうがくさんねんせい

高校一年生 (n) – high school, first year student (10th grader)
こうこういちねんせい

高校二年生 (n) – high school, second year student (11th grader)
こうこうにねんせい

高校三年生 (n) – high school, third year student (12th grader)
こうこうさんねんせい

大学一年生 (n) – first year college/university student
だいがくいちねんせい

■ 漢字 Kanji
かんじ

高　小　中　大　学　校　年　先　生　山

高	コウ; たか (い) – tall, expensive, high こう	、	亠	产	亨	古	亨	高	高
10 strokes	高 (校) – high school; 高 (い) – tall, expensive, high こう こう / たか	高	高						
	This looks like the TALL pagodas found all over East Asia. Many of these TALL pagodas would also be quite EXPENSIVE to build.								

小	ショウ; ちい (さい) – small しょう	亅	八	小					
3 strokes	小 (学校) – elementary school; 小 (さい) – small しょう がっこう / ちい								
	This is a drawing of a person pulling his/her arms down and closer to his/her body, so as to appear SMALLer.								

中 4 strokes	チュウ；なか – middle, inside	丶	口	口	中				
	中 (学校) – middle school; 中 – medium; ちゅう がっこう　　　　　　　　ちゅう 中 – middle, inside なか								
	One stroke divides this character right down the MIDDLE.								

大 3 strokes	ダイ；おお (きい) – big, large	一	ナ	大					
	大 – big, large; 大 (きい) – big, large; 大 (学) – だい　　　　　　　 おお　　　　　　　　　 だい がく college, university								
	This is a drawing of a person with arms stretched out to appear BIG or LARGE.								

学 8 strokes	ガク – to learn	丶	丷	丷	丷	兴	学	学	学
	学 (校) – school; (中) 学 (生) – middle school がっ こう　　　 ちゅう がく せい student								
	This character is a child (子) under a roof with large drops of "LEARNing" pouring down into the child's head through the roof of the SCHOOL.								

校 10 strokes	コウ – school	一	十	才	木	朴	扩	栌	杉
	学 (校) – school; (高) 校 (生) – high school student がっ こう　　　 こう こう せい	杉	校						
	Tree/wood (木) and a father (父) wearing a top hat (strokes 5 and 6). Years ago a SCHOOL was often no more than a wooden building where a father put on a top hat to teach.								

年 6 strokes	ネン；とし – year	丿	亠	仁	午	乍	年		
	(何) 年 – what year?; (何) 年 (生) – what grade?; なん ねん　　　　　　　 なん ねん せい (今) 年 – this year こ とし								
	The best way to remember this is through repetition by writing the year on all homework and tests from now on. For example: 1492年, 1967年…								

先 6 strokes	セン – earlier, future	丿	一	牛	生	步	先		
	先 (生) – teacher; 先 (週) – last week せん せい　　　　　 せん しゅう								
	This kanji is a picture of a very big pot of earth (土) with a small sprout planted EARLIER, growing on the left. It is being carried by a MASTER gardener whose legs can be seen below the tray.								

生	セイ – life; う(まれる) – to be born	ノ	⺧	牛	牛	生	
	(先)生 – teacher; (何年)生 – what grade?						
5 strokes	The earth/soil (土) is the basis of LIFE. This kanji has a new branch, just BORN, near the top.						

山	～サン – Mt. ～; やま– mountain	l	凵	山			
	(富士)山 – Mt. Fuji; (大きい)山 – big mountain						
3 strokes	This is a primitive drawing of a MOUNTAIN.						

■ 言葉の探索 Language Detection

1. いません/ありません - does not exist
   To change these verbs (います/あります) from the affirmative to the negative, change the ～ます ending to ～ません.
   　When affirmative statements are made with ～います/あります where people or things exist or are possessed, you use the particle が after the subject. When you make negative statements with いません/ありません, you *often* use は after the subject.

   あります - exists (for inanimate objects)
   ありません - (does not exist)
   います - exists (for animate objects)
   いません - (does not exist)

   A) あそこに 小学校が あります。でも　中学校は ありません。
   = There is an elementary school over there. But there is no middle school over there.
   B) 犬が います。でも ねこは いません。= There is a dog. But there is no cat.
   C) 中学校が あります。でも 高校は ありません。
   = There is a junior high school. But there is no high school.

2. 大きい / 小さい and とても / 少し - The basics of using adverbs and adjectives
   Use the following pattern to use adjectives and/or adverbs to make basic A=B or A は B です sentences. The adjective or adverb quite often comes after the は.

   Topic は (adverb) adjectiveです。
   A   B

   A) 私の 学校は 大きい です。　　　　　　= My school is big.
   B) 私の ぼうしは 少し 小さい です。　　　= My hat is a little small.
   C) じゅん君の バックパックは とても 大きい です。= Jun's backpack is very big.
   D) そのノートは 大きいですね。　　　　　= That notebook is big, isn't it?

■ 自習 Self Check

1. Say the following out loud to yourself in Japanese. Use affirmative and negative variations of あります and います "to exist" as needed.

    A) There is no junior high school. ⇨ 中学校は _____ 。

    B) There are two second year students. ⇨ 二年生が 二人 _____ 。

    C) There is no high school. ⇨ _____ 。

    D) There are four siblings. ⇨ _____ 。

    E) I have 4 friends. ⇨ _____ 。

    F) There is no cat. ⇨ _____ 。

    G) There are no bags over there. ⇨ _____ 。

    H) There are a pencil and 2 erasers over there. ⇨ _____ 。

2. Say the following out loud to yourself in Japanese. Include the words for *big*, *small*, *a little*, and *very* as needed.

    A) My Japanese class is large. ⇨ 私の 日本語の クラスは _____ です。

    B) My eraser is small. ⇨ 私の 消しゴムは _____ です。

    C) The Japanese classroom is a little small. ⇨ _____ 。

    D) The University of _____ is very large. ⇨ _____ 。

    E) My friend's school is very small. ⇨ _____ 。

■ 練習の時間 Time for Practice

1. Pair Work

Use objects on your desk, in the classroom, and in the pictures below for this activity. Take turns using Japanese to ask if each of the objects exists or not (on the desk or in the room). Answer the questions using あります／ありません or います／いません. (Note: Use the particle は in questions about existence.)

> A-さん： ぼうしは　ありますか。　　　　　= Do you have a hat?/Is there a hat?
> B-さん： はい、ぼうしが　あります。　　　 = Yes, I have a hat./Yes, there is a hat.
> 　　　　 -OR-
> 　　　　 いいえ、ぼうしは　ありません。　 = No, I don't have a hat./No, there is no hat.

2. Pair Work

Compare this list of people with the picture of Kiara's family. Using your Japanese, take turns stating whether these people are in the picture with Kiara's family or not. Use います/いません. (Note: は is the particle used in the question.)
wa

A-さん: お父さんは　いますか？	= Is father here?
B-さん: はい、います。	= Yes, he is (here).
-OR-　いいえ、いません。	= No, he is not (here).

お父さん

お母さん

お兄さん

お姉さん

弟さん

妹さん

おばあさん

おばさん

おじいさん

おじさん

3. Class Activity – Information Gap

A) Your 先生 will choose six to seven students who will stand equally spaced around the perimeter of the classroom.
せんせい
Each student will be holding a card with an object on it. The card pictures will be familiar nouns which you have learned such as 高校, 寿司, 鉛筆, 猫, 犬, 家, あめ, and ぼうし. On the backs of the cards, the instructor will have
こうこう　す し　えんぴつ　ねこ　いぬ　いえ
written "small," "large," "a little small," "very big," etc.

B) The remaining students will pair up and work together to figure out the sizes of each object, and then redraw that object on a piece of scrap paper.

C) A-さん will interview one person standing and ask the size of the object on that picture card.
- A-さん: ぼうしは　ありますか。 = Is there a hat?
- B-さん: はい、あります。 = Yes, there is.
- A-さん: ぼうしは　大きいですか。 = Is it big?
  おお
- B-さん: はい。ぼうしは　とても　大きい　です。 = Yes, the hat is very big.
  おお
  -OR-
- いいえ。 = No.

D) A-さん then reports that information to B-さん who draws what he/she hears and writes a sentence about it.
- A-さん to B-さん: ぼうしは　とても　大きい　です。
  おお
  B-さん must draw the object so that the relative size is clear and write a sentence about it. For example, 友達
  の　ぼうしは　大きいです。   とも だち
  おお

4. Interview Practice

Draw the chart below on a piece of scrap paper. Interview at least five classmates. Ask each his/her name and what grade he/she is in and record that information on your chart, in English. When everyone has finished interviewing, use your Japanese to report the grade level of one of your interviewees to the class.

	A:	お名前は　何　ですか。	= What is your name?
例	B:	Chelsea　です。	= It is Chelsea.
EXAMPLE	A:	Chelsea-さん、何年生　ですか。	= Chelsea, what year are you?
	B:	高校 二年生　です。	= (I'm a) 2ⁿᵈ year high school student.
	A:	はい、分かりました。	= Oh, I understand.
		-OR-	
		ああ、そうですか。	= Oh, really?

名前	年生

■ 文化箱 Culture Chest

School System

Japan has a variety of public and private schools. Students in Japan almost all go through twelve years of public or private education and most advance to some type of post-secondary education. Typical schools are organized as follows:

Elementary School: 6 years
Junior High School: 3 years
High School: 3 years

Most students also go to nursery school (幼稚園) and kindergarten (保育園). During their ninth year of school (中学 三年生), students are busy studying for entrance examinations to get into the high school of their choice. Similarly, during their twelfth year of school (高校 三年生), students must study for the college entrance exams. In their last year of junior high and in their last year of high school, students are often expected to focus their time on working to pass these exams. This is why it is rare for high school students to have part-time jobs, or even to be involved in other activities outside of schoolwork during their last year of high school. Students even eliminate their club activities during their final year of high school to provide more time for exam preparation. Parents generally feel that the student's main "job" is to successfully pass the entrance exams for high school and then for college or university.

Many Japanese students go to じゅく (cram schools) for extra study and practice for these entrance exams. Some students even start attending じゅく as early as elementary school. Many families feel that the amount of time and money spent preparing for entrance exams is worth it, since Japanese society places much social status on the high school and college one attends. One benefit of this system for students is that their parents care so much about this exam that many high schoolers have almost no chores to do at home while they are preparing for the exams!

■ キアラのジャーナル Kiara's Journal
きあら　　じゃーなる

Read the journal entry below, and then answer these questions.

❶ What grade levels are in high schools in Japan?
❷ Where did Kiara's teacher study English?
❸ Describe Kiara's school.

Dear Journal,

We had our first day of school today. To get to our 学校, we had to change trains twice, and then walk
がっこう
about five blocks. It took about thirty minutes. At home, I usually ride the school bus, but じゅん君 said
くん
that they don't use school buses in Japan.

小学校 consists of 一年生 から 六年生、中学校 は grades 7-9 or 中学 一年生 から 中学
しょうがっこう　　　　　　　　　ねんせい　　　　　　　ねんせい　　ちゅうがっこう　　　　　　　　　　　　　　　ちゅうがく　　ねんせい　　　　　　　ちゅうがく
三年生、as they are called. 高校 is grades 10-12 or 高校 一年生から 高校 三年生. Since 高
さんねんせい　　　　　　　　　　　こうこう　　　　　　　　　　　　　　　　　　こうこう　　　　　　　　　　こうこう　　さんねんせい
校 is not mandatory, everyone who attends 高校 in Japan has to pass an entrance exam in order to be
accepted. Nearly everyone in the entire country goes to 高校. It's a lot different from home, where it is
easy to enter 高校. ベン君 is still a 中学生. ベン君は中学三年生。じゅん君 は 高校 一年生で
くん
す。私は 高校二年生です。

My homeroom teacher, 山本先生, is really kind. He's from 横浜 and travels almost an hour every day
よこはま
to get to this 高校. He is one of the English teachers here. He studied at 東京大学, one of the best and
こうこう
oldest universities in Japan. Right after college, he lived in New Zealand for one year, so he speaks English
with a New Zealand accent. I never really thought about how many different kinds of accents there are
just in my own language.

この 高校は とても 大きい です. It's three stories tall, like most schools, complete with a
こい pond in the middle of the courtyard. I think I'm going to like going out there to draw. My homeroom's
on the first floor, and I stay in that one room most of the day. In Japan, teachers move from classroom
to classroom more than the students do. Each teacher has a desk in the large faculty room next to the
principal's office, and they usually carry their things around with them from classroom to classroom like
students do in the U.S.

After classes, we all had to clean the floors, blackboard, and the hallway outside of our room, empty the
trash can, and clean up part of the schoolyard. My 先生 in the U.S. told me about this, but I thought that
it was a joke! It wasn't too bad, though; I actually enjoyed getting a bit of exercise in the afternoon.

■ テクノの時間 Techno Time
て く の　　じ かん

1. Though you've not been introduced to them all, type all the vocabulary words from this chapter into your digital
   dictionary. Remember to use your file labeled "JISHO" (in *romaji*).

社会と 音楽と 英語が あります。
You will have social studies, music and English.

2) おはよう。

1) 先生、おはよう ございます。

3) 今日の スケジュールを おしえて下さい。

4) はい。学校は 八時から です。今日は、社会と 国語と 体育と 美術と 音楽と 英語が あります。しつもんは ありますか。

5) はい、あります。明日の スケジュールと 今日の スケジュールは ちがいますね。毎日スケジュールは ちがいますか。

6) 時間割 ですか。ええ、毎日ちがいます。

■ 会話 Dialogue
かいわ

キアラ　　　：　先生、おはよう　ございます。
きあら

山本先生　：　おはよう。
やまもと

キアラ　　　：　今日の　スケジュールを　*おしえて　下さい。
きあら　　　　　きょう　　　すけじゅーる　　　　　　　　　　くだ

山本先生　：　はい。学校は　八時　から　です。今日は、社会と　国語と　体育と　美術と　音楽
やまもと　　　　　　　　　　はちじ　　　　　　　　きょう　　　しゃかい　こくご　　たいいく　　びじゅつ　　おんがく
　　　　　　　　　と　英語が　あります。しつもんは　ありますか。
　　　　　　　　　　えいご

キアラ　　　：　はい、あります。明日の　スケジュールと　今日の　スケジュールは　ちがいます
きあら　　　　　　　　　　　　　あした　　すけじゅーる　　　きょう　　すけじゅーる
　　　　　　　　　ね。スケジュールは　毎日違いますか。
　　　　　　　　　　　すけじゅーる　　　まいにちちが

山本先生　：　時間割　ですか。ええ、毎日　ちがいます。
やまもと　　　　じかんわり　　　　　　　　まいにち

*おしえて　下さい – please teach (tell) me
　　　　　　くだ

■ 単語 New Words
たんご

科目 (n) – subject, course
かもく

スケジュール (n) すけじゅーる	クラス (n) くらす	教室 (n) きょうしつ	英語 (n) えいご	国語 (n) こくご
数学 (n) すうがく	科学 (n) かがく	体育 (n) たいいく	美術 (n) びじゅつ	音楽 (n) おんがく
授業 (n) じゅぎょう	ホームルーム (n) ほーむるーむ	昼休み (n) ひる	宿題 (n) しゅくだい	小テスト (n) しょうてすと
テスト (n) てすと	試験 (n) しけん	作文 (n) さくぶん	楽しい (い adj.) たの	難しい (い adj.) むずか

Hours and Minutes

一時 いち じ	1:00	八時 はち じ	8:00	一分 いっぷん	:01	十　分 じゅっぷん/じっぷん	:10
二時 に じ	2:00	*九時 く じ	9:00	二分 に ふん	:02	十一分 じゅういっぷん	:11
三時 さん じ	3:00	十時 じゅう じ	10:00	三分 さん ぷん	:03	十二分 じゅうにふん	:12
*四時 よ じ	4:00	十一時 じゅう いち じ	11:00	四分 よん ぷん	:04	十三分 じゅうさんぷん	:13
五時 ご じ	5:00	十二時 じゅうに じ	12:00	五分 ご ふん	:05	二　十　分 にじゅっぷん/にじっぷん	:20
六時 ろく じ	6:00	何時 (inter.) なん じ	what time?	六分 ろっぷん	:06	二十一分 に じゅう いっぷん	:21
七 時 なな じ/しち じ	7:00			七分 なな ふん	:07	四十三分 よんじゅうさんぷん	:43
				八　分 はっぷん/はちふん	:08	何分 (inter.) なん ぷん	how many minutes?
				九 分 きゅう ふん	:09		

*Note the pronunciations for 4 o'clock and 9 o'clock.

a.m.	p.m.			日月火水木金土 X X X X X X X		
午前 (n) ごぜん	午後 (n) ご ご	今 (n) いま	今日 (n) きょう	毎日 (n) まいにち	昨日 (n) きのう	明日 (n) あした

時々 (n/adv.) – ときどき sometimes	ちょっと (adv.) – a little	前 (n/adv.) – まえ in front, before	～すぎ – past, after, too (much)	～ごろ – about	から (part.) – from ～はん (n) – half

Other words you might like to use:

生物学 (n) せいぶつがく	biology	一　秒 (n) いち びょう	1 second
保健体育 (n) ほけんたい いく	health education	二　秒 (n) に びょう	2 seconds
家庭科 (n) か てい か	home economics	三　秒 (n) さん びょう	3 seconds
歴史 (n) れき し	history	四　秒 (n) よん びょう	4 seconds
アメリカ史 (n) あ めり か し	American history	五　秒 (n) ご びょう	5 seconds
日本史 (n) に ほん し	Japanese history	六　秒 (n) ろく びょう	6 seconds
世界史 (n) せ かい し	world history	七　秒 (n) なな びょう	7 seconds
経済学 (n) けい ざい がく	economics	八　秒 (n) はち びょう	8 seconds
心理学 (n) しん り がく	psychology	九　秒 (n) きゅう びょう	9 seconds
物理学 (n) ぶつ り がく	physics	十　秒 (n) じゅう びょう	10 seconds
事務所 (n) じ む しょ	office	何秒 (inter.) なんびょう	how many seconds?

■ 漢字 Kanji
かんじ

英 **8 strokes**	エイ – gifted, talented えい 英(語) – English えい ご The first three strokes are the plant radical, while the rest looks like a flower box on the big (大) stand of a TALENTED ENGLISH gardener who speaks ENGLISH to the plants to make them grow.	一　十　艹　艹　苎　苎　英　英

国 **8 strokes**	～コク, ～ごく, くに – country, nation こく (中)国 – China; (韓)国 – Korea; ちゅう ごく　　　かん こく (母)国 – mother country ぼ こく This shows a king (王), bouncing a ball (玉) in his four-walled kingdom (country). It shows that it is easy to have a ball in your own COUNTRY, but cool things can also happen in other COUNTRIES. おう　　　　たま	丨　冂　冂　冃　冃　囯　国　国

音 **9 strokes**	オン, おと – sound おん 音(楽) – music; 音 – sound おん がく　　　　おと This kanji consists of two parts. To stand (立) is on top of the sun (日). Imagine the SOUND someone would want to make standing on the sun!	丶　亠　亠　立　产　音　音 音

楽 **13 strokes**	ガク, たの(しい) – fun, enjoyable がく 音(楽) – music; 楽 (しい) – fun, enjoyable おん がく　　　　　たの This kanji looks like a white (白) bird chirping HAPPILY and with great JOY on top of a short tree (木).	丶　亻　白　白　白　泊　泊 泊　渔　楽　楽　楽

今 **4 strokes**	コン – this, いま – now こん 今(日 は) – hello; 今(何時) – What time is it now? こん にち　　　　　いま なんじ This shows a two-story house with a roof held up by only one wall: the house leans to the right under the weight. The owner needs to fix it NOW!	𠆢　𠆢　今　今

分 **4 strokes**	ブン, フン, プン – minute, portion; ぶん ふん ぷん わ(かる) – to understand (一)分, (二)分, (三)分 – one minute, two minutes, いっ ぷん　に ふん　さん ぷん three minutes; 分(かります) – to understand わ This kanji has an eight (八) on top of a sword (刀). When you use a sword to cut something into eight small parts, like reducing an hour down to MINUTES, you can more easily UNDERSTAND it.	丿　八　分　分

■ 言葉の探索 Language Detection
こ と ば   たん さく

1. The direct object particle – を

The direct object is the object or person that receives the action of a verb. The particle を, the direct object indicator, is pronounced "o," just like the hiragana お. It is found in the "w" column on the hiragana chart, though, and is typed "wo." The particle を comes after the direct object.

A) 漫画を 読んで 下さい。	= Please read the manga.
B) えんぴつを 出して 下さい	= Please take out a pencil.
C) 本を 開いて 下さい。	= Please open the book.
D) 紙を 貸して 下さい。	= Please lend me paper.

In the first example, the 漫画 is receiving the action of the verb (what is being read). In the second example, the えんぴつ is receiving the action of the verb (it is what is being taken out). Therefore, 漫画 and えんぴつ are direct objects and are followed by the particle を.

2. Telling time

A. **Hours:** 時 is the counter for hours. It is used like "o'clock" in English, following the number. Unlike *o'clock*, 時 cannot be cut when telling time. For instance, for 5:00 it is OK to say "It is five" in English but incorrect to say「五です」in Japanese. You must say 「五時 です」.
ご じ

2:00 –	二時
6:00 –	六時
4:00 –	四時
9:00 –	九時

Use 前 or すぎ to talk about "before # o'clock" or "after # o'clock." These words always follow the time expression, never preceding it.
まえ

九時前   before 9
く じ まえ

十一時すぎ   after 11
じゅういちじ

五時十分前   ten minutes before 5
ご じ じゅっぷん まえ

八時二十分すぎ   twenty minutes after 8
はち じ に じゅっぷん

Use the particle から (*from*) after the time expression to talk about when something starts.

学校は 七時半から です。   School starts (is from) 7:30.
がっこう しちじ/なな じ はん

英語の 授業は 九時十五分から です。   English class starts at (is from) 9:15.
えい ご じゅぎょう く じ じゅう ご ふん

ばんごはんは、まいにち 六時四十五分から です。   Every day, dinner starts at (is from) 6:45.
ろく じ よんじゅう ご ふん

B. **Minutes:** 分 or 分 is the counter for minutes. The pronunciation of 分
ふん   ふん   ふん
or 分 changes slightly depending on the number that precedes it.
ふん

1:05 –	一時五分
3:45 –	三時四十五分
11:20 –	十一時二十分
7:30 –	七時三十分

3.   **Time words**

There are two types of time words in Japanese, GENERAL and SPECIFIC.

A.   General time words used as adverbs do not need any particle after them. General time words include:

今 (now) いま	毎日 (every day) まいにち	明日 (tomorrow) あした
今日 (today) きょう	毎月 (every month) まいつき/まいげつ	毎年 (every year) まいとし/まいねん

General time words <u>may</u> be followed by the particle は, to indicate emphasis or that the time is the actual topic. Time
WA
words can appear in many different places in a sentence, but they usually come toward the beginning.

B.   The particle に follows immediately after specific time words (when we would use the prepositions *on*, *in*, or *at* in English). Specific time words include:

二時三十分に   at 2:30
に　じ さんじゅっぷん

六時に   at 6 o'clock
ろくじ

2058年に   in the year 2058
にせんごじゅうはちねん

Below are some example sentences showing how to use both general and specific time words and expressions.

A) 明日　この本を　貸して　下さい。   = Tomorrow, please lend me this book.
    あした   か   くだ
B) そのあと　紙を　出して　下さい。   = After that, please take out some paper.
              かみ   だ   くだ
C) 八時半に　黒板を　見て　下さい。   = Please look at the blackboard at 8:30.
    はちじ はん こくばん み   くだ

Notice which time words are followed by the particle に.

■ 自習 Self Check
    じ しゅう

I.   Say the following in Japanese, inserting particles as needed.

⤳ その漢字＿＿＿＿＿＿読んで　下さい。 (Please read that kanji.)
        かんじ   よ   くだ

⤳ まど＿＿＿＿＿＿ 開けて　下さい。 (Please open the window.)
                    あ   くだ

⤳ 八時＿＿＿＿＿＿宿題＿＿＿＿＿＿出して　下さい。 (At 8:00, please take out your homework.)
    はちじ   しゅくだい   だ   くだ

⤳ 毎日＿＿＿＿＿Ｅメール＿＿＿＿＿＿書いて　下さい。 (Please write an e-mail every day.)
    まいにち   め ー る   か   くだ

⤳ Please read your kanji every day. ⇨ ＿＿＿＿＿＿＿＿＿＿＿＿＿＿＿＿＿

⤳ Please close your book at 3:00. ⇨ ＿＿＿＿＿＿＿＿＿＿＿＿＿＿＿＿＿

2. Cover up the right column with your hand or a piece of paper as you say the times in the left column out loud to yourself in Japanese. Check yourself by looking at the right column.

a. 7:00	しちじ
b. 1:30	いちじ　はん
c. before 3:00	さんじ　まえ
d. after 9:15	くじじゅうごふん　すぎ
e. 5:20	ごじにじゅっぷん
f. 12:33	じゅうにじさんじゅうさんぷん

■ 練習の時間 Time for Practice
れんしゅう　じかん

1. Small Group Work

Take turns giving each other commands. If A-さん is speaking, B-さん should act out the command. A-さん should pay close attention to the particles in the commands.

A) この本を　開いて　下さい。
B) あのドアを　しめて　下さい。
C) 漢字を　書いて　下さい。
D) 鉛筆を　出して　下さい。

E) 紙を　見せて　下さい。
F) この　ひらがなを　読んで　下さい。
G) あの　黒板を　見て　下さい。
H) 日本の　音楽を　聞いて　下さい。

2. Pair Practice

What time is it? Information Gap Activity

Your teacher has placed clocks on opposite walls of the room. A-さん should go to one of the clocks, read the time silently and remember it, and then go back and say the time in Japanese to B-さん. Repeat this until half of the clocks are recorded. Switch roles and finish.

Q 今何時 ですか。
いまなんじ

A 今、＿＿＿＿＿＿＿＿＿＿＿＿＿＿＿＿＿ です。
いま

3. Pair Work

Copy the chart below onto a scrap piece of paper. Your partner will ask you if you have the following classes or subjects and who the teacher is. Answer using one of these general time words: 毎日、時々、明日、or 今日. If you don't
まいにち　ときどき　あした　きょう
have a class this semester, answer ありません. Your partner will write down your answers in the correct columns.

A-さん:　美術の　授業は　毎日 ありますか。 = Do you have art class every day?
びじゅつ　じゅぎょう　まいにち
B-さん:　はい、毎日 あります。 = Yes, I have (art class) every day.
まいにち
-OR- いいえ、毎日 じゃありません。 = No, not every day.
まいにち
(if they have the class):
A-さん:　そう ですか。美術の 先生の 名前は 何 ですか。 = Really. What is the name of your art teacher?
びじゅつ　なまえ
B-さん:　＿＿＿先生 です。 = It's Mr./Ms. ＿＿＿＿.
せんせい

Class	every day	sometimes	today	tomorrow	no	Teacher
英語 えいご						
数学 すうがく						
体育 たいいく						
音楽 おんがく						
国語 こくご						
科学 かがく						
美術 びじゅつ						
(other)						

4. **Pair Work**

Draw six clocks on a piece of scrap paper, numbering them from 1 to 6. A-さん should draw in times on clocks 1 through 3 and B-さん should draw in times on clocks 4 through 6. Don't let your partner see the times you write down. Next, take turns asking what time it is.

(assume B has drawn in 5:15 on clock number 4)

A-さん： 四は　何時　ですか。　　　 = What time is (clock) 4?
　　　　よん　なんじ

B-さん： 四は　五時十五分　です。 = (Clock) 4 is 5:15.
　　　　よん　ごじじゅうごふん

■ 文化箱 Culture Chest
ぶんかばこ

High School Courses

Most courses offered in a Japanese high school can be found in other countries as well. However, some Japanese high schools offer classes you might not see in a typical non-Japanese high school, such as 書道 (calligraphy), 古文 (classical
しょどう   こぶん
Japanese) and 倫理 (ethics). English classes are required study beginning in middle school.
りんり

■ キアラのジャーナル Kiara's Journal
きあら　　じゃーなる

Read the journal entry below, and then answer these questions.

❶ List three of Kiara's six classes.
❷ What is Kiara's favorite class? Which will be her most difficult class? Why?
❸ Give a specific example of how Kiara's language skills have improved.
❹ Make a sentence in Japanese using a specific time expression about your own daily schedule.

Dear Journal,

I had my second day of 高校 today. 毎日　六つの　クラスが　あります。社会と　国語と　数学と　美術と　音楽と　英語が　あります。美術が　とても　楽しい　です。日本の　学校　の　国語のクラスは　日本語　です。私の　数学の　先生は　とても　いい人　です。先生は　この　高校に九年間　います。Most teachers are transferred to other schools every five years or so. It's not that common to have a 先生 at the same school for as long as 私の　数学の　先生。山本先生は　この　高校に　三年間　います。

クラスは　ちょっと　大きい　です。生徒が　四十一人　います。The rest of my classes are about the same size. 高校は　一年生から　三年生まで　です。私の　社会の　先生は　とても　いい　先生　です。She lived in the U.S. for two years right after college as an assistant Japanese teacher in a high school in Seattle. She really liked it there. She said that the weather there was similar to the weather where she grew up, in 金沢.

私の　国語の　先生も　いい　先生　です。It's still going to be my hardest 授業 by far. I only know a little Japanese and I'm going to have to find a lot of ways to help myself remember new 単語 and 漢字 as I go through the year. I should be able to learn a lot this year, as long as I remember to review my 単語 and 漢字　毎日。

国語、which of course is what we would call 日本語 in America, is an interesting term. It makes sense. "Nation's language." While there are Koreans, Chinese, English, Australians, Americans, and other people from all over the world living here, Japan is basically a country where the vast majority of people are ethnic Japanese and Japanese is the official language.

美術 is still my favorite class. We are starting out this year drawing from a still life, but we're also keeping a sketchbook where we can draw whatever we like, after we finish our assignment.

私の　日本語 is improving a little more each day. One of the things that I realized today was how to use the particle を。For example, じゅん君 asked me, "漫画を　読みますか。" 後で, he said "ドアを　開けて下さい。" So when I wanted to ask him for a pencil, I knew that pencil is "鉛筆" and that "貸して下さい" means "please lend." And after listening to じゅん君の requests, I realized which particle I need to use between "pencil" and "please lend me." じゅん君 said that if the "pencil" is what is borrowed, or the "漫画" is what is read, or if the "door" is what is to be opened, the object (or sometimes it is a person) that has the action done to it must be followed by "を." That's the direct object.

The other language point I picked up today was about time. It seems that whenever anyone refers to a specific time to do something, like 一時に (*at one o'clock*) or 2051年に (*in the year 2051*), the time is followed by the particle に. If you are using words that don't talk about specific times but are more general like 今年 (*this year*) or 毎日 (*every day*) you don't use に after the word. I was excited—my language skills are growing so quickly!

第3課の3　次は　何時間目　ですか。
What period is next?

1) ここは コンピューターラボ です。あそこは 体育館 です。

2) そう です か。図書館は どこ ですか。

3) あそこ です。

4) この 高校は とても 大きい ですね。次は 何時間目 ですか。

5) ええと。次は 四時間目 です。四時間目は 数学 です。

6) 五時間目は 何 ですか。

7) 五時間目は 英語 です。六時間目は 美術 です。授業の 後、 部活が あります。私の クラブは 柔道部 です。

8) そう ですか。私は、茶色 帯 三だん です。

9) ええっ！ 三だん ですか。すごい ですね。

■ 会話 Dialogue

じゅん： ここは　コンピューターラボ　です。あそこは　体育館　です。

キアラ： そう　ですか。　図書館は　どこ　ですか。

じゅん： あそこ　です。

キアラ： この　高校は　とても　大きい　ですね。次は　何時間目　ですか。

じゅん： ええと。次は　*四時間目　です。四時間目は　数学　です。

キアラ： 五時間目は　何　ですか。

じゅん： 五時間目は　英語　です。六時間目は　美術　です。
　　　　　授業　の　後、部活が　あります。私　の　クラブは　柔道部　です。

キアラ： そう　です　か。私は、+茶色　帯　三だん　です。

じゅん： ええっ！三段　ですか。すごい　ですね。

* Notice this is pronounced <u>YOJIKANME</u>, *dropping the "N" sound of* YON.

+ 茶色　帯　三段 – third degree brown belt

■ 単語 New Words

一時間目 (n) – 1st period

二時間目 (n) – 2nd period

三時間目 (n) – 3rd period

四時間目* (n) – 4th period

五時間目 (n) – 5th period

六時間目 (n) – 6th period

何時間目 (inter.) – what period?

放課後 (n/adv.) – after school

後 – after

後で – afterwards

次 (adv.) – next

部活 (n) – school clubs/activities

* To refer to the club (部活) of a sport or group, put 部 after the sport or group. For example バスケ is *basketball* while バスケ部 is *basketball team* or *club*.

図書館 (n)

体育館 (n)

コンピューターラボ (n)

成績 (n)

野球 or ベースボール (n)

バスケ (n)

柔道 (n)

がっしょう (n)

寺 (n)

神社 (n)

> ## Other words you might like to use:

ブラスバンド部 (n)　陸上部 (n)　たっきゅう部 (n)　けんどう部 (n)　バスケ部 (n)　バレーボール部 (n)
ぶらすばんどぶ　りくじょうぶ　　　　　　　　　　　　　　　　　　ばすけぶ　　　ばれーぼーるぶ

■ 漢字 Kanji
かんじ

書　寺　時　門　間　下

書 10 strokes	ショ, か(く/きます) – write しょ	¬	⊐	∃	⊒	⊒	聿	書	書
	書(きます) – to write; (図)書(館) – library か　　　　　　としょかん	書	書						
	This is a large hand with all four fingers gripping a brush moving forward and backward WRITING the character for sun (日).								

寺 6 strokes	ジ, てら – temple じ	一	十	土	圭	寺	寺		
	(東大)寺 – Todaiji Temple in Nara; (お)寺 – temple とうだい じ　　　　　　　　　　てら								
	The upper part of this character is "ground" (土), while the lower part means "an inch," or a "little bit." In general, TEMPLES are built on ground that is a little bit more peaceful.								

時 10 strokes	ジ, とき – time じ	丨	冂	日	日	日	日	旪	旪
	(一)時 – 1:00; 時(々) – sometimes いち じ　　 とき どき	時	時						
	The left side of this kanji is the kanji for sun (日) while the right is the kanji for temple (寺). Long ago, temple bells rang to tell the TIME which was measured in the temple by the position of the sun.								

門 8 strokes	モン – gate もん	丨	冂	冂	冂	冂	門	門	門
	(寺の)門 – gate of the temple てら　もん								
	This is a drawing of a GATE. It looks like swinging doors or a swinging GATE.								

間 12 strokes	カン, あいだ – interval, space	丨	冂	冂	冃	冃	門	門	門
	(時)間 – hour (interval) of time; 間 – space between	門	門	間	間				
	This is a drawing of a GATE with the sun poking through the SPACE for an INTERVAL of time.									

下 3 strokes	力, した – below, under; くだ(る) – descend, give	一	下	下					
	下(さい) – please; 下 – below, under								
	The second stroke of this kanji is pointing DOWN, indicating something BELOW or UNDERNEATH. Point at some money on the ground and ask your friend to GIVE it to you.									

■ 言葉の探索 Language Detection

Class periods

The Japanese words for class periods are formed from several root words. Here is an example for 2nd period, 二時間目.

二 = two ⇨ 二時 = two o'clock ⇨ 二時間 = a two hour period of time

⇨ 二時間目 = second period

■ 自習 Self Check

⊃ Count from 1st period to 7th period in Japanese.

⊃ Now count backwards from 7th period to 1st period.

⊃ Count odd periods only.

⊃ What are your three best/favorite periods?

■ 練習の時間 Time for Practice

1. Pair Practice

The class schedule below is Jun's schedule for today. Use this schedule to ask your partner what period Jun has which class. Take turns asking and answering.

A-さん: 英語は 何時間目 ですか。= What period is English?
B-さん: 英語は 四時間目 です。 = English is 4th period.

今日の 時間割

時間目	一時間目	二時間目	三時間目	四時間目	ひる休み	五時間目	六時間目	ほうかご
じゅぎょう	びじゅつ	かがく	しゃかい	英語		たいいく	すうがく	ぶかつどう

2. **Class Practice**

Copy the chart below on a piece of scrap paper. Fill in the 授業(じゅぎょう) column with the following classes. Be sure to mix up the order:

英語(えいご)　　美術(びじゅつ)　　数学(すうがく)　　音楽(おんがく)　　社会(しゃかい)　　日本語　　自習(じしゅう)

今日(きょう)の　時間割(じかんね)り

時間目(じかんめ)	授業(じゅぎょう)	生徒(せいと)の名前(なまえ)
一時間目(いちじかんめ)		
二時間目(にじかんめ)		
三時間目(さんじかんめ)		
四時間目(よじかんめ)		
五時間目(ごじかんめ)		
六時間目(ろくじかんめ)		

Use Japanese to survey your classmates, one at a time, until you find a person with one of the exact classes you have on your schedule at the exact same period. Use Japanese to ask that student to sign their name in the box on your form. Begin when your teacher says "HAI, HAJIMEMASHOU." Once your survey form is completely signed or when your teacher tells you to stop, sit down. Be prepared to report some of your survey results to the class. You may ask each student you interview what class they have each period.

A-さん：　二時間目(にじかんめ)は　何(なん)ですか。　　= What class do you have second period?
B-さん：　美術(びじゅつ)です。　　　　　　　= I have art.
If this is the same class that A-さん has second period, A-さん then says:
名前(なまえ)を　書(か)いて下(くだ)さい。　　= Please write your name.

■ 文化箱(ぶんかばこ) Culture Chest

部活(ぶかつ) School Clubs

　　In Japan, sports teams are considered to be after-school clubs just like the various culture- and music-related groups are. Students in Japan join one club or sport when they enter high school, rather than many. They usually practice with this club, or 部活(ぶかつ), every day after school for the entire school year and stay with the same group until they graduate. There is often a wide range of sports 部活 such as 柔道部(じゅうどうぶ), 空手部(からてぶ), けんどう部(ぶ), バスケ部(ばすけぶ), 野球部(やきゅうぶ), and バレーボール部(ばれーぼーるぶ). Other clubs might include the broadcasting club, art club, tea ceremony club, and English club. The members of clubs often become very close and this bond can be an important part of a student's school life.

■ キアラのジャーナル Kiara's Journal
きあら　じゃーなる

Read the journal entry below, and then answer these questions.

❶ What adjective does Kiara use to describe the sport of kendo?
❷ What are some differences between Shinto shrines and Buddhist temples?
❸ What is a good thing to do if you miss your stop on the Tokyo subway?

Dear Journal,

　　Today was so busy. We had our first full day of 学校の　クラス。
これは　今日の　クラスの　スケジュール　です。始めは
ホームルーム　です。一時間目は　国語　です。次は　音楽　です。
三時間目　は　社会　です。明日、社会の　授業　は　図書館で　あります。午後の
クラスの　後で、じゅん君と私 met in the 体育館。I wanted to see the 剣道部。剣道は　とても
難しい　です。

　　昨日、on our way home, we passed by an amazing 神社、a Shinto shrine. Shinto is one of Japan's major religions; Buddhism is the other. Buddhism originated in India, and spread from China to Korea, and then to Japan. Buddhist temples are called お寺。You can easily tell the difference between shrines and temples, because the entrance to the grounds of 神社 are set off by a large gate, usually orange, called a 鳥居。Often there is a straw rope hung across the top. White paper zigzag cutouts hang from the rope, letting us know that the space inside this 鳥居 is purified and sacred. In front of a 寺, you can usually find a large elaborate wooden 門, with two huge and ferocious guardian deities keeping watch from either side of the gate.

　　The 鳥居 in front of the shrine on the way home looked really familiar, like I'd seen it someplace before. Jun, Ben, and I go most of the way home from school together, so I asked Jun if we could stop and walk up to the 神社 sometime. He sent a text message to his お母さん, asking if we had time before 晩ご飯。お母さん said OK です。Up close, the 鳥居は　とても　大きいです。Some 鳥居 are made from 木, some are made of stone or concrete, but this one seemed to be made of some sort of metal, which Jun said is not as common. すごい　です。Inside the shrine grounds, a long row of lanterns (in the shape of the 東京の　京) led up the hill to the big red 神社 building. The path had large stone fox statues on both sides. These foxes had an intense stare; they were actually a little freaky. It was as if they wanted to speak, but had been frozen in time. Beyond the fox statues, at the base of the staircase up to another, higher, 神社 building, something big and hairy scurried through the bushes. I only caught a glimpse of it out of the corner of my eye; and neither じゅん君 nor ベン君 saw it. It really made me nervous, so I asked them if we could go home and come back 明日。

　　We finally made it back to the subway station, just in time for the next train to 銀座。That was where we had to transfer to catch 次の train home. I was tired, and not really paying attention, so before I knew it, the others had walked off the train, onto the platform, and the doors were closing, with me still sitting there inside the train. This just wasn't turning out to be my day! じゅん君 had already told me, though, that if I got lost or separated like this, I should just get out at the 次の

station and wait for him. So I did, and sure enough, he and ベン君 showed up about five minutes later, with とても　大きい grins on their faces.

■ テクノ の時間 Techno Time

じゅん君 has just written you the following e-mail from Japan. Open your digi journal and type your reply to his message. Title it "103-3TT" followed by the first three letters of your last name and the first three of your first name. Good luck!

Dear Friend,

あなたの　高校の　スケジュールを　教えて　下さい (please teach [tell] me)。毎日　どんな　科目 がありますか。

一時間目 〜
二時間目 〜

よろしく　お願いします。
じゅん

今日、宿題は ありません。
きょう　しゅくだい
There is no homework today.

1) 先生、すみません。ちょっと暑いです。まどを開けてもいいですか。

2) いい ですよ。その まどと あの まどを 開けて 下さい。皆さん、今日、宿題は ありません。でも、小テストが あります。それでは、教科書と 紙一 枚を 出して 下さい。鉛筆も 出して 下さい。

4) ペンは だめ です。鉛筆で 書いて 下さい。みなさん 鉛筆は ありますか。

3) 先生、すみません。ペン で 書いて も いい ですか。

5) はい、あります。

6)はい、じゃあ 始めましょう。

■ 会話 Dialogue
（かいわ）

キアラ　　　：先生、すみません。ちょっと　暑い　です。まどを　開けても　いい　ですか。
（きあら）　　　（せんせい）　　　　　　　　　（あつ）　　　　　　　　　　　　（あ）

山本先生　：いい　ですよ。その　まどと　あの　まどを　開けて　下さい。皆さん、今日、
（やまもとせんせい）　　　　　　　　　　　　　　　　　　　　　　　（あ）　（くだ）　（みな）　　（きょう）

　　　　　　　しゅくだいは　ありません。でも、小テストが　あります。それでは、教科書と
　　　（きょう　しょ）

　　　　　　　紙　一枚を　出して　下さい。鉛筆も　出して　下さい。
　　　　　　　（かみ）（いちまい）　（だ）　（くだ）　（えんぴつ）　（だ）　（くだ）

キアラ　　　：先生、すみません。ペンで　書いても　いい　ですか。
（きあら）　　　（せんせい）　　　　　　　　　　　　（か）

山本先生　：ペンは　だめ　です。鉛筆で　書いて　下さい。皆さん　鉛筆は　ありますか。
（やまもとせんせい）　（ぺん）　　　　　　（えんぴつ）（か）　（くだ）　（みな）　（えんぴつ）

皆　　　　　：はい、あります。
（みんな）

山本先生　：はい、じゃあ　始めましょう。
（やまもとせんせい）　　　　　　　　（はじ）

■ 単語 New Words
（たんご）

だめ (な adj.)	暑い (い adj.)（あつ）	寒い (い adj.)（さむ）	涼しい (い adj.)（すず）	蒸し暑い (い adj.)（む）（あつ）

ドア (n) – door　　窓 (n) – window　　でも (part./conj.)　　開ける／開けます (v) –　　閉める／閉めます (v) –
（ど　あ）　　　（まど）　　　　　　　　　　　　– but　　（あ）　to open (doors/windows)　（し）to close (doors, windows)

■ 漢字 Kanji
（かんじ）

暑　寒　神　社

暑 12 strokes	あつ(い) – hot (weather/temp.)（あつ）	丶	冂	冃	日	旦	早	星	暑
	暑(い) – hot (weather/temp.)（あつ）	暑	暑	暑	暑				
	This kanji is made up of a very HOT sun (日) on top of the land (土) with a blazing HOT sword cutting into it and another very HOT sun (日) below, making it twice as HOT!								

寒 12 strokes	さむ(い) – cold (weather/temp.)（さむ）	丶	丷	宀	宀	宀	宀	宀	宭
	寒(い) – cold (weather/temp.)（さむ）	宭	寒	寒	寒				
	Under the roof of this kanji is a grid shape of a radiator trying to heat up a very COLD room. At the bottom of the kanji are two snowflakes representing winter (冬) which makes things even COLDER!								

シン, ジン, かみ – God/god, spirits しん じん かみ	`	ラ	ネ	ネ	ネ	ネ	初	初	神
神(社) – Shinto shrine; 神(道) – Shinto religion, じん じゃ　　　　　　　　しん とう literally "the way of the gods"; 神(様) – god(s) 　　　　　　　　　　　　かみ さま	神								
The left side is a version of the radical that means "to show" (示); the right side is a rice field (田) with a long line extending from ground to the heavens. It is very important to show the GODS how hard you are trying to grow a good crop.									

9 strokes

シャ, ジャ – association, company しゃ じゃ	`	ラ	ネ	ネ	ネ	社	社
神(社) – Shinto shrine; (会)社 – company or じん じゃ　　　　　かい しゃ corporation; 社(会) – society; social studies しゃ かい							
The right side is the earth (土), which shows (示) the solid foundation upon which SOCIETY is based! 神 is the character for god while 社 implies ASSOCIATION. So 神社 is an association of gods and the SHRINE where they all gather.							

7 strokes

■ 言葉の探索 Language Detection
ことば たんさく

1. でも、...

   でも means "but" or "however," and is often used to link two sentences. The first sentence ends with a period. でも, followed by a comma, comes at the beginning of the second sentence.

    中学校　と　高校が　あります。でも、小学校　は　ありません。= There is junior high school and a
   ちゅうがっこう　　こうこう　　　　　　　　　　しょうがっこう　　　　　　　　　　　　　　　　　high school. However, there is no elementary school.

   今日は　暑い　です。でも、エアコンは　ありません。= Today is hot. But there isn't any air conditioning.
   きょう　あつ　　　　　　えあこん

2. で (by means of)

   The particle で, when it follows a noun, means to do something "by means of" X, or to use X as a tool or instrument.

    ボールペンで　書いて　下さい。　= Please write by (means of) pen.
   ぼーるぺん　　か　　くだ
   漢字で　書いて　下さい。　= Please write (using) kanji.
   かんじ　か　くだ
   英語で　話して　下さい。　= Please speak in (by means of) English.
   えいご　はな　くだ

■ 自習 Self Check
じしゅう

1. Link each of the two sentences using でも.

   今日は　暑いです。　明日は　寒い　です。
   きょう　あつ　　　　あした　　さむ
   (Today is hot. Tomorrow will be cold.)

   じゅん君が　います。かずひさ君　は　いません。
   くん　　　　　　　　　くん
   (Jun is here. Kazuhisa is not here.)

   明日、英語　の　授業　が　あります。　数学の　授業は　ありません。
   あした　えいご　　じゅぎょう　　　　　　　すうがく　じゅぎょう
   (Tomorrow, I have English class. I do not have math class.)

2. Using で, "by means of," translate these phrases into 日本語.

by means of paper _____

by means of chopsticks _____

by means of a pencil _____

by means of money _____

■ 練習の時間 Time for Practice
れんしゅう　 じ かん

1. Pair Work

With a partner, link each of the two sentences using でも.

A) 今日は　涼しい　です。　明日は　蒸し暑い　です。
きょう　　すず　　　　　あした　　む　あつ

B) これは　鉛筆　です。　それは　鉛筆　では　ありません。
えんぴつ　　　　　　えんぴつ

C) 六時間目が　あります。　七時間目は　ありません。
ろくじ かんめ　　　　　　ななじ かんめ

D) 猫が　います。犬は　いません。
ねこ　　　　　いぬ

E) 兄が　います。弟は　いません。

2. Pair Work

Add a second sentence beginning with でも to each of the sentences below. Make sure the information in the second sentence is different enough that the use of でも is appropriate. Take turns.

A) 今日は　寒い　です。
きょう　　さむ

B) あれは　本　です。

C) 姉が　います。

D) 三時間目に　数学が　あります。
さんじ かんめ　　すうがく

3. Pair Work

Making a request

Review requests then ask your partner permission to do the following things. Your partner will either give or deny permission. Use the ～てもいい　ですか pattern. Take turns.

Open the book

A: 本を　開いてもいい　ですか。
ひら

B (*granting permission*): はい、開いても　いい　です。
ひら

-OR- B (*denying permission*): いいえ、開いては　だめ　です。
ひら

⊃ shut the door

⊃ take out some paper

⊃ read this hiragana

⊃ listen to Japanese music

⊃ write kanji

⊃ take out a pencil

⊃ look at that blackboard over there

⊃ (a request of your choice)

■ 文化箱 Culture Chest
ぶん か ばこ

School Calendar

The Japanese school year begins in April and ends in March. It is usually divided into three terms. Summer vacation lasts for a month, from late July through much of August, when the second term begins. Winter vacation, which lasts a month or less, centers around the New Year's holiday, and separates the second and third terms. College entrance exams begin in January for the national standardized test and continue into February and early March, for individual university tests. The graduation ceremony (卒業式) is held in March. The opening ceremony marking the new school year (入学式) happens in early or mid-April.

There are many seasonal events on the school calendar. These include school trips called 修学旅行 that last for one or more days, school sports festivals often held in early fall, and school cultural festivals or 文化祭 in late fall. These events entail a great deal of planning and group work and are considered part of a young person's education.

むし暑い　ですね。
It's muggy, isn't it.

■ 会話 Dialogue

(After school)

じゅん ： ベン君、こんにちは。

ベン ： こんにちは。暑い です ねえ。キアラさん、日本の 学校は どう ですか。

キアラ ： 楽しい です。でもむし暑い ですね。私達の学校には エアコンが ありません。
中学校は どう ですか。

ベン ： 涼しい です。私の 中学校は エアコンが ありますよ。

(a very strong wind comes out of nowhere)

ベン ： わっ！すごい風 ですね。

じゅん ： あの 神社の 鳥居に *行きましょう。

キアラ ： ええ！ここは どこ ですか。

*行きましょう – Let's go.

■ 単語 New Words

エアコン (n)	風 (n)	行きましょう(v)	速く (adv.)

鳥居 (n) – shrine gate

どう (interj.) – how?

わっ! (interj.) – Wow!

さあ (interj.) – now, well (then)

■ 漢字 Kanji

風 9 strokes	かぜ – wind	ノ 几 凡 凡 風 風 風 風
	風 – wind; (神)風 – divine wind	風
	The first two strokes represent a WIND tunnel in which the insect inside (虫) is annoyed. You can tell the bug is annoyed because its antenna (the third stroke) is bent and tilted.	

友 4 strokes	ユウ, とも – friend	一 ナ 方 友
	友(達), 友人 – friend	
	The first two strokes of this kanji for FRIEND are a person, reaching an arm across a table (又) to shake hands with a new FRIEND.	

■ 言葉の探索 Language Detection
<ruby>言葉<rt>こ と ば</rt></ruby> <ruby>探索<rt>たん さく</rt></ruby>

1. ね/ねえ

    When using these two, inflection is everything. Think about how, in English, the phrase "It's cold" can have several different meanings, depending on your inflection: "It's cold." "It's cold!" or "It's cold?" The same is true with the use of ね and ねえ, particles that come at the end of the Japanese sentence to express a range of emotions or intensities. They can be used:

A. to confirm something in the form of a rhetorical question, or when seeking agreement from the person listening, as in "... right?"

    明日は　寒い　ですね。 = Tomorrow will be cold, won't it?
    <ruby>明日<rt>あした</rt></ruby>　<ruby>寒<rt>さむ</rt></ruby>

B. as an exclamation mark.

    寒い　ですねえ。 = It's cold!
    <ruby>寒<rt>さむ</rt></ruby>

    Note: It is common in Japan to repeat a question before giving the answer. Often the repeated part will have the particle ね at the end to confirm that the question was understood. You can also use ね after you repeat directions or new information to confirm that you accurately understood what the speaker said. This is a great communication strategy, so try to use it when you get new information from your pair practice partners.

2. よ

    よ comes at the end of the sentence and is used to make a definite statement that the listener should agree with such as "I am telling you ..." or "Hey ..."   In some contexts, it acts like an exclamation mark in English. よ should be used sparingly, especially when speaking to superiors, as it can easily be construed as a bit too direct, even rude.

    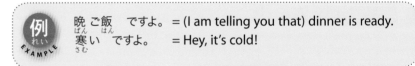

    例 | 晩 ご飯　ですよ。 = (I am telling you that) dinner is ready.
    れい | <ruby>晩<rt>ばん</rt></ruby> ご<ruby>飯<rt>はん</rt></ruby>
    EXAMPLE | 寒い　ですよ。 = Hey, it's cold!
    | <ruby>寒<rt>さむ</rt></ruby>

■ 自習 Self Check
<ruby>自習<rt>じ しゅう</rt></ruby>

1. Say the following, using ね:

    It's cool, isn't it?　　　　　　= 涼しい　です_____。
    <ruby>涼<rt>すず</rt></ruby>

    It's hot, isn't it?　　　　　　 = _____。

2. Say the following, using よ:

    I'm telling you, it's muggy.　 = むし暑い　です_____。
    <ruby>暑<rt>あつ</rt></ruby>

    I'm telling you, this is sushi. = _____。

■ 練習の時間 Time for Practice
<ruby>練習<rt>れんしゅう</rt></ruby> <ruby>時間<rt>じ かん</rt></ruby>

1. Pair Practice

Pointing out as many classroom objects as you can (refer to Appendix 4 as needed), confirm that you are using the correct Japanese word by asking a confirmation question with ね. Your partner will answer authoritatively using よ.

例　A-さん: (*Points to a desk*) あれは　つくえ　ですね。 = That over there is a desk, isn't it?
れい
EXAMPLE　B-さん: はい、あれは　つくえ　ですよ。 = Yes, that over there is a desk!

2. Pair Practice

Your teacher has asked your class to find out information about pen pals. Assume you and your partner have had many pen pals, and that you have much information to share (see Table A and Table B, below). Decide which table each of you will use, then copy your table onto a separate piece of paper, and take turns asking/answering questions. Use ね, ねえ, and よ in your answers as appropriate. When all the blanks on your questionnaire are filled in, say 「できました」. You may be asked to share some of your information with your class.

Note: ね generally is used in a statement where the speaker is hoping for/expecting agreement. ねえ is generally used where an exclamation mark would be used in English.

(location)
B-さん： Maria は どこに いますか。　　= Where is Maria?
A-さん： Maria は Barcelona に いますよ。　= Maria is in Barcelona, you know.

(weather — both are in same city)
B-さん： Barcelonaは 涼しい ですね。　　= Barcelona's weather is cool, isn't it?
A-さん： そうですね。Barcelonaは とても 涼しい ですねえ。
　　　　　= Yes (I agree). The weather in Barcelona is very cool!

(club activities)
B-さん： Mariaの 部活は 何ですか。　　= What is Maria's club activity?
A-さん： Mariaの 部活は サッカーです。　= Maria is in the soccer club.

Table A

名前	場所 (location)	年生 (学年)	天気	家族	部活
Maria	Barcelona (BARUSERONA)	10th	cool	five	soccer
Martin					
Bruce					
Meilin	Taiwan	2nd year college	muggy	three	English Club
Aimee					
Sergei	Moscow (MOSUKUWA)	8th	hot	four	basketball
Phillip					
Kazumi	Tokyo	12th	cool	six	kendo

■ 文化箱 Culture Chest

1. 鳥居 Shinto Shrine Gate

The literal meaning of 鳥居, the red gates at the entrances to Shinto shrines, is 鳥の居るところ or 鳥が居ます which could be translated as "place where the bird is." Some birds are thought of as very powerful. This may mean actual power, like birds of prey (eagles, hawks, or owls), or a "powerful presence," such as great blue herons or white cranes or storks. Other powerful birds are mythological, such as the thunderbird or the phoenix in Western tales or the garuda of Indonesian legends. Large cranes and other birds often perch on high places to scout for prey or to sun themselves. Japanese hope that these birds will land on a TORII and stay there for as long as possible. What grander perch could a special bird have than a TORII at the entrance of a 神社?

2. **制服 Uniforms**
　せいふく

Most high school students in Japan wear school uniforms. Rules about wearing proper uniforms differ from school to school and can be quite specific. Wearing a uniform outside of school identifies students as part of a particular school and shows school pride. Some students push the limits of what is acceptable within the school rules just as they do in many other places. Rules related to makeup, piercing, and hair also differ from high school to high school, although few Japanese high schools allow their students to wear jewelry or even makeup at school.

What are some good arguments for and against having school uniforms?

Table B

名前	場所 (location) ばしょ	年生 (学年)	天気 てんき	家族 かぞく	部活 ぶかつ
Maria					
Martin	Manila (MANIRA)	1st year college	muggy	eight	volleyball
Bruce	Sydney (SHIDONI-)	12th	cold	four	Ping-Pong
Meilin					
Aimee	Paris (PARI)	11th	cool	three	brass band
Sergei					
Phillip	Toronto (TORONTO)	9th	muggy	five	choir
Kazumi					

■ キアラのジャーナル Kiara's Journal
　　きあら　じゃーなる

Read the journal entry below, and then answer these questions.

❶ Where did the students run to seek shelter from the storm?
❷ What kind of animal did Jun think the hairy beast was?
❸ What is a 時 の 門?
　　　　　　とき　　もん
❹ Ben compared the hairy animal to what other creature?
❺ Make a prediction about the content of Kiara's next journal entry.

ジャーナルへ
じゃーなる

This was such a bizarre day! No one's ever going to believe what happened, but here goes.

The three of us had just left our 部活、heading toward the subway station. We stopped in to get some
　　　　　　　　　　　　　　　　ぶかつ
あめ at our favorite Seven-Eleven, but as soon as we left the store, winds blew up, whipping everything around. The closest building was the 神社, so we ran toward it, dodging papers and cardboard and plastic bags. A bicycle, knocked over by the wind, almost hit じゅん君。At the 鳥居 gate, that same hairy animal
　　　　　　　　　　　　　　　　　　　　　　　くん　　　　　　とりい
I saw the other day darted out of the bushes and ran through the 鳥居 with us.

Suddenly, everything stopped! The wind vanished, the garden and 神社 vanished too! Instead, we were in some sort of tunnel. Right in front of us, flying forward, was that same hairy animal!

I screamed at じゅん君と　ベン君 to see if they knew where we were and what was going on.
じゅん君 yelled back "分かりません！But that looks like the 狸 we saw earlier!"
　　　　　　　　　　わ　　べん　　　　　　　　　　　　　　たぬき

ベン君 said "I didn't think 狸 were real! And even if they are real, what's it doing here? And where are we going?"

All that I could contribute was, "What's a 狸?"

At this point, the animal ... he, ... it, turned and stared at us in surprise. He spoke. "How did you get here? Who are you?"

ベン君 whimpered, "We don't know. We were just trying to get out of the storm, and now we're in this wind tunnel or something. We headed for the 神社、 and the next thing we knew, we were, umm, here."

じゅん君 interjected, "Speaking of here, where is here? And who, or what, are you?"

The 狸 replied, "僕は 友 です。 これは 私の 時の 門 です。"

"時の門?" じゅん君 repeated, "それは 何 ですか。"

友さん replied, "It's not a word commonly used in 日本語 yet since few creatures know that these gates can be used for time travel. でも、百年後 (in 100 years), it will be a very common word! 僕は 2125年 から 来ました。 Something must have gone wrong, though, because you are not supposed to be here! That 風 must have affected the gate, but there's nothing that I can do now. We're on our way!"

I was starting to freak out, with all this talk about the past and the future and mistakes. I had to ask, "How can we be talking to a little fur ball? Animals aren't supposed to talk!"

Ben answered, "Japanese folk tales mention 狸 and 狐 (foxes) as having supernatural powers. They're supposed to be shape-shifters, animals that can change their appearance at will. Normally, they're portrayed as being quite tricky, but these are just stories. It's not real, of course."

"That may be," 友 sniffed, "but could one of you go over there to that switch please. We're coming in for a landing, and with your extra weight, we're descending much faster than we should be. I need help slowing us down. Hang on. We're almost there!"

■ テクノの時間 Techno Time

高山ゆみ, a high school student in Japan, has sent you the following e-mail. Reply to her e-mail.

日本語の 生徒 さんへ

この でんしメール(e-mail)は 私の 宿題 です。 あなたの お名前は 何ですか。 先生の 名前と 学校の 名前は 何 ですか。 今 何年生 ですか。 科目は 何が ありますか。 何が 楽しい ですか。

返事 (reply)を 待って います (waiting)。ありがとう。
では また。

高山 ゆみ

To gain your passport stamp for this chapter, and to prove that you've mastered the survival skills necessary to move forward, you will make a presentation on your school life. Be prepared to briefly talk about your classes and clubs. You must use a visual (poster or PowerPoint) to assist you.

■ 単語チェックリスト New Word Checklist
たんごちぇっくりすと

Japanese	Location	English
3-1		
いちねんせい　　一年生 (n)	3-1	first year student
えむぴすりー ぷれーやー　　MP3 プレーヤー (n)	3-1	MP3 player
おおきい　　大きい (い adj.)	3-1	big, large
がくせい　　学生 (n)	3-1	student
がっこう　　学校 (n)	3-1	school
けいたい (でんわ)　　けいたい (電話) (n)	3-1	cellular phone
こうこう　　高校 (n)	3-1	high school
こうこういちねんせい　　高校一年生 (n)	3-1	tenth grader
こうこうさんねんせい　　高校三年生 (n)	3-1	twelfth grader
こうこうせい　　高校生 (n)	3-1	high school student
こうこうにねんせい　　高校二年生 (n)	3-1	eleventh grader
さんねんせい　　三年生 (n)	3-1	third year student
しょうがくせい　　小学生 (n)	3-1	elementary school student
しょうがっこう　　小学校 (n)	3-1	elementary school
すこし　　少し (adv.)	3-1	little
せいと　　生徒 (n)	3-1	student
だいがく　　大学 (n)	3-1	college/university
だいがくせい　　大学生 (n)	3-1	college/university student
たくさん (n)	3-1	many, a lot
ちいさい　　小さい (い adj.)	3-1	small
ちゅうがくいちねんせい　　中学一年生 (n)	3-1	seventh grader
ちゅうがくさんねんせい　　中学三年生 (n)	3-1	ninth grader
ちゅうがくせい　　中学生 (n)	3-1	middle school student
ちゅうがくにねんせい　　中学二年生 (n)	3-1	eighth grader
ちゅうがっこう　　中学校 (n)	3-1	middle school
とても (adv.)	3-1	very
なんねんせい　　何年生 (inter.)	3-1	what grade/year
にねんせい　　二年生 (n)	3-1	second year student
ほいくえん　　保育園 (n)	3-1	kindergarten
みなさん　　皆さん (n)	3-1	everyone (polite)
みんな　　皆 (n)	3-1	everyone, all
やま　　山 (n)	3-1	mountain
やまもと　　山本 (n)	3-1	Yamamoto (family name)
ようちえん　　幼稚園 (n)	3-1	nursery school

Japanese	Location	English
3-2		
あした　明日 (*n*)	3-2	tomorrow
あめりかし　アメリカ史 (*n*)	3-2	American history
いちじ　一時 (*n*)	3-2	one o'clock
いっぷん　一分 (*n*)	3-2	one minute
いま　今 (*n/adv.*)	3-2	now
えいご　英語 (*n*)	3-2	English language
おんがく　音楽 (*n*)	3-2	music
かがく　科学 (*n*)	3-2	science
かていか　家庭科 (*n*)	3-2	family consumer science
かもく　科目 (*n*)	3-2	school subject
から (*part*)	3-2	from
きのう　昨日 (*n/adv.*)	3-2	yesterday
きゅうふん　九分 (*n*)	3-2	nine minutes
きょう　今日 (*n*)	3-2	today
きょうしつ　教室 (*n*)	3-2	classroom
くじ　九時 (*n*)	3-2	nine o'clock
くらす　クラス (*n*)	3-2	class
こくご　国語 (*n*)	3-2	national language (Japanese language)
ごご　午後 (*n*)	3-2	p.m.
ごじ　五時 (*n*)	3-2	five o'clock
ごぜん　午前 (*n*)	3-2	a.m.
ごふん　五分 (*n*)	3-2	five minutes
～ごろ	3-2	about
さくぶん　作文 (*n*)	3-2	essay
さんじ　三時 (*n*)	3-2	three o'clock
さんぷん　三分 (*n*)	3-2	three minutes
しけん　試験 (*n*)	3-2	test, exam
しちじ or ななじ　七時 (*n*)	3-2	seven o'clock
じゅういちじ　十一時 (*n*)	3-2	eleven o'clock
じゅうじ　十時 (*n*)	3-2	ten o'clock
じゅうにじ　十二時 (*n*)	3-2	twelve o'clock
じゅぎょう　授業 (*n*)	3-2	class
しゅくだい　宿題 (*n*)	3-2	homework
じゅっぷん or じっぷん　十分 (*n*)	3-2	ten minutes
しょうてすと　小テスト (*n*)	3-2	small test, quiz
しんりがく　心理学 (*n*)	3-2	psychology
すうがく　数学 (*n*)	3-2	math
～すぎ	3-2	past, after, (too) much
すけじゅーる　スケジュール (*n*)	3-2	schedule
せいぶつがく　生物学 (*n*)	3-2	biology
せかいし　世界史 (*n*)	3-2	world history
たいいく　体育 (*n*)	3-2	physical education
たのしい　楽しい (*い adj.*)	3-2	fun, enjoyable
ちょっと (*adv.*)	3-2	little, somewhat
てすと　テスト (*n*)	3-2	test

Japanese	Location	English
ときどき　時々 (*adv.*)	3-2	sometimes
ななふん　七分 (*n*)	3-2	seven minutes
なんじ　何時 (*inter.*)	3-2	what time
なんぷん　何分 (*inter.*)	3-2	how many minutes
にじ　二時 (*n*)	3-2	two o'clock
にじゅっぷん　二十分 (*n*)	3-2	twenty minutes
にぷん　二分 (*n*)	3-2	two minutes
にほんし　日本史 (*n*)	3-2	Japanese history
はちじ　八時 (*n*)	3-2	eight o'clock
はっぷん　八分 (*n*)	3-2	eight minutes
はん　半 (*n*)	3-2	half hour
びじゅつ　美術 (*n*)	3-2	art
ひるやすみ　昼休み (*n*)	3-2	lunch break
ぶつりがく　物理学 (*n*)	3-2	physics
ほーむるーむ　ホームルーム (*n*)	3-2	homeroom
ほけんたいいく　保健体育 (*n*)	3-2	health (class)
まいにち　毎日 (*n*)	3-2	every day
むずかしい　難しい (い *adj.*)	3-2	difficult
よじ　四時 (*n*)	3-2	four o'clock
よんぷん　四分 (*n*)	3-2	four minutes
れきし　歴史 (*n*)	3-2	history
ろくじ　六時 (*n*)	3-2	six o'clock
ろっぷん　六分 (*n*)	3-2	six minutes

3-3

Japanese	Location	English
あと　後	3-3	after
あとで　後で	3-3	afterwards
いちじかんめ　一時間目 (*n*)	3-3	first period
がっしょう　合唱 (*n*)	3-3	chorus; choir
けんどう　剣道 (*n*)	3-3	kendo
けんどうぶ　剣道部 (*n*)	3-3	kendo club
ごじかんめ　五時間目 (*n*)	3-3	fifth period
こんぴゅーたらーぼ　コンピューターラボ (*n*)	3-3	computer lab
さんじかんめ　三時間目 (*n*)	3-3	third period
じゅうどう　柔道 (*n*)	3-3	judo
じんじゃ　神社 (*n*)	3-3	shrine
せいせき　成績 (*n*)	3-3	score, grade
たいいくかん　体育館 (*n*)	3-3	gymnasium
たっきゅうぶ　たっきゅう部 (*n*)	3-3	Ping-Pong club
つぎ　次 (*adv.*)	3-3	next
てら　寺 (*n*)	3-3	temple
としょかん　図書館 (*n*)	3-3	library
なんじかんめ　何時間目 (*inter.*)	3-3	what period
にじかんめ　二時間目 (*n*)	3-3	second period
ばすけぶ　バスケ部 (*n*)	3-3	basketball team
ばれーぼーるぶ　バレーボル部 (*n*)	3-3	volleyball club (team)

Japanese	Location	English
ぶかつ　部活 (n)	3-3	club activity
ぶらすばんど　ブラスバンド (n)	3-3	brass band
ほうかご　放課後 (n/adv.)	3-3	time after school
やきゅうぶ　野球部 (n)	3-3	baseball team
よじかんめ　四時間目 (n)	3-3	fourth period
りくじょうぶ　陸上部 (n)	3-3	track and field club
ろくじかんめ　六時間目 (n)	3-3	sixth period

3-4

Japanese	Location	English
あける/あけます　開ける/開けます (開けて) (v)	3-4	(to) open (door/window)
あつい　暑い (い adj.)	3-4	hot (weather)
さむい　寒い (い adj.)	3-4	cold (weather)
しめる/しめます　閉める/閉めます (閉めて) (v)	3-4	(to) close (doors/windows)
すずしい　涼しい (い adj.)	3-4	cool (weather)
だめ (な adj.)	3-4	is bad
でも (part./conj.)	3-4	but
むしあつい　蒸し暑い (い adj.)	3-4	humid (weather)

3–5

Japanese	Location	English
いきましょう　行きましょう (v)	3-5	let's go
えあこん　エアコン (n)	3-5	air conditioner
かぜ　風 (n)	3-5	wind
さあ (interj.)	3-5	well...
どう (inter.)	3-5	how
とりい　鳥居 (n)	3-5	Shinto shrine gate
はやく　速く (adv.)	3-5	quickly
わっ! (interj.)	3-5	similar to "wow!"

People and Places of Nagasaki

第 **4** 課

✔ Learning Goals

By the end of this chapter you will learn:

A) a little about trade in Japan in during the Tokugawa period (1603–1868)

B) where Kyushu (one of Japan's four main islands) is on a map and some of its geographical features

C) about interesting sites on the island of Kyushu

D) the origins of some Japanese foods and other goods

E) 11 new kanji

✔ Performance Goals

By the end of this chapter you will be able to:

A) interview someone about what country she/he is from, what language is spoken there, and what sorts of food are eaten there

B) use three directional verbs (行きます *to go*, 来ます *to come*, and 帰ります *to return home*) in asking and answering questions about coming to school, going to a friend's house, or returning home

C) create simple non-past and non-past negative sentences. For instance, if your friend invites you to a party, you will be able to say whether or not you are going

D) read and write 11 additional kanji

Hakata Port, Kyushu

■ 会話 Dialogue
<small>かいわ</small>

ベン   :   あなたは、だれ　ですか。
<small>べん</small>

じゅん: それは何　ですか。

キアラ: あの　風は　どこから　ですか。
<small>き　あ　ら</small> <small>かぜ</small>

友   :   皆さん、ちょっと　待って　下さい。僕の　名前は　友　です。あの風は　あの鳥居か
<small>とも</small>   <small>みな</small>   <small>ま</small>   <small>ぼく</small>   <small>なまえ</small>   <small>とも</small>   <small>かぜ</small>   <small>とりい</small>
        ら　です。あの　鳥居は　時の門　です。
                      <small>とりい</small>   <small>とき</small> <small>もん</small>

じゅん: 時の門？
            <small>とき</small> <small>もん</small>

ベン＆キアラ: それは、何　ですか。
<small>べん</small> <small>き　あ　ら</small>

友   :   ちょっと、静かに　して　下さい。
<small>とも</small>   <small>しず</small>
        ところで、あなた達は、何人　ですか。
               <small>たち</small>   <small>なにじん</small>

■ 単語 New Words
<small>たんご</small>

アメリカ (n) <small>あめりか</small>	アメリカ人 (n) <small>あめりかじん</small>	カナダ (n) <small>かなだ</small>	カナダ人 (n) <small>かなだじん</small>
オーストラリア (n) <small>おーすとらりあ</small>	オーストラリア人 (n) <small>おーすとらりあじん</small>	ニュージーランド (n) <small>にゅーじーらんど</small>	ニュージーランド人 (n) <small>にゅーじーらんどじん</small>

For nationalities such as the ones below, you may designate that the person is of that country's descent rather than a "citizen of" by replacing "人" with "系." For example:
<small>じん</small>   <small>けい</small>

イギリス (n) <small>いぎりす</small>	イギリス人 (n) <small>いぎりすじん</small> イギリス系 (n) <small>いぎりすけい</small>	オランダ (n) <small>おらんだ</small>	オランダ人 (n) <small>おらんだじん</small>	ロシア (n) <small>ろしあ</small>	ロシア人 (n) <small>ろしあじん</small>

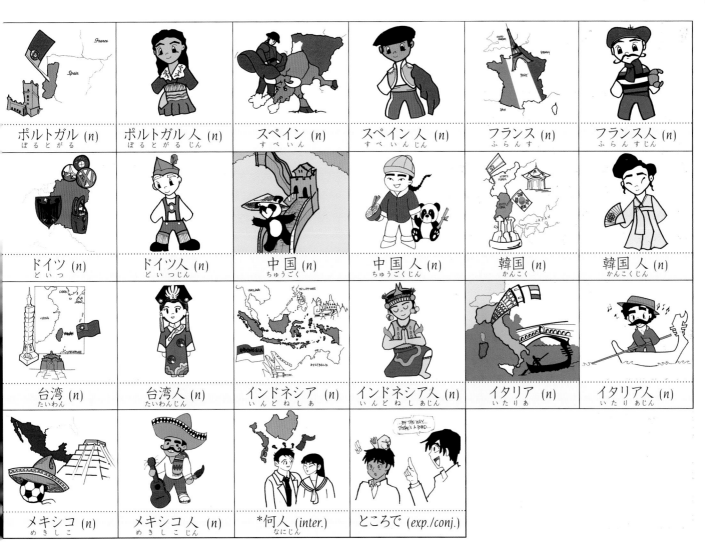

ポルトガル (n) ぽるとがる	ポルトガル人 (n) ぽるとがるじん
スペイン (n) すぺいん	スペイン人 (n) すぺいんじん
フランス (n) ふらんす	フランス人 (n) ふらんすじん
ドイツ (n) どいつ	ドイツ人 (n) どいつじん
中国 (n) ちゅうごく	中国人 (n) ちゅうごくじん
韓国 (n) かんこく	韓国人 (n) かんこくじん
台湾 (n) たいわん	台湾人 (n) たいわんじん
インドネシア (n) いんどねしあ	インドネシア人 (n) いんどねしあじん
イタリア (n) いたりあ	イタリア人 (n) いたりあじん
メキシコ (n) めきしこ	メキシコ人 (n) めきしこじん
*何人 (inter.) なにじん	ところで (exp./conj.)

日系人 (n) – of Japanese descent
にっけいじん

何系 (inter.) – of what ethnicity?
なにけい

外国 (n) – foreign country
がいこく

外国人 (n) – foreigner
がいこくじん

から (part.) – from

（手伝う）手伝います (v) – to help
てつだ　　てつだ

（言う）言います (v) – to say
い　　　い

* You were previously introduced to this kanji compound read as なんにん. Depending upon the context, you should be able to tell whether the kanji compound means "how many people?" (なんにんですか) or "what nationality?" (なにじんですか).

■ 漢字 Kanji
かんじ

言　外

		、	一	亠	言	言	言	言	
言 7 strokes	ゲン, い(う), こと – to speak げん								
	言(語) – language; 言(う) – to say; 言(葉) げん ご　　　　　い　　　　　こと ば – words, language								
	This kanji shows a face. The first stroke is the forehead and is often drawn vertically. The second stroke is a "unibrow." Subsequent strokes form the eyes, then the nose, and finally the open mouth that is SPEAKING.								

外	ガイ, そと – outside	ノ	ク	タ	列	外			
5 strokes	外 – outside; 外(国) – foreign country; 外(国人) – foreigner, foreign person								

This kanji combines the katakana タ and ト. How to put タ+ト together for a memorization hint lies OUTSIDE my creative abilities.

■ 言葉の探索 Language Detection

1. 何人ですか。/ 何系ですか。
    When asking about someone's nationality or ethnicity, you can use these two questions.

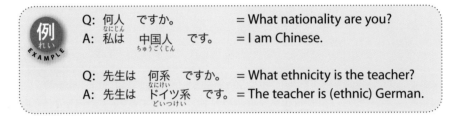

例 EXAMPLE
Q: 何人　ですか。　　　= What nationality are you?
A: 私は　中国人　です。　= I am Chinese.

Q: 先生は　何系　ですか。　= What ethnicity is the teacher?
A: 先生は　ドイツ系　です。 = The teacher is (ethnic) German.

2. 友さんは、「＿＿＿＿＿。」と　言いました。 - Tomo said, "＿＿＿＿＿."
    The most common way to quote someone is to say the person's name, followed by は to show that he or she is the topic, followed by the quote, then the quotation particle と, and finally the verb "said" 言いました.

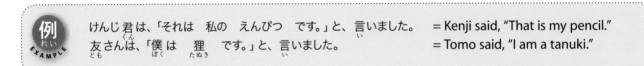

例 EXAMPLE
けんじ君は、「それは　私の　えんぴつ　です。」と、言いました。　= Kenji said, "That is my pencil."
友さんは、「僕は　狸　です。」と、言いました。　= Tomo said, "I am a tanuki."

3. あなた - you
    あなた means *you*. However, あなた is not as commonly used as "you" in English. It is more common to address the person you are talking to by his or her name. あなた can be useful, however, when you do not know the name of the person you are talking to. Usually, it is best to use the person's name or title if you know it.

■ 自習 Self Check

1. 何人 or 何系 - what nationality/ethnicity
    Practice asking what country someone is from or what ethnicity they are, using 何人 or 何系.

    A) What nationality is the teacher?
    B) What nationality is (my friend's) mother?
    C) What nationality is the English teacher?
    D) What nationality is Tomo?
    E) What ethnicity is that person over there?

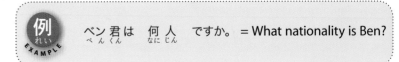

例 EXAMPLE
ベン君は　何人　ですか。 = What nationality is Ben?

2. 〜と　言いました。

Read these two sentences, aloud, to yourself, and translate them into English.

A) キアラさん　は、「これは　本　です。」と　言いました。

B) 母は、「座って　下さい。」と　言いました。

3. あなた

With which of the following could you use あなた?

| your teacher | your younger sister | your friend |
| your dog | Mr. Smith | Mrs. Miyazaki |

■ 練習の時間 Time for Practice

1. Pair Practice

Ask three partners about the national origin or ethnicity of their families. Be prepared to report your findings. (Take turns.)

A-さん:	ご家族は　何人　ですか。	= What is your family's nationality?
B-さん:	私の　家族は　イギリス人　です。	= My family is English.
A-さん:	ご家族は　何系　ですか。	= What is your family's heritage?
B-さん:	家族は　イギリス系と　ドイツ系　です。	= My family heritage is English and German.

2. Pair Practice

Use this picture to talk about where each student is from.

Pierre　Anna　Will

Adam　Sam　Ben

Younge　Mark　Paolo

A-さん:	パオロさんは　何人　ですか。
	= What nationality is Paolo?
B-さん:	パオロさんは　スペイン人　です。
	= Paolo is Spanish.

3. Group Practice

Survey six classmates. Ask them where their grandparents came from. If you don't know the answer when you are asked, say 知りません. Report your results to the class.

A-さん:	おばあさんと　おじいさんは　何人　ですか。
	= What nationalities are your grandmother and grandfather?
B-さん:	おじいさんは　中国人　です。でも、おばあさんは　知りません。
	= Grandfather is Chinese. But I don't know about grandmother.

■ 文化箱 Culture Chest
ぶん か ばこ

九 州
きゅうしゅう

One of the largest and most famous cities on the southern island of 九州 is 長崎.
きゅうしゅう   ながさき
The name 九州 was given to the island for the nine feudal states that made up this island.
きゅうしゅう
九州 is the site of some of the oldest evidence of Japanese civilization. On the eastern
きゅうしゅう
coast of the island, clay funerary statues called はにわ, dating from 1,500 to 1,800 years ago,
have been unearthed. These statues of houses, warriors, horses, and other animals were
placed around the graves of important people.

Much of the Tom Cruise movie *The Last Samurai* centers around rebels in southern 九
州. Far away from the power of the Imperial Court, this part of Japan had always been one
of the least controlled by feudal governments. The samurai of さつま in southern 九州, and
長州 in far western 本州 (Japan's largest island), were instrumental in the overthrow of
ちょうしゅう   ほんしゅう
the shogun-dominated 徳川 government (1600–1868). These rebels were also interested in
とくがわ
the restoration of power to the Emperor, just after the Tokugawa Period. Eventually, though,
some of these same samurai came to disagree with Japan's path toward westernization and
trade with the outside, and they attempted the second rebellion that lies at the heart of the
film *The Last Samurai*.

■ 地図 Map Skills
ち ず

長崎 is an ancient Japanese city. It is close to Korea and has long been a gateway to Japan from the
ながさき
Asian continent. Use the map here and available resources to answer the following questions.

❶ 長崎は　日本の　どこに　ありますか。
　ながさき

❷ 長崎 is located on which island?
　ながさき

❸ Which Western power was the first to set foot in 長崎?
　　　　　　　　　　　　　　　　　　　　　　　ながさき

■ キアラのジャーナル Kiara's Journal
き あ ら　　じゃー なる

Read the journal entry below, and then answer these questions.

❶ What is a tanuki? See if you can find a picture of one.
❷ What is the time tunnel called in Japanese?
❸ Where did the travelers arrive?
❹ In what year did they arrive?
❺ What does 海 mean?
❻ Describe or draw a picture of the people and clothing Kiara and her friends might have seen in their new location.

ジャーナルへ

You're never going to believe what happened today. We were running for cover from a sudden windstorm toward the nearest shelter, a Shinto 神社。 As we ducked under the 鳥居 gate, lights flashed and the next thing we knew, we were inside some sort of room, or tunnel, but there were no walls! It was very strange. The furry little animal we had seen the day before, rustling around in the bushes near the 神社、 ran through the 鳥居 with us, and that must have triggered the "door" to this place. Ben said that the creature was a 狸 or a "raccoon dog." We have raccoons at home, but they don't look anything like this. The creature could talk too! 「僕の 名前は 友 です。」と 言いました。 He was sort of cute, but seemed to be a bit cranky. Here's what happened next ...

　じゅん君は、「それは いい です けど・・・・ ここは どこ ですか！」と 言いました。 We seemed to be flying through this tunnel of darkness lit only by small glowing lights. 友さんは、「これは タイム トンネル、時の 門 です。今から 日本の 1601年へ 行きます。」と 言いました。じゅん君は、「ええ？ 1601年 ですか。うそ！」と 言いました。 "How is that possible?" 友さんは、「それは 後で。長崎へ ようこそ。」と 言いました。ベン君は、「1601年の 長崎 に は 色々な 外国人が います。ポルトガル人 と スペイン人と フィリピン人と 中国人と 韓国人が います。」と 言いました。

　As we walked out the gate, I turned around to look at it. We were right in front of yet another, different 神社！ I'm not sure how this whole 時の 門 thing works yet, but walking into this live history lesson, set over 四百年前、 is very strange indeed! From our hillside, we could see the 海 below us, with a few large sailing ships anchored in the bay. People walked here and there, many carrying baskets. We started down the hill on a hard-packed dirt road, lined on both sides with shops and houses. People were wearing clothes that looked like the pictures in 私の 高校の 世界史の 教科書。 Some had on traditional 日本の 着物、 others were wearing 大きい ぼうし with feathers, big baggy pants, and funny shoes.

　友さんは、「その 人達は スペインから 来た 人達 です。あの人は イギリス人 です。」と 言いました。「はい、あそこへ 行きましょう。」

　And with that, 友さん led us off in the other direction.

■ テクノの時間 Techno Time

Though you've not been introduced to them all yet, type all the vocabulary words from this chapter into your digital dictionary. Be sure to follow the pattern you began earlier and to use your file called "JISHO" (in *romaji*).

何語を　話しますか。
What language do you speak?

■ 会話 Dialogue
（かいわ）

ベン	： ええ〜っ！あの 歴史の 教科書の 中の ウィリアム・アダムズ？
（べん）	（れきし）（きょうかしょ）（なか）（うぃりあむ・あだむず）
じゅん	： サイン お願いします！
	（さいん）（ねが）
キアラ	： 写真 お願いします！
（きあら）	（しゃしん）（ねが）
ベン	： あくしゅも お願いします。
（べん）	（ねが）
ウィリアム：	写真 ですか。 それは 何 ですか。 あなた達は だれ ですか。 どこから
（うぃりあむ）	（しゃしん）（たち）
	ですか。 なぜ 私の 名前が 分かりますか。
	（なまえ）（わ）

■ 単語 New Words
（たんご）

オランダ 語 (n)（おらんだご）	ロシア 語 (n)（ろしあご）
ポルトガル 語 (n)（ぽるとがるご）	スペイン 語 (n)（すぺいんご）
フランス 語 (n)（ふらんすご）	中国語 (n)（ちゅうごくご）
韓国語 (n)（かんこくご）	インドネシア 語 (n)（いんどねしあご）
イタリア 語 (n)（いたりあご）	ドイツ 語 (n)（どいつご）

写真を 撮っても いい ですか。
（しゃしん）（と）
– May I take a photo?

(話す) 話します (v) – to speak
（はな）

(知る) 知ります (v) – to know something/someone
（し）（し）

サイン (n)（さいん）
あくしゅ (n)
写真を 撮ります (v)（しゃしん）（と）

sheets of.../ flat things	number/quantity	pages	sheets of.../ flat things	number/quantity	pages
一枚（いちまい）	one	一ページ（いちぺーじ）	七枚（ななまい）	seven	七ページ（ななぺーじ）
二枚（にまい）	two	二ページ（にぺーじ）	八枚（はちまい）	eight	八ページ（はちぺーじ）
三枚（さんまい）	three	三ページ（さんぺーじ）	九枚（きゅうまい）	nine	九ページ（きゅうぺーじ）
四枚（よんまい）	four	四ページ（よんぺーじ）	十枚（じゅうまい）	ten	十ページ（じゅっぺーじ）
五枚（ごまい）	five	五ページ（ごぺーじ）	十一枚（じゅういちまい）	eleven	十一ページ（じゅういちぺーじ）
六枚（ろくまい）	six	六ページ（ろくぺーじ）	何枚（なんまい）	how many?	何ページ（なんぺーじ）

■ 漢字 Kanji

		、	㇗	㇗	늘	言	言	言	言
 13 strokes	ワ; はなし, はな(す) – to speak, conversation	言	訂	訐	話	話			
	話(す) – to talk (to someone/something else); (電)話 – telephone (literally, electric talking)								
	The left seven strokes of this kanji form a radical, 言, that is in many words related to speaking. The right side has a tongue (舌) which is 1,000 (千) on top of a mouth (口). Imagine 1,000 mouths forming one tongue in order to SPEAK.								

■ 言葉の探索 Language Detection

～ます

The ～ます form of Japanese verbs is used for the non-past tense. The non-past tense can have one of two meanings depending on the situation:

a. Present or continuous action.

A) 私は　日本語を　話します。　　　　　= I speak Japanese.
B) 母は　韓国語と　英語を　話します。　= My mother speaks Korean and English.
C) 私は　毎日　手伝います。　　　　　　= I help out every day.

b. Future tense.

キアラは　あした　手伝います。　= Kiara will help tomorrow.
でも、友さんは　手伝いません。　= But Tomo-san won't help out.

■ 自習 Self Check

～ます　話します

Give the two possible translations, continuous action and future tense, for the following:

A)　ベン君は　　日本語を話します。
B)　愛子さんは　手伝います。

■ 練習の時間 Time for Practice

1. **Small Group Practice**

Bring a picture of a famous personality from another country to class. Introduce this personality to your group, including their name, nationality, and what language(s) they speak. Trade pictures and introduce the new personality to a different classmate.

例
れい
EXAMPLE

こちら は サム君 です。 メキシコ人 です。 スペイン語と 英語を 話します。
さむくん   めきしこじん   すぺいんご えいご はな
= This is Sam. He is from Mexico. He speaks Spanish and English.

2. Pair Practice

何ページ
なに ぺーじ

Take turns giving each other a page number to find in your textbook. See how quickly you can locate the correct page. Use the counter ページ.
                                                                          ぺーじ

例
れい
EXAMPLE

A-さん: 四十三ページを 開いて 下さい。 = Please open your book to page 43.
        よんじゅうさん ぺーじ ひら
B-さん: (should open his/her book to page 43)

■ 文化箱 Culture Chest
    ぶんかばこ

サイン　お願いします！
   さいん   ねが

サイン is one of the many foreign "loan" words that have become integrated into the
さいん
Japanese language. You will learn many other words in the course of your study of Japanese.
サイン　お願いします！ "Please give me your signature!" is a phrase that foreigners of-
さいん   ねが
ten hear when visiting Japanese schools or famous sites in Japan, especially in the popular
tourist cities of Nara or Kyoto. This might make you feel like a rock star, but it is often an
assignment for timid, yet eager Japanese school children. Japanese students from all over
Japan visit these famous sites on school field trips, and one aspect of going to these sites is the opportunity to practice
their English language speaking skills with foreign tourists. Taking photos with visitors and getting signatures in another
language is a highlight for many school children in Japan.

■ キアラのジャーナル Kiara's Journal
    きあら じゃーなる

Read the journal entry below, and then answer these questions.

❶ What did Tomo want to show Kiara, Ben, and Jun at the fruit and vegetable store?
❷ Where did this object originally come from? How did it get to Japan?
❸ Near the end of the journal entry, Ben gasps. Why is he so surprised?

ジャーナルへ
じゃーなる

友さんと　じゅん君と　ベン君 walked farther into the town down the narrow dirt street. This was
とも   くん
totally weird on so many levels! I mean, what seems like only a few hours ago, we were deciding what club to visit
after school, and now we're wandering around dirt streets in medieval Nagasaki. My friends are never going to
believe this. I knew that I was embarking on an adventure when I came to Japan, but I never imagined...

友さん stopped us in front of a fruit and vegetable store. そして　友さんは、「これを　見て下さい。」と　言いました。He held up a small brown round object.「これは　スペインからです。」私は、「What's special about　その　potato?」と　言いました。友さんは、「これは　ジャガイモ　です。ジャガイモは　オランダ人が　持って来ました(brought)。」と　言いました。「First, スペイン人は　南米 (South America) から　ヨーロッパ (Europe) へ　持って行きました (took)。And then, オランダ人は　インドネシアの　ジャカルタ (Jakarta) へ持って行きました。そして　オランダ人は　ジャカルタから　ここに　持って来ました。」と　言いました。ベン君は　とても surprised でした。そして、「そう　ですか。That must be why they are called ジャガイモ。イモ means potato, and the fact that they came from Jakarta, Indonesia is why this particular kind of potato is called ジャガイモ。ジャガ is short for Jakarta! なるほど!」と　言いました。The store owner smiled widely, leaned forward, and asked,「何人　ですか。」じゅん君は、「この人は　アメリカ人　です。その人は　オーストラリア人　です。僕は日本人　です。」と言いました。

The　おじさん asked、「そう　ですか。アメリカは　オランダに　ありますか。」Realizing that America had not even become a country yet, all that I could say was 「それは　ちょっと　違います (a little different)。」おじさん asked、「何語を　話しますか。スペイン語を　話しますか。」私は、「いいえ、英語を　話します。日本語も　ちょっと　話します。」と　言いました。He then looked at ベン君 and said 「何語を　話しますか。」ベン君は、「僕も　英語を　話します。」と言いました。He stared again at me, then at ベン君、and then glanced at the tall, thin Caucasian man waiting next door at the calligrapher's stall. He mumbled something to himself, then smiled and said、「あの人も　英語を　話しますよ。」Surprised, we turned toward the tall man wearing an old British sailor's uniform. I asked,「何語を　話しますか。」He answered,「私は　オランダ語と　英語と日本語も　話します。なぜ　ですか。」I said,「私と　この　人も　英語を　話します。あなたは、何人　ですか。」「僕は　イギリス人　です。でも　オランダから　来ました。僕の名前は　ウイリアム　アダムズ　です。」the man replied in good 日本語、but with a pretty serious accent.

"THE William Adams?" ベン君 gasped. "You're the one who was shipwrecked here and later met..." Before he could finish his sentence, 友さん jumped into the conversation. "That vegetable store owner, over there, that's who you met. And that's how these kids heard about you." 友さん then turned to us with, 「はい、アダムズさんは very busy でしょう。」友さん bowed to アダムズさん、「すみません。」と言いました。Then he turned back to us. 友さんは、「あそこに　とても　いい　寿司屋が　ありますよ。」と　言いました。

I realized that my stomach was actually a bit ペコペコ、and I also realized that it was probably good that ベン君 was not able to finish his sentence to Mr. Adams. If he had, he would have told Mr. Adams about the future. From all of the sci-fi books and 漫画 that I've read, I know that this would definitely not have been a good thing to do.

私は　ここで　食べません。

I won't eat here.

■ 会話 Dialogue
（かいわ）

【ラーメン屋　で】
（らーめんや）

店員　　：　いらっしゃいませ！ようこそ！
（てんいん）
　　　　　　あ、すみません。狸は、ちょっと・・・。
　　　　　　　　　　　　　（たぬき）

キアラ　：　この　狸は　私達の　友達　です。
（きあら）　　　　　（たぬき）　（わたしたち）　（ともだち）

ベン　　：　日本語も　分かります。
（べん）　　　　　　　　　　（わ）

店員　　：　すみません。狸は、ちょっと・・・。
（てんいん）　　　　　　　（たぬき）

友　　　：　はい、分かりました。私は　ここで　食べません。
（とも）　　　　　　（わ）　　　　　　　　　　　　（た）
　　　　　　ちょっと　待って　下さい。
　　　　　　　　　　　　（ま）
　　　　　　大丈夫ですよ・・・。
　　　　　　（だいじょうぶ）

友　　　：　こんにちは。
（とも）

店員　　：　いらっしゃいませ！
（てんいん）

ベン　　：　アダムズさん、ここで　私達は　ラーメンを　食べます。一緒に　どうぞ。
（べん）　　（あだむず）　　　　　（わたしたち）　（らーめん）　　（た）　　　（いっしょ）

友　　　：　ありがとう　ございます。
（とも）

店員　　：　お飲み物は？
（てんいん）　　（の）（もの）

友　　　：　お茶を　お願いします。
（とも）　　（ちゃ）　　（ねが）

■ 単語 New Words
（たんご）

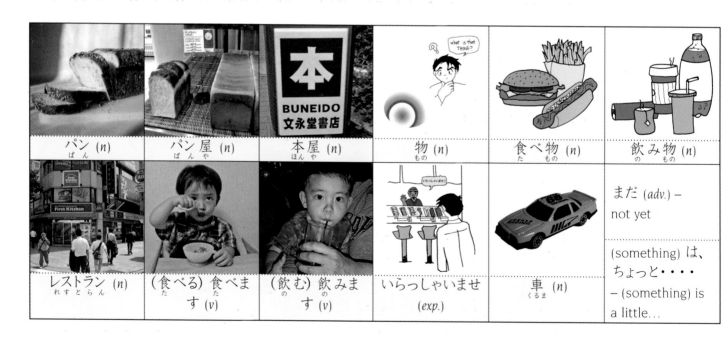

パン (n) （ぱん）	パン屋 (n) （ぱんや）	本屋 (n) （ほんや）	物 (n) （もの）	食べ物 (n) （た　もの）	飲み物 (n) （の　もの）
レストラン (n) （れすとらん）	（食べる）食べます (v) （た）（た）	（飲む）飲みます (v) （の）（の）	いらっしゃいませ (exp.)	車 (n) （くるま）	まだ (adv.) – not yet · (something) は、ちょっと・・・ – (something) is a little…

■ 漢字 Kanji

食　飲　物

食 9 strokes	ショク; た(べる) – food, eat	ノ	人	亽	今	今	仐	佇	食
	食(べる) – to eat; 食(べ物) – food/foods; 食(事) – to dine	食							
	The top two strokes here represent a roof, and below the roof is the kanji for good (良). It is always good to EAT under a roof.								

飲 12 strokes	の(む) – drink	ノ	人	亽	今	今	仐	佇	食
	飲(む) – to drink; 飲(み物) – drink/drinks	飮	飮	飲	飲				
	The left side of this kanji is the radical for "to eat" (食) and the right side means lacking (欠). It is fine to live with a lack of food as long as you have something to DRINK.								

物 8 strokes	ブツ, もの – thing, object	ノ	ヒ	牛	牛	牛	牤	物	物
	物 – thing, object; (本)物 – the real thing, genuine object; (動)物 – animal, lit. a moving thing								
	The left side of this kanji is the radical for "cow" (牛). The right side looks like it could be long hair on a cow or some THING. We don't know what it is, but it is a THING.								

■ 言葉の探索 Language Detection

1. 食べません – negative of ～ます verbs
   To change a ～ます verb to its negative form, simply change the ～ます ending to ～ません. (Note that as in the examples below, the particle after the direct object usually changes from を to は for negative sentences.)

寿司を　食べます。	= I eat sushi.
いもは　食べません。	= I do not eat potatoes.
Q:　スペイン語を　話しますか。	= Do you speak Spanish?
A:　スペイン語は　話しません。	= (I) do not speak Spanish.
Q:　お父さんは　日本語を　話しますか。	= Does your father speak Japanese?
A:　いいえ、日本語は　話しません。	= No, he does not speak Japanese.

2. 日本で　すしを　食べます。
   We learned earlier that the particle で can mean "by means of." The particle で also indicates the place of action. In the sentence above, 日本 is the place of action (where the sushi is being eaten) and therefore is followed by で.

A) レストランで　お茶を　飲みます。　　= At the restaurant, I will drink green tea.
B) 家で　手伝います。　　= At home, I help out.
C) 学校で　お昼ご飯を　食べません。　= I don't eat lunch at school.

3.　ちょっと・・・・

ちょっと can be used to say "no thank you" to someone without giving a specific reason why. ちょっと literally means "a little."

A-さん：　この寿司を　どうぞ。　　= Here, try this sushi.
B-さん：　すみません。寿司は　ちょっと・・・ = I'm sorry, but sushi is a little . . .

■ 自習 Self Check

1.　～ません

Change the following into the negative:

A)　話します
B)　手伝います
C)　あります

D)　言います
E)　食べます
F)　飲みます

2.　で

Practice using で in Japanese for the place of action:

中国で　ご飯を　食べます。　= I eat rice in China.

A)　I will speak Japanese in Japan.
B)　I will not speak English in Japan.
C)　My mother speaks Korean at home.
D)　My younger sister eats lunch in the cafeteria.
E)　I read manga at home.
F)　I help my teacher in the computer lab.

■ 練習の時間 Time for Practice
れんしゅう　じ　かん

---

1. Pair Practice

With a partner, take turns asking what you would eat or drink at the following places in Japanese. Use the list of foods and drinks below to help you with your answers.

A-さん：　お寿司屋さんで　何を　食べますか。そして、何を　飲みますか。
　　　　　すし や　　　　　なに　　た　　　　　　　　　なに　　の
　　　　= What do you eat at the sushi restaurant? What do you drink?

B-さん：　お寿司屋さんで　巻き寿司を　食べます。そして、お茶を　飲みます。
　　　　　すし や　　　　ま　ず し　　た　　　　　　　　ちゃ　の
　　　　= At the sushi restaurant, I eat rolled sushi. I drink green tea.

ラーメン屋　　イタリアンレストラン　　ケンタッキー・フライド・チキン　　マクドナルド　　メキシカンレストラン　　寿司屋
ら　ー　め　ん　や　　いたりあんれすとらん　　けんたっきー・ふらいど・ちきん　　ま　く　ど　な　る　ど　　めきしかんれすとらん　　す　し　や

食べ物	飲み物
た もの	の もの
ハンバーガー	コーラ
は ん ば ー が ー	こ ー ら
チキン	オレンジ・ジュース
ち き ん	お れ ん じ じゅ ー す
ピザ	ミルク
ぴ ざ	み る く
タコス	お茶
た こ す	お ちゃ
たこ	お水
	お みず

---

2. Pair Practice

With a partner, read through the words listed below. Then take turns using one word from each column to make questions and answer them. Add particles and/or conjunctions when necessary.

母 and 話します
はな

A-さん：　お母さんは　日本語を　話しますか。　　　　= Does your mother speak Japanese?
　　　　　　　　　　　　　　　はな
B-さん：　はい、母は　日本語を　話します。　　　　　= Yes, my mother speaks Japanese.
　　　　　　　　　　　　　　はな
-OR- いいえ、母は　日本語を　話しません。　　　　= No, my mother doesn't speak Japanese.
　　　　　　　　　　　　　　はな

妹さん　　　　　　　　食べます
　　　　　　　　　　　た
お兄さん　　　　　　　飲みます
　　　　　　　　　　　の
おばあさん　　　　　　話します
　　　　　　　　　　　はな
先生　　　　　　　　　見ます
　　　　　　　　　　　み
お母さん

お父さん

■ 文化箱 Culture Chest
ぶんかばこ

狸
たぬき

What's a 狸? 狸 is the Japanese name for a "raccoon-dog," an animal that lives throughout Japan. It is somewhat
たぬき たぬき
larger than a North American raccoon. 狸 are mischievous creatures with the reputation of being tricksters. They are said
to have the ability to "shape-shift," or turn into other beings. According to Japanese folklore, when a 狸 places a large
たぬき
leaf on its head, it can change shape, often becoming a Buddhist monk or priest.

■ キアラのジャーナル Kiara's Journal
きあら じゃーなる

Read the journal entry below, and then answer these questions.

❶ What nationalities might you find in 17th-century Nagasaki?
❷ Nagasaki is famous for two types of food. What are they?
❸ To find a traditional-style restaurant in Japan today, what sign would you look for?

ジャーナルへ
じゃーなる

We've been in Nagasaki only a few hours, but I wanted to update you on what I've done so far. I'm
learning a lot about Japanese food!

友さんは、「ここには 韓国の 食べ物と 中国の 食べ物と スペインの 食べ物と日本の
とも かんこく た もの ちゅうごく た もの すぺいん
食べ物が あります。オランダ人は 二年前 日本へ 来ました。だから、オランダの
た もの おらんだだ
食べ物は まだ ありません。長崎は とても いい ところ です。あそこの お寿司屋
ながさき すしや
さんに たこが あります。スペインと ポルトガルでも たこを たくさん 食べます。
すぺいん ぽるとがる
長崎は、ラーメンと ぎょうざも 有名 です。何を 食べますか。」と、言いました。
ながさき らーめん なに
ベン君は、「中国人が たくさん います ね。ここは ラーメンが とても おいしい
べん ちゅうごくじん
です。ラーメンと ぎょうざを 食べませんか。アダムズさんも ラーメン屋さんへ 行き
あだむず らーめんや い
ました。」

「いい ですよ。何でも いい ですよ。」と、友さんは、言いました。

友さんは sure gets excited about his food. He's really quite chunky for a たぬき of only about 三 feet.
Eating seems to be a top priority for the little guy. In fact, he doesn't want to stop.

そして 友さんは、「後で あの寿司屋へも 行きませんか。とても いい レストラン
あと すしや れすとらん
ですよ！」と 言いました。

At the entrance to the ラーメン屋 hung a long のれん curtain. You see these outside Japanese
や
restaurants even in the 21st century, covering the door. That was とても 小さな レストラン でした。
ラーメン屋の 人 took our order. ベン君は、「私は みそラーメンを 食べます。」と 言い
や べん
ました。わたしは、とんこつラーメンを 食べました。とんこつラーメン is pork broth noodle
くん
soup. 友さんは、5 dishesを 食べました。He eats a lot!

また 後で。
あと

私は　江戸に　行きます。
I will go to Edo.

1) 明日 私は 江戸に 行きます。

2) え、東京 ですか？ 私達も 一緒に 行きます！

3) 私達は 東京から です。だから、アダムズさんと 一緒に 東京に 帰ります！

4) いいえ、東京では ありません。私は、江戸に 行きます。

5) 江戸と 東京は 同じ です。

6) よく、分かりません ？？？？

7) とにかく、江戸に 私達も、一緒に 行っても いい ですか。

8) だめ です。あ！人が 来ます。静かにして下さい。旅館へ 行きましょう。

■ 会話 Dialogue
かいわ

アダムズ　：　明日　私は　江戸に　行きます。
あだむず　あした　　　えど　　い

ベン　：　え、東京　ですか？　私達も　一緒に　行きます！
べん　　　　わたしたち　いっしょ　い

じゅん　：　私達は　東京から　です。だから、アダムズさんと　一緒に　東京に　帰ります！
わたしたち　　　　　　　　　　あだむず　　　　いっしょ　　　　　　かえ

アダムズ　：　いいえ、東京では　ありません。私は、江戸に　行きます。
あだむず　　　　　　　　　　　　　　えど　　い

じゅん　：　江戸と、東京は　同じ　です。
えど　　　　　おな

アダムズ　：　よく　分かりません？？？？
あだむず

キアラ　：　とにかく、江戸に　私達も、一緒に　行っても　いい　です か。
きあら　　　　　えど　わたしたち　いっしょ　い

友　：　だめ　です。あ！人が　来ます。静かに　して下さい。旅館へ　行きましょう。
とも　　　　　　　　　　き　　しず　　　　　　りょかん　い

■ 単語 New Words
たんご

 （行く）行きます (v) い　い	 （来る）来ます (v) く　き	 （帰る）帰ります (v) かえ　かえ	（する）します (v) – to do だから (conj.) – so, therefore

■ 漢字 Kanji
かんじ

行　来　帰

行 6 strokes	コウ– journey; い（く）– to go	`	` ｀	ｸ	彳	行	行	行		
	行（く）– go;（旅）行 – a trip, travel い　りょこう									
	The left three strokes show a person with a hat about to GO to the crossroads, represented by the three strokes on the right.									

来 7 strokes	ライ – next/coming; く（る）– to come らい　く	一	一	ｱ	平	平	来	来		
	来（る）– to come; 来（週）– next week く　らいしゅう									
	This kanji consists of one (一) and rice (米). One COMES to rice, one grain at a time, to get food in Japan.									

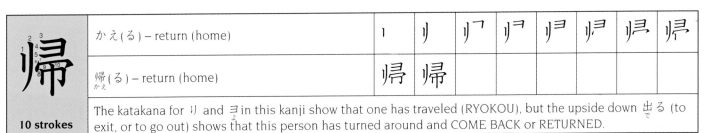

	かえ(る) – return (home)	l	リ	リ冖	リⱻ	リヨ	リ帚	帰	帰
帰	帰(る) – return (home)	帰	帰						

10 strokes

The katakana for リ and ヨ in this kanji show that one has traveled (RYOKOU), but the upside down 出る (to exit, or to go out) shows that this person has turned around and COME BACK or RETURNED.

■ 言葉の探索 Language Detection

1. へ／に direction particles
   Three verbs of movement you have just learned are 行く/行きます　来る/来ます　帰る/帰ります (go, come, return). Verbs of movement often have a goal of movement (a destination) which takes either the particle へ or に. In this case, these two particles are interchangeable. Note that when へ is a particle, it is always pronounced "E".

   > 例
   > EXAMPLE
   > A) ベン君は　日本へ　帰ります。　　　　= Ben will return to Japan.
   > B) キアラさんは　イタリアに　行きます。= Kiara will go to Italy.
   > C) じゅん君は　僕の　家に　来ません。　= Jun will not come to my house.
   > D) 明日、アメリカへ　行きますか。　　　= Tomorrow, are you going to the U.S.?

2. The point of view of the speaker determines which direction verb is used in Japanese.

   > 例
   > EXAMPLE
   > *A-さん: 私の　家へ　来ますか。　　= Will you come to my house?
   > B-さん: はい、行きます。　　　　　 = Yes, I will go.
   > A-さん (at school): 放課後、部活 に　行きますか。　= After school, are you going to club?
   > B-さん (at school): 今日 は　行きません。帰ります。= Today I'm not going. I'm going home.

   * Note: In English, Person B can say that he/she will "come" to the house. In Japanese, Person B must say he will "go" to the house since from B's point of view the house is away from him/her so he/she will actually be "going" to the house from somewhere else.

■ 自習 Self Check

1. 私は　東京に/へ行きます。　(I will go to Tokyo.)
   Now try to say these in Japanese:

   A) Kiara will go to school.
   B) Jun will return to Japan.
   C) Keita goes to the gymnasium.
   D) Keiko will go to the cafeteria.
   E) Keita will go to the gymnasium.

   F) My older brother will go to the bakery.
   G) My teacher returns to Japan.
   H) My mother will go to Japan tomorrow.
   I) I go to school at 7:30.

2.   **Direction words based on speaker's point of view**
Say the following in Japanese:

A) Will you come to Japan? (Asked by your friend in Japan)
B) Yes, I will go to Japan. (You are currently not in Japan.)
C) No. I will not go to Japan. (You are currently not in Japan.)

■ 練習の時間 Time for Practice
れんしゅう　じかん

1. Pair Practice

Ask your partner questions in Japanese about places where you might come, go, or return to. Take turns and alternate between affirmative and negative answers.

A-さん:	数学の教室へ　行きます／来ますか。	= Will you go/come to the math classroom?
B-さん:	はい、　行きます/来ます。	= Yes, I will go/come.
-OR-	いいえ、　行きません/来ません。	= No, I will not go/come.

➲ school
➲ library
➲ gymnasium
➲ friend's house
➲ restaurant

■ 文化箱 Culture Chest
ぶんかばこ

中国　と　日本
ちゅうごく

China and Japan have a long history of interaction, dating back at least 1,800 years. Many traditions, customs, and foods from China made their way to Japan and took on a uniquely Japanese shape. One aspect of Chinese culture that remains much the same is Chinese food. Though slightly tempered for Japanese tastes, Chinese restaurants all around Japan serve up large bowls of ラーメン (ramen noodles), served with a side of steaming hot ぎょうざ (pot-stickers). ぎょうざ are pan-fried wonton wrappers that have usually been stuffed with a pork and vegetable filling.

■ キアラのジャーナル Kiara's Journal

Read the journal entry below, and then answer these questions.

❶ Who is Will Adams going to meet and what does this person's title mean?
❷ Where were foreigners allowed to live in early medieval Japan?
❸ What are Kiara, Jun, and Ben going to drink later?
❹ What will they eat for dinner?

ジャーナルへ

　　今日は　とても　amazing　です。東京から　長崎へ　来ました。長崎で　ウイリアム　アダムズ　さんに　会いました。(met)アダムズさんは　イギリス人です。でも、彼は　オランダ人と　一緒に　オランダから　日本へ　来ました。とても　いい　人　です。アダムズさんは　very smart man。I heard from Ben that the main character in *Shogun* was based on William Adams. Ben told me that the book was a best-selling novel (and a popular TV mini-series) about the early contact between Westerners and Japanese. 明日、私達は　家へ　帰ります (I think)。その　前に、アダムズさんと　もう　一度　会いたい (want to meet again)　です。アダムズさんと　写真を　撮ります (at least I want to)。今、私達は　旅館に (a traditional inn)　います。後で　お茶を　すこし飲みます。そして、晩ご飯を　食べます。晩ご飯に　天ぷらを　食べます。

　　また。

この　寿司を　食べて　下さい。
すし　　た
Please eat this sushi.

■ 動詞の　練習 Verb Review
どうし　　れんしゅう

います	to exist (animate people and animals)	*閉じます と	to close	*立ちます た	to stand
		*書きます か	to write	*座ります すわ	to sit
あります	to exist (inanimate objects)	*聞きます き	to listen	食べます た	to eat
		*読みます よ	to read	話します はな	to speak
分かります わ	to understand	*飲みます の	to drink	手伝います てつだ	to help
*始めます はじ	to begin	*見ます み	to look	来ます き	to come
*出します だ	to take out	*言います	to say	帰ります かえ	to return
*開きます ひら	to open	*行きます い	to go	します	to do

* Previously introduced as part of requests and commands.

■ 漢字 Kanji
かんじ

見 **7 strokes**	み(る) – see; み – visible, can be seen	一 冂 冃 目 目 貝 見
	見(る) – see; 見(える) – visible, can be seen み　　　　　み	
	An eye (目) walking around on two legs (the last two strokes). Imagine SEEING that or even worse, being SEEN by it.	

聞 **14 strokes**	き(く) – to listen, to ask; き(こえる) – can be heard	丨 冂 冂 冃 冃 門 門 門
	聞(く) – to hear, listen; 聞(こえる) – can hear き　　　　　　　　き	門 門 門 門 聞 聞
	When you LISTEN, you sometimes have to place your ear (耳) up against the temple gate (門). To be sure that you HEARD correctly, later you should ASK if you were HEARing correctly.	

■ 言葉の探索 Language Detection

Japanese verbs can be broken down into three main types. Understanding each type will help you understand how to conjugate verbs and use them in different ways.

The ~MASU form

Throughout this book, you have been introduced to verbs in the ~MASU forms. For example, 食べます (*I eat*), or 中国語を 話します (*I speak Chinese*). This form is generally referred to as the です/ます form in Japanese (and sometimes the "polite form" in English).

The dictionary form

Whenever a new verb is introduced in the New Words list, the dictionary form of that verb (which is shorter) is also provided. This form is used to look up verbs in dictionaries. Other uses will be introduced later.

The ~TE form

Early on in this text you learned a number of classroom phrases. Many of these expressions utilize the ~TE form. This is the form you can use when making a polite request or command. It is also one of the most useful of Japanese verb forms. In addition to the request or command, it can be used to say things in the present progressive tense, like お水を 飲んで います。 (*I "am drinking" water*) rather than 水を 飲みます。 (*I drink water*).

You will learn how to conjugate ~て-form verbs and use them in a number of different ways in Chapter 6.

These charts will help you to review the verbs you've learned up to this point and to clearly see how they are conjugated. Look for patterns in the verb conjugations below.

Type 1, or ～う, verbs through Chapter 4

non-past (～ます)	non-past negative (～ません)	～て-form	dictionary (infinitive) form	English meaning
飲みます	飲みません	飲んで	飲む	to drink
読みます	読みません	読んで	読む	to read
手伝います	手伝いません	手伝って	手伝う	to help, assist
立ちます	立ちません	立って	立つ	to stand
あります	ありません	あって	ある	to exist (inanimate)
帰ります	帰りません	帰って	帰る	to return
座ります	座りません	座って	座る	to sit
分かります	分かりません	分かって	分かる	to understand
書きます	書きません	書いて	書く	to write
聞きます	聞きません	聞いて	聞く	to listen, hear
開きます	開きません	開いて	開く	to open (books)
出します	出しません	出して	出す	to get out, go out
話します	話しません	話して	話す	to speak

Type 2, or 〜る, verbs through Chapter 4

non-past (〜ます)	non-past negative (〜ません)	〜て-form	dictionary (infinitive) form	English meaning
開_あけます	開_あけません	開_あけて	開_あける	to open
います	いません	いて	いる	to exist (animate)
食_たべます	食_たべません	食_たべて	食_たべる	to eat
閉_とじます	閉_とじません	閉_とじて	閉_とじる	to close
始_{はじ}めます	始_{はじ}めません	始_{はじ}めて	始_{はじ}める	to begin, start
見_みます	見_みません	見_みて	見_みる	to look
見_みせます	見_みせません	見_みせて	見_みせる	to show

Irregular verbs through Chapter 4

non-past (〜ます)	non-past negative (〜ません)	〜て-form	dictionary (infinitive) form	English meaning
来_きます	来_きません	来_きて	来_くる	to come
します	しません	して	する	to do

Exception:

non-past (〜ます)	non-past negative (〜ません)	〜て-form	dictionary (infinitive) form	English meaning
行_いきます	行_いきません	行_いって	行_いく	to go

■ 自習_{じしゅう} Self Check

1. Change these verbs into the non-past negative. Try not to look at the chart:

    ➲ 食_たべます   ➲ 来_きます

    ➲ 飲_のみます   ➲ 行_いきます

    ➲ 手伝_{てつだ}います   ➲ 開_{ひら}きます

    ➲ 分_わかります

2. Put these requests into 日本語:

    ➲ Please write.   ➲ Please drink this cola.

    ➲ Please listen.   ➲ Please go to the cafeteria.

    ➲ Please sit down.   ➲ Please read this kanji.

    ➲ Please open the window.   ➲ Please go home now.

■ 練習の時間 Time for Practice
れんしゅう じかん

1. Small Group Activity

In this book's Introduction, you learned several types of graphic organizers that might help you in your language learning. You've probably been using one frequently. As a small group activity, compare the graphic organizer that works best for you with those of your partners. Try to come to a consensus about a graphic organizer that is different than what you usually use but is also effective. Then, on a separate piece of paper, use this graphic organizer to group the ます form of the verbs in the charts on pages 151–152 into as many different categories as possible (e.g., verbs related to motion, actions that happen at home, verbs related to being bored). Be creative!

2. Small Group Activity

Play verb "pictionary." One group member silently selects one verb from the verb charts on the preceding pages. That person then has one minute to draw a picture so that the other group members can identify that verb. The first person to correctly say the NEGATIVE form of the verb becomes the next "artist."

3. Pair Work

You have thirty seconds to give as many commands as you can to your partner. Your partner must act them out. When done, switch roles.

■ 文化箱 Culture Chest
ぶんかばこ

Exploring 九州
きゅうしゅう

九州 is a wonderful island to tour. You may want to start in Beppu,
きゅうしゅう
the hot spring mecca in Oita Prefecture which is home to over 4,000 natural hot springs. Next visitors can see the HANIWA statues mentioned in section 1 of this chapter, in Miyazaki, after taking a break from the beaches there. For a different beach experience, you can head west to be buried up to your neck in naturally hot black sands on one of the beaches in Kagoshima. If this thermal energy is not enough for you, Kagoshima Prefecture is also home to Sakurajima, one of the most active volcanoes in the world. Next you might want to travel north to visit Kumamoto, home of beautiful Mt. Aso and Kumamoto City, a charming castle town in the central part of the island. You can head farther west, past Mt. Unzen, another active volcano, to the seaport of 長崎 City. You may want to enjoy
ながさき
the northernmost part of the island, with its ancient ceramic kiln sites, by also stopping in dynamic Fukuoka City, the largest city in Kyushu, before getting on a train that links 九州 with the main island of 本州 .
きゅうしゅう   ほんしゅう

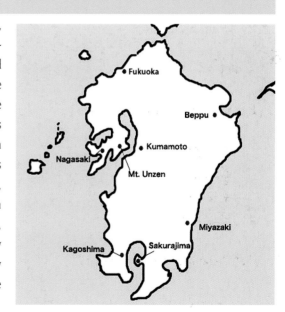

■ キアラのジャーナル Kiara's Journal (A)
きあら　　じゃーなる

Read the journal entry below, and then answer these questions.

❶ What did Kiara do at the 本屋?
　　　　　　　　　　　　　　　ほんや

❷ While Kiara was writing in her journal, what was Ben doing?

❸ After Tomo made his startling announcement, what did he do?

❹ How did Ben respond to the announcement?

ジャーナルへ
じゃーなる

After lunch we had a busy afternoon visiting different places. Here is the list of what we did:

1.　本屋へ　行きました。そこで　本を　買いました。

2.　私は　ジャーナルを　書きました。でも、ベン君は　漫画を　少し　読みました。

3.　じゅん君は　アダムズおじさんと　ちょっと　話しました。でも、友さんは　また　ラーメンを　食べました。

4.　後で　みんな　お茶を　少し　飲みました。そして　晩ご飯を　食べました。晩ご飯に　天ぷらを　食べました。（天ぷらは　ポルトガルと　スペインから　来ました。）

We had just about finished eating our tempura, and were getting ready to return to the 旅館 when 友
　　　　　　　　　　　　　　　　　　　　　　　　　　　　　　　　　　　　　　　りょかん
さん said, 「明日　東京へ　行きます。でも・・・・」 There was a really long pause.

じゅん君は、「でも・・・・?」と　友さんに、聞きました。

そして、友さんは、「ちょっと、問題が　あります。I've not yet perfected navigation to an exact time period.」と　言って、その後 quickly　外へ　出て　行きました。

私は、「ええっ! What are we going to do? The time gate is the only way to get back!」

ベン君 stayed calm and said, 「この　部屋は　ちょっと　暑い　ですね。その　まどを　開けて　下さい。」

じゅん君も tried to make it sound as if it wasn't going to be too bad. Look on the bright side: my trip to 日本 is definitely going to be one no one else has ever experienced!

■ キアラのジャーナル Kiara's Journal (B)
きあら　じゃーなる

Read the journal entry below, and then answer these questions.

❶ How many Portuguese sailors were staying at the inn?
❷ How long had these men been in Nagasaki?
❸ Name at least two things the Portuguese brought to Japan.
❹ Are the Portuguese the only foreigners to be trading with Japan? Support your answer.

ジャーナルへ
じゃーなる

I'm actually really concerned about what 友さん said last night. If he can't control when we land, we might actually never get home! He did say that he's working on it and that he's almost got it fixed. I just hope that he's telling the truth.

Despite these worries, we went to sleep すこし early last night in the 旅館、after a terrific 晩ご飯。ここの 天ぷらは とても delicious です。At the 旅館、四人の ポルトガル人も いました。They were very friendly. We communicated in 日本語、although theirs was much better than ours, since they had lived here for several years. 私の 日本語は ちょっと improving. 晩ご飯の 後で音楽の performance が ありました。ポルトガル人 really enjoyed it.

その ポルトガル人たちは 五年前に ここに 来ました。でも、ポルトガルと 日本は 1543年から trade を 始めました。Everything had been going very well here for nearly 六十年間。その ポルトガル人 brought guns, which the 大名、or feudal lords, really wanted. Ultimately, each 大名 wanted to gain control over the other small fiefdoms and eventually rule the entire archipelago. その ポルトガル人 also brought 食べ物、especially vegetables, from the various parts of the world they had visited in their travels. The king of ポルトガル人 was very interested in promoting Christianity and sent many Jesuit monks, including St. Francis Xavier, to East Asia. Xavier は スペイン から です。In Japan, the ポルトガル人 had been quite successful at trade, until 1600, when this group of オランダ人 arrived.

Last year, rumors abounded about a 船 shipwrecked off an island near Nagasaki. The sailors rescued in that wreck have been here for a few months. ポルトガル人は、「The first few months were とても horrible for the オランダ人。」と 言いました。Evidently the オランダ人 were trying to cut into the Portuguese trade, so the two nationalities didn't get along at all. でも、since they have gotten to know each other, they've become friendlier. ポルトガル人は、「アダムズさんは とても いい 人 です。」と 言いました。The オランダ人 seem to be recovering from this rough experience. 彼は、「早く家へ 帰りたいです。」と 私達に 言いました。

To gain your passport stamp for this chapter, you have two choices. You may cook or bring samples of food from another country and say (in Japanese) where it is from, or you can create a poster with your class schedule on it in Japanese on one half and on the other, your schedule in a language other than English. Good luck!

■ 単語チェックリスト New Word Checklist

Japanese	Location	English
4-1		
あめりか　　アメリカ (n)	4-1	United States of America
あめりかじん　　アメリカ人 (n)	4-1	American
いう/いいます　　言う/ 言います (言って) (v)	4-1	(to) say
いぎりす　　イギリス (n)	4-1	England
いぎりすけい　　イギリス系 (n)	4-1	English descent
いぎりすじん　　イギリス人 (n)	4-1	English (person)
いたりあ　　イタリア (n)	4-1	Italy
いたりあじん　　イタリア人 (n)	4-1	Italian (person)
いんどねしあ　　インドネシア (n)	4-1	Indonesia
いんどねしあじん　　インドネシア人 (n)	4-1	Indonesian (person)
おーすとらりあ　　オーストラリア (n)	4-1	Australia
おーすとらりあじん　　オーストラリア人 (n)	4-1	Australian
おらんだ　　オランダ (n)	4-1	Holland
おらんだじん　　オランダ人 (n)	4-1	Dutch person
がいこく　　外国 (n)	4-1	foreign country
がいこくじん　　外国人 (n)	4-1	foreigner
かなだ　　カナダ (n)	4-1	Canada
かなだじん　　カナダ人 (n)	4-1	Canadian
かんこく　　韓国 (n)	4-1	South Korea
かんこくけい　　韓国系 (n)	4-1	Korean descent
かんこくじん　　韓国人 (n)	4-1	Korean (person)
すぺいん　　スペイン (n)	4-1	Spain
すぺいんじん　　スペイン人 (n)	4-1	Spaniard
たいわん　　台湾 (n)	4-1	Taiwan
たいわんじん　　台湾人 (n)	4-1	Taiwanese (person)
ちゅうごく　　中国 (n)	4-1	China
ちゅうごくけい　　中国系 (n)	4-1	of Chinese descent
ちゅうごくじん　　中国人 (n)	4-1	Chinese (person)
てつだう/てつだいます　　手伝う/手伝います (手伝って) (v)	4-1	(to) help, to assist
どいつ　　ドイツ (n)	4-1	Germany
どいつじん　　ドイツ人 (n)	4-1	German (person)
ところで (exp./conj.)	4-1	by the way
ながさき　　長崎 (n)	4-1	Nagasaki (city name)
なにけい　　何系 (inter.)	4-1	what ethnicity or heritage
なにじん　　何人 (inter.)	4-1	what nationality

Japanese	Location	English
にっけいじん　日系人 (n)	4-1	Japanese descent
にほんじん　日本人 (n)	4-1	Japanese person
にゅーじーらんど　ニュージーランド (n)	4-1	New Zealand
にゅーじーらんどじん　ニュージーランド人 (n)	4-1	New Zealander
ふらんす　フランス (n)	4-1	France
ふらんすじん　フランス人 (n)	4-1	French (person)
ぽるとがる　ポルトガル (n)	4-1	Portugal
めきしこ　メキシコ (n)	4-1	Mexico
めきしこけい　メキシコ系 (n)	4-1	Mexican descent (person of)
めきしこじん　メキシコ人 (n)	4-1	Mexican (person)
ろしあ　ロシア (n)	4-1	Russia

4-2

Japanese	Location	English
あくしゅ (n)	4-2	handshake
いたりあご　イタリア語 (n)	4-2	Italian language
いちまい　一枚 (n)	4-2	one sheet/piece
いちぺーじ/いっぺーじ　一ページ (n)	4-2	one page/page one
いんどねしあご　インドネシア語 (n)	4-2	Indonesian (language)
おらんだご　オランダ語 (n)	4-2	Dutch language
かんこくご　韓国語 (n)	4-2	Korean language
きゅうぺーじ　九ページ (n)	4-2	nine pages, page nine
きゅうまい　九枚 (n)	4-2	nine sheets
ごぺーじ　五ページ (n)	4-2	page five
ごまい　五枚 (n)	4-2	five sheets, five pages
さいん　サイン (n)	4-2	signature
さんぺーじ　三ページ (n)	4-2	three pages, page three
さんまい　三枚 (n)	4-2	three sheets
しゃしん(を) とる/とります　写真(を) 撮る/撮ります (撮って) (v)	4-2	(to) take a photo
じゅうぺーじ　十ページ (n)	4-2	ten pages, page ten
じゅうまい　十枚 (n)	4-2	ten sheets
しる/しります　知る/知ります (知って) (v)	4-2	(to) know something/someone
すぺいんご　スペイン語 (n)	4-2	Spanish
ちゅごくご　中国語 (n)	4-2	Chinese
どいつご　ドイツ語 (n)	4-2	German
ななぺーじ/しちぺーじ　七ページ (n)	4-2	seven pages, page seven
ななまい/しちまい　七枚 (n)	4-2	seven sheets
なんぺーじ　何ページ (inter.)	4-2	how many pages, what page
なんまい　何枚 (inter.)	4-2	how many sheets
にぺーじ　二ページ (n)	4-2	two pages, page two
にまい　二枚 (n)	4-2	two sheets
はちぺーじ/はっぺーじ　ハページ (n)	4-2	eight pages, page eight
はちまい　八枚 (n)	4-2	eight sheets
はなす/はなします　話す/話します (話して) (v)	4-2	(to) speak
ふらんすご　フランス語 (n)	4-2	French language
ぽるとがるご　ポルトガル語 (n)	4-2	Portuguese

Japanese	Location	English
よんぺーじ　四ページ (n)	4-2	four pages, page four
よんまい　四枚 (n)	4-2	four sheets
ろくぺーじ　六ページ (n)	4-2	six pages, page six
ろくまい　六枚 (n)	4-2	six sheets
ろしあご　ロシア語 (n)	4-2	Russian (language)

4-3

いらっしゃいませ (exp.)	4-3	welcome (usually used at a place of business)
くるま　車 (n)	4-3	car, vehicle
たべもの　食べ物 (n)	4-3	food(s)
たべる/たべます　食べる/食べます (食べて) (v)	4-3	(to) eat
(_____は、)ちょっと・・・ (exp.)	4-3	little … (something is)
のみもの　飲み物 (n)	4-3	drink(s)
のむ/のみます　飲む/飲みます (飲んで) (v)	4-3	(to) drink
ぱん　パン (n)	4-3	bread
ぱんやさん　パン屋さん (n)	4-3	bakery
ほんや　本屋 (n)	4-3	bookstore
まだ (adv.)	4-3	not yet
もの　物 (n)	4-3	thing

4-4

いく/いきます　行く/行きます (行って) (v)	4-4	(to) go
かえる/かえります　帰る/帰ります (帰って) (v)	4-4	(to) return
くる/きます　来る/来ます (来て) (v)	4-4	(to) come
する/します (して) (v)	4-4	(to) do; (to) wear
だから (conj.)	4-4	because of that

Time in Nara

第 **5** 課

✔ Learning Goals

By the end of this chapter you will learn:

A) how to form the past tense and the past negative tense of verbs

B) about past, future, and present schedules

C) basic details of the Nara period (710–794) and the traditional Japanese calendar

D) how to read basic schedules

E) 15 additional kanji

✔ Performance Goals

By the end of this chapter you will be able to:

A) talk about birthday dates

B) state your address and today's complete date

C) talk about what you did last week or last month

D) talk about what you will do next week or next month

E) read and write 15 additional kanji

Daibutsu (Big Buddha) of Todaiji Temple, Nara

毎週　月曜日の　12時に　私に、電話して　下さい。

会話 Dialogue
（かいわ）

キアラ　：　*月、火、水、木、金、土、日。月、火、水、木、金、土、日。
（きあら）　（げつ）（か）（すい）（もく）（きん）（ど）（にち）（げつ）（か）（すい）（もく）（きん）（ど）（にち）

ベン　：　キアラさん、それは　何　ですか。
（べん）　　　（きあら）　　　　　（なに）

キアラ　：　曜日の　練習　です。じゅん君　から、聞きました。
（きあら）　（ようび）（れんしゅう）　　　　　　（くん）　　　（き）

ベン　：　月は、月曜日、火は　火曜日　ですね。
（べん）　　（げつ）（げつようび）（か）（かようび）

キアラ　：　よく　出来ました！
（きあら）　　　（でき）

あ！今、何時　ですか。母は、「毎週　月曜日　12時に　私に、電話して　下さい。」
（いま）（なんじ）　　（はは）　（まいしゅう）（げつようび）　　　（わたし）（でんわ）　　（くだ）
と　言いました。今日は、月曜日　ですね。
（い）　　　　（きょう）（げつようび）

じゅん　：　はい、今日は、月曜日　です。今　11時59分　ですよ。
（きょう）（げつようび）　　（いま）

キアラ　：　後　一分！でも、今は、７５１年です。ここに　電話は　ありませんね。
（きあら）　（あと）（いっぷん）　　　（いま）　　　　　　　　（でんわ）

ベン　：　僕は　ここから　母に　電子メールを
（べん）　　（ぼく）　　　　（はは）　（でんしめーる）
＋送りましたよ。キアラさんも、お母さん　に、メールを　送りますか。
（おく）　　　　（きあら）　　　（かあ）　　　（めーる）　（おく）

キアラ　：　それは　いい　アイデア　です　ねえ！
（きあら）　　　　　　　　（あいであ）

---

* Note about counting days of the week: The readings of the kanji for days of the week are normally different when they stand alone (not in conjunction with other kanji), but do not change when referring to days of the week.

送ります – to send
（おく）

単語 New Words
（たんご）

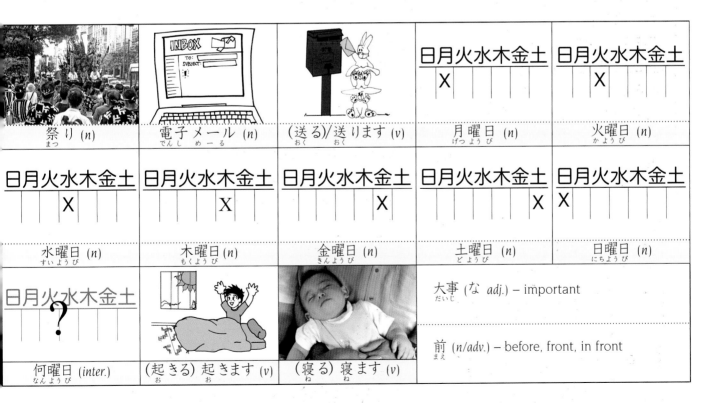

祭り (n) （まつ）	電子メール (n) （でんし めーる）	（送る）/送ります (v) （おく）（おく）	日月**火**水木金土 月曜日 (n) （げつようび）	日月水**火**木金土 火曜日 (n) （かようび）
日月火**水**木金土 水曜日 (n) （すいようび）	日月火水**木**金土 木曜日 (n) （もくようび）	日月火水木**金**土 金曜日 (n) （きんようび）	日月火水木金**土** 土曜日 (n) （どようび）	**日**月火水木金土 日曜日 (n) （にちようび）
日月火水木金土 **?** 何曜日 (inter.) （なんようび）	（起きる）起きます (v) （お）（お）	（寝る）寝ます (v) （ね）（ね）	大事 (な adj.) – important （だいじ） 前 (n/adv.) – before, front, in front （まえ）	

■ 漢字 Kanji

午　後　良　月　火　水　金　土　曜

午 4 strokes	ゴ – noon	丿	㇑	仁	午			
	午 – noon							
	Noon is when the clock is at 12. The last two strokes of this kanji mean 10 (十). Add 2 (the first two strokes) to the ten and you have 12, which represents NOON.							

後 9 strokes	ゴ；あと – after, afterward	丿	㇇	彳	彳	行	従	後
	後 – after; (午)後 – p.m., afternoon	後						
	The FIRST three strokes are also in the left side in the kanji for the verb "to go" (行). The next three strokes are the top part of thread (糸). The last three strokes are the top part of winter (冬). Imagine someone going out with a piece of thread in the winter to measure the snow AFTER a snowfall.							

良 7 strokes	よ(い) – good	`	㇗	彐	彐	自	良	良
	良(い) – good							
	良 or GOOD is the same as what is below the roof in "to eat" — 食. We all know that eating is very GOOD!							

月 4 strokes	ゲツ、がつ – month; つき – moon	丿	刀	月	月			
	(今)月 – this month; 月(曜日) – Monday							
	This is a stylized picture of a MOON with clouds moving across it. "Moon-day" sounds just like MONDAY.							

火 4 strokes	カ、ひ – fire	`	㇔	少	火			
	火(曜日) – Tuesday							
	See the person standing in the middle, surrounded on each side by FLAMES and FIRE? This kanji also looks like some sticks standing against each other with sparks or FIRE coming out. TUESDAY is FIRE day.							

水 4 strokes	スイ、みず – water	亅	刁	水	水			
	水 – water; 水(曜日) – Wednesday							
	The first stroke is the fishhook breaking into the smooth WATER represented by the remaining three strokes. WEDNESDAY is WATER day.							

金 8 strokes	キン – gold; かね – money	ノ	八	스	仐	仐	仐	金	金
	金 – gold; 金(曜日) – Friday								
	This kanji is a king (王) under his roof with two large pieces of gold at his feet. That is some serious GOLD! FRIDAY is usually payday or GOLD day.								

土 3 strokes	ド、つち – soil, ground	一	十	土					
	土 – earth, soil; 土(曜日) – Saturday								
	"DIRT Day" is SATURDAY, when you have free time to dig in the DIRT in your garden.								

曜 18 strokes	ヨウ – day of the week	丨	冂	日	日	日ㄱ	日ㅋ	日ㅋ	日ㅋㄱ	日ㅋㅋ
	(何)曜(日) – what day of the week?	日ㅋㅋ	日ㅋㅋ	明ㅋ	明ㅋ	瞬	曜	曜	曜	
	This kanji has the radical for DAY on the left. Two katakana ヨ on top of a short-tailed bird (strokes 11–18) gives this character its pronunciation. Every day (日) that you can hear birds chirping is a good day です ヨ!									

■ 言葉の探索 Language Detection

1. Review of the time particle に

   You learned in Chapter 3 that the particle に is used after specific time words and not after general time words. Specific time words include hours and minutes, and *occasionally* the days of the week or month, and months themselves. General time words, such as 毎日 (every day) or 明日 (tomorrow), are NOT followed by any particle.

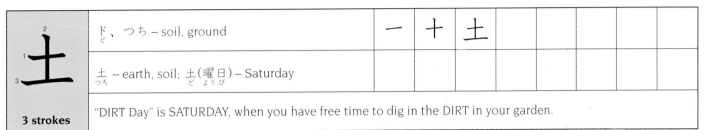

   A) 一時に 宿題を します。 = At one o'clock I will do homework.
   B) 午後 六時三十五分に 寿司を 食べます。 = At 6:35 p.m. I eat sushi.
   C) 火曜日に バスケを します。 = On Tuesday I play basketball.
   D) 毎日 午前七時三十分に 学校へ 行きます。 = Every day I go to school at 7:30 a.m.
   E) 明日 部活は 何時に ありますか。 = What time do you have club tomorrow?

■ 自習 Self Check

1. Which time words can be followed by に?

   a. 五時
   b. 毎日
   c. 木曜日
   d. 十六日
   e. 明日
   f. 五月

2. Review the following by covering up the right column with your hand or a piece of paper as you say the words in the left column out loud to yourself in Japanese. Check yourself by looking at the right column.

a. 5:00	ごじ
b. after 9:00	くじ　すぎ
c. before 8:00	はちじ　まえ
d. 1:02	いちじにふん
e. 10:25	じゅうじにじゅうごふん
f. 11:38	じゅういちじさんじゅうはっぷん

3. Say the seven days of the week out loud to yourself in Japanese:

a. Monday　　　月曜日
　　　　　　　　げつ よう び

b. Tuesday　　　_____

c. Wednesday　　_____

d. Thursday　　　_____

e. Friday　　　　_____

f. Saturday　　　_____

g. Sunday　　　_____

■ 練習の時間 Time for Practice
　　れんしゅう　　じかん

1. Pair Practice

Schedule Information Gap

Tetsuya's family has some communication gaps. His mother and father did not talk to each other about what he should do on Sunday before heading out for the day, and therefore each parent left him a different schedule for chores to do for the day. A-さん's job, with B-さん, is to read each schedule and find the differences. To begin, A-さん goes to the wall where Tetsuya's mother's schedule is posted, and reports each activity to B-さん, in Japanese, so that B-さん can write down the schedule. Switch roles; B-さん goes to the wall where Tetsuya's father's schedule is posted, and reports back to A-さん, so that A-さん can write it down. Finally, write what both of you think is the best schedule of activities for Tetsuya today. DO NOT WRITE IN THIS BOOK.

時間 じかん	Mother's schedule	Father's schedule	Ideal schedule
6:30			
7:05			
7:35			
11:35			
3:05			
4:30			
5:00			
6:45			
8:00			
11:00			

■ 文化箱 Culture Chest

Nara (奈良)

The city of 奈良 is a wonderful place to explore, full of ancient temples and shrines. The huge Buddhist temple of 東大寺, one of the great architectural treasures of Japan, is located here. Can you tell the meaning of this temple's name from its kanji? The temple, and the "big" Buddha inside, were completed and the temple officially opened in 752. At the time of construction, 東大寺 was the largest wooden structure in the world, and it is said to still hold that title. The Buddhist statue inside is also the largest gilt bronze Buddha in the world at 15 meters. The building has burned down twice, and the current structure, rebuilt in the early 1700s, is actually 30% smaller than the original!

Originally called 平城京, 奈良 was the earliest established capital of Japan. During what became known as the Nara Period (奈良時代, 710–794), the burgeoning court and nobles enjoyed writing poetry in Chinese and studying popular Buddhist scriptures imported from China and Korea. Chinese influence was so strong at the time that the city, with its north-south orientation and straight-line streets, was modeled after the Chinese capital of Chang-an (present-day Xian). 奈良 remains famous today for its many temples (including Todaiji) and parks, some of which are now part of a UNESCO World Heritage Site.* Every year millions of tourists visit Nara to see these attractions and its other main feature, the 1,200 tame deer that roam freely, looking for tourists to feed them しかせんべい (deer crackers). The deer are considered sacred and are protected by law.

*UNESCO: United Nations Educational, Scientific, and Cultural Organization

■ 地図 Map Skills

奈良 is the first capital of the nation of Japan. It was the capital from 七百十年　から　七百九十四年までです. It was laid out on a grid pattern modeled after Chinese capital cities. The city was quickly filled with Buddhist temples and monasteries that were favored by the emperors at the time. Today, when you go to Nara, the feel of the city is much closer to that of a large town rather than a city. Popular sites include Todaiji Temple, Kasuga Taisha, the Nara Deer Park, and Horyuji Temple.

❶ 奈良は　日本の　どこに　ありますか。

❷ 奈良 is located on which island?

❸ What is the name of the largest statue in 奈良?

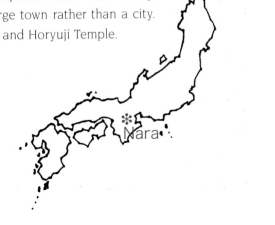

■ キアラのジャーナル Kiara's Journal
きあら　　　じゃーなる

Read the journal entry below, and then answer these questions.

❶ What day of the week did Kiara mention having school?
❷ What day of the week did the strong winds come?
❸ What city are they in as Kiara writes this journal entry?
❹ What did Ben tell Kiara to look at?

ジャーナルへ
じゃーなる

　　先週 (last week) の　木曜日に　学校が　ありました。そして、金曜日に　大風が　あって、
時の門を　通りました。It must have taken all night to get to 長崎、since we arrived on 土曜日。
今日は、月曜日です。月曜日 is usually considered the first day of the week in Japan. 今日の　あさ、
we activated the 時の門 again and we are off on another adventure ending up in 奈良。I was hoping that
we would luck out and get home, but this is really pretty exciting.

　　When we go through the 時の門、for some reason、ベン君 is able to send text messages using his
cell phone. I don't know why, but he received a message from his mother about doing something 昨日の晩。
I'm going to try to send an e-mail to my family on my laptop the next time we go through the 時の門。I
hope it will work.

　　今朝、as we were about to leave 長崎、アダムズさんを　見ました。徳川家康、the future 将軍
of 日本、was in town, and アダムズさんと　徳川家康 were supposed to have a meeting. 友さんは
「早く　時の門に　行きましょう。ここは　ちょっと　危ない　ですよ。」と　言いました。As
we reached the 鳥居、友さん took the dipper from the fountain in front of the gate. Then he grabbed
a pinch of salt from his かばん and sprinkled the salt in the 水。The 門 glazed over and 友さん told us
to jump through. 三時間後 we walked out. じゅん君は、「ここは　どこ　ですか。」と　言いま
した。

　　ベン君は、「あれを　見て　下さい！」と　言いました。私は、「あの寺は　東大寺　です
か。」と　聞きました。A Buddhist monk overheard us and replied 「はい、そう　です。あの　お
寺は　世界で　一番　大きい　木の　建物　です。」と　言いました。東大寺は、21st century
の　今でも、世界で　一番　大きい　木で　作った　建物　です。すばらしい　ですね。

　　私は、「友さん、私は　ちょっと　東大寺へ　行きます。私は　美術が　大好き (really like)
です。あそこを　見に行きます。」と、言いました。

　　でも、友さん was nowhere to be found。じゅん君　は、「友さんは　どこに　います
か。一分前　ここに　いました。でも、今は　どこ　ですか。」と、言いました。

■ テクノの時間 Techno Time
てくの　　じかん

Though you've not been introduced to them all yet, type all the vocabulary words from this chapter into your digital dictionary. Remember to type in your file called "JISHO" (in *romaji*).

私も、アメリカ で、漢字を　ちょっと　勉強しました。
I also studied some kanji in the U.S.

■ 会話 Dialogue

中国語の先生 ： 先週の　水曜日、奈良で　中国語の　授業を　始めました。皆さん、次の　授業に
　　　　　　　　来て　下さい。

ベン 　　　　： どこ　ですか。

中国語の先生 ： 東大寺　です。東大寺は　分かりますか。

じゅん 　　　： はい、分かります。

キアラ 　　　： 女性も、中国語を　勉強しますか。

中国語の先生 ： いいえ、女性は　中国語を　勉強　しません。でも、キアラさん、来て　下さ
　　　　　　　　いね。

キアラ 　　　： はい、分かりました。

ベン 　　　　： 僕は、漢字が　*好き　です。

キアラ 　　　： 私も、アメリカで　漢字を　ちょっと　勉強しました。

中国語の先生 ： ええっ？！

*好き – to like

■ 単語 New Words

誕生日 (n)	(生まれる) 生まれます (v)	(始める) 始めます (v)	(勉強(を)する) 勉強(を) します (v)

一月 (n) – January

二月 (n) – February

三月 (n) – March

四月 (n) – April

五月 (n) – May

六月 (n) – June

七月 (n) – July

八月 (n) – August

九月 (n) – September

十月 (n) – October

十一月 (n) – November

十二月 (n) – December

何月 (inter.) – What month?

(終わる)終わります (v) – to finish

いつ (inter.) – when

■ 漢字 Kanji

千　末　毎　週

千 3 strokes	セン – thousand せん	ノ	二	千				
	千 – one thousand; 二千 – two thousand せん　　　　　　　に せん							
	The second two strokes are the kanji for 10 (十) to show this is a number. The 3 total strokes represent the 3 zeros in 1,000.								

末 5 strokes	マツ – end まっ	一	二	十	未	末		
	(週)末 – weekend しゅう まっ							
	This character is a tree (木) with the addition of a long branch (the first stroke) which causes it to be so top heavy that a little wind will END its life. Note that the top branch is longer here than in "not yet" (未).								

毎 6 strokes	マイ – every まい	ノ	ﾉ	ﾆ	勹	毎	毎	
	毎(日) – every day; 毎(週) – every week; まい にち　　　　　まい しゅう 毎(年), 毎(年) – every year まい ねん　まい とし							
	The grid part of this kanji looks like a calendar. Think of the top two strokes as a hand pulling sheets of the calendar across EVERY day.								

週 11 strokes	シュウ – week しゅう	ノ	几	月	冃	用	用	周
	(今)週 – this week; (来)週 – next week こん しゅう　　　　　らい しゅう	冂	凋	週				
	The first two strokes show the walls surrounding many working people, who have to follow the path (the last 3 strokes) and work in the dirt (土) to feed their mouths (口) all WEEK.								

■ 言葉の探索 Language Detection

1. **Past tense of 〜ます verbs**

   To form the past tense of a ~ます verb, change the ~ます ending to ~ました.

   例
EXAMPLE

私は　食べます。	= I eat.
私は　食べました。	= I ate.
一月に　愛子さんは　中国に　<u>行きます</u>。	= Aiko will go to China in January.
八月に　愛子さんは　中国に　<u>行きました</u>。	= Aiko went to China in August.
明日　先生と　<u>話します</u>。 あした	= I will speak to the teacher tomorrow.
キアラさんは　友さんと　日本語で　<u>話しました</u>。	= Kiara spoke to Tomo in Japanese.

2. Negative past tense of ～ます verbs

To form the negative past tense of a ます verb, add でした to the negative tense.

ベン君は　手伝いません。	= Ben does not help.
キアラさんは　手伝いません　でした。	= Kiara did not help.
僕は　飲みません。	= I will not drink.
太郎さんは　飲みません　でした。	= Tarou did not drink.

Verb tense overview

～ます non-past	～ました past	～ません negative non-past	～ませんでした negative past	(英語)
話します	話しました	話しません	話しませんでした	to speak
来ます	来ました	来ません	来ませんでした	to come
あります	ありました	ありません	ありませんでした	to exist (inanimate)
勉強します	勉強しました	勉強しません	勉強しませんでした	to study

■ 自習 Self Check

1. Past

Say the following out loud to yourself in Japanese.

A) Mayumi talked.

B) Daisuke went to Canada.

C) I ate rice.

D) Ken came to school.

E) Tomoko ate sushi at lunch.

F) Mayumi studied Japanese

2. Past negative

Say the following out loud to yourself in Japanese.

A) Kenji did not eat.

B) Kiara did not go.

C) Jun did not play basketball.

D) Ben did not drink water.

E) Yesterday, Tomo didn't go to Shikoku.

F) For breakfast, I did not eat bread.

3. Say the following in Japanese:

A) Tuesday

B) Friday

C) January

D) October

E) Monday

F) June

G) April

H) Saturday

I) Thursday

J) March

K) June

L) November

■ 練習の時間 Time for Practice
れんしゅう　じ　かん

1. Class Practice

何月　生まれ　ですか。
なんがつ　う

Survey 8 to 10 classmates in Japanese to find out their birth month and write down your findings. Tabulate the responses and report to the class.

Which month has the most birthdays?

Q 何月　生まれ　ですか。　= What month were you born?
なんがつ　う

A 一月　生まれ　です。　= I was born in January.
いちがつ　う

2. Pair Practice

Emiko's schedule of activities

Emiko has had a busy year. Take turns with your partner putting these activities into 日本語. Remember to use the past tense and the particle after the time word.

A) In April, Emiko went to Kyoto.

B) In February, Emiko went to a Shinto shrine.

C) In August, Emiko returned home.

D) In September, Emiko helped out at home.

E) In October, Emiko went to the beach.

F) In January, Emiko went to Sapporo.

G) In July, Emiko went to Okinawa.

H) In December, Emiko did not eat ice cream.

I) In June, Emiko ate ice cream.

J) In May, Emiko did not go to a party.

3. Pair Practice

Yesterday's schedule

Use the vocabulary words below to ask your partner whether or not she/he studied each subject yesterday. Answer based upon fact.

 例
れい
EXAMPLE

A-さん：　きのう、社会を　勉強しましたか。
しゃかい　べんきょう
B-さん：　いいえ、社会は　勉強しませんでした。
べんきょう

歴史　数学　英語　美術
れき　し　すう　がく　えい　ご　び　じゅつ
体育　音楽　日本語　ドイツ語
たい　いく　おん　がく　ど　い　つ　ご

■ 文化箱 Culture Chest
ぶん　か　ばこ

Chinese Influence during the Nara Period

During the Nara Period (奈良時代, 710–794), Nara was the capital of all that was unified Japan (from Kyushu in the south to near present-day Tokyo in the northeast). At this time, China was undergoing a "golden age" that resulted in its culture being admired and imitated around Asia. The Japanese emperors were very interested in Chinese philosophy and culture, including Buddhism, Confucianism, Daoism, art, architecture, and literature. They sent teachers and scholars to China to study and bring back what they learned. Once they reached Japan, these new Chinese ideas began to take on a Japanese style that deeply influenced subsequent development of Japanese art, architecture, writing, and even martial arts and fashion. Can you think of an example of how another culture has influenced the one where you live?

■ キアラのジャーナル Kiara's Journal
きあら　じゃーなる

Read the journal entry below, and then answer these questions.

❶ What time was the music going to start?
❷ Who was the Emperor during the early Nara Period?
❸ What were some of the Chinese things that the Emperor had seen and heard?
❹ What did early spiritual religions and practice in Japan come to be known as?
❺ Where did Kiara, Ben, and Jun speak to the Chinese teacher?

ジャーナルへ
じゃーなる

　　今日は 751年1月20日 です。奈良の 人達は とても 忙しい です。752年に この 寺の dedication ceremony が あります。毎日、十二時半に construction workers は 一緒に お昼ご飯を 食べます。そして 一時半から また 仕事をします。今日、午後六時二十分から音楽会が ありました。奈良時代 (Nara Period) の 音楽は 私達の 音楽と すごく 違います。At first the music was pretty painful to listen to, since the beat and tones are totally different from music in the 21st century. But now I'm a bit more used to the different sound. 午後七時四十五分から 晩ご飯を 食べました。

　　しょうむ天皇 (the Emperor) は、中国の 美術が 大好きでした。中国の 音楽も たくさん 聞きました。食べ物は 日本と 中国の 食べ物がありました。今まで 日本の 宗教 (religion) は mainly indigenous religions which later became known as 神道 (Shintoism) でした。でも、奈良時代から 仏教 (Buddhism) も 入りました (entered)。今、奈良は 日本の 首都 (capital) です。天皇 (Emperor) は 奈良に います。中国人と 韓国人も たくさん います。The Korean Peninsula から、奈良時代に たくさんの 人が 日本に 来ました。Nara seems like quite an international place right now for me.

　　At the 音楽の コンサート、中国語の 先生と 話しました。その 先生は、「先週の 水曜日に 奈良で 中国語の 授業を 始めました。」と 言いました。「次の 授業に 来て 下さい。先週は 三十五人 来ました。仏教 (Buddhism) の お経 (scriptures) は 中国語 です。今は、まだ 日本に、there is no other writing system. 中国語を copying them is how writing was practiced and taught in here.」と 言いました。

　　ベン君は、「僕は 漢字が 好き です。でも 中国語は 分かりません。」と 言いました。

　　友さんは私に、「こうぼう だいしを 知っていますか。」と 言いました。

　　私は、「知りません。奈良の 人 ですか。」と 言いました。

　　友さんは、「僕の 友達の 友達 です。」と 言いました。それから、友さんは 私に、「空海は (otherwise known as Koubou Daishi) 774年に 生まれました。Some people say that 彼 (he) は 高野山で ひらがなと かたかなを 作りました。」と、言いました。

　　奈良は とても すばらしい です。本当に いい 所 です。

テクノの時間 Techno Time
て　く　の　　　じ　かん

Approach to Todaiji Temple, Nara

China, Korea, and Japan significantly influenced each other throughout their histories as neighbors often do. Can you find more information about the Chinese and Korean presence in Japan during the Nara Period? Choose to research this topic or one of the topics below. Try to find information and interesting images that you can use to create a poster to share with your class. Most of the information you have written on the poster can be in English, but your poster should contain at least some information in Japanese. Try to find interesting points that your classmates won't be able to find!

Kuukai (Koubou Daishi)
UNESCO sites in Japan
Japanese writing (hiragana)
Temples in Nara
the City of Nara
traditional Japanese music
Emperor Shomu
the deer of Nara

朝から、晩まで、ずっと　食べます。
I eat from morning all the way until night.

■ 会話 Dialogue

キアラ ： 友さんは、本当に　たくさん　食べますね。

友 ： はい、朝から　晩まで　ずっと　食べます。

ベン ： 日本の　食べ物から、中国の　食べ物まで、何でも　食べますね。

じゅん ： それは、いつから　ですか。

友 ： 生まれた時から、今日まで、ずっと　です。ここから、ここまで、食べ物　です。

あっ、この　寿司は、だれも　食べませんね。

じゅん ： だれも　何も　食べませんよ。

友 ： じゃ、私が、全部　食べます！

■ 単語 New Words

から (*part.*) – from   まで (*part.*) – until, to   何日 (*inter.*) – what day (of the month)?

Calendar						
月	火	水	木	金	土	日
	1 一日 ついたち	2 二日 ふつか	3 三日 みっか	4 四日 よっか	5 五日 いつか	6 六日 むいか
7 七日 なのか	8 八日 ようか	9 九日 ここのか	10 十日 とおか	11 十一日 じゅういちにち	12 十二日 じゅうににち	13 十三日 じゅうさんにち
14 十四日 じゅうよっか	15 十五日 じゅうごにち	16 十六日 じゅうろくにち	17 十七日 じゅうしちにち	18 十八日 じゅうはちにち	19 十九日 じゅうくにち	20 二十日 はつか
21 二十一日 にじゅういちにち	22 二十二日 にじゅうににち	23 二十三日 にじゅうさんにち	24 二十四日 にじゅうよっか	25 二十五日 にじゅうごにち	26 二十六日 にじゅうろくにち	27 二十七日 にじゅうしちにち
28 二十八日 にじゅうはちにち	29 二十九日 にじゅうくにち	30 三十日 さんじゅうにち	31 三十一日 さんじゅういちにち			

■ 言葉の探索 Language Detection

1. から－まで

   These two words are used to mean "from" and "until." Together with specific times or places, they mean "from this time until that time" or "from this place until that place." Both から and まで come after the time or place words they modify.

A) けん君は　一時から　二時まで　寝ました。 = Ken slept from 1:00 until 2:00.

B) 英語の　授業は　九時十分から　十時まで　です。 = English class is from 9:10 until 10:00.

C) 学校は　四月から　三月まで　です。 = School is from April until March.

D) 学校は　月曜日から　金曜日まで　です。 = School is from Monday until Friday.

E) 家から　学校まで　来ました。 = I came from home to school.

F) アメリカから　日本まで　行きます。 = I will go from the U.S. to Japan.

2. だれも、何も

A question word followed by も generates a negative expression. A few examples are だれも "nobody," or 何も "nothing." These words are followed by the NEGATIVE form of the verb.

A) 日曜日 は、だれも　学校に　いません。 = Nobody is at school on Sunday.
B) 昨日　だれもベースボールを　しません　でした。 = No one played baseball yesterday.
C) 私は　何も　知りません。 = I don't know anything.
D) 昨日は　キアラさんは　何も　しません　でした。 = Kiara didn't do anything yesterday.

3. Years and addresses

When time and addresses are given, larger units such as years, months, countries, or states come before smaller units such as hours, minutes, street addresses, or apartment numbers. Basically the order goes from largest to smallest unit.

In Example C, 〒106-0047 is the postal code which is the first thing you write for Japanese mailing addresses. 東京 is the city, 港区 = Minato Ward, 南麻布 = South Azabu (the neighborhood within the district), and 4–23–2 is the block, building, and house number. Tarou Satou is a person the mail is going to. 様 is typically used as an honorific suffix at the end of names when writing addresses on letters instead of さん, 先生, ちゃん, etc. which are used when speaking.

A) 1918年11月11日　火曜日　午前11時
B) 平成14年1月20日 = Heisei year 14, January, 20th
C) 〒106-0047

東京都　港区
南麻布　4−23−2
佐藤太郎 様

■ 自習 Self Check

Say the following out loud to yourself in Japanese:

1. ＿＿＿＿＿＿＿＿から . . . ＿＿＿＿＿＿＿＿まで

A) I played volleyball from 8:00 until 9:30.
B) I helped from September until December.
C) I went from Tokyo to Kyoto.
D) I ate dinner from 5:00 until 5:30.
E) Mayumi talked to her friend from 6:00 until 8:00.

2. だれも/何も

A) Nobody will go to Tokyo.
B) Kiara did not drink anything.
C) My father did not eat anything.
D) My friend didn't study anything.
E) Ben will not go anywhere on Saturday.
F) My older sister did not eat anything for breakfast.
G) Michio will not study anything on Sunday.

3. Dates

A) November 6   D) January 20
B) Say your birthday (including the year)   E) March 14
C) July 1   F) May 2

4. Write your home address using the Japanese general rule of writing the most general information first and the most specific information last.

練習の時間 Time for Practice
<ruby>練<rt>れん</rt>習<rt>しゅう</rt></ruby>の<ruby>時<rt>じ</rt>間<rt>かん</rt></ruby>

---

1. Pair Practice

いつ　ですか。
Use Japanese to ask your partner the dates below. Take turns asking and answering.

> A) A-さん：　<ruby>地球<rt>ちきゅう</rt></ruby>の　日は　いつ　ですか。　= When is Earth Day?
>   B-さん：　4月22日です。　　　　　　　　= It's April 22.
> B) A-さん：　お母さんの　<ruby>誕生日<rt>たんじょうび</rt></ruby>は　<ruby>何月何日<rt>なんがつなんにち</rt></ruby>　ですか。= What month and date is your mother's birthday?
>   B-さん：　母の　<ruby>誕生日<rt>たんじょうび</rt></ruby>は　<ruby>八月六日<rt>むいか</rt></ruby>　です。　　= My mother's birthday is August 6th.

➲ New Year's Eve – おおみそか (December 31)   ➲ Boxing Day – クリスマスの<ruby>翌日<rt>よくじつ</rt></ruby> (December 26)
➲ New Year's Day – <ruby>元日<rt>がんじつ</rt></ruby> (January 1)   ➲ your birthday
➲ Halloween – ハロウィーン (October 31)   ➲ your 先生's birthday
➲ spring equinox – <ruby>春分<rt>しゅんぶん</rt></ruby>の<ruby>日<rt>ひ</rt></ruby> (March 21)   ➲ a holiday of your choice
➲ Greenery Day – みどりの<ruby>日<rt>ひ</rt></ruby> (May 4)

---

2. Pair Practice

いつ　から、　いつ　まで　ですか。
Using the particles から and まで, make sentences with your partner in Japanese about when the following activities begin and end. Use the tense indicated.

> 私の　<ruby>日本語<rt>にほんご</rt></ruby>の　クラスは　<ruby>九時十五分<rt>くじ</rt></ruby>から　<ruby>十時五分<rt>じゅうじ</rt></ruby>まで　です。
> = My Japanese class is from 9:15 until 10:05.

A)	Jun	1:17	2:30	studies	math
B)	Kiara	June 18	July 2	Japan	will go
C)	Jun's mother	Dec. 14	Dec. 17	Tokyo	went
D)	My father	Friday	Sunday	Chicago	will go
E)	My friend	10 p.m.	11 p.m.	party	was there
F)	My teacher	today	day after tomorrow		on vacation

■ 文化箱 Culture Chest
ぶん か ばこ

Imperial Years and Dates

The Japanese system of using era names, or 年号, for dating has been in use since the 7th century and is still in use
ねんごう
today.

An example of this system is using the term Heisei 20年 for the year 2008. Adopted from the Chinese tradition, these
Imperial reign period names are closely linked to the imperial family and were originally chosen by court officials when a
new emperor was installed or if something auspicious, or disastrous, happened. The reign period of Heisei 平成 began in
へいせい
1989 when the previous emperor passed away. The first year of his reign was the year one. What reign year is it now, based
upon this system?

Japan also uses the Western system for counting years so a Japanese person is just as likely to say 1998年 as Heisei
10年。This is a good example of how Japan adapts elements from ancient China and other modern cultures into its own
unique ways of doing things.

Kasuga Taisha gate, Nara

■ キアラのジャーナル Kiara's Journal
きあら じゃーなる

Read the journal entry below, and then answer these questions.

❶ What is the name of the building that Kiara entered?
❷ What does Tomo eat in this entry?
❸ What did he eat yesterday?
❹ How many pages of notes has Tomo written about important food items?
❺ What was special about Kouken?

ジャーナルへ
じゃーなる

今日　東大寺の　中に　入りました (went into). 金曜日から　今日まで　友さんと　一緒に
とうだいじ　　　　　　　　　　　　　　　　　　　　　　　　　　　　　　　　いっしょ
いました。友さんは　毎日　たくさんの　食べ物を　食べました。彼は何でも　食べます！
　　　　　　　　　　　　　　　　　　　　　　　　　　　かれ
友さんは　お魚 (fish)と　芋(ポテト)と　漬け物も　食べました。昨日は、晩ご飯に　中国の
　　　　　さかな　　　いも　　　　つ　もの
食べ物を　たくさん　食べました。お酒も　いっぱい　飲みました。友さんは　食べ物の
　　　　　　　　　　　　　　　　　　さけ
事を　ノートに　三ページ　ぐらい　書きました。その　ノートに　天平勝宝　三年と
　　　の　と　　ぺ　じ　　　　　　　　き　　　　　　　　　　　　てんぴょうしょうほう
書きました。私は、「むずかしい！ (Difficult!) 友さん、それは　何ですか。」と、聞きました。
　　　　　　　　　　　　　　　　　　　　　　　　　なん　　　　　　き
友さんは、「考謙天皇の　年号です。今年は、考謙天皇の　三年目　です。」と、言いました。
　　　　　こうけんてんのう　ねんごう　ことし　　　　　　　　　　　　　　　　　　い
孝謙天皇は one of very few female emperors in Japanese 歴史。今、私 達は、その very unusual era
こうけん てんのう　　　　　　　　　　　　　　　　　　　れきし　いま　わたしたち
に　います。面白い　ですね。
　　　　　おもしろ
　ああ、今日は　とても　眠い　です。We've been so busy every day. I just have to take a break
　　　　　　　　　　　　　　ねむ
now and get some sleep.
　お休み。

■ テクノの時間 Techno Time
てくの　じかん

In which imperial reign year were you born? Check online to see if you can find out. Look for the reign year when your parents or guardians were born as well. Using this dating system, what year is it now?

来週は　私の　誕生日　です。
Next week is my birthday.

1) 毎日、
とても　早い　です。

2) 先週は、二千十年に　いました。
そして、ベン君の　家族に　会いました。
それから　学校に　行きました。
そして、今は、七百五十一年です。

3) 先週も、
あちこちに
行きました。
来週も、
奈良時代に
いますね。

6) 友さんは、
毎日、どこでも
おいしい物を
食べますよ。

5) 私は、毎年、
奈良のお祭りで、
美味しい物を
食べます。

4) はい。来週は、
奈良の　お祭りが
あります。

会話 Dialogue
（かいわ）

ベン　　：　毎日、とても　早い　です。
（べん）　　（まいにち）　　　　（はや）

キアラ　：　先週　は、二千十年に　いました。そして、ベン君の　家族に　会いました。それから、
（きあら）　（せんしゅう）　（にせんじゅうねん）　　　　　　　（べん）（くん）　　（かぞく）　（あ）

　　　　　　学校に　行きました。そして、今は、七百五十一年　です。
　　　　　　　　　（い）

ベン　　：　先週　も、あちこちに　行きました。来週　も、奈良時代に　いますね。
（べん）　（せんしゅう）　　　　　　　　（い）　　　（らいしゅう）（ならじだい）

じゅん　：　はい。来週　は、奈良の　お祭りが　あります。
　　　　　　　　　（らいしゅう）　（なら）　（まつ）

友　　　：　私は、毎年、奈良の　お祭りで、おいしい物を　食べます。
（とも）　　　　（まいとし）（なら）　（まつ）

キアラ　：　友さんは、毎日、どこでも　おいしい物を　食べますよ。
（きあら）　（とも）　　　（まいにち）

■ 単語 New Words
（たんご）

散歩 (n)　　去年 (n)　　今年 (n)　　来年 (n)　　　　毎年 (n)　　忙 しい (い adj.)
（さんぽ）　　（きょねん）　　（ことし）　　（らいねん）　　　（まいとし／まいねん）　　（いそが）

散歩(を) する/散歩(を)し ます (v) – to take a walk
（さんぽ）　　　　　　（さんぽ）

先週 (n) – last week
（せんしゅう）

今週 (n) – this week
（こんしゅう）

来週 (n) – next week
（らいしゅう）

毎週 (n) – every week
（まいしゅう）

先月 (n) – last month
（せんげつ）

今月 (n) – this month
（こんげつ）

来月 (n) – next month
（らいげつ）

毎月 (n) – every month
（まいつき）

何年 (inter.) – what year?
（なんねん）

■ 漢字 Kanji
（かんじ）

電	デン – electricity （でん）	一	厂	戸	币	乕	雨	雨
（13 strokes）	電 (気) – electricity; 電 (話) – telephone （でん）（き）　　　　　（でん）（わ）	雫	雫	雪	雪	電		

The top half of this kanji is the radical for rain (雨). The last strokes look like a kite with a long tail. Imagine Benjamin Franklin flying that kite under the rain in his famous experiment to discover ELECTRICITY.

達 12 strokes	ダツ, タチ, ダチ – to reach or arrive at; pluralizes some words	一	十	土	寺	去	幸	幸	幸
	(友)達 – friend; (私)達 – we; (先生)達 – teachers; 達 します – to arrive	幸	達	達	達				
	The dirt (土), sheep (羊), and a road (the last 3 strokes) here show how a GROUP (the pluralization part) of sheep can follow a long dirt road to REACH their destination.								

■ 言葉の探索 Language Detection

1. This week, next week, last week, every week/month/year

The prefixes 先 (before), 今 (this), and 来 (next) are placed in front of some time expressions:

先週	last week
今週	this week
来週	next week
先月	last month
今月	this month
来月	next month

Years are slightly different:

去年	last year
今年	this year
来年	next year

Deer in Nara are considered sacred and a National Treasure.

2. Every day/week/month/year

The prefix 毎 (every) can be used in front of many time expressions.

毎日	every day
毎週	every week
毎月	every month
毎年 or 毎年	every year

■ 自習 Self Check

1. Without looking at the above section, try to say each of the following out loud in Japanese:

A) last week

B) next week

C) this month

D) every day

E) every month

F) this week

G) last month

H) next month

I) every week

J) every year

■ 練習の時間 Time for Practice
れんしゅう　じかん

1. Tic-Tac-Toe

Place your marker on a spot and say the phrase for that square out loud to your partner in Japanese. If your partner feels that you are correct, you get to keep the square. If they challenge you, they may take the square. If they challenge you and are wrong, they lose a turn. Take turns. Try to get three in a row. Check your answers on the last page of this chapter.

(a)

this week	every year	next year
next week	yesterday	today
last Tuesday	this year	next month

(b)

this month	last year	every week
this Friday	tomorrow	last week
every day	next Saturday	last month

2. Pair Practice

Takes turns asking and answering the following questions with your partner in Japanese.

Partner's answers

A) 来年 は 何年 ですか。　　　　　A) _____
　らいねん　　なんねん

B) 今月 は 何月 ですか。　　　　　B) _____
　こんげつ　　なんがつ

C) 来週 の 月曜日 は 何日 ですか。　C) _____
　らいしゅう　げつようび　なんにち

D) 明日 は 何曜日 ですか。　　　　　D) _____
　あした　　なんようび

E) 今日 は 何曜日 ですか。　　　　　E) _____
　きょう　　なんようび

F) 今日 は 何日 ですか。　　　　　　F) _____
　きょう　　なんにち

G) 先週 の 金曜日 は 何日 でしたか。　G) _____
　せんしゅう　きんようび　なんにち

H) 去年 は 何年 でしたか。　　　　　H) _____
　きょねん　　なんねん

I) 来週 の 水曜日 は 何日 ですか。　I) _____
　らいしゅう　すいようび　なんにち

J) 先月 は 何月 でしたか。　　　　　J) _____
　せんげつ　　なんがつ

K) あなたの 誕生日 は いつ ですか。　K) _____
　　　たんじょうび

L) お母さんの 誕生日 は いつ ですか。　L) _____
　　　　たんじょうび

3. Pair Practice

Information gap

Help Jun fill out his three-month schedule. On a separate piece of paper, assign all the activities listed under (A) to specific dates on the calendar here. Your partner will assign dates to all the activities listed under (B) in the same manner. Then, take turns asking and answering questions about Jun's schedule. Notice the date for today. If the activity happened before "today," be sure to use the past tense of the verb. Write the answers you hear on the calendar. By the time you have finished, Jun's summer schedule should be completed.

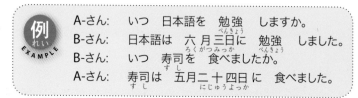

A-さん：　いつ　日本語を　勉強　しますか。
B-さん：　日本語は　六月三日に　勉強　しました。
B-さん：　いつ　寿司を　食べましたか。
A-さん：　寿司は　五月二十四日　に　食べました。

じゅんの　スケジュール

五月						六月						七月					
月	火	水	木	金	土/日	月	火	水	木	金	土/日	月	火	水	木	金	土/日
	1	2	3	4	5-6					1	2-3	1	2	3	4	5	6-7
7	8	9	10	11	12-13	4	5	6	7	8	9-10	8	9	10	11	12	13-14
14	15	16	17	18	19-20	11	12	13	14 今日	15	16-17	15	16	17	18	19	20-21
21	22	23	24	25	26-27	18	19	20	21	22	23-24	22	23	24	25	26	27-28
28	29	30	31			25	26	27	28	29	30-31	29	30	31			

A
1. basketball
2. study Japanese
3. math test
4. judo club
5. (free choice)

B
6. tennis
7. sushi restaurant
8. friend's birthday
9. English test
10. (free choice)

■ 文化箱 Culture Chest

Cross-Cultural Holidays

As people migrate from place to place, they carry their celebrations and holidays with them. For instance, some Americans of Mexican heritage celebrate Dia de los Muertos (Day of the Dead) in November to honor the deceased, Irish in Germany celebrate St. Patrick's Day, and Chinese all over the world celebrate Chinese New Year. Japan is culturally more homogeneous, but Western and other influences have crept into its holiday celebrations as well. For instance, Christmas and Valentine's Day (two Western holidays) are celebrated in Japan, but not exactly as they might be celebrated in the West. Another example is White Day, a holiday related to Valentine's Day and observed on March 14. Do a web search to find pictures of how these holidays are celebrated in Japan. What strikes you as different? Does your family honor a holiday special to your cultural heritage?

Paper lanterns at Kyoto's Gion Matsuri

■ キアラのジャーナル Kiara's Journal

Read the journal entry below, and then answer these questions.

❶ When did Kiara meet Jun's family?
❷ To whom is Kiara going to try to write an email tomorrow?
❸ What is Kiara going to do at Todaiji Temple?

ジャーナルへ

先週　じゅん君の　ご家族に　会いました。それから　学校へ　行きました。今週　友さんに　会いました。アメリカの　友達の　学校は　来週から　です。They are never going to believe the trip I'm having. 来週　私は　どこで　だれと　会うでしょう？ この experience は　毎日　surprising です。

明日　母に　電子メールを　書きます。Maybe it will go through. 友さんと　じゅん君とベン君と　私は、毎日　忙しい　です。私達は　たくさん　いい　人達と　会いましたが、ちょっと　休みたい　です。奈良で　来週　大祭が　あります。その　前に　東大寺でちょっと　お手伝いします。東大寺で　絵を　描きます (drawing). 私は、絵が　好き　です。その　絵を　電子メールで　母に　送ります。

■ テクノの時間 Techno Time

Jun has written you an e-mail message. Write a response. Be sure to use the proper greetings and endings. Answer his questions and ask him some questions in return to encourage him to write back and begin an ongoing dialogue.

初めまして。

僕は　じゅん　です。　僕の　家族は　五人　です。　僕は　一月生まれ　です。　母は　七月生まれ　です。　そして、父は　二月　生まれ　です。　兄は　十一月　生まれで、　妹の　愛子は四月　生まれ　です。東京に　ある　僕の　学校は　四月　から　三月まで　です。　期末テスト(final exams)　は　三月に　あります。僕は　週末にも　勉強します。　でも、時々、友達と　話します。

あなたの　ご家族は　何人　ですか？　お父さんは、　何月　生まれ　ですか。　お母さんは、　何月生まれ　ですか。　学校は、　いつから　ですか。　いつ　終わりますか。　毎週、何曜日が　休みですか。　週末に　何を　しますか。

では。

じゅん

第5課の5　Verb Review

■ ベンの話

Answer the following based upon Ben's story below.

❶ Where was Ben born?
❷ What is Ben's birthday?
❸ How old was Ben when his family moved to Tokyo?
❹ What school subject does Ben really like?
❺ What century are Ben and his friends in as he is writing?

Ben's Story

僕は　オーストラリアで　生まれました。誕生日は　七月八日　です。家族は　六人です。父と　母と　兄と　妹が　二人います。キャンベラの　幼稚園に　行きました。九年前、６才の時、東京へ　来ました。その四月、　日本の　小学校に　入りました。四年生の　時に、じゅん君と　会いました。じゅん君は　今も　とても　いい　友達　です。そして、１３才で、中学一年生に　なりました。今は、１５才で、中学三年生　です。今、中学校で　日本語と　英語と　数学と　科学を　勉強　しています。歴史も　勉強しています。歴史はとても　おもしろいです。僕は、歴史が　大好きです。先週、友達と　時の門に　入りました。今日は、７５１年１月２０日　です。２１世紀から　８世紀まで　来ました。

■ 練習の時間 Time for Practice

I. **Small Group Activity**

Grid game

Copy this grid onto a piece of scrap paper. This is your "game board." Then, fill in each blank with a different date or time (for example, May 20 or 1:30 p.m. or 1776) in English, and exchange papers with your fellow group members. To play, roll two dice. The total of the two dice tells you which grid space to go to. For that grid space, say the date and/or time in Japanese as you wrote it. If no one in your group challenges your answer, write your initials in that box and pass the dice to the next person. If you roll a number that you have already completed, you may try to answer (and initial) someone else's grid space. The winner is the player whose initials are in the most grid spaces on all the game boards in the group.

START	2	3	4	5	6
7	8	9	10	11	12

2. **Small Group Verb Review**

Ready, Set, Action!

Use flash cards (either cards you have already made or cards from your teacher) for all verbs you have studied thus far. Then make four additional "tense" flash cards labelled "non-past," "negative," "past," and "negative past." Put the verb flash cards in one pile and the four "tense" cards in another, upside down. Take turns flipping over the top card in each pile and conjugating the verb into the specified tense. If your new verb is correct, keep that card. If you conjugate the verb incorrectly, put the card back at the bottom of the pile. For Round Two, you must use the verb in the designated tense in a sentence. If your partners approve of your sentence, you may keep the card. The player with the most cards at the end of Round Two is the winner.

■ テクノの時間 Techno Time
てくのじかん

To gain your passport stamp for this chapter you have two options:

1. Create a yearlong activity calendar (年中行事表) for your family; write in family events that
ねんちゅうぎょうじひょう
   are important to you (birthdays, anniversaries, favorite family holidays or vacations, etc.). Colorfully label and illustrate all these dates in Japanese. Take one day in the calendar and with a balloon bubble write in a detailed schedule with the times you will do various things. Display your calendar in the classroom. Good luck (がんばって)!
2. Put together a PowerPoint presentation of a family vacation or your weekend, giving detailed day-by-day descriptions with photos of events, specifying what you did from what date (or time) until what date (or time).

■ 単語チェックリスト New Word Checklist
たんごちぇっくりすと

Japanese		Location	English
5-1			
おきる/おきます	起きる/起きます（起きて）(v)	5-1	(to) wake (up)
おくる/おくります	送る/送ります（送って）(v)	5-1	(to) send
かようび	火曜日 (n)	5-1	Tuesday
きんようび	金曜日 (n)	5-1	Friday
げつようび	月曜日 (n)	5-1	Monday
すいようび	水曜日 (n)	5-1	Wednesday
する/します (v)		5-1	(to) do
だいじ	大事 (な adj.)	5-1	important
でんしめーる	電子メール (n)	5-1	e-mail
どようび	土曜日 (n)	5-1	Saturday
なんようび	何曜日 (inter.)	5-1	what day of the week
にちようび	日曜日 (n)	5-1	Sunday
ねる/ねます	寝る/寝ます（寝て）(v)	5-1	(to) sleep
まえ	前 (n/adv.)	5-1	front, in front, before
まつり	祭り (n)	5-1	festival
もくようび	木曜日 (n)	5-1	Thursday

Japanese	Location	English
5-2		
いちがつ　一月 (n)	5-2	January
いつ (inter.)	5-2	when?
うまれる/うまれます　生まれる/ 生まれます(生まれて) (v)	5-2	(to) be born
おわる/おわります　終わる/ 終わります (終わって) (v)	5-2	(to) finish
くがつ　九月 (n)	5-2	September
ごがつ　五月 (n)	5-2	May
さんがつ　三月 (n)	5-2	March
しがつ　四月 (n)	5-2	April
しちがつ/なながつ　七月 (n)	5-2	July
じゅういちがつ　十一月 (n)	5-2	November
じゅうがつ　十月 (n)	5-2	October
じゅうきゅうまん　十九万 (n)	5-2	one hundred ninety thousand
じゅうにがつ　十二月 (n)	5-2	December
たんじょうび　誕生日 (n)	5-2	birthday
なんがつ　何月 (inter.)	5-2	what month?
にがつ　二月 (n)	5-2	February
はじめる/はじめます　始める/始めます (v)	5-2	(to) begin
はちがつ　八月 (n)	5-2	August
べんきょう(を) する/します　勉強する/勉強(を) します (v)	5-2	(to) study
ろくがつ　六月 (n)	5-2	June
5-3		
いつか　五日 (n)	5-3	fifth (day of the month)
ここのか　九日 (n)	5-3	ninth (day of the month)
さんじゅういちにち　三十一日 (n)	5-3	thirty-first (day of the month)
さんじゅうにち　三十日 (n)	5-3	thirtieth (day of the month)
じゅういちにち　十一日 (n)	5-3	eleventh (day of the month)
じゅうくにち　十九日 (n)	5-3	nineteenth (day of the month)
じゅうごにち　十五日 (n)	5-3	fifteenth (day of the month)
じゅうさんにち　十三日 (n)	5-3	thirteenth (day of the month)
じゅうしちにち　十七日 (n)	5-3	seventeenth (day of the month)
じゅうににち　十二日 (n)	5-3	twelfth (day of the month)
じゅうはちにち　十八日 (n)	5-3	eighteenth (day of the month)
じゅうよっか　十四日 (n)	5-3	fourteenth (day of the month)
じゅうろくにち　十六日 (n)	5-3	sixteenth (day of the month)
ついたち　一日 (n)	5-3	first (day of the month)
とおか　十日 (n)	5-3	tenth (day of the month)
なのか　七日 (n)	5-3	seventh (day of the month)
なんにち　何日 (inter.)	5-3	what day of the month?
にじゅういちにち　二十一日 (n)	5-3	twenty-first (day of the month)
にじゅうくにち　二十九日 (n)	5-3	twenty-ninth (day of the month)
にじゅうごにち　二十五日 (n)	5-3	twenty-fifth (day of the month)
にじゅうさんにち　二十三日 (n)	5-3	twenty-third (day of the month)
にじゅうしちにち　二十七日 (n)	5-3	twenty-seventh (day of the month)
にじゅうににち　二十二日 (n)	5-3	twenty-second (day of the month)
にじゅうはちにち　二十八日 (n)	5-3	twenty-eighth (day of the month)
にじゅうよっか　二十四日 (n)	5-3	twenty-fourth (day of the month)
にじゅうろくにち　二十六日 (n)	5-3	twenty-sixth (day of the month)

Japanese	Location	English
はつか　　二十日 (*n*)	5-3	twentieth (day of the month)
ふつか　　二日 (*n*)	5-3	second (day of the month)
まで (*part.*)	5-3	until
みっか　　三日 (*n*)	5-3	third (day of the month)
むいか　　六日 (*n*)	5-3	sixth (day of the month)
ようか　　八日 (*n*)	5-3	eighth (day of the month)
よっか　　四日 (*n*)	5-3	fourth (day of the month)

5-4

Japanese	Location	English
いそがしい　　忙しい (い *adj.*)	5-4	busy
きょねん　　去年 (*n*)	5-4	last year
ことし　　今年 (*n*)	5-4	this year
こんげつ　　今月 (*n*)	5-4	this month
こんしゅう　　今週 (*n*)	5-4	this week
さんぽ　　散歩 (*n*)	5-4	walk
さんぽ(を) する/します　　散歩(を) する/します (*v*)	5-4	(to) take a walk
せんげつ　　先月 (*n*)	5-4	last month
せんしゅう　　先週 (*n*)	5-4	last week
なんねん　　何年 (*inter.*)	5-4	what year?
まいしゅう　　毎週 (*n*)	5-4	every week
まいつき　　毎月 (*n*)	5-4	every month
まいねん/まいとし　　毎年 (*n*)	5-4	every year
らいげつ　　来月 (*n*)	5-4	next month
らいしゅう　　来週 (*n*)	5-4	next week
らいねん　　来年 (*n*)	5-4	next year

5-4 Key, Tic-Tac-Toe:

(a)

今週	まいねん（まいとし）	来年
来週	きのう	今日
先週の　火曜日	ことし	来月

(b)

今月	きょねん	まいしゅう
今週の　金曜日	明日 あした	せんしゅう
毎日	来週の　土曜日	せんげつ

Body Parts and Clothing in Hiraizumi

✓ Learning Goals

By the end of this chapter you will learn:

A) names of basic body parts
B) adverbs
C) expressions that describe physical features
D) how to give, or deny, permission
E) how to talk about wearing clothing and accessories
F) 18 additional kanji

✓ Performance Goals

By the end of this chapter you will be able to:

A) distinguish between basic body parts and talk on a basic level about these parts
B) talk about physical features at a basic level
C) use adverbs in the present positive and present negative tenses
D) talk about personal health at a basic level
E) ask, give, and deny permission for a variety of activities
F) talk about what someone is wearing
G) answer the question "What are you doing?" with a series of actions (verbs) in one sentence
H) read and write 18 additional kanji

Steps leading to the Konjikido, Hiraizumi, Iwate

頭が とても いい です。
あたま

■ 会話 Dialogue
かいわ

ベン　　：あなたが、あの　弁慶さん　ですか。
べん　　　　　　　　　　べんけい

弁慶　　：そう　です。私は　弁慶　です。
べんけい　　　　　　　　　べんけい

ベン　　：あなたは　とても　有名　ですね！
べん　　　　　　　　　　　ゆうめい

キアラ：とても　強い　侍　ですね。心も　強い　ですね。それに　頭が　とても　いい　で
きあら　　　　つよ　さむらい　　　こころ　つよ　　　　　　あたま
すね。

友　　　：そして、いい　人　ですね。

ベン　　：目も、鼻も、口も、耳も、頭も、顔も足も、皆　大きい　ですね！
べん　　め　　はな　　くち　　みみ　　あたま　かお　あし　みんな

■ 単語 New Words
たんご

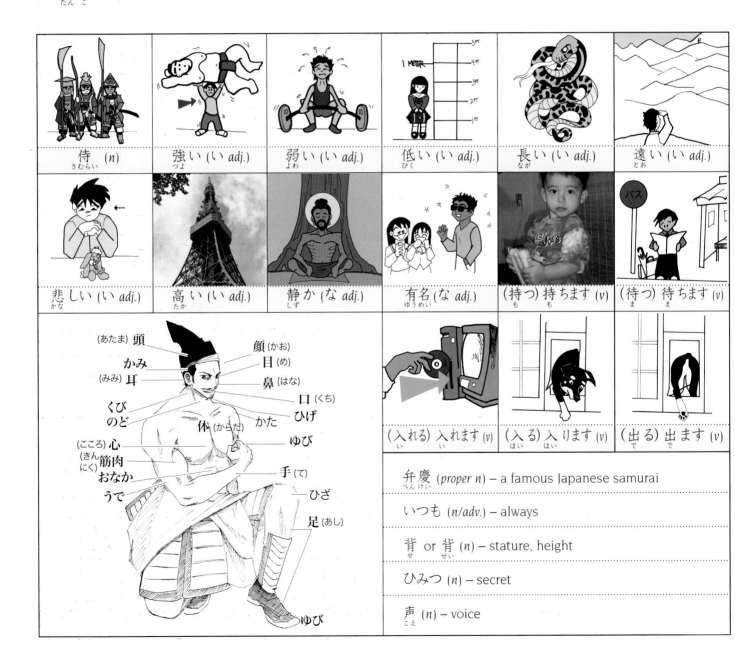

侍 (n) さむらい

強い (い adj.) つよ

弱い (い adj.) よわ

低い (い adj.) ひく

長い (い adj.) なが

遠い (い adj.) とお

悲しい (い adj.) かな

高い (い adj.) たか

静か (な adj.) しず

有名 (な adj.) ゆうめい

(持つ) 持ちます (v) も　　も

(待つ) 待ちます (v) ま　　ま

(あたま) 頭　　顔 (かお)
かみ　　目 (め)
(みみ) 耳　　鼻 (はな)
くび　　口 (くち)
のど　　ひげ
体 (からだ)　かた
(こころ) 心　　ゆび
(きんにく) 筋肉
おなか　　手 (て)
うで　　ひざ
足 (あし)
ゆび

(入れる) 入れます (v) い　　い

(入る) 入ります (v) はい　はい

(出る) 出ます (v) で　　で

弁慶 (proper n) – a famous Japanese samurai
べんけい

いつも (n/adv.) – always

背 or 背 (n) – stature, height
せ　　せい

ひみつ (n) – secret

声 (n) – voice
こえ

漢字 Kanji

体 目 口 耳 手 足 心 持 待 強

---

7 strokes

タイ；からだ – body	ノ	イ	仁	什	仚	休	体	
体 - body; 体(重) - (physical) weight								

The left two strokes are a person (人) leaning his BODY on the world's largest book (本)!

目

5 strokes

モク；め - eye	l	冂	冃	月	目	
目 – eye; (科)目 – subject						

This is a picture of an EYEBALL turned 90 degrees. The 3rd and 4th strokes represent the pupil in the middle.

口

3 strokes

くち/ぐち – mouth	l	冂	口	
口 – mouth; (入)口 – entrance; (出)口 – exit				

This kanji is a picture of a MOUTH opened really wide.

耳

6 strokes

みみ – ear	一	丅	下	肀	玨	耳	
耳 – ear							

Starting with your eye (目), go over a little to your left and right, then down a little (represented by the lines that extend to the left and right and down) to get to your EARS (耳).

---

4 strokes

シュ；て – hand	ノ	二	三	手	
手 – hand (from the shoulder down to the tips of the fingers); (上)手 – skillful; (下)手 – unskillful					

Think of the first stroke as the thumb and the second stroke as the main part of the HAND, with two fingers to the right and two fingers to the left. You can imagine how this HAND (手) got so disfigured!

---

7 strokes

ソク；あし – foot, leg; た (りる) – to be enough, sufficient	丶	口	口	早	早	足	足	
足 – leg, foot; (一)足 – a pair of socks/shoes								

The top of this character is the mouth (口) on the body of a runner who is showing off his really big FEET at the end of his LEGS.

	シン, こころ – heart, spirit	丶	心	心	心				
	心（臓）– the heart (organ); 心 – heart, spirit								
4 strokes	This kanji (心) has four strokes, one representing each chamber of the HEART. They are drawn best when the calligrapher uses a lot of strong SPIRIT.								

	も（つ）– to hold, to have	一	十	扌	扩	扩	拃	拌	持
	持つ – to hold, to have	持							
9 strokes	The first three strokes represent the hand (手) radical. The right side of this kanji is a Buddhist temple (寺). Think of something you HAVE or HOLD in your hand as you visit a Buddhist temple.								

	ま（つ）– to wait	ノ	ク	彳	彳	彳	往	待	待
	待（つ）– to wait	待							
9 strokes	The first three strokes are the left side of the character "to go" (行), while the right side is a Buddhist temple (寺). Think of how annoying it would be to go to a Buddhist temple only to have TO WAIT for a long time.								

強	キョウ; つよ（い）– to be strong	ラ	コ	弓	弘	弘	殆	殆	弘
	強（い）– to be strong; 勉強 する – to study (i.e., to exert strong effort even against your natural inclination)	弹	強	強					
11 strokes	The left side of this kanji (弓) is a Japanese bow while the right side is 虫 (MUSHI), or bug, with a katakana ム (MU) on top. If a bug is STRONG enough to pull this bow, he must be a very STRONG bug indeed!								

■ 言葉の探索 Language Detection

1. 強い / 弱い:
   強い and 弱い literally mean "strong" and "weak."

A) じゅん君の 体は 強い です。 = Jun('s body) is strong.
B) 私の 足は 弱い です。 = My legs are weak.
C) 一郎の 心は 強い です。 = Ichirou has a lot of heart. (Ichirou has a strong heart.)

強い and 弱い can also be used to talk about being good or bad at something.

A) この 高校の サッカー部は 強い です。 = This high school's soccer club (team) is strong.
B) その 学校の 野球部は 弱いです。 = That school's baseball club is weak.

2. When referring to physical features in Japanese, the part of the body is followed by the particle が then an adjective descriptor.

頭が いい	=	is smart/intelligent
背が 高い/低い	=	is tall/short (used for people's height)
目が いい	=	good eyesight
体が 弱い/強い	=	has a strong/weak body
足が 長い	=	long legged
耳が 遠い	=	hard of hearing
鼻が 高い	=	tall/high nosed*

* When describing facial features of people of European descent, Japanese often use the term "high" nose when describing an aquiline nose or classical "Greek" nose. This term can have a complimentary meaning. As an idiom, this phrase implies that someone is proud of something. When used to refer to someone else's excessive pride it can be a negative term. Take care in using it.

■ 自習 Self Check

1. 強い/弱い
How would you say the following in Japanese?

A) (name of your school's rival) is weak in baseball.
B) The kendo club is strong.
C) My (insert school club/team of your choice) is strong (or weak).

2. **Body parts and adjectives**
Try to say the following in Japanese using the names of people you know.

A) _____ is tall.
B) _____ is smart.
C) _____ has long legs.
D) _____ has good eyesight.

■ 練習の時間 Time for Practice

1. **Pair Practice**

Parts of the body
Point to a body part and ask your partner what it is. Your partner will say the name of that body part in Japanese. If correct, switch. If incorrect, teach your

 A-さん： (*point to your eye*) これは 何 ですか。
B-さん： それは 目です。

partner what the correct word is until he or she can say it, then switch roles. Keep speaking until both partners can smoothly say all the body parts introduced in this section.

2. **Whole Class Activity**

Here are the words for "Heads, Shoulders, Knees, and Toes" in Japanese. Practice singing with your class. Once you have mastered it, sing it faster, double-time!

3. **Pair Practice**

Kanji slapjack

Spread out your kanji cards for body parts on the table, face up. You will also need a picture of Benkei; draw one or enlarge the one on page 192. To play, choose one of the versions below, or come up with your own version.

- Version 1: Spread out your kanji cards for body parts on the table, face up. Your teacher, or another friend, calls out a Japanese vocabulary word. You and your partner see who can be the first to slap the correct kanji. The quickest "slapper" gets to keep the card.

- Version 2: You and your partner take turns picking up a kanji card and placing it in the correct place on the picture of Benkei. You must say the name of the body part as you set it in place. See how quickly you can move all the cards onto the picture of Benkei. Try to beat your time in the second round.

- Version 3: With the kanji cards already in place on the picture of Benkei, take turns saying a body part in Japanese. Your partner has two seconds to slap the correct card. If your partner slaps the correct card, that card belongs to him/her and is removed from play. If your partner slaps the wrong card, the card stays in play. Play ends when all the cards have been removed from Benkei. The player holding the most cards wins.

4. **Group Practice**

先生 Says

One person, the "leader," calls out a body part and then the verb "to touch" (*さわって下さい), with or without "先生 says" in front. When the "leader" uses "先生 says," everyone touches that body part, just like "Simon says. . ." When the leader omits this and only gives the command, no action should be taken. The last one standing gets to lead the next round.

> **例**
> **EXAMPLE**
>
> Leader: 先生 says "耳"を さわって下さい。 (Please touch your ear.)
> (Action: Everyone in the class should touch their ears.)
>
> Leader: 足を さわって下さい。
> (Action: No one in the class should touch their leg.)

* SAWATTE KUDASAI means "Please touch."

■ 文化箱 Culture Chest

平泉

Hiraizumi, with a population of about 9,000, is a small town in Iwate Prefecture in northern 本州. Around 1100, it served as the northern capital for the ruling Fujiwara Clan, and rivaled Kyoto in wealth and power for the next 100 years. Estimates vary, but at its peak the city's population may have reached one million, making Hiraizumi one of the largest cities in the world at the time.

The glory of Hiraizumi crashed in 1189 when Minamoto no Yoritomo destroyed the city as part of his plan to unite all Japan.

Two victims of the destruction of Hiraizumi are legendary today: Yoshitsune and Benkei. Yoshitsune, younger brother of the 将軍 (military ruler of all of Japan) Yoritomo, had helped his older brother in his rise to power. Mistrust and intrigue led Yoritomo to turn on his younger brother, forcing Yoshitsune to commit 切腹 (ritual suicide).

Benkei, Yoshitsune's samurai retainer (家来 in Japanese; a retainer is a type of servant or attendant), is legendary throughout Japan for his size, physical strength, and steadfast loyalty to his master. Saito Musashibō Benkei (1155–1189), known simply as Benkei, was a 僧兵 (Buddhist monk warrior). There are so many legends about Benkei that it is impossible to distinguish between fact and fiction. He is reported to have been over two meters tall at age seventeen. Legend has it that Benkei remained standing even after he died in Hiraizumi defending a bridge as he continued to fight to the end against all odds to save his master Yoshitsune from an invading army.

Tourists posing behind a faceless cutout of Benkei. Hiraizumi, Iwate.

■ キアラのジャーナル Kiara's Journal
きあら　　　じゃーなる

Read the journal entry below, and then answer these questions.

❶ What time of day did the TOKI no MON arrive at its next stop?
❷ What was the first thing Ben saw when he went outside?
❸ Who do Jun, Ben, and Kiara meet? What does this person invite them to do?

ジャーナルへ
じゃーなる

　　今朝、奈良の　友達に　さようならと　言いました。そして、また　時の門に　入りました。今、私は　ちょっと　寂しいです。でも　この　adventureは　楽しい　です。それと、時々　ちょっと　危ない　です。The way that　友さん　activates the　時の門は　まだ　ひみつです。時の門を　出た時は、午後4時　でした。友さんは、「ええっ・・・ここ　ですか。」と　言いました。

　　ベン君は、「どこですか。」と　聞きました。そして、「わあ！あの　家は　とても　大きい　ですね。あの　人達は　侍　ですか。」と、言いました。

　　じゅん君は、「そう　です。でも、ちょっと、静かに　して下さい。」と　言いました。

　　一人の　侍が　近くに　来ました。そして、「あなた達は、だれ　ですか。」と言いました。

　　友さんは、「私は　友です。あなたの　敵 (enemy) では　ありません。こちらは　じゅんと　ベンと　キアラ　です。私達は、あの　神社から　来ました。」と　言いました。

　　その侍さんは、「僕は　弁慶　です。源義経の　家来 (servant)です。」と　言いました。そして、「敵は　明日、will attack　と思います。」と言いました。

　　ベン君は、「弁慶さん　ですか。あなたは　とても有名　です。強い　侍　で、心も　広いですね。」と、言いました。そして、「ここは　平泉ですか。」と、聞きました。

　　友さんは、「そう　です。今は　1181年　です。弁慶さんは　とても　いい人　です。」と言いました。

　　ベン君 was excited and whispered、「弁慶は　昔話 (legend)の　中　だけの　人　だと思っていました！」

　　友さんは、「今、ベン君の　目の　前 (front)　に　いる　人は、本物 (real)　の弁慶さんですよ。」と、小さい　声で　言って、wink しました。

　　弁慶さんは、「私の　家に　来ませんか。八時半から　晩ご飯を　食べます。今晩は友達が、美味しい (tasty)　米 (uncooked rice) を　持って来ます。どうぞ来て下さい」と　言いました。

■ テクノの時間 Techno Time
てくの　　じかん

Though you've not been introduced to them all yet, type all of the vocabulary words from this chapter into your digital dictionary. Be sure to type first the kanji, then hiragana, and then the meaning in English as you have been doing. Remember to use your file labeled "JISHO" (in *romaji*). When you finish, go to TimeForJapanese.com and practice the vocabulary and kanji reviews for this chapter.

弁慶さんは、 とても 背が 高い ですね。
Benkei is very tall, isn't he!

1) 弁慶さんは、とても 背が 高い ですね。格好 いい です。

2) 父も、背が 高い です。

3) へえ。キアラさんの、お父さんは どんな 人 ですか。

4) 父は 目が 大きい です。ちょっと 太って います。足が 長い です。手がとても 大きい です。そして バスケット ボールが とても 上手 です。ベン君の お父さんは、背が 高い ですか。

5) 父ですか。ええ、まあまあ 高い です。鼻も 高い です。足は ちょっと 短い です。友さんの お父さんは どんな 狸 ですか。

6) 僕の父は、とても 背が 低いです。顔と 頭が 大きい です。おなかも 大きい です。太って います。そして、手と 足が 短い です。

7) 写真を 見せて 下さい。

8) ほら、これが お父さんの 写真 です。見て 下さい。とても かっこ いい 狸 です。

■ 会話 Dialogue
かいわ

ベン　　：弁慶さんは、とても　背が　高い　ですね。格好　いい　です。
べん　　べんけい　　　　せ　たか　　　　　　　かっこう

キアラ：父も、背が　高い　です。
きあら　　　　せ　たか

じゅん：へえ。キアラさんの、お父さんは、どんな　人　ですか。
　　　　　　　きあら

キアラ：父は、目が　大きい　です。ちょっと　太っています。足が　長い　です。手が　とて
きあら　　　め　　　　　　　　　　　　　ふと　　　　　　あし　なが　　　　　　
　　　　も　大きい　です。そして　*バスケットボールが　とても　上手　です。ベン君の　お
　　　　　　　　　　　　　　　ばすけっとぼーる　　　　　　じょうず　　べんくん
　　　　父さんは、背が　高い　ですか。
　　　　　　　せ　たか

ベン　　：父　ですか。ええ、まあまあ　高い　です。鼻も　高い　です。足は　ちょっと　短い
べん　　　　　　　　　　　　　たか　　　はな　たか　　　　　　　　　　　　みじか
　　　　です。友さんの　お父さんは、どんな　狸　ですか。
　　　　　　　　　　　　　　　　　たぬき

友　　　：僕の　父は、とても　背が　低い　です。顔と　頭が大きい　です。おなかも　大きい
　　　　ぼく　　　　　　せ　ひく　　かお　あたま　　　　　　　　　　　　　
　　　　です。太っています。そして、手と　足が　短い　です。
　　　　　ふと　　　　　　　　　　　　あし　みじか

ベンと　キアラと　じゅん：　写真を　見せて下さい。
べん　　きあら　　　　　　　しゃしん

友　　　：ほら、これが　お父さんの　写真　です。見て下さい。とても　かっこいい　狸です。
　　　　　　　　　　　　　　しゃしん　　　　　　　　　　　　　　　　たぬき

* バスケットボール is the former version of what most Japanese have shortened to just バスケ. It is common for "loan" words to be shortened
ばすけっとぼーる　　　　　　　　　　　　　　　　　　　　　　　　　　　　ばすけ
in Japanese.

■ 単語 New Words
たんご

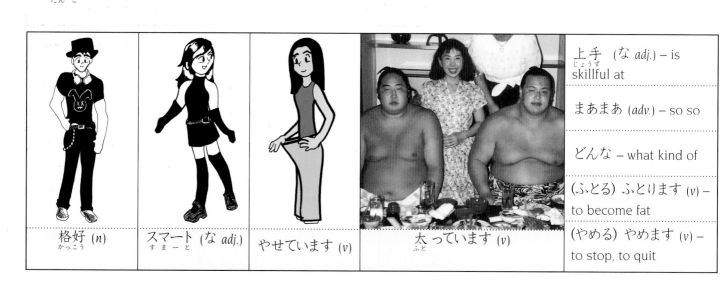

格好 (n) かっこう	スマート (な adj.) すまーと	やせています (v)	太っています (v) ふと	上手 (な adj.) – is じょうず skillful at
				まあまあ (adv.) – so so
				どんな – what kind of
				(ふとる) ふとります (v) – to become fat
				(やめる) やめます (v) – to stop, to quit

> ### Other words you might like to use:
>
> 渋い (い adj.) – tasteful, subtle
> しぶ
>
> おしゃれ (な adj.) – fashionable

■ 漢字 Kanji
_{かんじ}

平 1 2 4 3 **5 strokes**	ヘイ; たいら – even, flat _{へ　い}		一	フ	ㄅ	立	平		
	平安時代 – the Heian Period; 平 – Taira (family _{へいあんじだい}　　　　　　　_{たいら} name), flat								
	This KANJI has a post firmly planted in the ground (the vertical stroke). Two strong horizontal supports keep the top roof EVEN and FLAT.								

和 **8 strokes**	ワ – peace and harmony; ancient name for Japan _わ	㇒	二	千	禾	禾	利	和	和
	平和 – peace; 和食 – Japanese meal; 和室 – Japanese- _{へいわ}　　_{わしょく}　　　　_{わしつ} style room; 和服 – Japanese-style clothing _{わふく}								
	The right side is mouth (口). We would have more PEACE AND HARMONY if everyone sat quietly under a tree (strokes 2–5), silently meditating without using their mouths.								

低 **7 strokes**	ひく (い) – short, low	ノ	イ	亻	仸	任	低	低	
	低い – short, low (height) _{ひく}								
	The left part of this kanji is a standing person (人). The right side is 氏, which means "clan" or "family" with the kanji for one (一) as the final stroke. Think of this as one entire clan of very SHORT (vertically-challenged) people with the final stroke representing a floor that the clan can barely rise above.								

太 **4 strokes**	タイ; ふと (い) – large, deep (voice); _{たい}　　　_い ふと (る) – to become fat	一	ナ	大	太				
	太る – to become large or fat; 太鼓 – large (fat) _{ふと}　　　　　　　　　_{たいこ} Japanese drum; 太平洋 – Pacific Ocean _{たいへいよう}								
	This is the KANJI for a big (大) dog (犬) that has just caught one too many biscuits and is beginning to get FAT.								

■ 言葉の探索 Language Detection
_{こと ば　　たんさく}

1. て-form of verbs

   Another conjugation for verbs in Japanese is the て-form. You were introduced to this form in Chapter 1, when you practiced classroom commands. The て-form has several uses:

   A. to give commands (section 6-2)

   B. to ask and give permission (or) to deny permission (6-3)

   C. to show the present progressive tense (i.e., "is doing something") (6-4)

   D. to connect two or more verbs (in the same sentence) (6-5)

How to form the TE form:

Type 1

The て-form conjugation for Type 1 verbs varies depending on the "verb stem" (the hiragana that comes just before the ます ending in the polite form of the verb). If that stem is a hiragana sound from the い row of the hiragana chart (い, き, ぎ, し, ち, に, ひ, び, み, or り), then it is a Type 1 verb.

<u>Verb Stem</u>   Examples:

Verb Stem			Examples		
み			読みます	→	読んで
に	→	んで	死にます	→	死んで
び			遊びます	→	遊んで
い			会います	→	会って
ち	→	って	待ちます	→	待って
り			とります	→	とって
き	→	いて	書きます	→	書いて
Exception to this rule:			いきます	→	いって
ぎ	→	いで	泳ぎます	→	泳いで
し	→	して	話します	→	話して

To remember how to convert Type 1 verbs to the て-form, sing this song to the tune of "Three Blind Mice."

て-Form Song

Type 1 Verbs (Chapters 1-6)

	non-past (〜ます)	non-past negative (〜ません)	〜て -form	dictionary form (infinitive form)	English meaning
み に び	飲みます	飲みません	飲んで	飲む	to drink
	読みます	読みません	読んで	読む	to read
い ち り	言います	言いません	言って	言う	to say
	手伝います	手伝いません	手伝って	手伝う	to help
	待ちます	待ちません	待って	待つ	to wait
	帰ります	帰りません	帰って	帰る	to return home
	座ります	座りません	座って	座る	to sit
	知ります	知りません	知って	知る	to know
	(写真)をとります	とりません	とって	とる	to take (a photo)
	入ります	入りません	入って	入る	to enter, go into
	あります	ありません	あって	ある	to exist (inanimate)
	太ります	太りません	太って	太る	to grow fat
	分かります	分かりません	分かって	分かる	to understand
き	聞きます	聞きません	聞いて	聞く	to listen, to hear
	開きます	開きません	開いて	開く	to open books
*	行きます	行きません	行って	行く	to go
ぎ	泳ぎます	泳ぎません	泳いで	泳ぐ	to swim
し	話します	話しません	話して	話す	to speak

*行きます is an exception to the song above because the き does not become いて but instead って。

Type 2 Verbs

To create the TE form from the ます form of Type 2 verbs , simply drop the ます and add て to the verb stem.

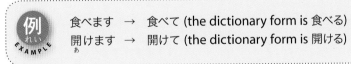

例 EXAMPLE 食べます　→　食べて (the dictionary form is 食べる)
　　　　　　　開けます　→　開けて (the dictionary form is 開ける)

Type 2 Verbs (Chapters 1–6)

non-past (〜ます)	non-past negative (〜ません)	〜て -form	dictionary form (infinitive form)	English meaning
開けます	開けません	開けて	開ける	to open (doors/windows)
います	いません	いて	いる	to exist (animate)
しめます	しめません	しめて	しめる	to close (doors/windows)
食べます	食べません	食べて	食べる	to eat
とじます	とじません	とじて	とじる	to close
はじめます	はじめません	はじめて	はじめる	to begin, start
見ます	見ません	見て	見る	to look or to see
見せます	見せません	見せて	見せる	to show

Irregular verbs (します and 来ます)

します (to do) and 来ます (to come) are exceptions because they are irregular verbs. Their て-forms are:

します　　→　　して (the dictionary form is する)
来ます　　→　　来て (the dictionary form is 来る)

Irregular Verbs

non-past (〜ます)	non-past negative (〜ません)	〜て -form	dictionary form (infinitive form)	English meaning
来ます	来ません	来て	来る	to come
します	しません	して	する	to do

2. Commands/requests

You can make familiar (or informal) commands in Japanese simply by putting verbs in the て-form.

A) 本を　読んで。　　= Read the book.
B) 立って。　　= Stand up.
C) 座って。　　= Sit down.

Polite requests can be made by adding 下さい (*please*) after the TE form verb:

A) 食べて　下さい。　　= Please eat.
B) 手伝って　下さい。　　= Please help.
C) 学校に　来て　下さい。 = Please come to school.

3. すこし、とても、ちょっと、まあまあ

Adverbs are words that modify adjectives, verbs, or other adverbs. As with English, in Japanese adverbs generally come before the words they modify. Notice the use of は (topic marker) and が (subject marker).

A) 久美子さんは　頭が　とても　いい　です。 = Kumiko is really smart.
B) ゆみさんは　体が　ちょっと　弱い　です。 = Yumi's body is a little weak.
C) 先生は　少し　ハンサム　です。 = The teacher is a little good looking.

■ 自習 Self Check

1. て-form

Say the following out loud to yourself in Japanese, putting the following verbs in their て-form. Is each a Type 1 verb or a Type 2 verb?

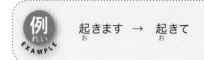

起きます　→　起きて

A) 言います
B) 飲みます
C) 食べます
D) 来ます
E) 帰ります

2. Polite commands

Try to say the following in Japanese, changing the verbs into the て-forms.

A) Please do it. (します)
B) Please return home. (帰ります)
C) Please go to the library. (行きます)

3. すこし、ちょっと、まあまあ、とても adverbs

Use one of these adverbs to say the following in Japanese:

Ichiro's eyes are a little weak.　→　一郎さんは　目が　ちょっと弱い　です。

A) Emi has very good vision.
B) Mr. Yamamoto is kind of long legged.
C) _____ is a little smart.

■ 練習の時間 Time for Practice

1. **Pair Practice**

Use the verbs in the verb charts on pages 203 and 204 to practice making the て-form. A-さん should read the verbs in the left column and B-さん should say the TE form (looking at the chart as little as possible). Take turns.

2. **Small Group Practice**

The leader calls out a verb in English (see pages 203–204 for a list of verbs). The first person in the group to raise his/her hand and correctly state the て-form becomes the next caller.

3. **Group Practice**

Play "Sensei Says (TE form of verb) 下さい." The "leader" calls out commands including both those you learned in Chapter 1-6 and those that use a body part plus さわって下さい from Chapter 6-1.

■ 文化箱 Culture Chest
ぶん か ばこ

松尾芭蕉
まつお ばしょう

Matsuo Basho, Japan's most famous haiku poet, is forever linked with Hiraizumi. He was famous for traveling the countryside to find inspiration for his haiku poems. In one work, 奥の細道 "The Narrow Road to the Back Country," おく　　ほそみち Basho traveled to and around northern Japan. In 1689, Basho gazed upon the abandoned fields of the former great city of Hiraizumi as he wrote:

夏草や　　　　　*Ah, summer grass!*
なつくさ

兵　どもが　　　*All that remains*
つわもの

夢の跡　　　　　*Of the warriors' dreams.*
ゆめ　あと

The 5-7-5 syllable pattern haiku is probably the most well known among the various types of Japanese poems. Can you make your own haiku in English and Japanese?

Here is one for inspiration with the 5-7-5 syllable pattern in both English and Japanese:

Time for Japanese　　　　この本を
　　　　　　　　　　　　　　ほん

If you study hard each day　毎日読んで
　　　　　　　　　　　　　　まいにち　よ

You will learn a lot!　　　よく学ぶ
　　　　　　　　　　　　　　　　まな

■ 地図 Map Skills
ち　ず

平泉 is an ancient Japanese city in northern Japan, a region called Tohoku. Use the map in the back of your
ひらいずみ
book to find the location of Hiraizumi on this map. Then use your book and other resources to answer the following questions.

❶ What modern-day prefecture is 平泉 located in?
　　　　　　　　　　　　　　　ひらいずみ

❷ When was 平泉 a thriving city and what was the name of the clan that controlled the area?
　　　　　ひらいずみ

❸ Name three of the surrounding prefectures (provinces).

❹ About how far (in kilometers) is 平泉 from Tokyo?
　　　　　　　　　　　　　　　ひらいずみ

キアラのジャーナル Kiara's Journal
きあら　じゃーなる

Read the journal entry below, and then answer these questions.

❶ What does Kiara say about Benkei's hair?
❷ What has been happening between Yoshitsune and his older brother?
❸ Where did Kiara see Benkei and Yoshitsune?

ジャーナルへ
じゃーなる

　昨日、弁慶さんに　会いました。そして、晩ご飯を　いっしょに (together)　食べました。弁慶さんは　目が　ちょっと　大きい　です。それから、髪の　毛が　とても　長いです。ちょっと　太っています。とても　強い　です。そして、弁慶さんは　とても　いい人です。

　でも、ここは　ちょっと　こわい　です。ベン君は、「源義経と　彼の　お兄さんは前から　けんかしていました (have been fighting).」と　言いました。

　今朝、私達は　お寺で、弁慶さんと　義経さんを　見ました。二人は、大きい　桜の木の　下 (under)　に　いました。義経さんには、ひげが　ありました。とても　かっこいいscenery　でした。そして、私は、それを　見て　びっくりしました (was very surprised).「皆さん、これを　見てください！」と　言って、私は、友さんと、じゅん君と、ベン君に、スケッチブックを　見せました。皆、「あっ！」と、びっくりしました。私は、「去年、アメリカの学校の　図書館で　この絵を　描きました。」と、言いました。友さんが、「義経さんと弁慶さんの　浮世絵 (woodblock print)ですね。」と、言いました。「はい、色鉛筆 (colored pencils)で、コピーしました。」と、私は、言いました。

　It was really interesting to see in real life what I had seen in an art book from my library last year!

　Just like in the picture, 義経さんは　ハンサムです。彼は、渋いです。弁慶さんは、目がとても　いいです。それに、背が　高い　です。そして、二人は、とても、かっこいいです。

■ テクノの時間 Techno Time
てくの　じかん

Using 15 new vocabulary words from this chapter, create a crossword puzzle. Use Japanese words (in hiragana) in the puzzle and their English definitions as the clues.

お茶を　飲んでも　いい　ですか。
May I drink some green tea?

1) キアラさん、大丈夫 ですか。

2) ちょっと、頭が 痛いです。

3) 少し 熱が ありますね。

4) 風邪 ですね。無理を しては いけません。この お茶を　飲んで 下さい。体に いい ですよ。

5) ありがとう。ちょっと 布団で 昼寝しても いい ですか。

6) 僕も、その お茶を 飲んでも いいですか。それと、僕も、昼寝しても いい ですか。

7) 友さんも、風邪 ですか。

8) いいえ。すみません、美味しい 飲み物と 昼寝が とても 好き ですから・・・・。

9) 友さん、キアラさんは、病気 ですよ！

会話 Dialogue
（かいわ）

じゅん　：　キアラさん、大丈夫　ですか。

キアラ　：　ちょっと、頭が　痛い　です。

弁慶　：　少し　熱が　ありますね。

ベン　：　風邪　ですね。無理を　してはいけません。このお茶を　飲んで下さい。体に　いい
です。よ。

キアラ　：　ありあがとう。ちょっと　布団で　昼寝しても　いい　ですか。

友　：　僕も、そのお茶を　飲んでも　いい　ですか。それと、僕も、昼寝　しても　いい
です。か。

弁慶　：　友さんも、風邪　ですか。

友　：　いいえ。すみません、美味しい飲み物と　昼寝が　とても　好きですから・・・・

ベン　：　友さん、キアラさんは、病気ですよ！

単語 New Words
（たんご）

熱 (n)（ねつ）	風邪 (n)（かぜ）	ジュース (n)（じゅーす）	布団 (n)（ふとん）	昼寝 (n)（ひるね）	医者 (n)（いしゃ）
病気 (n) -（びょうき）- illness, sickness	病院 (n)（びょういん）	薬 (n)（くすり）	無理 (な adj.)（むり）	大丈夫 (な adj.)（だいじょうぶ）	痛い (い adj.)（いた）

昼寝 (を)　する/します (v) – to take a nap
（ひるね）

* 薬 (を)　飲む/飲みます (v) – to take medicine
（くすり）（の）（の）
*Note: when medicine is consumed, the verb for "to drink" is used.

具合が悪い (exp.) – sick, feel bad
（ぐあい）（わる）

心配 (を)　する/（しんぱい）します (v)	けが (を)　する/します (v)	無理しないで下さい (exp.)

風邪 (を)　引く/引きます (v) – to catch a cold
（かぜ）（ひ）（ひ）

> **Other useful health related expressions you might like to know:**
>
> 救急車 (を)　呼んで下さい。　(exp.) – Please call an ambulance.
> きゅうきゅうしゃ　　よ
> 看護婦 (n) – nurse
> かんごふ
> 健康 (n) – health
> けんこう
> 健康に　いい　です (exp.) – It is good for your health.
> けんこう

■ 漢字 Kanji
かんじ

7 strokes	イ – related to medicine or the medical field	一	丆	亐	三	歪	矢	医
	医(者) – doctor; 医(学) – study of medicine							
	矢 is an arrow and this one is enclosed on three sides in a shelter. If this arrow were to puncture the outer surface, a lot of MEDICINE would surely be needed!							

者　8 strokes	シャ, もの – person	一	十	土	耂	耂	者	者	者
	(医)者 – doctor ; (学)者 – scholar							
	The top of this kanji is soil (土) or earth, while the bottom is sun (日). A PERSON has started tying these two together with one large stitch of the needle and thread.							

薬　16 strokes	くすり – medicine	一	十	艹	丗	艹	苧	苩	苩
	薬 – medicine; 薬 (屋) – drugstore, apothecary	苩	洭	渶	蓙	蓙	薬	薬	薬
	A leafy plant (the first three strokes appear in kanji related to plants) is growing up a tree (木), but it is sickly and white (白), with drops of sap shooting out all over (the 4 strokes to the side of white). It seems in need of some tender loving care and some MEDICINE.							

■ 言葉の探索 Language Detection
ことば　たんさく

1. ・・・てもいい　です。　You may . . .

    You learned several phrases using this pattern in the Classroom Expressions section of Chapter 1. Here, you will learn how to create more phrases that grant permission. This pattern uses a verb in the て-form followed by もいい です. To ask permission, add a か to the end.

    Note that it is common, but not mandatory, to put よ at the end of a sentence in which you are giving someone permission.

お寿司を　食べても　いい　ですか。	= May I eat sushi?
はい、(お寿司を)　食べても　いい　です(よ)。	= Yes, you may eat (it).
ロッカーへ　行っても　いい　ですか。	= May I go to my locker?
はい、(ロッカーへ) 行っても　いい　です(よ)。	= Yes, you may go (to your locker).
スペイン語で　話しても　いい　ですか。	= May I speak in Spanish?
はい、(スペイン語で) 話しても　いい　です(よ)。	= Yes, you may speak (in Spanish).

2. ・・・ては　いけません

To deny someone permission to do something, use the て-form of a verb followed by は いけません (the は here is the particle は, using the "wa" sound).

この　まどを　開けても　いい　ですか。	= May I open this window?
いいえ、(まどを)　開けては　いけません。	= No, you may not open it.
その　薬を　飲んでも　いい　ですか。	= May I take that medicine?
いいえ、この　薬を　飲んでは　いけません。	= No, you may not take this medicine.
けん君の　家へ　行っても　いいですか。	= May I go to Ken's house?
いいえ、　行っては　いけません。	= No, you may not.

A more casual way to deny permission is to use だめ in place of いけません。

| ペンで　書いてもいいですか。 | = May I write with a pen? |
| いいえ、ペンで　書いては　だめです。 | = No, you cannot write with a pen. |

3. Review of で meaning "by means of" or "using such and such"

The particle で can mean "by means of" or "using such and such" as you learned in Chapter 3 section 4.

先生は　英語で　話します。	= The teacher speaks in (using) English.
日本人は　箸で　食べます。	= Japanese eat by means of chopsticks.
私は　鉛筆で　漢字を　書きます。	= I write kanji with (using) a pencil.

As introduced in Chapter 4 section 3, the particle で can also indicate the place of action (for example, 学校で 昼ご飯 を食べました。= At school I ate lunch).

■ 自習 Self Check

1. Use the 〜てもいいですか pattern to ask permission to do the following.

A) May I stand up?　　　立って＿＿＿＿＿＿＿ですか。
B) May I sit down?　　　＿＿＿＿＿＿＿も　いい　ですか。
C) May I write?
D) May I read the book?

2.　Use the 〜てもいい　です pattern to give permission to do the following:

A)　You may look.

B)　You may eat.

C)　You may return home.

D)　You may go to the cafeteria.

E)　On Saturday, you may go to Tokyo.

F)　In March you may go to your grandmother's house.

G)　On Tuesday you may eat pizza.

3.　Use Japanese to tell someone they may not do the following:

A)　You may not drink.　　　　　　飲んで＿＿＿＿＿＿＿＿いけません。

B)　You may not go.　　　　　　　　行って　＿＿＿＿＿＿＿＿＿＿＿。

C)　You may not go to the restroom.

D)　You may not go to your locker.

E)　You may not eat.

4.　Use the particle で after the word (tool), which is the "means" by which something is done. Say the following in Japanese:

A)　May I write with a pen?　　　　＿＿＿＿＿＿＿＿書いても　いい　ですか。

B)　You may eat sushi with chopsticks.

C)　You may not speak in English.

■ 練習の時間 Time for Practice
れんしゅう　　じかん

1.　**Pair Practice**

Politely request each of the following. Your partner can grant or deny your request as he/she sees fit. Take turns.

> *You want to write in hiragana.*
> **You:** ひらがなで　書いてもいいですか。
> **Your partner:** いいえ、ひらがなで　書いてはいけません。 -OR- はい、ひらがなで　書いてもいいです。

A)　You are thirsty.

B)　You want to eat cake.

C)　You want to sit down.

D)　You want to take a nap.

E)　You want to go to the library.

F)　You want to return home at 11 p.m.

G)　You want to play tennis today.

H)　You want to eat dinner at 9:30 p.m.

2.　**Pair Practice**

Use the cues below to create questions using the particle で. Your partner should answer according to his/her own circumstances. Take turns.

> (Do you) come to school by bus?
> **You:** バスで　学校へ　来ますか。
> ばす
> **Your partner:** いいえ、私は、バスで　学校へ　来ません。-OR- はい、私は、毎日　バスで　学校へ　来ます。

A)　eat spaghetti with chopsticks

B)　do homework with a pencil

C)　go to the bookstore by taxi（タクシー）
たくしー

D)　go to France by boat（ふね）

E)　play tennis using a racquet（ラケット）
らけっと

F)　type（タイプを　します）a letter on a computer
たいぷ
（コンピューター）
こんぴゅーたー

3. Charades

Take a slip of paper from your teacher. Your job is to silently act out the illness or physical problem. Your classmates will try to guess what your problem is.

Class: どう　しましたか。　= What happened?
熱が　ありますか。　= Do you have a fever?

■ 文化箱 Culture Chest
ぶん　か　ばこ

Chinese and Japanese Medicine

Did you know that Japanese men and women often live to be among the oldest people in the world? Credit for this longevity goes partly to Japan's modern medical care and national health insurance system, but no doubt in large measure to the extremely healthy traditional Japanese diet.

If you get sick while in Japan, you are likely to be taken to a hospital since Japanese tend to use hospitals, clinics, and doctor's offices more often than in some other cultures. As modern as Japan's medical system is, traditional Chinese herbs, remedies, and medical practices are also widely available in Japan and have been used to some extent since the Nara Period in the 700s.

The 20th century saw a tremendous increase in the import of Western foods and drinks into Japan. While the traditional Japanese diet is heavily based upon fish products and rice, the influx of sugars and meats is affecting the height and weight of many Japanese. It will be interesting to see what impact Western foods and drinks such as cheeseburgers and colas will have on the health and lifespan of Japanese people in the future.

■ キアラのジャーナル Kiara's Journal
きあら　じゃーなる

Read the journal entry below, and then answer these questions.

❶ What was the weather like in Hiraizumi at the time that Kiara and her friends were there?
❷ What did Benkei loan Kiara?
❸ How was Kiara feeling?
❹ What changed how Kiara was feeling?

ジャーナルへ
じゃーなる

　今、平泉は　ちょっと　寒い　です。弁慶さんは、いい　ジャケットを　着ていました。
ひらいずみ　　　　　　　　　　べんけい　　　　　　　　　じゃけっと
私は　弁慶さんに、「ジャケット (jacket)を　借りても　いい　です か。」と　言いました。He
じゃけっと　　　か
didn't really understand the word "jacket," but through my gestures, he caught on.

　弁慶さんは、「いい　ですよ。」と　言いました。彼は、やさしい　人です。

　私は　ちょっと　風邪を　引きました。ここには、ティッシュは、ありません。お医者さんも
かぜ　ひ　　　　　　　　　　　　　　　　　　　　　　　いしゃ
いません。薬も　ありません。弁慶さんは　私の　事を　心配しました。(The rest were a little worried
こと　しんぱい
too.)　そして、「キアラさん、大丈夫　ですか。少し　熱が　ありますね。」と　言いました。
だいじょうぶ　　　すこ　ねつ

　私は、「はい、少し　あります。でも、大丈夫　です。もう　ちょっと　寝ます。」と　言い
ました。

　ベン君は、「キアラさん、この　お茶を　飲んで下さい。体に　いいですよ。」と　言いました。
くん　　　　　　　　　　　ちゃ
私は、「いただきます。どうも　有り難う。」と　言いました。その後、六時間ぐらい　昼寝
あと　じかん　ひるね
しました。そして、元気に　なりました。
げんき

私達は　洋服を　着ています。

第6課の4　**We are wearing Western clothing.**

■ 会話 Dialogue
（かいわ）

弁慶　　：　あなた達の　服は　とても　かっこ　いい　ですね。
（べんけい）

じゅん　：　これは　学校の　制服　です。
（せいふく）

ベン　　：　*21世紀の　学校の　服　です。
（べん）（せいき）（ふく）

弁慶　　：　着物では　ありませんね。
（べんけい）（きもの）

じゅん　：　そう　ですね。私達は　洋服を　着ています。
（ようふく）（き）

ベン　　：　見て下さい。私達は、シャツと　ジャケットを　着ています。そして、パンツを　はい
（べん）（み）（しゃ）（じゃけっと）（き）（ぱんっ）
　　　　　ています。靴下と　靴も、はいています。
　　　　　（くつした）（くつ）

キアラ　：　私は、スカートを　はいています。。
（きあら）（すかーと）

弁慶　　：　それは　侍の　服　ですね。あなたは　侍　ですか。私も、その　スカートを　はい
（べんけい）（さむらい）（ふく）（さむらい）（すかーと）
　　　　　ても　いい　ですか。

キアラ　：　いいえ、私は　侍では　ありません。そして、これは、侍の　服では　ありません。
（きあら）（さむらい）（さむらい）（ふく）
　　　　　この　スカートは　女の子の　制服　です。
　　　　　（すかーと）（おんなのこ）（せいふく）

弁慶　　：　21世紀は　へん　ですね。
（べんけい）

* 21世紀 – 21st century

■ 単語 New Words
（たんご）

服 (n) ふく	着物 (n) きもの	洋服 (n) ようふく	ジャケット (n) じゃけっと	ズボン (n)
靴 (n) くつ	靴下 (n) くつした	スカート (n) すかーと	ジーンズ (n) じーんず	眼鏡 (n) めがね
スーツ (n) すーつ	ネクタイ (n) ねくたい	ドレス (n) どれす	イヤリング (n) いやりんぐ	メイク (n) めいく

| 女の人 (n) おんな ひと | 女の子 (n) おんな こ | 男の人 (n) おとこ ひと | 男の子 (n) おとこ こ | 着る/着ます (v) き き |
| 被る/被ります (v) かぶ かぶ | 履く/履きます (v) は は | する/します (v) | かける/かけます (v) | 住む/住みます (v) す す |

(お)餅 (n) – pounded rice cake
もち

下着 (n) – underwear
したぎ

パンツ (n) – underwear
ぱん つ

シンプル (な adj.) – simple
しんぷる

普通 (な adj./adv) – ordinary, usual
ふつう

すてき (な adj.) – lovely, beautiful

人 (n) – person/people
ひと

ハンサム (な adj.) – handsome
はんさむ

*する or します means "to wear" (as in jewelry) and "to do." It can be used alone or in conjunction with some nouns to form a variety of verbs. Some examples of this usage include:

| タイプ(を)　する/します たいぷ |
| ハイキング(を)　する/します はいきんぐ |
| すもう(を)　する/します |
| 空手(を)　する/します からて |

■ 漢字 Kanji
かんじ

着

1 2 3 5 6 着 12 strokes	き(る) – to wear	丶	丷	丷	丷	半	半	羊
	着(る) – to wear (above the waist); き 着(物) – traditional Japanese dress き もの	着	着	着	着			
	The top section of this kanji looks like 羊 or "sheep." And the bottom half is 目 or "eye." What sort of outfit could you WEAR to catch ひつじ the sheep's eye? Another way that you might remember it is that the eye that you see is WEARing a really nice wool sweater.							

■ 言葉の探索 Language Detection

1. **The present progressive tense: て-form + います。**
   To say that someone is in the process of doing something, use the て-form of a verb plus います。

   A) キアラ さんは　せんべいを　食べて　います。　　= Kiara is eating senbei.
   B) 山口先生は　平泉に　住んで　います。　　= Mr. Yamaguchi lives in Hiraizumi.
   C) 花子さんは　ながいスカーフを　しています。　　= Hanako is wearing a long scarf.

2. **Verbs for "to wear"**
   Japanese uses many verbs for the English word "wear." To say someone is wearing an article of clothing or an accessory, use the correct verb in the ています form.

   A) 着て　います (wearing something from the waist up or something like a robe or a kimono)
   B) 履いて　います (wearing something below the waist, such as pants, shoes, or socks)
   C) 被って　います (wearing something on the head, such as a hat or helmet)
   D) して　います (wearing jewelry or other accessories such as a scarf)
   E) かけて　います (wearing glasses or sunglasses)

   A) 森山君は　ずぼんを　履いて　います。　　= Mr. Moriyama is wearing slacks.
   B) 高橋先生は　帽子を　被って　います。　　= Ms. Takahashi is wearing a hat.
   C) けい子さんは　ネックレスを　して　います。　　= Keiko is wearing a necklace.

3. **The negative present progressive: て-form + いません。**
   To say someone is NOT in the process of doing something, use the verb in the て-form plus いません。

   A) キアラさんは　靴下を　履いて　いません。　= Kiara is not wearing any socks.
   B) 花子さんは　日本に　住んで　いません。　= Hanako is not living in Japan.
   C) けい子さんは　メガネを　かけていません。　= Keiko is not wearing glasses.

■ 自習 Self Check

1. **The present progressive tense, positive and negative: て-form + います／いません**
   Try to say the following in Japanese:

   A) I am reading a good book.　　　　　　私は　いい　本を　_____。
   B) I live in Nagoya.
   C) The first year students are eating with chopsticks.
   D) The third year high school students are not living here.　高校三年生は　_____。
   E) Grandmother is not drinking green tea.

2.   **Verbs for wearing**

Try to say the following in Japanese:

A) Tomo is wearing a hat.
B) Kenji's older sister is wearing a kimono.
C) Ben's younger brother is not wearing any pants!

友さんは　ぼうしを　_____。

■ 練習の時間 Time for Practice
れんしゅう　じかん

1.   **Pair Practice**

Use the cards provided by your sensei. Person A uses the ています form to describe what the figures on his/her card are doing. Person B draws a picture of it.

2.   **Pair Practice**

Use verbs of wearing and the ています form to describe someone in the photo here or someone near you. Your partner should try to guess who you are describing. Keep adding clues until your partner guesses correctly. Take turns.

例
れい
EXAMPLE

Tーシャツを　着ています。
しゃつ　き
-OR- スカートを　はいています。
すか－と

3.   **Pair Practice**

Use the pictures below and the actions of the people around you to practice saying what others are doing. Use the て います pattern with verbs of action to make your statements.

例
れい
EXAMPLE

本を　読んでいます。
タコスを　食べています。

■ 文化箱 Culture Chest
ぶんかばこ

岩手県 Iwate Prefecture
いわてけん

Hiraizumi lies in Iwate Prefecture in northern Japan. The name 岩手 comes from a legend in which a demon was driven
いわて
out of the prefecture and forced to put his hand (手) print in a rock (岩) to symbolize his promise to never come back.

Iwate is the home of the beloved Japanese children's story writer Kenji Miyazawa (1896–1933), beautiful Mt. Iwate, saw-toothed coastline, and a number of good ski resorts. One of the most famous foods in Morioka, the capital of Iwate, is 煎餅, a snack that is a combination of a cracker and cookie. There are a wide variety of types and flavors of senbei and they can be found all over Japan.

Hiraizumi is famous for 餅, a type of sticky rice cake. Perhaps Hiraizumi became famous for mochi due to the name of one type of mochi sold in Hiraizumi, 弁慶 の 力餅. The name is a pun since "chikaramochi" usually means someone who has strength (力持ち), so the name of the Hiraizumi treat can also mean "Benkei the Strongman." Mochi is extremely popular throughout Japan, especially during the New Year's holidays.

■ キアラのジャーナル Kiara's Journal

Read the journal entry below, and then answer these questions.

❶ What are traditional pants called in Japanese?
❷ What did Tomo do when he was away from the group?
❸ Who does Kiara want to give mochi to?

ジャーナルへ

弁慶さんは、侍の 服を 着ています。恰好いい です。とても ハンサム です。ベン君は 弁慶さんの 侍の 服を 着たかったです。じゅん君は、「その ぼうしを かぶっても いい です か。」と、弁慶さんに 聞きました。

弁慶さんは、「いい ですよ。この はかま (traditional pants)も 履きますか。ジャケットも 着ますか。」と 言いました。

じゅん君は、「すごい！ どうも ありがとう ございます。」と言って、「ベン君、侍の ぼうしを かぶりませんか。」と、ベン君に 聞きました。

ベン君は、「侍の ぼうしを かぶっても いい ですか。」と 弁慶さんに 聞きました。

弁慶さんは、「ええ、大丈夫 ですよ。かぶってみて下さい。あれ、ところで (by the way) 友さんは どこ ですか。」と 言いました。

その時 (at that time)、友さんが 来ました。彼は、「僕は お餅を 少し 食べて 来ました。ここの お餅は とても おいしいですよ！」と 言いました。

私は、「わ！私達に、お餅の おみやげを 持って 来ましたか。昨日その お餅を 見ました。」と 言いました。

友さんは、「ア・・・ア・・・ ごめんなさい。忘れました。でも、あちこち (here and there) に たくさん ありますよ。」と 言いました。

後でみんなで、お餅を 食べに 行きました。平泉の お餅は とても おいしい です。母にも あげたいです。

弁慶さんに　会って、たくさん　話して、歴史を　勉強しました。
We met Benkei, talked a lot, and studied history.

■ 会話 Dialogue

弁慶　：　平泉 は、どう でしたか。

ベン　：　とても きれい でした。

じゅん：　弁慶 さんに 会って、たくさん 話して、歴史を 勉強 して、文化も 勉強 して、・・・

キアラ：　日本語も たくさん 勉強 して、病気もして・・・・

ベン　：　キアラ さん、ここで 冗談を 言っては いけません。

友：　　　おいしい 食べ物を 食べて、おいしい 飲み物も 飲みました。

弁慶　：　キアラさん、どんな 単語を 勉強 しましたか。

キアラ：　これは 目、これは 鼻、これは 口、これは 耳、これは 頭、そして、これは 手、
　　　　　これは 足です。もっと 言っても いい ですか。

友　　：　もう時間 です。皆さん、行きますよ！弁慶さん、さようなら。

弁慶　：　さようなら。*21世紀の、+弁慶の ファンに よろしく。

皆　　：　分かりました。では、さようなら。ありがとう。

*21世紀 – 21st century

+弁慶 の ファン – a fan of Benkei

■ 単語 New Words

文化 (n)	どう でしたか。(inter.)	経験 (n) – (an) experience
		素晴しい (い adj.) – wonderful
		…に よろしく (exp.) – say hello to … (for me)
		習う/習います (v) – to learn

■ 言葉の探索 Language Detection

I. Multiple verbs using the て-form

To list a series of actions in one sentence, put all of the verbs into the て-form except for the last verb. The tense of the entire sentence is determined by the tense of the final verb.

1. 私は 朝ご飯を 食べて、音楽を 聞いて、学校へ 行きました。 = I ate breakfast, listened to music, and went to school.

2. 友は ラーメンを 食べて、ジュースを 飲んで 寝ます。 = Tomo eats ramen, drinks juice, and then sleeps.

■ 自習 Self Check
じしゅう

1. Multiple verbs using the て-form
    How would you say the following in Japanese?

    A) Ben put on his shirt, ate breakfast, and then came to the high school.
    B) I will eat ramen (noodles), take a nap, and then go to the library.
    C) I read the book, did homework, and then went to sleep.

■ 練習の時間 Time for Practice
れんしゅう　じかん

---

1. **Pair Practice**

    Translate the following sentences into Japanese. Take turns, remembering to use the て-form to link the actions. Also remember that the tense of the sentence is determined by the final verb.

    A) I woke up, ate breakfast, and came to school.
    B) I will go home, eat some mochi, and study.
    C) I ate lunch, went to English class, and talked with my friend.
    D) I studied, did/practiced judo, and returned home.
    E) I talked with my friend, ate dinner, and read a book.
    F) I caught a cold, took some medicine, and took a nap.
    G) I will go to baseball practice, eat dinner, and watch TV.

---

2. **Pair Practice**

    Using the verb list in section 6-2, think of a short story with lots of action (use at least five verbs). Tell your story to your partner, who will try to illustrate it. Do not look at the drawing until it is finished! Use the past tense. Take turns.

    You might say: 私は、朝ご飯を　食べて、学校へ　行って、友だちと　話して　音楽のクラスに　行きました。
    あさ　はん　　　　　　　　　　　　　　　　　　　　　　　　　　　　　おんが　くらす
    勉強　して、それから、部活を　しました。テストの　成績は　だめ　でした。
    べんきょう　　　　　　　　　ぶかつ　　　　　　　　　　　せいせき

    Your partner draws a picture showing you eating breakfast, going to school, talking to your friends, and going to music class. Then he/she draws you studying, participating in a club activity, and not doing very well on a test.

---

3. **Group Practice**

    Take turns going to the front of the classroom and miming an action (without speaking). The class has to call out the action in Japanese, using the ています form.

■ 文化箱 Culture Chest

東北

The northern six prefectures, or provinces, of 本州 are referred to collectively as 東北. The characters for east (東) and north (北) are used in this order. (In English the reverse, "northeast," is normally used.) This is one of the more rural parts of the country. 東北 had a reputation in Japan as being a remote and distant countryside long before Basho wandered through in the 1600s looking for poetic inspiration.

Some of the extraordinary sites of 東北 include famous destinations such as 松島 (Pine Islands) near 仙台; the 雪国 skiing region in the west-central area; 田沢湖, the deepest lake in Japan; and the snow monkeys of northern 青森.

Thousands of people visit 東北 every summer for its festivals. They include the 青森ねぶた祭り every August, with its brilliantly illuminated floats and colorfully-dressed participants, the 竿燈祭り in 秋田市, with its long poles with dozens of hanging lanterns balanced by participants, and the 七夕祭り of 仙台, where streets are almost flooded with brightly colored streamers seemingly hanging from the stars.

■ キアラのジャーナル Kiara's Journal

Read the journal entry below, and then answer these questions.

❶ Kiara's Japanese language skills are getting better. List three areas of Japanese language where she improved quite a bit while in Hiraizumi.

❷ Retell what you know about Benkei.

❸ When you travel to Tohoku, what will you want to see and do first?

ジャーナルへ

平泉 は とても いい 所 です。昔、ここで 大きいwarが ありました。弁慶さんの story は とても sad です。東京へ 帰って インターネット リサーチを します。ベン 君は、この story は 面白いと 言いました。

私は 平泉で 日本語を たくさん 勉強しました。体の partsの 名前を 習いました。手と 目と 耳などの 名前を 習いました。And now I can describe what people look like. For example, ベン君は 背が 高い ですから、バスケが 上手です。I learned how to use adverbs like 少し、ちょっと、とても・・・。And now I can talk about health, too. Things like おなかが 痛い、とか、かぜを 引きました。 Good thing, too. I'm feeling a bit sick! Oh, and if we had a fashion show here on this side of the 時の門、I could be the M.C. For instance, ベン君は 今、とても ステキな 侍の ぼうしを かぶっています。

Even though my body feels a bit weak, I'm feeling good about how my language is progressing. Being able to use my language in context really helps, of course, and I have a great time with it!

■ テクノの時間 Techno Time
たくののじかん

Visit the www.TimeForJapanese.com website and practice the review activities for Chapter 6. Your best score is what counts, not how quickly you finish.

To gain your passport stamp for this chapter you have two options:

1. Make a large poster with one or more people in it. Label all of the body parts you learned in this chapter and describe what the person or people are wearing.

2. MC a fashion show in which you describe what your models are wearing. If you are too shy to do this live in front of the class, you can make a video to show the class.

■ 単語チェックリスト New Word Checklist
たんごちぇっくりすと

Japanese	Location	English
6-1		
あし　　足 (n)	6-1	leg, foot
あたま　　頭 (n)	6-1	head
いつも (n/adv.)	6-1	always
いれる/いれます　　入れる/入れます (入れて) (v)	6-1	put into
うで (n)	6-1	arm
おなか (n)	6-1	stomach
かお　　顔 (n)	6-1	face
かた　　肩 (n)	6-1	shoulder
かなしい　　悲しい (い adj.)	6-1	sad
かみ(のけ)　　髪(の毛) (n)	6-1	hair
きんにく　　筋肉 (n)	6-1	muscle
くち　　口 (n)	6-1	mouth
くび　　首 (n)	6-1	neck
こえ　　声 (n)	6-1	voice
こころ　　心 (n)	6-1	heart (not one's physical heart); soul
さむらい　　侍 (n)	6-1	samurai
しずか　　静か (な adj.)	6-1	quiet
せ/せい　　背 (n)	6-1	stature, height
たかい　　高い (い adj.)	6-1	high, tall, expensive
つよい　　強い (い adj.)	6-1	strong
て　　手 (n)	6-1	hand
でる/でます　　出る/出ます (出て) (v)	6-1	(to) go out, leave, get out
とおい　　遠い (い adj.)	6-1	far, distant
ながい　　長い (い adj.)	6-1	long
のど　　咽喉 (n)	6-1	throat
はいる/はいります　　入る/入ります (入って) (v)	6-1	(to) come in, go in, enter
はな　　鼻 (n)	6-1	nose
ひくい　　低い (い adj.)	6-1	low, short (height)
ひげ (n)	6-1	mustache, beard
ひざ　　膝 (n)	6-1	knee

Japanese	Location	English
ひみつ　　秘密 (n)	6-1	secret
べんけい　　　弁慶 (proper n)	6-1	Benkei (famous samurai name)
まつ/まちます　　待つ/待ちます (待って) (v)	6-1	(to) wait
みみ　　耳 (n)	6-1	ear
め　　目 (n)	6-1	eye
もつ/もちます　　持つ/持ちます (持って) (v)	6-1	(to) have, hold, carry
ゆうめい　　有名 (な adj.)	6-1	famous
ゆび　　指 (n)	6-1	finger(s)
よわい　　弱い (い adj.)	6-1	weak

6-2

Japanese	Location	English
おしゃれ (な adj.)	6-2	fashionable
かっこう　　格好 (n)	6-2	appearance
しぶい　　渋い (い adj.)	6-2	tasteful, subtle
じょうず　　上手 (な adj.)	6-2	skillful
すまーと　　スマート (な adj.)	6-2	slim, stylish
どんな	6-2	What/which kind of
ふとっている/ふとっています　　太っている/太っています (v)	6-2	(to) be fat
ふとる/ふとります　　太る/太ります (太って) (v)	6-2	(to) get fat
まあまあ (adv.)	6-2	so so, not bad, moderate
やせて いる/やせて います (v)	6-2	(to) be/is skinny

6-3

Japanese	Location	English
いしゃ　　医者 (n)	6-3	doctor
いたい　　痛い (い adj.)	6-3	painful
かぜ　　風邪 (n)	6-3	cold (a)
かぜ(を) ひく/ひきます　　風邪(を) ひく/ひきます (v)	6-3	(to) catch a cold
かんごふ　　看護婦 (n)	6-3	nurse
きゅうきゅうしゃ(を) よんで　　救急車(を) 呼んで (exp.)	6-3	Call an ambulance.
ぐあいが わるい　　具合が 悪い (exp.)	6-3	sick, feel bad
くすり　　薬 (n)	6-3	medicine
くすり(を) のむ/のみます　　薬(を) 飲む/飲みます (v)	6-3	(to) take medicine
けが(を) する/します　　怪我(を) する/します (v)	6-3	(to) be hurt, get wounded
けんこう　　健康 (n)	6-3	health
けんこうに いい です　　健康に いい です (exp.)	6-3	good for your health
じゅーす　　ジュース (n)	6-3	juice
しんぱい(を) する/します　　心配(を) する/します (v)	6-3	(to) worry
だいじょうぶ　　大丈夫 (な adj.)	6-3	all right
ねつ　　熱 (n)	6-3	fever
びょういん　　病院 (n)	6-3	hospital
びょうき　　病気 (n)	6-3	illness, sickness
ひるね　　昼寝 (n)	6-3	nap
ひるね(を) する/します　　昼寝(を) する/します (v)	6-3	(to) nap
ふとん　　布団 (n)	6-3	futon
むり　　無理 (な adj.)	6-3	impossible, unreasonable
むりしないで ください　　無理しないで 下さい (exp.)	6-3	Don't overexert.

Japanese	Location	English
6-4		
いやりんぐ　イヤリング (n)	6-4	earring
おとこ　男 (n)	6-4	man, male
おとこのこ　男の子 (n)	6-4	boy
おんな　女 (n)	6-4	woman, female
おんなのこ　女の子 (n)	6-4	girl
かける/かけます (かけて) (v)	6-4	(to) wear glasses or sunglasses
かぶる/かぶります　被る/被ります (v)	6-4	wear something on your head
きもの　着物 (n)	6-4	kimono (Japanese traditional clothing)
きる/きます　着る/着ます (v)	6-4	(to) wear (for things above the waist or dresses)
くつ　靴 (n)	6-4	shoes
くつした　靴下 (n)	6-4	socks
じーんず　ジーンズ (n)	6-4	jeans
したぎ　下着 (n)	6-4	underwear
じゃけっと　ジャケット (n)	6-4	jacket
しゃつ　シャツ (n)	6-4	shirt
しんぷる　シンプル (な adj.)	6-4	simple
すーつ　スーツ (n)	6-4	suit
すかーと　スカート (n)	6-4	skirt
すてき　素敵 (な adj.)	6-4	wonderful, nice
ずぼん　ズボン (n)	6-4	pants, trousers
すむ/すみます　住む/住みます (住んで) (v)	6-4	(to) live/reside
する/します (して) (v)	6-4	(to) do; (to) wear
どれす　ドレス (n)	6-4	dress (a)
ねくたい　ネクタイ (n)	6-4	necktie
はく/はきます　履く/履きます (履いて) (v)	6-4	(to) wear (items below the waist)
はんさむ　ハンサム (な adj.)	6-4	handsome, good-looking
ぱんつ　パンツ (n)	6-4	underwear
ふく　服 (n)	6-4	clothes
ふつう　普通 (な adj./adv.)	6-4	usual, normal
めいく　メイク (n)	6-4	makeup
めがね　眼鏡 (n)	6-4	eyeglasses
もち　餅 (n)	6-4	sticky rice cake
ようふく　洋服 (n)	6-4	clothes, Western clothes
6-5		
けいけん　経験 (n)	6-5	experience
すばらしい　素晴らしい (い adj.)	6-5	wonderful
どう　でしたか。 (inter.)	6-5	How was it?
ならう/ならいます　習う/習います (習って) (v)	6-5	(to) learn
に　よろしく (exp.)	6-5	Say hello to . . .
ぶんか　文化 (n)	6-5	culture

Hobbies in the Ancient City of Heian-kyou

第 **7** 課

✓ Learning Goals

By the end of this chapter you will learn:

A) how to talk about your hobbies and to ask others about theirs

B) ways to combine two sentences using conjunctions

C) how to state your likes, dislikes, and the sort of things you are good or bad at

D) color words

E) about the Heian period (794–1185)

F) 14 additional kanji

✓ Performance Goals

By the end of this chapter you will be able to:

A) state your hobbies and ask others what their hobbies are

B) talk about foods, drinks, music, etc., that you like or dislike

C) describe which activities you are good at and which you are poor at

D) point to something and say, or ask, what color it is

E) tell your friends about Heian Period Japan and a little about some of the well-known literary styles from that period

F) to read and write 14 additional kanji

Fountain at Ryoanji Temple, Kyoto

僕の　趣味は　食べる事です。
My hobby is eating.

■ 会話 Dialogue
（かいわ）

キアラ ： 友さん、あなたの　趣味は、何　ですか。

友　　 ： 僕の　趣味は　食べる事　です。キアラさんの　趣味は、何　ですか。
（ぼく）（しゅみ）（た）（こと）（きあら）（しゅみ）（なん）

キアラ ： 私の　趣味は、絵を　描く事　です。それから、歌を　歌う事と、柔道を　する事
（しゅみ）（え）（か）（こと）（うた）（うた）（こと）（じゅうどう）（こと）
　　　　 です。ベン君の　趣味は、何　ですか。
（べん）（くん）（しゅみ）（なん）

ベン　 ： そう　ですね。僕の　趣味は、歴史と　読書　です。そして、ビデオゲームも　趣味
（ぼく）（しゅみ）（れきし）（どくしょ）（びでおげーむ）（しゅみ）
　　　　 です。

キアラ ： じゅん君、あなたの　趣味は、何　ですか。
（くん）（しゅみ）（なん）

じゅん ： え？　僕の　趣味　ですか。*ひみつ　です。
（ぼく）（しゅみ）

友　　 ： じゅん君の　趣味は、寝る事　ですよ。
（くん）（しゅみ）（ね）（こと）

* ひみつ － secret

■ 単語 New Words
（たんご）

趣味 (n) （しゅみ）	生け花 (n) （い）（ばな）	茶道 (n) （さどう/ちゃどう）	スポーツ (n)	アメフト (n) （アメリカン)フットボール
スケボー (n) スケートボード	ピアノ (n)	ギター (n)	水泳 (n) or 泳ぐ事 (n) （すいえい）（およ）（こと） （泳ぐ）泳ぎます (v) （およ）（およ）	歌 (n) － song （うた） 歌う事 (n) － singing （うた）（こと） （歌う）歌います (v) － （うた）（うた） to sing
食べる事 (n) （た）（こと）	寝る事 (n) （ね）（こと） （寝る）寝ます (v) （ね）（ね）	読書 (n) （どくしょ）	ゴルフ (n)	旅行 (n) （りょこう）

		それに *(conj.)* – moreover, furthermore
		それから *(conj.)* – and then
トランプ *(n)*	（弾く）弾きます *(v)* ひ　　ひ	そして *(conj.)* – and then

Other vocabulary you might like to know:

乗馬 *(n)*　　踊り *(n)*　　スキー *(n)*　　料理 *(n)*　　ビデオゲーム *(n)*
じょうば　　　おど　　　　　　　　　　　　りょうり

■ 漢字 Kanji
　かんじ

花　池　趣　味　事

花 **7 strokes**	はな – flower	一	ナ	サ	ナ	艿	花	花
	花 – flower; 花（子） – a girl's name; （生け）花 – はな　　はな こ　　　　　　　い　　 ばな Japanese flower arranging; 花（火） – fireworks はな び							
	The first three strokes here make up a radical related to plants. The final 4 strokes mean change (化). When FLOWERS bloom, plants change their appearance.							

池 **6 strokes**	チ, いけ – pond	丶	氵	氵	汀	汕	池	
	池 – pond いけ							
	The first three strokes are the water radical (a simplified form of 水), and the right side of this kanji means "to be." A POND is rainwater becoming another kind of water.							

趣 **15 strokes**	シュ – gist, tend (to), become	一	十	土	丰	丰	走	走
	趣（味） – hobby しゅ み	赴	赴	赴	赳	趄	趣	趣
	The radical for run (走) is on the left side of this kanji. To get the GIST of someone using this kanji, you should run to it and put your ear (耳) closer, and BECOME better at things by practicing them again (又) and again (又).							

味	み, あじ – taste/flavor, to taste or appreciate		｜	ㅁ	ロ	口	口二	吽	味	味
	味 – taste or flavor; 味（わう）– to taste or appreciate; 趣味 – hobby									
8 strokes	The mouth (口) has not yet (未) savored the TASTE or FLAVOR of the delicious food.									

事	ジ、こと – intangible thing		一	一	亓	写	写	写	写	事
	事 – intangible thing;（大）事 – important									
8 strokes	The THING about this kanji is that it starts with one (一) mouth (口) and a backwards capital E (ヨ which is also the katakana for YO) with the middle line longer than the other horizontal lines. This kanji ends with a hooked line through the middle of the entire THING.									

■ 言葉の探索 Language Detection

1. (私の) 趣味は、読書 です。 = (My) hobby is reading.

A) 私の 趣味は、音楽 です。　　　= My hobby is music.
B) キアラの趣味は、柔道 です。　　= Kiara's hobby is judo.
C) 母の 趣味は ピアノです。　　　　= My mother's hobby is the piano.
D) 友達の 趣味は 読書では ありません。 = My friend's hobby is not reading.

2. が used for new information

A second way to talk about hobbies uses the particle が. This is a common pattern in Japanese.

(私は) 読書が 趣味 です。 = Reading is my hobby.

The topic of this sentence is 私, followed by は. The actual "hobby" is followed by the "new information marker" が. In this pattern, the word for *hobby*, 趣味, is not followed by a particle.

A) 私は 音楽が 趣味 です。　　　　= As for me, music is a hobby.
B) キアラさんは 柔道が 趣味 です。 = As for Kiara, judo is a hobby.
C) 母は ピアノ が 趣味 です。　　　= As for my mother, piano is a hobby.
D) 友達は 読書が 趣味です。　　　　= As for my friend, reading is a hobby.

3. The dictionary form, sometimes called the "plain" form of verbs, is very useful for talking about hobbies.

書く事が　趣味　です。　= Writing is my hobby.

Since the beginning of this book, you've seen references to the dictionary form of the verb. You may have not really understood what that meant, but basically the "dictionary form" is exactly what it sounds like: it is the form used to look up a verb in the dictionary. Here is where you will start learning other uses for the dictionary form. To say that your hobby is writing, eating, sleeping, etc., add 事 to the end of the dictionary form of the verb. This changes the verb into a gerund, a type of noun. To check and review the dictionary forms of verbs you have learned, refer to Appendix 1. Some examples are:

書く事 (writing), 話す事 (conversing), 食べる事 (eating), 寝る事 (sleeping). Can you think of more?

This form can be used to say things like:

書く事が　上手　です。	= I/he/she am/is good at writing.
話す事が　下手　です。	= I/he/she am/is bad at talking.
日本語を 勉強する事が　趣味　です。	= Studying Japanese is my/his/her hobby.
姉の　趣味は　ゴルフを　する事　です。	= My older sister's hobby is golf.
歌う事は　母の　趣味　です。	= Singing is my mother's hobby.

物 is also translated as "thing" or "object." But it is only used for tangible things. 事 can be translated as an intangible "thing."

4. それから = after that, and そして = and/and then
Both それから and そして are transitional words. They can be used as conjunctions to tie the content of two sentences together. Using transitional words helps make your language clearer and more interesting.

A) 私は　朝ご飯を　食べました。それから、学校へ　行きました。
= I ate breakfast. <u>After that</u>, I went to school.
B) 学校へ　行きました。それから、友達と　話しました。
= I went to school. <u>After that</u>, I spoke with my friends.
C) うちへ　帰りました。それから、スナックを　食べました。
= I returned home. <u>Then</u>, I ate a snack.
D) 本を　読みました。そして、テレビを　見ました。
= I read a book. <u>And then</u> I watched TV.
E) サラさんの　趣味は　テニスです。そして、お姉さんの　趣味も　テニスです。
= Sara's hobby is tennis. <u>And</u> her older sister's hobby is also tennis.

■ 自習 Self Check

1. 私の趣味は_____です。
Use this pattern to say the following out loud to yourself in Japanese.

A) My hobby is skateboarding.

B) _____'s hobby is volleyball.

C) Jun's mother's hobbies are tea ceremony and karate.

D) Tom's little sister's hobby is reading.

E) The math teacher's hobby is golf.

F) (make your own sentence)

2. Dictionary form + こと

Using the dictionary form of a verb as a gerund (a form of a noun) try to say the following out loud to yourself in Japanese.

A) My hobby is singing.

B) Ben's friend's hobby is swimming.

C) Tomo's hobbies are eating and sleeping.

D) Playing guitar is Sara's hobby.

E) My grandfather's hobby is jogging.

F) (make your own sentence)

3. それから and そして

Combine these sentences using first それから and then again using そして and say them out loud to yourself in Japanese.

A) I came to school. I studied English.

B) I ate sushi. I drank tea.

C) (Make another sentence combination of your own choosing.)

■ 練習の時間 Time for Practice
れんしゅう　じかん

1. Group Practice

Copy the form below onto a piece of scrap paper. Interview six classmates in Japanese about their hobbies. Follow the sample dialogue provided here. Begin when your teacher says "始めましょう。" はじ
Write your answers in English. Stop and return to your seats when your 先生 says "はい、時間 です！" (It's time!). Review your findings and be prepared to report them in Japanese to the class.

A-さん:　お名前は　何ですか。
B-さん:　私は　Aliciaです。なまえ
A-さん:　Aliciaさんの　趣味は　何ですか。
B-さん:　私の　趣味は　ギターです。それから、読書です。

名前 なまえ	趣味
Alicia	guitar, reading

2. Pair Practice

Use Japanese to interview your partner about his/her family members' hobbies. Follow the sample dialogue here. Write down the answers (in English) on a piece of scrap paper. Be prepared to report your results to the class.

A-さん: ご家族は　何人　ですか。かぞく　なんにん
B-さん: 僕と　父と　母と　兄の　四人です。ぼく　　　　あに　よにん
A-さん: お父さんの　趣味は　何　ですか。しゅみ
B-さん: 父の　趣味は　ゴルフ　です。しゅみ

■ 文化箱 Culture Chest
ぶんかばこ

Heian Period (794–1185)

In 794, at the beginning of the Heian period, Emperor Kanmu moved the capital of Japan to the site of modern-day Kyoto. The stability this move lent to Japanese society led to a flourishing of Japanese culture, including the Buddhist religion, literature, and the arts. The invention of hiragana and katakana allowed for the writing of literature in Japanese for the first time. Hiragana and katakana were largely considered writing systems for the less educated, so, while the more educated male elite still wrote in classical Chinese, early pioneers of truly "Japanese" literature were court women who had not been trained in Chinese literary techniques.

Activities enjoyed by the aristocracy during the Heian Period included writing poetry, relaxing while enjoying views of the moon or cherry blossoms, and participating in Buddhist practices and rituals. This cultural period is revered in Japan as a high point in Japanese history by many; however, it is also considered a time when the influence of China dominated Japanese society. To some, a more truly Japanese culture developed later.

■ キアラのジャーナル Kiara's Journal
きあらじゃーなる

Read the journal entry below, and then answer these questions.

1. Why was Tomo anxious about going to the gate?
2. Where did they exit the gate?
3. What do you think is meant by "紫式部さんの時代"?
4. What was 紫式部's hobby?
5. Tomo said to Ben and Jun, 「けんかしないで下さい。」 Given the context, what do you think that means?

ジャーナルへ
じゃーなる

　弁慶さんは　いい人　でした。彼の　体が　とても　大きかったので、being around him I felt とても　安全。However, this morning we overheard an old man talking about hearing rumors that a group of soldiers loyal to 頼朝 were planning something bad。友さんは、「早く　時の門へ　行きましょう！危ない　です。」と、言いました。私達は、いそいで　静かに　時の門に　行きました。

　The next thing we know、時の門から　大きな　お寺の　前に　出ました。ベン君は、「ここは　どこ　ですか！わあ！あれは　清水寺　ですか。すばらしい　ですね。」と、言いました。

　じゅん君は、「あれが　清水寺なら、ここは　京都ですね。」と、言いました。

　友さんは、「そう　ですね。でも、今の　時代、ここは　京都と　いいません。ここは　今、平安京、と　言います。多分 1010 C.E. ぐらい　です。」と、言いました。

　私は、「うそ　でしょう！じゃあ、ここは、今、紫式部の　時代ですか。彼女の(her)　趣味は　本を　書く事でした。とても　すてきな　女の人　です。」と、言いました。

じゅん君は、「そう　ですね。彼女の　本の　名前は　何　でしたか。」と、聞きました。

ベン君は was surprised and,「本当に　知りませんか！とても　有名　ですよ！」と、言いました。

じゅん君は、「うるさいな。友さん、教えて下さい。」と　言いました。

友さんは、「ベン君、じゅん君、だめ　ですよ。けんかしないで下さい。紫式部さんの　本の　名前は　『源氏物語』ですよ。とても　有名な　本　です。」と　言いました。そして、「紫式部さんと　会いましょうか。紫さんは　僕の　友達ですよ。」と、言いました！

私は、「ええーっ！？」と　大きい声で　いいました。でも、友さんは already walking past the great temple 清水寺、そして、「今日は　水曜日　ですね。紫さんは　いつも　水曜日に和歌を　習っています(is learning)。紫さんの　趣味は　本を書く事と　和歌を　詠むこと　です。」と、言いました。

This was the second time that I had heard the word 趣味。I felt like I understood what it meant, so I tried to use it in a sentence to see if it worked the way I thought it would。私は、「友さん、あなたの　趣味は何　ですか。」と　聞きました。

友さんは、「僕の　趣味は　食べる事　です。キアラさんの　趣味は　何　ですか。」と、言いました。

「私の　趣味は　絵を描く事と　歌を歌う事と　生け花と　柔道です。ベン君の　趣味は何　ですか。」と　私は、次に (next)、ベン君に、聞きました。

ベン君は、「そう　ですねえ。僕の　趣味は　歴史と　読書　です。」と　言いました。

■ テクノの時間 Techno Time

Though you've not been introduced to them all yet, type all the vocabulary words from this chapter into your digital dictionary. Remember to use your file labeled "JISHO" (in *romaji*).

キアラさんは、日本が　大好きですね。
Kiara, you really love Japan, don't you?

■ 会話 Dialogue

キアラ ： 私は、この 『時の門』の 旅行が、大好き です。

じゅん ： 学校は、好き ですか。

キアラ ： はい、日本の 学校も 大好き です。友達も、家族も、食べ物も 大好き です。

ベン ： キアラさんは、日本が 大好き ですね。

キアラ ： はい。それに、アメリカも 大好き ですよ。

友   ： キアラさんは どんな物が、嫌い ですか。

キアラ ： そう ですねえ・・・・。蛙が 嫌い ですね。

友   ： え？蛙ですか？
       ごめん、ごめん。冗談 ですよ。私は、冗談が、大好き です。

キアラ ： *面白くない です！もう、帰る！

友   ： はい、これが 蛙。

*面白くない – not fun or amusing

■ 単語 New Words

鼠 (n)	蛙 (n)	冗談 (n)	好き (な adj.)
大好き (な adj.)	嫌い (な adj.)	大嫌い (な adj.)	(思う) 思います (v)

たいてい (adv.) – usually

どんな – what kind of (thing)

動物 (n) – animal

■ 漢字 Kanji
かんじ

好 6 strokes	す（き）– like	く	夕	女	好	好	好		
	好（き）– to like								
	This character combines woman 女 and child 子 to make something that everyone LIKES—a mother hugging a child.								

■ 言葉の探索 Language Detection
ことば　たんさく

1. 好き、大好き、嫌い、大嫌い
   す　だいす　きら　だいきら
   Whatever or whomever is liked or disliked is almost always followed by the particle が.

   私は ＿＿＿＿＿＿ が 好き　です。　　　　= I like . . .
   　　　　　　　　　　す
   　　　　　　大好き　です。　　　　= I love (really like) . . .
   　　　　　　だいす
   　　　　　　嫌い　です。　　　　　= I dislike . . .
   　　　　　　きら
   　　　　　　大嫌い　です。　　　　= I hate (really dislike). . .
   　　　　　　だいきら

   Contrast can be shown by using は instead of が.

   天ぷらが　好き　です。　= I like tempura.
   てん　　　　す
   天ぷらは　好き　です。　でも　お寿司は　嫌いです。
   てん　　　　す　　　　　　　　　　　きら
   　　　　　　　　　　　= I like tempura. But I don't like sushi.

   Both statements above mean "I like tempura." However, in the example using は, the emphasis is slightly different. This statement could be restated as "I like tempura. But as for sushi, I dislike it."

   > 例 (for affirmative statements:)
   > れい
   > EXAMPLE
   > A) 私は　あなたが　好き　です。　= I like you. (*Note: in some contexts, this could mean you have a romantic interest, so be careful!!!*)
   > B) 弟は　食べる事が　好き　です。　= My little brother likes to eat.
   > C) 友達は　旅行が　きらい　です。　= My friend dislikes travelling.
   > 　　　　りょこう

   The negative forms of these four words are created just like other nouns, by replacing です with では　ありません or 〜じゃ　ありません.

   > 例
   > れい
   > EXAMPLE
   > A) 私は　おすしが　好きでは　ありません。　= I don't like sushi.
   > B) 犬は　豆腐が　好きでは　ありません。　= Dogs don't like tofu.
   > 　　　とうふ
   > C) 友さんは　歌う事が　好きじゃ　ありません。　= Tomo does not like to sing.
   > 　　　　　うた　こと

2. どんな (what kind of / what sort of) + noun

The question word どんな means "what kind" or "what sort" and precedes the noun in question.

* Note: When you ask a preference or for new, specific information which you do not know, the particle following that subject is が.

Q: どんな 動物が 好き ですか。 = What sort of animals do you like?
A: 犬と 猫が 大好き です。 = I love dogs and cats.

Q: どんな 科目が 好き ですか。 = What sort of subjects do you like?
A: そう ですね。科学が 好き です。それから、数学も 好き です。
                                                = Let me see. I like science. And I also like math.

Q: お母さんは どんな スポーツが 好き ですか。 = What kind of sports does your mother like?
A: 母は スポーツが 好きでは ありません。でも、料理は 好き です。
                                = My mother does not like sports. But she likes cooking.

■ 自習 Self Check

1. **Talking about things you like and don't like**
    Say the following out loud to yourself in Japanese.

    A) I like (the art of) flower arranging.
    B) Yuki dislikes American football.
    C) Ben really likes swimming.
    D) Ken really dislikes playing the guitar.

    E) My mother doesn't like tennis (テニス).
    F) My grandmother really likes ramen (noodles).
    G) My friends really like Japan.

2. **Asking what kind of...**
    Say the following out loud to yourself in Japanese.

    A) What kind of food do you like?
    B) What kind of animals does your mother like?
    C) What kind of drink does your little brother like?
    D) What country does your grandmother like?

    E) What kind of class do you like?
    F) What kind of car (くるま) do you like?
    G) What kind of music does your mother like?

■ 練習の時間 Time for Practice

1. **Pair Practice**

    Ask your partner if he/she likes the following things. Partners should use 大好き, 好き, きらい, or 大きらい in their answers.

    A-さん: お寿司は 好き ですか。
    B-さん: はい、私は、お寿司が 好き です。 -OR-
            いいえ、私は、寿司が 嫌い です。

サッカー	アイスクリーム
さしみ	テニス
コーラ	フットボール
読書 どくしょ	野球 やきゅう
チョコレート	お茶 ちゃ
犬 いぬ	蛙 かえる
猫 ねこ	花 はな

2. **Pair Practice**

Ask your partner to identify a specific thing he or she likes, and one he or she dislikes, from each category below. Then switch.

> 例
れい
EXAMPLE
>
> A-さん:　どんな　動物 が　好きですか。
どうぶつ
> B-さん:　狸 が　好きです。
たぬき
> A-さん:　そう　ですか。どんな　動物 が　嫌い　ですか。
どうぶつ　きら
> B-さん:　＿＿＿＿＿が　嫌いです。

A) 動物
どうぶつ
B) 食べ物
た もの
C) 飲み物
の もの

D) 科目
か もく
E) 音楽
おんがく
F) 本

G) 映画 (movie)
えいが
H) 車 (car)
くるま
I) (any other category you can think of)

■ 文化箱 Culture Chest
ぶん か ばこ

紫式部
むらさきしきぶ

　紫式部 is the name of the author of 源氏物語, or *The Tale of Genji*, a story about the relations between aristocratic
むらさきしきぶ　　　　　　　　　　　　　　　げんじものがたり
men and women in the capital city of Kyoto, then called 平安京. It is sometimes called the world's first novel.
へいあんきょう

　Murasaki Shikibu was born about 973 C.E. and died either in 1014 C.E. or 1025 C.E.; the records are unclear. Murasaki was not her real name—she served Empress Shoshi and Murasaki (referring to purple wisteria flowers) may have been a nickname. She is considered one of the great writers in Japanese history and her portrait and a scene from *The Tale of Genji* appear on the two thousand yen note.

■ キアラのジャーナル Kiara's Journal
きあら　じゃーなる

Read the journal entry below, and then answer these questions.

❶ Where did they first go when they arrived in Heian-kyou, current-day Kyoto?
❷ Why did Tomo want to introduce the trio to Lady Murasaki?
❸ What secret did Lady Murasaki share?
❹ Why was Lady Murasaki a little sad at the restaurant?
❺ Why does Kiara think that Lady Murasaki is a great author?

ジャーナルへ
じゃーなる

　　1010年、平安京は　日本の　capital　でした。中国から　たくさんの　ideasが　日本に　来ました。紫式部さんは　この時　平安京に　いました。

　　紫さんの　家へ　皆で　行きました。友さんは、「紫さん、ひさしぶり　です！お元気ですか。」と　言いました。

　　「まあ、友さん　ですか。ようこそ。いつ　ここに　来ましたか。この　人達は　だれですか。」と　言いました。

　　友さんは、「昨日　来ました。それから、こちらは　キアラさんと　じゅん君と　ベン君です。この　人達は　読書が　好き　です。ですから、紫さんに　introduce　したいと　思いました。(thought)」と　言いました。

　　紫さんは、「そう　ですか。初めまして。よろしく　お願いします。　私も　読書が　好きです。詩を　書く事も　好き　です。」と、言いました。

　　私達は、「どうぞ　よろしく　お願いします。」と　言いました。

　　紫さんは、「キアラさんは　平安京が　好き　ですか。」と　聞きました。

　　私は、「ええ、大好き　です。特に清水寺が　大好き　です。紫さんの　趣味は　和歌を作ること　ですね。」と　言いました。

　　「はい、私は　毎週　和歌の　勉強を　しています。でも、ひみつ　ですが、読書や和歌を　作ること　より、物を　食べることが　もっと(more)　大好きです。」と　言いました。

　　友さんは、「だから、紫さんと、私は、友達なんです！」と、私達にsmileしました。そして、「紫さん、晩ご飯を食べましたか。僕は　おなかが　ペコペコ　です。食事を　しましょう。」と　言いました。

　　じゅん君は、「僕も　ペコペコです。僕は　お豆腐(tofu)が　好き　です。美味しい*湯豆腐屋さんは　ありますか。」と、言いました。
ゆどうふや

　　紫さんは、「ええ、川の　そばに(river side)　いい　湯豆腐屋さんが　ありますよ。」と　言いました。「こちらへ　どうぞ」。
かわ

　　それから、a really cute little　湯豆腐やに　入りました。There was no signage at all outside, but inside,　人が　たくさん　いました。すばらしい　畳の部屋 (tatami room)　が　いっぱい　ありました。友さんは　私に、「ここで　いい　ですか。」と　言いました。そして、「僕は何年か前に　ここに　来た事が　あると　思いますが・・・・。」と、紫さんに　言いました。

*湯豆腐屋: Restaurant specializing in tofu boiled in broth. Kyoto has many ゆどうふや。
ゆどうふや

紫さんは、「そう　ですよ。わたしと　一緒に　来ましたよ。」と　言いました。友さんが、一緒に　来たことを　忘れていたので、紫さんは　ちょっと　さびしそうでした。

Actually, it seemed like it did not matter for her, but I thought to myself that she probably will write about her slight sadness in her next poem or book. I think Lady Murasaki is skilled at observing details and commenting on people's emotions. She also has a very good imagination。だから、紫さんは、素晴らしい作家(author)です。

食べ物は　とても　おいしかったです。それに、私は　紫さんが　本当に　好き　です。いい友だちに　なりたいです。

あ、もう　遅い(late)　時間　です。

お休み。

Samples of moss varieties, Kyoto

キアラさんは、日本語が　とても上手です。
Kiara's Japanese is very good.

■ 会話 Dialogue
かいわ

ベン　　：　今日は、紫式部さんの　パーティー　です。皆で和歌を　詠むパーティーです。
　　　　　きょう　むらさきしきぶ　　　　　　　　　　　　　　みんな　わか　　よ

じゅん　：　キアラさんは、日本語が　とても　上手　です。いい　和歌を　作って下さいね。
　　　　　　　　　　　　　　　　　　　じょうず　　　　わか　　つく

キアラ　：　ありがとう！　　がんばります！

ベン　　：　友さんは、食べる事が　得意　ですね。
　　　　　　　　　　　　　　とくい

友　　　：　ありがとう！がんばります！

ベン　　：　友さん、和歌も、がんばりますか。
　　　　　　　　わか

友　　　：　いいえ、和歌は、ちょっと・・・・。和歌は　苦手　ですから、がんばりません。でも、
　　　　　　　　わか　　　　　　　　　　　わか　にがて
　　　　　食べる事は　得意　ですから、　がんばりますよ〜！
　　　　　　　　とくい

■ 単語 New Words
たんご

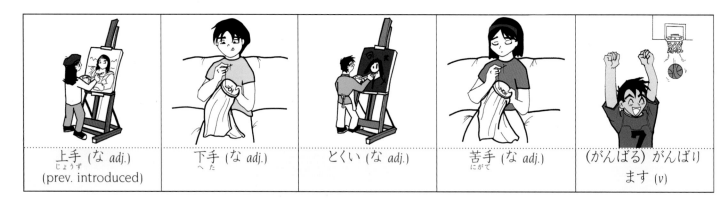

上手 (な adj.) じょうず (prev. introduced)	下手 (な adj.) へた	とくい (な adj.)	苦手 (な adj.) にがて	(がんばる) がんばります (v)

(やる) やります (v) – to do (informal)　　　　(やってみる) やってみます (v) – try to do

■ 漢字 Kanji
かんじ

上

	ジョウ, うえ, あ(がる), のぼ(る) – above, upper; climbing up (a hill), going up (to the capital)	一	十	上					
上	上手 – to be skilled at something (lit., to have the upper hand); 上がる – to go up (to the capital, for instance, or to the emperor's throne)								
3 strokes	This kanji shows a diving board on which one bounces to go UPWARDS and so this means UP, ABOVE, or ON TOP OF.								

■ 言葉の探索 Language Detection

1. 上手、下手
   The words 上手 (*to be good at something*) and its opposite 下手 (*to be bad at something*) are used in the same way as 好き and 嫌い.

   A) 由美子さんは バスケが 上手 です。 = Yumiko is good at basketball.
   B) 私は サッカーが 下手 です。 = I am bad at soccer.

2. 得意、苦手
   得意 (*skilled*) and 苦手 (*unskilled*) are similar to 上手 and 下手, but 得意 implies that someone specializes in the activity he/she is skilled at, and that he/she enjoys it. Similarly, 苦手 implies that he/she dislikes whatever they are unskilled at and would like to avoid it if possible.

   A) 山田先生は 柔道が 得意 ですよ。 = Mr./Ms. Yamada is good (specializes) at judo (you know).
   B) 山本先生は 英語が 得意 ですね。 = Mr. Yamamoto is skilled at English, isn't he?
   C) 私は 数学が 苦手 です。 = I am not good at (and I dislike) math.

3. The particle が can function as a conjunction that means "but," joining two contrasting sentences. Note that が comes at the end of the first part of the sentence.

   A) キアラさんは 柔道が 得意 ですが、水泳は 苦手 です。
      = Kiara is skilled at judo, but she is not skilled at swimming.
   B) 母は ゴルフが 上手 ですが、父は 下手 です。
      = My mother is good at golf, but my father is poor at it.
   C) ハンバーガーが 嫌い ですが、ステーキは 大好き です。
      = I dislike hamburgers, but I love steak.

   Note that が can be used more than once in a sentence, each time for a different purpose. Also note how は is used in some of the examples to provide contrast.

■ 自習 Self Check

1. 上手、下手
   Try to say the following in Japanese.

   A) Junko is good at tea ceremony.

   B) Junkichi is bad at cards.

   C) I am bad at drawing manga.

   D) Keiko's younger sister is good at playing the guitar.

   E) (compose your own example)

   F) (compose your own example)

2. 得意、苦手
   とくい　にがて
   Try to say the following in Japanese.

   A) Keiko is good (specializes) at music.
   B) My friends are not good at skateboarding.
   C) My father is good (specializes) at kendo.
   D) My friend is not good at Korean. But he is good at French.

3. Combine these sentences using が.

> 例
> れい
> EXAMPLE
> Junkichi is bad at cards, but Tomoko is good at it.
> じゅんきち君は　トランプが下手ですが、友子さんは　上手です。
> 　　　　くん　　　　　　　　へた　　　　　　こ　　　　　じょうず

   A) I hate sushi. I love tempura.
   B) My older sister is good at math. My little brother is good at history.
   C) Tomohisa specializes in golf. He is not skilled at tennis.

■ 練習の時間 Time for Practice
     れんしゅう　じかん

---

1. Pair Practice

Point to one of the illustrations below and ask your partner in Japanese if he or she is good at the activity. Answer according to your own personal situation. Take turns.

> 例
> れい
> EXAMPLE
> A-さん(*pointing to soccer*): サッカーが　上手　ですか。
> 　　　　　　　　　　　　　　　　　　　　　じょうず
> B-さん:　いいえ、サッカーは　下手　です。嫌い　です。
> 　　　　　　　　　　　　　　　　へた　　　　きら
> A-さん:　そう　ですか。私も　サツカーが　苦手　です。
> 　　　　　　　　　　　　　　　　　　　　　にがて

2. Pair Practice

Ask your partner if he or she is skilled or unskilled at each of these activities. You can use a chart like the one below to record the answers. Then switch.

A-さん：　料理は　得意　ですか。
B-さん：　はい、得意　です。料理を　する事が　好き　です。
A-さん：　そう　ですか。
-OR-
A-さん：　スキーは　得意　ですか。
B-さん：　いいえ、苦手　です。
A-さん：　そう　ですか。私も　スキーが　苦手　です。

Activity	得意/苦手
cooking	
baseball	
playing guitar	
playing piano	
math	
skiing	
music	
drawing	
an activity of your choice	

■ 文化箱 Culture Chest

Paying Compliments

Japanese tend not to brag, so they rarely use the expression 上手 when talking about their own abilities or those of their family members. They are usually quite complimentary of others, however, and often compliment even the simplest things, even if the compliment is not necessarily one hundred percent true. For example, Japanese will often tell 外国人 (foreigners in Japan) the following:

お箸を使うのが　（お）上手　ですね。 = You are good at using chopsticks.
日本語が　（お）上手　ですね。 = You are very good at Japanese.

A proper reply to most compliments (rather than どうも　ありがとう) would be いいえ、いいえ, implying that you are not so good at that and that there is no need to pay such a compliment in the first place.

和歌

The kanji for WA in WAKA means "Japanese" and the KA means "songs." 和歌 are poems that have been written in Japan for centuries. Various types of long and short 和歌 were composed on special occasions (such as the new year, or when viewing the full moon), at parties, or as letters between lovers. 紫式部 included nearly 800 和歌 in her 源氏物語 novel.

■ キアラのジャーナル Kiara's Journal
きあら　じゃーなる

Read the journal entry below, and then answer these questions.

❶ How does Lady Murasaki feel about making waka?
❷ How skillful is Lady Murasaki at waka?
❸ What does Kiara like now that she did not like before coming to Japan?
❹ At the end of this journal entry, how does Kiara feel about her waka experience?

ジャーナルへ
じゃーなる

　今日、紫式部さんが　和歌の　勉強　しているのを　少し　見ました。紫さんは「和歌を作る事が　大好き　です。」、と　言いました。和歌を　作る事を、和歌を　詠む、といいます。本を　読む、とは、違う　漢字です。

　紫さんは　和歌が　とても　上手　です。ベン君も　和歌を　少し　がんばりました。でも、ベン君は　和歌を　詠む事が　ちょっと　下手　です。

　友さんは　また　disappeared. 彼は　食べる事が　得意　です。じゅん君は　どこでも　寝る事が　得意　です。ベン君も、寝る事が　好き　ですが、歴史も　好き　です。彼はスポーツが　下手　です。日本へ　来る前、私は　勉強が　あまり　好きではありませんでしたが、今は　好きです。明日、紫式部さんと　友達と　和歌を　作ってみます (make and see how it sounds).

　私は、高校の　日本語の　クラスで、俳句を　作りました。でも、和歌の事が　ちょっと分かりません。The number of syllables for a 俳句 is 5-7-5, while the waka is longer, 5-7-5-7-7. 長いですね。私は　俳句が　ちょっと　上手　ですが、　和歌が　あまり　上手では　ありません。紫式部さんは、「私は　友達と　いつも　パーティーで　和歌を　作ります。とても　楽しいです。」と言いました。

　じゅん君は、「パーティーで　和歌を　作るんですか。それは　楽しい　ですか。平安時代と　21ᵗʰ centuryは　とても　違いますね。」と　言いました。そして、「だから　紫さんは　和歌が　上手　なんですね。僕は下手です。」と言いました。

　そこへ、友さんが、帰って　来ました。ベン君は、「どこへ　行っていましたか。ご飯は、もう　食べましたか。」と　聞きました。

　友さんは「ちょっと　だけ　食べました。後で　また　一緒に　食べますよ。大丈夫です。」と、言いました。私は、「友さんは、やっぱり　食べる事が、得意　ですね。」と言いました。

　晩ご飯は　紫さんの　友達と　一緒に　食べました。遅くまで　和歌を　詠みました。私は　あまり　上手では　ありませんでしたが、和歌を詠む事が、とても　好きでした。Believe it or not, it's a little like writing a rap song.

　お休みなさい。

■ テクノの時間 Techno Time

Use the Internet to find a photo of a family. It can be a famous family, or a not-so famous family. The family can be a human family or not. Copy and paste the photo into a document. Your teacher will tell you what to name your document file. Above the photo, write a paragraph in Japanese introducing the characters. Use at least ten sentences to describe the people or creatures in the photo. Use five adverbs (such as とても, ときどき, or ちょっと) and include introductory and closing remarks (こんにちは at the beginning, or ありがとうございました at the end). Here are some topics you may wish to include in your paragraph:

- how many members in the family, and who they are
- activities at which the family is skilled or unskilled
- likes/dislikes
- physical features
- ages, grades, or dates of birth
- what subjects they study

友さんの 銀色の着物も、かっこいいですよ。
Tomo's silver-colored kimono also looks great!

1) 紫さん、おはよう ございます。

2) おはよう ございます、みなさん。

3) わ！紫さん、きれいな 着物ですね！

4) ありがとう。紫は、私の色です。この 白い 花と もも色の 花は 友さんが 好きなので・・・。

5) ありがとう ございます。私は、ファッションは、あまり 得意ではありません。でも、紫さんの その 着物が 本当に 大好きです。

6) ありがとう。友さんの 銀色の 着物も、とても かっこう いい ですよ。ベン君と じゅん君の 黒の 着物も、いい ですね。キアラさんの、黄色と 青の 花も、とても かわいい です。さ、朝ご飯 ですよ。

■ 会話 Dialogue

皆　　：　紫 さん、おはよう ございます。

紫　　：　おはよう ございます、みんなさん。

キアラ：　わ！ 紫 さん、きれいな 着物 ですね！

紫　　：　ありがとう。紫 は、私の 色 です。この白い花と もも色の 花は、友さんが
　　　　　好きなので・・・。

友　　：　ありがとう ございます。私は、ファッションは、あまり 得意では ありません。
　　　　　でも、 紫 さんの その 着物が 本当に 大好き です。

紫　　：　ありがとう。友さんの 銀色の 着物も、とても かっこいい ですよ。ベン君と
　　　　　じゅん君の 黒の 着物も、いい ですね。キアラさんの、黄色と 青の 花も、とても
　　　　　かわいい です。さ、朝ご飯 ですよ。

■ 単語 New Words

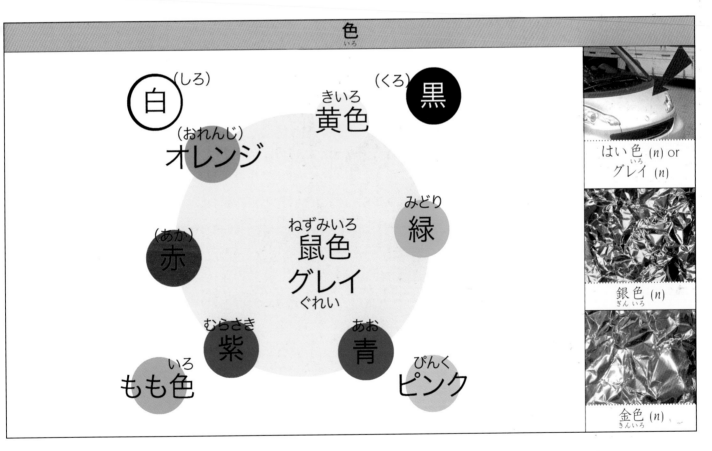

色 (いろ)

白 (しろ)
(くろ) 黒
きいろ 黄色
(おれんじ) オレンジ
みどり 緑
ねずみいろ 鼠色 グレイ ぐれい
(あか) 赤
むらさき 紫
あお 青
もも色 いろ
ぴんく ピンク

はい色 (n) or グレイ (n)

銀色 (n)

金色 (n)

| 色 (n) – color(s) | 色々 (な adj.) – various | 何色 (inter.) – what color? | 彼 (pron.) – he/him | 彼女 (pron.) – she/her | あまり (adv.) – not very | 全然 (adv.) – not at all |

Other words you might like to know:

橙色 (n) – orange
だいだいいろ

金髪 (n) – blond
きんぱつ

茶髪 (n) – hair dyed brown
ちゃぱつ

■ 漢字 Kanji
かんじ

色	いろ – color	ノ	ク	ク	名	多	色		
6 strokes	色 – color; (黄)色 – yellow								
	The first two strokes are a cuckoo bird (the kind of bird you see in a cuckoo clock); ク is the katakana for KU on top of a two-COLOR flag. The bottom of this kanji represents the shadow from the flag.								

白	ハク、しろ、しろ(い) – white	ノ	亻	白	白	白			
5 strokes	白 – white; 白い – white (adj.); 白(人) – Caucasian								
	Take the sun (日) and add a small flash of light (the first small stroke). The WHITE color is blindingly bright!								

黒	コク；くろ、くろ (い) – black	丶	冂	円	日	甲	甲	里	黒
11 strokes	黒 – black; 黒い – black (adj.); 黒(板) – blackboard	黒	黒	黒					
	The ground (土) of the rice field (田) is burnt BLACK by the fire (火) which you can see in the four strokes on the bottom.								

赤	セキ；あか、あか(い) – red, crimson, scarlet	一	十	土	宇	亦	赤	赤	
7 strokes	赤 – red; 赤い – red (adj.); 赤(ちゃん) – baby								
	The first three strokes are earth or soil (土). The bottom four strokes represent fiery RED lava pushing up on the earth.								

青	セイ；あお、あお(い) – blue, green; inexperienced	一	十	主	主	丰	青	青	青
8 strokes	青 – blue; 青い – blue (adj.); 青(年) youth								
	One (一) way to remember this 漢字 is to think how BLUE the soil of earth (土) looks under the light of the 月.								

■ 言葉の探索 Language Detection
ことば たんさく

1. 赤、赤色 - Colors (nouns)

   Colors in Japanese can appear as nouns, as you can see below, or as adjectives, as you will learn in the next chapter.

   A) 私は 赤が 好き です。　　　　　　　　= I like the color red.
   　　　 あか
   B) この Tシャツは 黒では ありません。　= This T-shirt is not black.
   C) 僕の ユニフォームの 色は 青と 赤 です。= My uniform's colors are blue and red.
   　 ぼく　　　　　　　　　　　　　 あお あか

2. あまり、全然
   　　　　 ぜんぜん

   あまり and 全然 are both adverbs that are used ONLY with the negative form of the verb. あまり means "not very,"
   　　　　　 ぜんぜん
   while 全然 means "not at all." These adverbs generally precede the verb they modify.
   　　 ぜんぜん

   A) ベン君は 数学が あまり 好きでは ありません。
   　　 くん　 すうがく
   　　= Ben does not like math very much.
   B) 私は お茶を 全然 飲みませんが、コーヒーは 時々 飲みます。
   　　　　 ちゃ　 ぜんぜん　　　　　　　　　　　 ときどき
   　　= I never drink green tea, but I sometimes drink coffee.
   C) 花子さんは 絵を 描く事が あまり 上手では ありません。
   　 はなこ　　 え　 か こと
   　　= Hanako is not very good at drawing.

■ 自習 Self Check
じしゅう

1. Say the following out loud to yourself in Japanese.

   A) Today my shirt is green.　　　　　　　D) I do not like purple very much.

   B) The paper is white.　　　　　　　　　E) I like yellow a little bit.

   C) I love orange.　　　　　　　　　　　　F) My father does not like blue at all.

■ 練習の時間 Time for Practice
れんしゅう じかん

Pair Practice

1. Point to something on or near your partner. Ask what color it is in Japanese. Take turns.

   A-さん: (pointing) それは 何色 ですか。
   　　　　　　　　　　　 なにいろ
   B-さん: これは 赤 です。
   　　　　　　 あか
   A-さん: そう ですね。

2. Ask your partner about his or her family members' favorite colors in Japanese. If you are unsure, either make up an answer or say that you don't know (しりません) in 日本語. You will first have to find out who is in your partner's family, as in the sample dialogue below. Take turns.

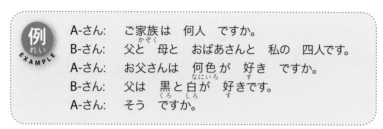

A-さん: ご家族は 何人 ですか。
B-さん: 父と 母と おばあさんと 私の 四人です。
A-さん: お父さんは 何色が 好き ですか。
B-さん: 父は 黒と白が 好きです。
A-さん: そう ですか。

3. Class Practice

だれ ですか。

Write down five statements, using color words, in Japanese, on a piece of scrap paper. The statements should describe one of the other students in the class. Next, one person reads his/her statements to the class; after three clues, the class can guess which classmate is being described. The first person to guess correctly reads his/her clues next.

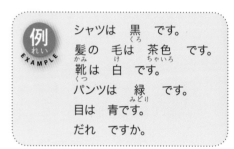

シャツは 黒 です。
髪の 毛は 茶色 です。
靴は 白 です。
パンツは 緑 です。
目は 青です。
だれ ですか。

■ 文化箱 Culture Chest

Fashion—Then and Now

Dress was very important to 10th- and 11th-century Japanese nobility, and they spent much time thinking about and planning what to wear. Elaborate layers of silk 着物 were time-consuming to weave and expensive to buy. Seasonal patterns were carefully considered by both the weavers and the wearers of 着物. Even something as simple as wearing an out-of-season under-kimono could be cause for gossip and comment at court. For instance, 清少納言, a contemporary of 紫式部, wrote in her collection of anecdotes and commentary called 枕草子 or *Pillow Book*, something that may be translated as "A woman with bad hair wearing a white cloth robe is not a pretty thing"!

Presently, the wearing of 着物 is generally limited to formal occasions such as weddings, funerals, tea ceremony or flower arranging occasions, or trips to temples or shrines. Visit Kyoto today, however, and you will see many a kimono-robed woman walking down the street.

■ キアラのジャーナル Kiara's Journal

Read the journal entry below, and then answer these questions.

❶ What colors were the flowers on Lady Murasaki's kimono?
❷ What color was Kiara's kimono?
❸ What was a little strange?
❹ What was delicious?

ジャーナルへ

　今朝、朝ご飯の　時に、紫さんは　着物を　着ました。とても　いい　着物　でした。彼女の着物に　花が　たくさん　ありました。その　花は　白と　もも色　でした。とても　きれいでした。私の　部屋にも　着物が　ありました。私の　着物は　黄色と　青の　花が　ありました。きれい　でした。じゅん君と　ベン君も　黒の　着物を　着ました。友さんは　銀色の着物を　着ました。男の子の　着物も　とてもきれいでした。朝ご飯の　時、音楽も　ありました。平安時代の　音楽は　とてもdifferent　でした。The tempo is quite slow and the scale is not anywhere near what I'm used to. ご飯は　とても　おいしかったです。白いご飯を　たくさん　食べました。緑の　漬け物と　オレンジ色の　魚 (fish)と　赤の　ストロベリーも　ありました。朝ご飯の　後で　色々な　お寺と　神社を　見に行きました。午後から　雅楽の　コンサートを　聞きました。紫さんは、「この　音楽の　皆さんは　とても　上手　です。」と、言いました。

僕も、雅楽は　とてもかっこいいと　思います。
I also think that gagaku is really cool!

■ 会話 Dialogue

キアラ　：　紫 さん、この音楽は、何と　言いますか。

紫　　　：　*雅楽　です。ベン君と　じゅん君と　キアラさんは、雅楽が　好き　ですか。

ベン　　：　すみません、僕は、ちょっと・・・・・　あまり　好きでは　ありません。

キアラ　：　私は、好き　です！　かっこいい　です！

じゅん　：　僕も、雅楽は　とても　かっこいいと　思います。僕は、色々な　音楽が　好きです。

友　　　：　私は、雅楽が、とても　好き　ですが、ベン君は、あまり　好きでは　ありませんね。

　　　　　　じゃあ、ベン君、私と　何か　食べに　行きましょう。

*雅楽 – court music during the Heian Period

■ 単語 New Words

歌舞伎 (n)　　　　　　能 (n)　　　　　　雅楽 (n)

■ 漢字 Kanji

歌　思

		一	一	一	一	可	可	哥
歌	カ、うた、うた(う) – song, sing	哥	哥	哥	歌	歌	歌	
14 strokes	歌 – a song; 歌(う) – to sing	The left side of this (可) looks like mouths open and SINGING SONGS on risers of a chorus while the right side looks similar to "next" (次). The singers are ready to SING the next SONG!						

	シ, おも(う) think, believe	丶	冂	冂	冃	田	甲	思	思
思	思(う) – to think, to believe おも	思							
9 strokes	When you are out working in the rice field (田), your heart (心) has nothing to do but THINK.								

■ 言葉の探索 Language Detection
こと ば　たん さく

1.　~と思います。 - I think . . .

~と思います is used when you want to express your own opinion. What comes before the ~と思います must be in the plain form. The plain form of the verb is the dictionary form, which was introduced in the first section of this chapter. The plain form of です is だ. Note the difference below between the polite form and the plain form for the non-past affirmative tense for the following types of words.

		Polite	Plain
1.	verbs	食べ ます	食べる
2.	nouns	すし です	すし だ
3.	い adjectives	美味しい です お　い	美味しい お　い
4.	な adjectives	静か です しず	静か だ しず

A)　私は 6時に 帰ると 思います。　　= I think that I will return at 6:00.
　　　　　　　かえ
B)　あの 人は 日本人だと 思います。　= I think that person over there is Japanese.
C)　ハンバーガーは 美味しい と 思います。 = I think hamburgers are delicious.
　　　　　　　　　お い
D)　あのフランス人は 有名だと 思います。 = I think that the French person over there is famous.
　　　　　　　　ゆうめい

■ 自習 Self Check
じ しゅう

1.　Say the following out loud to yourself in Japanese.

A) I think I will go to Japan.

B) I think Japanese is fun.

C) I think the first year students are quiet.

D) I think that this is a Chinese language book.

E) I think (finish this sentence based upon what you really think about something or someone).

■ 練習の時間 Time for Practice
れんしゅう　　じ かん

1.　**Pair Practice**

Point to something colorful near you and your partner. Make a statement about the object, using the phrase と思
います. If your statement is correct, your partner should agree. If your statement is not correct, your partner should correct you. Each of you should make at least 4 statements.

A-さん: (*pointing to a notebook*) この　ノートは　先生の　だと　思います。
= I think that this notebook is the teacher's.
B-さん: いいえ、違います。私の　ですよ。　= No, that's incorrect. It is mine.
-OR- はい、そう　ですね。　= Yes, it is (so).

2. Pair Practice

Use the following cues to ask your partner questions about which of the following he/she likes or is skilled at. B-さん should always answer negatively, using the adverbs あまり or 全然. Take turns.

Aさん: アイスクリームは　好き　ですか。
Bさん: いいえ、アイスクリームは　全然 好き　ではありません。
-OR-
Aさん: ダンスは　とくいですか。
Bさん: いいえ、あまり　とくい　ではありません。

liver (レバー)	disco (ディスコ)
okra (オクラ)	spiders (くも)
broccoli (ブロッコリー)	mountain climbing (山のぼり)
grapefruit (グレープフルーツ)	cactus (サボテン)

■ 文化箱 Culture Chest

雅楽 Gagaku

雅楽, or "elegant music," is a style of court music that dates back to the Nara period (奈良時代) and combines influences from Tang-dynasty China, Korea, and Shinto. It is performed with traditional wind, string, and percussion instruments and is often accompanied by classical dance. Theater also developed in conjunction with 雅楽; 能 (Noh theater) became especially popular in the 14th century. 雅楽 uses a pentatonic scale, that is, a musical scale with five pitches per octave. Touru Takemitsu is one well-known modern Japanese composer (he wrote the soundtracks for the movies *Ran* and *Kwaidan*, among others) who has used traditional Japanese music in his compositions. See if you can find some of Touru's music to listen to online. Can you hear the influence of 雅楽 in any of his pieces?

■ キアラのジャーナル Kiara's Journal

Read the journal entry below, and then answer these questions.

❶ What did Kiara and Murasaki spend the day doing?
❷ What is your favorite color? Would you find it on a kimono?
❸ Do you think Heian-kyou was a colorful town? Why or why not?

ジャーナルへ

　　今日は、紫式部さんと　九時から　三時まで　いっしょに　いました。とても　楽しかったです。いっしょに　平安京の　お寺と　神社を　見ました。平安時代にも　お寺と　神社は、たくさん　ありました。

　　紫さんと　よく　話しました。私は　色の　名前と　趣味の事を　勉強しました。Color words come in noun form and adjective form. I started off practicing with the noun form, like 赤 and 青 for red and blue. For example、「この着物は　赤と青です。とても　きれいです。」 じゅん君 told me there is another way to use color words as adjectives, but I decided to practice that later. それから、I learned that after hobby words, you use 'は' when the hobby is the topic. For example、「私の　趣味は　絵を　描く事　です。」 is how I would say "My hobby is drawing pictures." もう少し　がんばって 日本語の　勉強を　しますね！

■ テクノの時間 Techno Time

Tomohiro, a first year high school student in Japan, is trying to find out what students in American schools like and what they are good at. He has asked you to write to him telling him the results of a survey of what ALL of the following people like and what they are good at:

A) at least two people in your family
B) two students

C) a teacher
D) yourself

Be sure to include an introductory remark and a closing remark in your letter. Use sentences similar to this one to complete your task:

三人は読書が　好き　です。　二人は　日本語が　上手　です。

Pick a friend or family member to interview about his/her hobbies, likes and dislikes, and skills. With the information you have gathered, introduce this person to your class, in Japanese. Use a poster with graphics or photographs or a slide show/PowerPoint format.

■ 単語チェックリスト New Word Checklist
たんごちぇっくりすと

Japanese	Location	English
7-1		
あめふと　　アメフト (n)	7-1	American football
いけばな　　生け花 (n)	7-1	flower arranging
うた　　歌 (n)	7-1	song
うたう/うたいます　　歌う/歌います (歌って) (v)	7-1	(to) sing
うたうこと　　歌う事 (n)	7-1	singing
おどり　　踊り (n)	7-1	dancing
およぐ/およぎます　　泳ぐ/泳ぎます (泳いで) (v)	7-1	(to) swim
およぐこと　　泳ぐ事 (n)	7-1	swimming
ぎたー　　ギター (n)	7-1	guitar
ぎたー(を) ひく/ひきます　　ギター(を) 弾く/弾きます (v)	7-1	(to) play guitar
ごるふ　　ゴルフ (n)	7-1	golf
さどう/ちゃどう　　茶道 (n)	7-1	tea ceremony
しゅみ　　趣味 (n)	7-1	hobby
じょうば　　乗馬 (n)	7-1	horseback riding
じょぎんぐ　　ジョギング (n)	7-1	jogging
すいえい　　水泳 (n)	7-1	swimming
すきー　　スキー (n)	7-1	skiing
すけぼー(を) する/します　　スケボー(を) する/します (v)	7-1	(to) skateboard
すぽーつ (を) する/します　　スポーツ(を) する/します (n)	7-1	sports
そして (conj.)	7-1	then; and then
それから (conj.)	7-1	then; and then
それに (conj.)	7-1	moreover; furthermore
たべること　　食べる事 (n)	7-1	eating
どくしょ　　読書 (n)	7-1	reading
とらんぷ　　トランプ (n)	7-1	playing cards; card game
ねること　　寝る事 (n)	7-1	sleeping
ぴあの　　ピアノ (n)	7-1	piano
ひく/ひきます　　弾く/弾きます (弾いて) (v)	7-1	(to) play (a stringed instrument)
びでおげーむ　　ビデオゲーム (n)	7-1	video games
やきゅう　　野球 (n)	7-1	baseball
りょうり　　料理 (n)	7-1	cooking
りょこう　　旅行 (n)	7-1	trip; travel
7-2		
おもう/おもいます　　思う/思います (思って) (v)	7-2	(to) think
かえる　　蛙 (n)	7-2	frog
きらい　　嫌い (な adj.)	7-2	dislike
じょうだん　　冗談 (n)	7-2	joke
すき　　好き (な adj.)	7-2	like
だいきらい　　大嫌い (な adj.)	7-2	dislike a lot, hate
だいすき　　大好き (な adj.)	7-2	love
たいてい (adv.)	7-2	usually

Japanese	Location	English
どうぶつ　動物 (n)	7-2	animals
ねずみ (n)	7-2	rat, mouse

7-3

Japanese	Location	English
がんばる/がんばります　頑張る/頑張ります（頑張って）(v)	7-3	(to) do one's best
とくい　得意 (な adj.)	7-3	skilled at
にがて　苦手 (な adj.)	7-3	unskilled at
へた　下手 (な adj.)	7-3	not good at
やってみる/やってみます（やってみて）(v)	7-3	(to) see if you can do (something); (to) try to do (something)
やる/やります（やって）(v)	7-3	(to) do

7-4

Japanese	Location	English
あお　青 (n)	7-4	blue
あか　赤 (n)	7-4	red
あまり (adv.)	7-4	not very
いろ　色 (n)	7-4	color
いろいろ　色々 (な adj.)	7-4	various, various colors
おれんじ　オレンジ (n)	7-4	orange
かのじょ　彼女 (pron.)	7-4	she; girlfriend
かれ　彼 (pron.)	7-4	he; boyfriend
きいろ　黄色 (n)	7-4	yellow
きんいろ　金色 (n)	7-4	gold
ぎんいろ　銀色 (n)	7-4	silver
きんぱつ　金髪 (n)	7-4	blond (hair)
ぐれい　グレイ (n)	7-4	gray
くろ　黒 (n)	7-4	black
しろ　白 (n)	7-4	white
ぜんぜん　全然 (adv.)	7-4	not at all
だいだいいろ　橙色 (n)	7-4	orange
ちゃばつ　茶髪 (n)	7-4	brown (hair)
なにいろ　何色 (inter.)	7-4	what color
ねずみいろ　鼠色 (n)	7-4	gray (mouse colored)
はいいろ　灰色 (n)	7-4	gray, ash-colored
ぴんく　ピンク (n)	7-4	pink
みどり　緑 (n)	7-4	green
むらさき　紫 (n)	7-4	purple

7-5

Japanese	Location	English
ががく　雅楽 (n)	7-5	gagaku, ancient Japanese court music
かっこいい (い adj.)	7-5	cool
かぶき　歌舞伎 (n)	7-5	kabuki theater
のう　能 (n)	7-5	Noh (a type of theater)

Adjectives in Amanohashidate

✓ **Learning Goals**

By the end of this chapter you will learn:

A) a larger number of adjectives

B) how to use adjectives as well as their negative, past, and past negative tenses

C) about the folk tale of Urashima Tarou

D) 14 additional kanji

✓ **Performance Goals**

By the end of this chapter you will be able to:

A) describe things using a variety of adjectives

B) describe what things used to be like

C) read and write 14 additional kanji

Amanohashidate, on the Sea of Japan, is said to be one of Japan's three most scenic views.

海が<ruby>海<rt>うみ</rt></ruby>がきれい　ですね。
The ocean is beautiful, isn't it?

1) わあ・・・・
海が きれい ですね。

2) ビーチも
美しい ですね。

3) そう
ですね。ここは
天橋立 です。

4) ほら！あそこに
おじいさんが います。

5) わあ、ひげが とても 長い
ですね。そして、あの はこは
とても 不思議 ですね。

■ 会話 Dialogue

キアラ ： わあ・・・・海が きれい ですね。

ベン ： ビーチも 美しい ですね。

友 ： そう ですね。ここは 天橋立 です。

ベン ： ほら！あそこに おじいさんが います。

キアラ： わあ、ひげが、とても 長い ですね。そして、あの はこは とても 不思議 ですね。

■ 単語 New Words

うるさい (い *adj.*)	小さい (い *adj.*)	強い (い *adj.*) (prev. introduced)	きたない (い *adj.*)	かわいい (い *adj.*)
不思議 (な *adj.*)	ひどい (い *adj.*)	こわい (い *adj.*)	つまらない (い *adj.*)	美味しい (い *adj.*)
きれい (な *adj.*)	ビーチ (*n*)	海 (*n*)	はこ (*n*)	美しい (い *adj.*) – beautiful 短い (い *adj.*) – short (in length)

Other words you might like to use:

危ない (い *adj.*) – dangerous

じれったい (い *adj.*) – irritating

きびしい (い *adj.*) – strict

ずるい (い *adj.*) – cunning

みにくい (い *adj.*) – ugly

ばかばかしい (い *adj.*) – foolish; silly

かしこい (い *adj.*) – wise; bright

嬉しい (い *adj.*) – glad, happy

わがまま (な *adj.*) – selfish

All of the adjectives in this bonus list except for the last are い adjectives.

■ 漢字 Kanji
かんじ

美 9 strokes	ビ; うつく（しい）– beautiful	丶	ソ	⺌	ꙮ	羊	羊	羊	美
	美（しい）– beautiful; 美（人）– beautiful person (woman) うつく / び・じん	美							
	The upper half of this kanji is a sheep (羊) and the bottom part is the kanji for big (大). In ancient China, the sheep was an important domesticated animal. Big wool coats and large wool carpets are certainly BEAUTIFUL.								

長 8 strokes	チョウ – head, chief; なが（い）– long (length)	l	⼁	F	E	토	長	長	長
	長（い）– long (adj.); 長（崎）– Nagasaki (city in Kyushu); （校）長（先生）– school principal; （班）長 – leader of the group, "head honcho." なが / ながさき / こう・せんせい / はん・ちょう								
	This is a picture of an old man whose hair is streaming in the wind. This kanji implies LENGTH, including time and spatial length. It also looks like a LONG table with a stack of books on it.								

短 12 strokes	みじか（い）– short (length)	ノ	⺦	⺇	午	矢	矢	知	知
	短（い）– short (length) みじか	知	知	短	短				
	The left half of this kanji is a bow, though one could imagine it as an archer. The right side is a bean. An arrow must be a SHORT one to go through a bean.								

海 9 strokes	カイ; うみ – ocean, sea	丶	⼆	⺡	冫	浐	汸	海	海
	海 – ocean, sea; （日本）海 – Sea of Japan うみ / にほん・かい	海							
	The left three strokes of this kanji are the radical for water. Imagine water splashing on a beach every (毎) day, eventually creating an OCEAN of water.								

Previously introduced kanji:

Kanji	Previous Pronunciation and Use	New Pronunciation and Use
大	大（学） だい・がく	大きい おお
小	小（学校） しょう・がっこう	小さい ちい

Notice that some kanji are in compounds of kanji called 漢語, while others are followed by
かんご
hiragana and make stand-alone words.

■ 言葉の探索 Language Detection

1. い and な adjectives

   An adjective is a word that describes a person, place, or thing. Notice that in Japanese there are two types of adjectives. They are classified as い adjectives or な adjectives as outlined below. Refer to the list of adjectives in Appendix 1 for more examples.

   A) all い adjectives end in "い."

   B) MOST な adjectives end in sounds other than "い" (two exceptions are 有名 and きれい).

Using い adjectives:

Just like in English, い adjectives can come before or after the nouns that they modify. Here are several examples.

A) あの 映画は こわい です。	= That movie is scary.
B) この 朝ご飯 は 美味しいです。	= This breakfast is delicious.
C) それは かわいい 猫 ですね。	= That is a cute cat.
D) この中学校は 大きい ですね。	= This middle school is large, isn't it?

Using な adjectives:

な adjectives can also come before or after the nouns that they modify. However, if they come before the noun, the adjective is followed by a な。

A) 教室は 静か です。	= The classroom is quiet.
B) マイケル・ジョーダンは 有名 な 人 です。	= Michael Jordan is a famous person.
C) 私の 犬は 元気 です。	= My dog is lively.
D) あれは 不思議な話ですね。	= That is a strange story, isn't it?

■ 自習 Self Check

Say each of the following out loud, and decide which are い adjectives and which are な adjectives.

- ⊃ 大きい
- ⊃ 小さい
- ⊃ 短い
- ⊃ 美しい
- ⊃ 美味しい
- ⊃ 不思議
- ⊃ かわいい
- ⊃ 長い
- ⊃ うるさい
- ⊃ きれい
- ⊃ 静か
- ⊃ こわい

■ 練習の時間 Time for Practice

1. Use the images below to ask and answer questions with your partner in Japanese.

A-さん: どれが 長い ですか。	= Which one is long?
B-さん: これが 長い です。	= (Point to the correct image.) This one is long.
A-さん: はい、そう です。	= Yes, that's right.

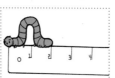

2. Use the adjectives below to ask your partner questions about people you both know. If the answer is negative, use a different adjective in the answer.

> **例 EXAMPLE**
> A-さん：　とも子さんは　足が　小さい　ですか。　　= Are Tomoko's feet small?

a. 静か
d. 大きい

b. うるさい
e. つまらない

c. 強い
f. 面白い

3. Use adjectives to talk about the pictures below with your partner. Use the sample dialogue as a pattern.

> **例 EXAMPLE**
> A-さん：　何が　美味しい　ですか。　　　= What is delicious (to you)?
> B-さん：　天ぷらが　美味しい　です。　　= The tempura is delicious.
> A-さん：　そうですか。　-OR-　そうですね。　= Is that so? -OR- That's so isn't it.

■ 文化箱 Culture Chest

The Tale of 浦島太郎

The folk story of 浦島太郎 is well known to all Japanese children. As with many folktales, there are several different versions. Here is one.

One day, the fisherman 浦島太郎 rescued a turtle on the beach. It was being tormented by a group of young boys, who were hitting it with a stick. In gratitude, the turtle returned the next day to invite 太郎 to visit the 竜宮城, the Dragon King's splendid palace at the bottom of the sea. The Princess 乙姫 welcomed 太郎 with delicious food and singing and dancing, and 太郎 spent much happy time there. Eventually, though, 太郎 began to miss his family and friends and decided to return to his home. As お土産, the Princess gave him a jewel-encrusted 玉手箱, or treasure chest, with the stern warning never to open the box. Again riding on the turtle's back, 太郎 returned to the beach near his home. To his surprise, 太郎 recognized not a soul. Desolate, he sat down on the beach and, forgetting the Princess's words, opened the treasure chest. Immediately, a puff of white smoke [some versions say "purple smoke"] emerged to envelop 太郎. He was transformed into an old man with a long beard. The days 太郎 thought he had spent under the sea actually numbered almost 300 years!

■ 地図 **Map Skills**

❶ 天橋立 は 日本の どこに ありますか。
❷ What body of water does it border?
❸ Which ancient capital is the closest to Amanohashidate?

The kanji for this town and its feature attraction are 天橋立, meaning "standing on heaven's bridge. Many visitors to Amanohashidate view the site by turning around, bending over, and looking at it upside down through their legs. Can you guess why?

AMANOHASHI DATE

■ キアラのジャーナル **Kiara's Journal**

Read the journal entry below, and then answer these questions.

❶ What was the weather like in Amanohashidate?
❷ How did Kiara feel about the weather?
❸ What was the name of the person Ben met on their walk?
❹ What was the most outstanding physical feature of that person?

ジャーナルへ

今日は、朝ご飯の　後、紫さんと　一緒に　清水寺の　となりの　神社の　鳥居に　行きました。紫さんは、とても　いい人でした。さようならを　言うのは、さびしかったですが、紫さんに　さよならを　言って、時の門に　入りました。

After some time passed、私達は、時の門を　出ました。友さんが、「天橋立と　いうところに　います。」と　言いました。天橋立の　漢字は'天橋'(heaven's bridge)と'立'(standing on or to stand) です。天橋立は、とても　きれい　です。

Not only are we not back in the 21st century, we're not even close. According to Tomo san, we're still only in the year 1388! I can't believe that we've been traveling together for about five months and now we're seeing things that happened in the 14th century! I'm thinking that I should learn to operate the 時の門 myself.

OK, it's time to get back to practicing my Japanese writing. I've been studying adjectives a lot lately so that I can better describe some of the things that I'm seeing. Here goes...

天橋立に　来ました。ここは　少し　あたたかい(warm)　です。私は、あたたかいのが　好きです。海の　真ん中に、まっすぐな　長い道が　あります。It looks like a bridge floating in the water, or if you look at it upside down, you could say, it looks like a bridge to heaven. 海も　空も、とても　きれい　です。母も、ここが　大好きだろうと　思います。

私達は、皆で　climbed up to the top of the hill. We could see 遠い　島。すばらしかった　です。その　後、天橋立の　ビーチで　散歩しました。そこで、おじいさんに　会いました。その　おじいさんの　名前は　浦島太郎　でした。かれの　ひげは、とても　長かったです。

■ テクノの時間 Techno Time

Though you've not been introduced to them all yet, type all the vocabulary words from this chapter into your digital dictionary. Be sure to type first the kanji, then hiragana, and then the meaning in English as you have been doing. Remember to use your file labeled "JISHO" (in *romaji*).

この海はもっときれいでした。
This ocean used to be prettier.

■ 会話 Dialogue
かい わ

キアラ ： こんにちは。

太郎　： こんにちは。

キアラ： おじいさん、ひげが とても 長い ですね。おじいさんは 何オ ですか。
なんさい

太郎　： 僕は 三百オ です。昔々、この 海は もっと きれい でした。そして かわいい
ぼく　　　　　さい　　　　　むかしむかし　　　　　　　　　　　　　　　　　　　　　　　　　　　　　　
亀が いました。五人の 子供達も いました。でも 彼らは 悪い ことを しました。
かめ　　　　　　　　　こどもたち　　　　　　　　　　　　かれ　　　わる

ベン　： ええっ・・・何を しましたか。

太郎　： 子供達は 亀を いじめました。僕は、「やめなさい！」と、言いました。*すると、
こどもたち　かめ　　　　　　　　ぼく　　　　　　　　　　　　　　　　
すぐに 子供達は、家に 帰りました。
こどもたち

じゅん： わあ。亀は こわかった でしょうね。
かめ

*すると – and then

■ 単語 New Words
たん ご

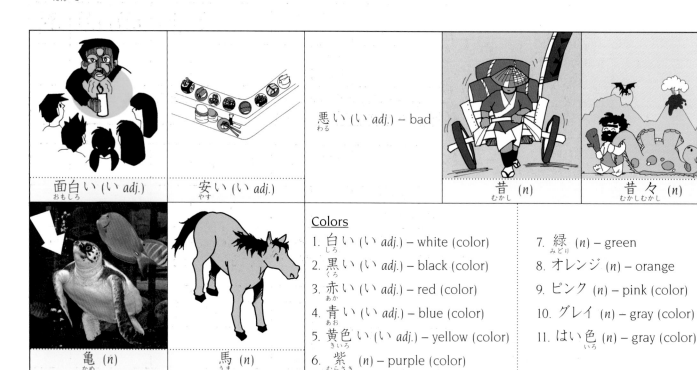

面白い (い adj.)
おもしろ

安い (い adj.)
やす

悪い (い adj.) – bad
わる

昔 (n)
むかし

昔々 (n)
むかしむかし

亀 (n)
かめ

馬 (n)
うま

<u>Colors</u>
1. 白い (い adj.) – white (color)
しろ
2. 黒い (い adj.) – black (color)
くろ
3. 赤い (い adj.) – red (color)
あか
4. 青い (い adj.) – blue (color)
あお
5. 黄色い (い adj.) – yellow (color)
きいろ
6. 紫 (n) – purple (color)
むらさき

7. 緑 (n) – green
みどり
8. オレンジ (n) – orange
9. ピンク (n) – pink (color)
10. グレイ (n) – gray (color)
11. はい色 (n) – gray (color)
いろ

天橋立 (n) –
あまのはしだて
place name

子供 (n) – child
こども

子供達 (n) –
こどもたち
children

彼ら (pron.) –
かれ
they (boys)

(やめる) やめます (v) –
to quit/stop

漢字 Kanji

安 悪 面 天 立 昔 々

安 6 strokes	アン – safe; やす(い) – cheap		ヽ	ソ	宀	宇	安	安		
	安(全) – safe; 安(い) – cheap あん ぜん　　　やす									
	The top half of this kanji is a roof, and the lower half represents a woman. You can think of this particular woman as someone who is CHEAP and paranoid so she is staying under her own roof to stay SAFE and to save money.									

悪 11 strokes	わる(い) – bad		一	匚	亓	戸	丏	丏	亜	亜
	悪(い) – bad わる		悪	悪	悪					
	The top half of this kanji (亜) is the kanji for Asia; the bottom part (心) is the kanji for heart or spirit. Just think, if all of Asia were pressing down on your heart, it would be very 悪い or BAD!									

面 9 strokes	メン; おも – face, mask		一	丆	厂	币	而	而	面	
	面(白い) – interesting, enjoyable おも しろ		面							
	Here is a FACE or a MASK with one huge eye (目) in the middle and a wig blowing off held on by only one thread of hair (the second stroke). Is this a funny MASK or a scary one?									

天 4 strokes	テン; あま – heaven		一	二	于	天				
	天(皇) – emperor; 天(ぷら) – Japanese batter fried てん のう　　　　てん vegetables, shrimp, and fish; 天(橋立) – place name 　　　　　　　　　　あまの はし だて									
	The kanji for big (大) is based on a person holding out his/her arms and legs to appear bigger. Here, the additional horizontal line above that person represents the space above humans, that is, the SKY or HEAVEN.									

立 5 strokes	た(つ) – to stand; リツ – to stand		ヽ	亠	六	立	立			
	立(つ) – to stand; 立って下さい – please stand; た　　　　　　　 た　　　くだ (起)立 – stand (at attention) き りつ									
	This kanji shows a person STANDing tall on the ground (bottom stroke) with a very wide brimmed hat on his head.									

昔 8 strokes	むかし – long ago		一	十	卄	世	芇	昔	昔	昔
	昔 – long ago; 昔(々) – long, long ago むかし　　　 むかし むかし									
	The top part of this kanji symbolizes "accumulation," with the kanji for ten (十) added to another 十. More and more "days" 日 accumulate and are multiplied by ten, making our story take place LONG, LONG AGO.									

			ノ	ケ	々			
々	人(々) – people; 木(々) – trees; ひとびと 昔(々) – long, long ago むかし むかし							
3 strokes	This mark has no pronunciation by itself and is not technically a kanji, but is rather a "kanji mark" or pluralizer.							

■ 言葉の探索 Language Detection
ことば　たんさく

1. Past tense of い adjectives

   The past tense of い adjectives is created by dropping the "い" and adding "かった" to the adjective stem and keeping です at the end of the sentence. The affirmative past tense of an い adjective is followed by です, not でした.

    大きい　です。 ⇨ 大きい+かった　です。 ⇨ 大きかった　です。 = It was big.
   涼しい　です。 ⇨ 涼しい+かった　です。 ⇨ 涼しかった　です。 = It was cool (weather).

2. Past tense of な adjectives

   The past tense of な adjectives is created by adding でした after the adjective without any other changes.

    元気　です。 ⇨ 元気　でした。 = He/she/it was fine (energetic/healthy).

Adjective conjugation chart: non-past and past

い adjectives	Non-past tense 〜いです	Past tense 〜かったです	英語
青い	青いです	青かったです	blue
面白い	面白いです	面白かったです	interesting

な adjectives			
静か しず	静かです しず	静かでした しず	quiet
ふしぎ	ふしぎです	ふしぎでした	strange

Irregular adjective			
いい or 良い	いいです 良いです	良かったです	good

■ 自習 Self Check

Say the words in the left column, followed by the past form.

1. い adjective conjugation

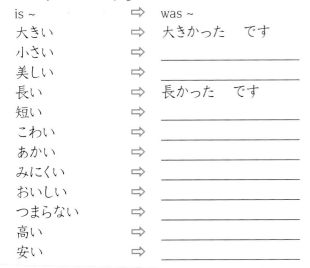

is ~	⇨	was ~
大きい	⇨	大きかった　です
小さい	⇨	＿＿＿＿＿＿＿
美しい	⇨	＿＿＿＿＿＿＿
長い	⇨	長かった　です
短い	⇨	＿＿＿＿＿＿＿
こわい	⇨	＿＿＿＿＿＿＿
あかい	⇨	＿＿＿＿＿＿＿
みにくい	⇨	＿＿＿＿＿＿＿
おいしい	⇨	＿＿＿＿＿＿＿
つまらない	⇨	＿＿＿＿＿＿＿
高い	⇨	＿＿＿＿＿＿＿
安い	⇨	＿＿＿＿＿＿＿

2. な adjective conjugation

is ~	⇨	was ~
きれい	⇨	きれい　でした
静か	⇨	＿＿＿＿＿＿＿
すてき	⇨	＿＿＿＿＿＿＿

3. Irregular いい adjective conjugation

is ~	⇨	was ~
いい／良い	⇨	良かった　です
かっこいい	⇨	＿＿＿＿＿＿＿

■ 練習の時間 Time for Practice

1. Pair Practice

Assume that you have just participated in the activities below. Ask and answer questions about how the activities were. Use as many adjectives as you can in your answers.

> 例 EXAMPLE
>
> A-さん:　宿題　は　どう　でしたか。 = How was the homework?
> B-さん:　つまらなかった　です。　そして、　長かった　です。 = It was boring. And it was long.
> A-さん:　本当。 = Really?

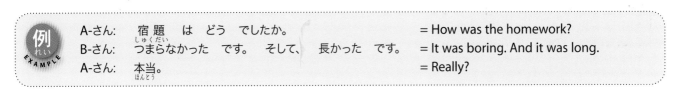

playing basketball	playing video games	reading manga
doing homework	swimming	doing karate

2. Pair Practice

With your partner, use as many Japanese adjectives in sentences to describe the following as you can until your teacher tells you to stop.

例
れい
EXAMPLE

A-さん： 映画は　どう　でしたか。 　　　　えいが	= How was the movie?
B-さん： (映画は)　面白しろかった　です。 　　　　　えいが　　　おもしろ	= The movie was interesting.
A-さん： そうですか。	= Is it/that so?

Note: If you do not know the vocabulary in the left-hand column, you can simply say something like 「5番は
　　　ばん
どう　でしたか。」(How was number 5?)

1. last movie you saw	
2. favorite elementary teacher	
3. middle school (building)	
4. memorable present you received	
5. something you did last night	
6. first day of high school	
7. a sport you played	
8. a singer/band you heard	
9. (your choice)	
10. (your choice)	

■ 文化箱 Culture Chest
　　ぶん か ばこ

昔々　(Long, Long Ago...)
むかしむかし

　　　Two common types of Japanese folklore are 昔話 (tales of long ago) and 伝説 (legends). Japanese and Western folk
　　　　　　　　　　　　　　　　　　　　　　　むかしばなし　　　　　　　　　でんせつ
tales have many similarities: both often contain important lessons and both are used to transmit morals and social customs to children. Unlike most Western folk tales, though, Japanese folk tales do not always have happy endings (a tradition
you can see continuing on in today's Japanese TV shows and movies). Japanese of all ages have long enjoyed listening to
these stories about 動物 (animals), 神 (spirits and gods), 鬼 (demons and ogres), and お化け (monsters and ghosts).
　　　　　　　　どうぶつ　　　　　かみ　　　　　　おに　　　　　　　　　　ば
In fact, the Japanese word for "interesting", 面白い, reflects a time when families would sit at home, around the fire pit,
　　　　　　　　　　　　　　　　　　　　　おもしろ
and listen to stories. As the plot grew more interesting, the audience would draw closer to the fire, with the white 白い
　　　しろ
light from the fire reflecting on their faces 面. 面白いですね！
　　　　　　　　　　　　　　　　　　　めん　おもしろ

■ キアラのジャーナル Kiara's Journal

Read the journal entry below, and then answer these questions.

❶ Where did Urashima Taro first see the turtle?
❷ Why did the turtle thank Urashima Taro?
❸ What sort of present did Urashima Taro receive from the princess?
❹ Did Urashima Taro follow the princess' advice about this present?
❺ How old is Urashima Taro now?

ジャーナルへ

天橋立に 来て すぐ、 ある おじいさんと 会いました。 その おじいさんの 名前は 浦島太郎 でした。 太郎さんは 三百才 だと 言いました。 (How it could be?!) 彼は とても 優しかったです。 若い 時に ビーチで 亀を rescue しました。 その 亀は ビーチで 寝て いましたが、 意地悪な 五人の 男の子達に、 teased with sticks and rocks. 太郎さんは その亀を rescued from the 意地悪な 男の子達。 その 亀は、「どうも 有り難う ございました。」と 言いました。

次の 日、太郎さんは また ビーチへ 行きました。 木の 下に 座って、昼ご飯を 食べていました。 そこへ、 その 亀が 来ました。 亀さんは、「きのうは、とても うれしか った です。」と 言いました。 そして、「私と 一緒に 海の中に 行きませんか。」と、 言いました。

太郎さんは、「いい ですね。 でも、私は 海の中に 行くと 死にますよ。」と、言い ました。

亀さんは、「大丈夫 です。 さあ、どうぞ。」と、言いました。

太郎さんは rode on the back of 亀さん、and 海の中に 行きました。 There was a beautiful castle under the sea. It was called『りゅうぐうじょう』。 太郎さんは、「そこは、とても すば らしかった です。」と、いいました。 金と 銀の treasures が たくさん ありました。 大 きい 部屋に 入りました。 そこに、とても きれいな 女の人が、来ました。 She was a princess of the castle, and she was called『おとひめさま』。 おとひめさまは、「私の 亀を 助けて(saved)下さって、本当に ありがとう ございました。 今日は、美味しい物を たくさん 食べてください。」と、言いました。 太郎さんは、寿司や 色々な 美味しい物 を たくさん 食べました。 それは、とても 楽しい 時間でした。 ご飯の 後で おと ひめさまは 太郎さんに プレゼントを あげました。 プレゼントは とても きれいな箱 でした。 おとひめさまは、「これは とても 大事な 物 です。 この 箱を never あけては いけません。」と、言いました。 その後、亀さんと 太郎さんは ビーチに 帰りました。 そして、 太郎さんは 家へ 帰りました。 でも、彼の お母さんと お父さんは、どこにも いませんでした。 友達も いませんでした。 There was nobody who Taro knew. それは、とても 不思議な 事 でした。 太郎さんは very confused で ビーチへ 行って、プレゼントの 箱を 開けました。 すると(And then)、とつぜん(suddenly)太郎さんは 三百才の おじいさんに なり

ました！太郎さんは、海の中で、一日、楽しい時間を、**enjoy**したと思っていました。でも、それは、一日では　ありませんでした。**About**三百年間　でした！だから、今、太郎さんは　三百才の　おじいさん　です。かわいそう　ですね。

　時の門は、すごいです！(awesome!) 私達を、昔話 (legend)　の　世界 (world) に、連れて　来てくれました！(brought)

■ テクノの時間 Techno Time

After school yesterday, you went with your friends to a new きっさてん (喫茶店 = coffee shop). Write a paragraph (6–8 lines) about the experience in your digi journal. Use the adjective list in the appendix to help you and remember to use the past tense. Include transitional words such as そして, それから, and が. Comment on:

- ⊃ how new the coffee shop was
- ⊃ how tasty, or horrible, the drinks were
- ⊃ the cost of the drinks
- ⊃ how quiet, or noisy, your friends were
- ⊃ the look or the style of the coffee shop
- ⊃ whether or not you would return to this coffee shop

これは美味しくありません。
This is not delicious.

■ 会話 Dialogue
(かいわ)

キアラ ： 友さん、ここに　いましたか・・・・。

友　　： おっと・・・　ごめんなさい。おなかが　ペコペコ　でした。この　かには　とても
　　　　　美味しかった　です。でも、この　漬物は　美味しく　ありません。
　　　　(おい)　　　　　　　　　　　　　　(つけもの)　　(おい)

ベン　： あれ、全部　食べましたか。ひどいなあ・・・。私達は　ずっと　友さんを　待っていま
　　　　　　　(ぜんぶ)
　　　　　したよ。

■ 単語 New Words
(たんご)

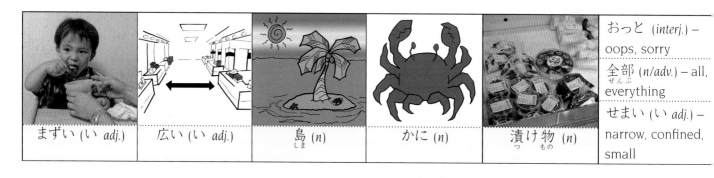

まずい (い *adj.*)	広い (い *adj.*)	島 (*n*) (しま)	かに (*n*)	漬け物 (*n*) (つ)(もの)	おっと (*interj.*) – oops, sorry

おっと (*interj.*) – oops, sorry

全部 (*n/adv.*) – all, everything
(ぜんぶ)

せまい (い *adj.*) – narrow, confined, small

■ 漢字 Kanji
(かんじ)

有 6 strokes	ユウ、あ(る) – to exist, to be	一　ナ　オ　有　有　有
	有(名) – famous (ゆう)(めい)	
	Imagine that the man in the moon (月) really EXISTS. Now imagine him spreading his arms out as he tries to jump over the moon (the first 2 strokes of this kanji).	

広 5 strokes	ひろ(い) – wide, spacious	` 亠 广 広 広
	広(い) – wide, spacious; (ひろ) 広(島) – (city of) Hiroshima (ひろ)(しま)	
	Under a canopy (the first three strokes) it is easier to move ム (katakana MU) around if it is WIDE and SPACIOUS. Let the "mu-ving" around remind you of the katakana ム.	

島 10 strokes	トウ, しま – island	´　亻　户　戶　自　鸟　鳥
	(広)島 – (city of) Hiroshima; (バリ)島 – the island (ひろ)(しま)　　　　　　　　　(とう) of Bali; (半)島 – peninsula (はん)(とう)	島　島
	This kanji resembles the kanji for bird 鳥, except there is a mountain 山 on the bottom. Just like a bird flies, an ISLAND, too, is a bit of the mainland that has flown off.	

■ 言葉の探索 Language Detection

1. Negating adjectives

   A. To put an い adjective in the non-past negative tense, drop the "い" and add "くないです" or "くありません" to the adjective stem.

   い adjective conjugation for adjectives in the negative tense

   | is ~ | ⇨ | is not ~ |

   is ~　　　⇨　　　is not ~

   大きい　⇨　　大きくないです
   　　　　　　　大きくありません

   小さい　⇨　　小さくないです
   　　　　　　　小さくありません

   美しい　⇨　　美しくないです
   　　　　　　　美しくありません

   長い　　⇨　　長くないです
   　　　　　　　長くありません

   B. To put a な adjective in the non-past negative tense, simply add ではありません/じゃありません or ではないです/じゃないです to the end of the adjective.

   きれい　⇨　　きれいでは　ないです／きれいじゃない　です。
   　　　　　　　きれいでは　ありません／きれいじゃ　ありません。

   静か　　⇨　　静かでは　ないです／静かじゃない　です。
   　　　　　　　静かでは　ありません／静かじゃ　ありません。

   IMPORTANT NOTE:
   The negative form of いい or 良い is 良くありません/良くないです。

Adjective conjugation chart: Non-past and negative

い adjectives	Non-past 〜いです	Negative 〜くありません 〜くないです	英語
面白い	面白いです	面白くありません 面白くないです	interesting
まずい	まずいです	まずくありません まずくないです	tastes bad
ひどい	ひどいです	ひどくありません ひどくないです	terrible

な adjectives			
有名	有名です	有名ではありません 〜じゃありません 〜ではないです 〜じゃないです	famous

すてき	すてきです	すてきではありません 〜じゃありません 〜ではないです 〜じゃないです	cool, nice
Irregular adjective			
いい or 良い	いいです 良いです	良くありません 良くないです	good

■ 自習 Self Check
（じ しゅう）

Say the words in the left column, followed by the negative form. The first one is done for you.

1. い adjective conjugation

is ~		is not ~
大きい	⇨	大きくありません
小さい	⇨	_____
高い	⇨	_____
長い	⇨	_____
短い	⇨	_____
こわい	⇨	_____
うるさい	⇨	_____
みにくい	⇨	_____
おいしい	⇨	_____
つまらない	⇨	_____
まずい	⇨	_____

Oga Peninsula, Akita

2. な adjective conjugation

is ~		is not ~
きれい	⇨	きれい ではありません
静か	⇨	_____
（しずか）		

■ 練習の時間 Time for Practice
（れんしゅう）

1. Pair Work

Play tic-tac-toe with your partner. To claim a square, state the correct negative form of each adjective. If you disagree with your partner's conjugation of the adjective, say "うそ！" and check the correct answer. If you are right, you get the square. If you are wrong, you forfeit your turn. Good luck!

美味しい （お）（い）	こわい	高い （たか）
面白い （おもしろ）	元気 （げんき）	短い （みじか）
小さい （ちい）	きれい	安い （やす）

つまらない	不思議 （ふしぎ）	うるさい
長い （なが）	まずい	静か （しず）
かわいい	みにくい	大きい

すてき	いい／良い	美しい （うつく）
わるい	きたない	美味しい （お・い）
静か （しず）	きれい	新しい （あたら）

2. Pair Practice

A-さん picks one picture and makes a positive comment, using the adjective supplied. B-さん disagrees, and responds with a comment using the negative form of the same adjective.

> **例（れい） EXAMPLE**
>
> 面白い（おもしろ）　interesting
>
> A: (この) 映画（えいが）は 面白い（おもしろ） ですね。　　= This movie is interesting, isn't it.
> B: いいえ、面白く（おもしろ）ない です。　　= No, it isn't interesting.
> 　　-OR-
> 　いいえ、面白く（おもしろ）ありません。　= No, it isn't interesting.

1. きれい

2. 大きい

3. 長い（なが）

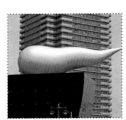

4. みじかい

5. 小さい

6. 新しい

7. 静か（しず）

8. じゃま

■ 文化箱（ぶんかばこ） Culture Chest

擬音語・擬態語（ぎおんご・ぎたいご）

As you learned in Chapter 2, 擬音語（ぎおんご）are onomatopoeic words that mimic or imitate sounds such as ワンワン (the sound a dog makes) and ニャーニャー (the sound a cat makes), and 擬態語（ぎたいご） are mimetic words such as the rumbling of a stomach (ペコペコ), the sound of a couch potato (ゴロゴロ), and the sound of someone speaking fluently (ペラペラ). 擬態語 and 擬音語 are used in Japanese quite often and understanding and being able to use them can be very useful for Japanese learners. Some of these sounds represent a state or an emotion and are repeated. Here are some other examples to broaden your repertoire.

ドキドキ – the sound of nervousness or a rapidly beating heart

トントン – a light repetitive beat of a drum or sound of knocking on a door

ドンドン – drumming (noise), or something done rapidly

ニコニコ – what smiling might "sound" like

カアカア – a bird's cry

ワンワン – a dog's bark

ニャーニャー – a cat's meow

■ キアラのジャーナル Kiara's Journal
きあら

Read the journal entry below, and then answer these questions.

❶ What word does Kiara use to describe what Amanohashidate was like?

❷ Both Osaka and Hiroshima are famous for what food?

❸ What food item is Amanohashidate famous for?

ジャーナルへ

天橋立は とても 面白かったです。 I was hoping to get here sometime, but didn't think that it
あまのはしだて
would be this way! I am still having a hard time believing that we're able to go back and forth in time. It's like something I've only seen on TV.

This Tomo character is a bit crazy! He keeps slipping away from the rest of us to find something to eat. 友さんは いつも 食べ物の メモを 書いています。 I knew that Japan had some places that were more famous than others for certain types of foods. There's so much more to Japanese cuisine than I had realized. 例えば (a new word that I just learned, which means "for example") 大阪は お好み焼き で 有名です。
たと　　おおさか　　　　　　　　　　　　　　　　　ゆうめい
広島も、 お好のみ焼きで 有名です。 でも、 大阪の お好み焼きと 広島の お好み焼きはと
ひろしま
ても 違います。 天橋立は かにで 有名 です。 ここの かには 本当に おいしい です。
ちが　　　　　あまのはしだて　　　　　　　　　　　　　　　　　　　　　　　　　　　　　　　ほんとう
母は かにが 大好き です。 母に この かにの 料理を 作ってあげたい です。
　　　　　　　　　　　　　　　　　　　　　　　　　　　　　りょうり　　　　　つく

*お好み焼き A type of Japanese food that resembles pancakes. Customers can choose which ingredients to put in it. お好み
　この　や
焼き literally means "fried or cooked as you like it."
や

■ テクノの時間 Techno Time

Visit TimeforJapanese.com and do review activity 1-08-3.

漬け物 は、美味しくありませんでした。
The pickles were not tasty!

友の日記
　そばは とても 美味しかった です。
つけ物は 美味しく ありません でした。
かには とても 美味しかった です。
レストランの ウェイトレスは あまり
　やさしく ありません でした。
浦島太郎さんは とても おだやかな 人 でした。

友の日記

そばは　とても　美味しかった　です。

漬け物は　美味しくありません　でした。

かには　とても　美味しかった　です。

レストランの　ウェイトレスは　あまり　やさしく　ありませんでした。

浦島太郎さんは　とても　おだやかな　人　でした。

■ 単語 New Words

暇 (な adj.)	おだやか (な adj.)	まったく (adv.) – really, indeed, truly

■ 言葉の探索 Language Detection

1. Negative past of adjectives

    A. To put an い adjective in the PAST NEGATIVE, drop the "い" and add "くありません　でした" to the adjective stem.

    い adjective conjugation for past negative

is	was not	
大きい	大きく　ありません　でした。	= It was not big.
小さい	小さく　ありません　でした。	= It was not small.

    B. To put "な" adjectives in the PAST NEGATIVE, simply add one of the following to the end of the adjective.
    　　〜では　ありません　でした
    　　〜じゃ　ありません　でした

    な adjective conjugation for past negative

きれい	きれいでは　ありません　でした。	= He/she/it was not pretty.
元気	元気じゃ　ありません　でした。	= He/she/it was not well.
静か	静かでは　ありません　でした。	= It was not quiet.

    NOTE:
    There is an alternative way to express "ありませんでした。"
    For example, 忙しくありません　でした could also be written 忙しくなかったです。
    暇じゃありませんでした　could also be written 暇じゃなかったです。Both versions are common and perfectly acceptable.

Adjective Conjugation Chart: Overview

い adjectives	Non-past tense ～いです	Past tense ～かったです	Negative ～くありません ～くないです	Negative past ～くありませんでした ～くなかったです	英語
まずい	まずいです	まずかったです	まずくありません まずくないです	まずくありませんでした まずくなかったです	tastes disgusting
ひどい	ひどいです	ひどかったです	ひどくありません ひどくないです	ひどくありませんでした ひどくなかったです	terrible
忙しい いそが	忙しい いそが です	忙しかったです いそが	忙しくありません いそが 忙しくないです いそが	忙しくありませんでした いそが 忙しくなかったです いそが	busy

な adjectives	～です	～でした	～ではありません ～ではないです (or じゃ in place of では)	～ではありませんでした ～ではなかったです (or じゃ in place of では)	
暇 ひま	暇です ひま	暇でした ひま	暇ではありません ひま 暇ではないです ひま	暇ではありませんでした ひま 暇ではなかったです ひま	free time
おだやか	おだやかです	おだやかでした	おだやかではありません おだやかではないです	おだやかではありませんでした おだやかではなかったです	calm, peaceful

Irregular adjective					
いい or 良い よ	いいです 良いです よ	良かったです よ	良くありません 良くないです	良くありませんでした 良くなかったです	good

■ 自習 Self Check
じしゅう

State out loud to yourself the words that should go in the blanks below.

Was not big ⇒ _____

_____ ⇒ 忙しく　ありません　でした
いそが

_____ ⇒ 美しくなかった　です。

Was not good ⇒ _____

_____ ⇒ かわいく　なかった　です。

Was not clean ⇒ _____

Did not have free time ⇒ _____

■ 練習の時間 Time for Practice
れんしゅう

Turn back to the 練習の時間 on page 282. Find a partner and play tic-tac-toe again, but this time you must say the negative past form of each adjective to win a point. Time yourself! Then discuss the pictures on page 283, again putting the adjectives into the negative past form.

OK, here's your chance to see how well you have learned how to conjugate adjectives. Try to fill in all the blanks on your own.

Time	Positive +/Negative −	Adjective (英語)	日本語
きょう	+	pretty	きれいです。
	−		大きくありませんでした。
きのう	−	busy	
あした	+		暇 です。 ひま
あした			まずくありません。
きのう	−	terrible	
あした	+	cute	
あさって	−		不思議 ではありません。 ふ し ぎ
あした			すてきではありません。
きのう	+	interesting	
おととい	−		良くありませんでした。

■ 練習の時間 Time for Practice
れんしゅう

Small Group Activity

Adjective conjugation review activity

Directions: Look at the calendar; ask the person to your left about a specific activity. Make sure to use the past tense if the activity has already occurred. The group members decide if the question is grammatically correct. If your question is correctly conjugated and makes sense, you win one point. If the answer is correctly conjugated and makes sense, the answerer wins one point. Keep going around the circle until all the activities have been discussed. Begin with finding "今日" (today) on the calendar.

A-さん：　*節分の　鬼　こわかった　ですか。
　　　　　　せつぶん　おに
B-さん：　いいえ、　全然　こわくなかった　です。
　　　　　　　　　　ぜんぜん
(Both A and B earn a point)

* 節分 is traditionally the day before each season. Nowadays, Setsubun is celebrated by children throwing beans at someone dressed as a goblin (typically the father of the house) while shouting 「鬼はそと。福はうち。」= "Out with the goblin. In with the good luck." The goblin represents bad luck so when he runs away he removes any bad luck from the household for the coming year. For most small children, it is a fun holiday that permits pelting your father with beans!

土・日	月	火	水	木	金
	1	2	3 節分 せつぶん	4	5 日本語のテスト
6/7 学校の ピクニック	8	9	10	11	12 買い物： チョコレート
13/14	15	16 今日	17 バンドの 練習 れんしゅう	18	19 イタリアン レストラン
20/21 カラオケ	22	23	24 数学 のテスト すうがく	25	26
27/28	29 母の誕生日				

■ テクノ の時間 Techno Time

You are going to participate in a text chat with Ben. Follow the directions for each prompt and reply appropriately to his entries. Use your "digi journal" or notebook for your responses. You should respond as fully and completely as possible. You will have 90 seconds to respond to each prompt.

Save your file with "8-4tc" immediately followed by the first three letters of your family name, then the first three letters of your given name. If your name is Ichiro Suzuki, for example, your file would be "8-4tcsuzich." Your teacher will provide you with the file for this or you can find it on the TimeForJapanese.com website. Use the file "1084technotime" for this exercise.

■ 単語チェックリスト New Word Checklist
たん ご

Japanese	Location	English
8-1		
あぶない　危ない (い adj.)	8-1	dangerous
うつくしい　美しい (い adj.)	8-1	beautiful
うみ　海 (n)	8-1	ocean, sea
うるさい (い adj.)	8-1	noisy, loud
うれしい　嬉しい (い adj.)	8-1	glad, happy
おいしい　美味しい (い adj.)	8-1	delicious
かしこい (い adj.)	8-1	wise; bright
かわいい (い adj.)	8-1	cute
きたない (い adj.)	8-1	dirty, messy

Japanese	Location	English
きびしい (い *adj.*)	8-1	strict
きれい (い *adj.*)	8-1	pretty; clean
こわい (い *adj.*)	8-1	scary
じれったい (い *adj.*)	8-1	irritating
ずるい (い *adj.*)	8-1	cunning
つまらない (い *adj.*)	8-1	boring
ばかばかしい (い *adj.*)	8-1	foolish; silly
はこ (*n*)	8-1	box
びーち　　ビーチ (*n*)	8-1	beach
ひどい (い *adj.*)	8-1	terrible
ふしぎ (な *adj.*)	8-1	mysterious
みじかい　　短い (い *adj.*)	8-1	short (length)
みにくい (い *adj.*)	8-1	ugly
わがまま (な *adj.*)	8-1	selfish

8-2

Japanese	Location	English
あおい　　青い (い *adj.*)	8-2	blue-colored
あかい　　赤い (い *adj.*)	8-2	red-colored
あまのはしだて　　天橋立 (*n*)	8-2	Amanohashidate (city)
うま　　馬 (*n*)	8-2	horse
おもしろい　　面白い (い *adj.*)	8-2	interesting
おれんじ　　オレンジ (*n*)	8-2	orange (colored)
かめ　　亀 (*n*)	8-2	turtle
かれら　　彼ら (*pron.*)	8-2	they, them
きいろい　　黄色い (い *adj.*)	8-2	yellow-colored
くろい　　黒い (い *adj.*)	8-2	black-colored
こどもたち　　子供達 (*n*)	8-2	children
しろい　　白い (い *adj.*)	8-2	white-colored
むかし　　昔 (*n*)	8-2	long ago
むかしむかし　　昔々 (*n*)	8-2	long long ago
やめる/やめます (やめて) (*v*)	8-2	(to) stop
わるい　　悪い (い *adj.*)	8-2	bad

8-3

Japanese	Location	English
おっと (*interj.*)	8-3	oops, uh-oh, sorry
かに (*n*)	8-3	crab
しま　　島 (*n*)	8-3	island
ぜんぶ　　全部 (*n/adv.*)	8-3	all, everything
つけもの　　漬け物 (*n*)	8-3	pickled vegetables
ひろい　　広い (い *adj.*)	8-3	wide, spacious
まずい (い *adj.*)	8-3	not tasty, not good
せまい (い *adj.*)	8-3	narrow, confined, small

8-4

Japanese	Location	English
おだやか (な *adj.*)	8-4	calm, peaceful
せまい　　狭い (い *adj.*)	8-4	narrow
ひま (な *adj.*)	8-4	free (time)
まったく　　全く (*adv.*)	8-4	really, indeed, truly

Purchasing and Giving Gifts in Edo

第 **9** 課

Learning Goals

By the end of this chapter you will learn:

A) how to use the verb する after a noun to create new verbal expressions

B) expressions useful when shopping, including the comparative

C) new counters for books, long cylindrical objects, and large sums of money

D) how to use the particle の to replace a noun

E) verbs for giving and receiving

F) 9 additional kanji

Performance Goals

By the end of this chapter you will be able to:

A) use the verb する with certain nouns to create many new verbal expressions

B) ask the price of something in a store, and ask for something bigger or cheaper

C) talk about presents you received for your last birthday and what presents you plan to give family members and friends for their birthdays

D) read and write 9 additional kanji

Zoujouji Temple Gate, Tokyo

第9課の1 買い物を します。 I'm going shopping.

■ 会話 Dialogue

じゅん： ここは、200年前の　東京　ですか。

友　　： はい。江戸時代　です。1603年から　1867年まで、東京の　名前は　江戸　でした。

ベン　： 本物の　江戸　ですね。かっこいい　ですね！

友　　： さて、皆さん、今日の　スケジュール　です。始めに、朝ご飯を　食べます。次に、
　　　　 ちょっと　散歩をします。それに、買い物を　します。

キアラ： 何を　買いますか。

友　　： 浮世絵　です。それから、食事を　します。

ベン　： 何を　食べますか。

友　　： *おでん　です。さ、行きますよ。

* おでん – a Japanese dish boiled in a soy flavored *dashi* (broth).

■ 単語 New Words

| （買う）/買います (v) | 買い物 (n) | （売る）/売ります (v) | 店 (n) |

| 絵 (n) | 映画 (n) | View from Tokyo Tower |

千 (n) – 1,000
せん

二千 (n) – 2,000
にせん

三千 (n) – 3,000
さんぜん

四千 (n) – 4,000
よんせん

五千 (n) – 5,000
ごせん

六千 (n) – 6,000
ろくせん

七千 (n) – 7,000
ななせん

八千 (n) – 8,000
はっせん

九千 (n) – 9,000
きゅうせん

何千 (inter.) – how many thousands?
なんぜん

万 (n) – 10,000
まん

一万 (n) – 10,000
いちまん

二万 (n) – 20,000
にまん

三万 (n) – 30,000
さんまん

四万 (n) – 40,000
よんまん

五万 (n) – 50,000
ごまん

六万 (n) – 60,000
ろくまん

七万 (n) – 70,000
ななまん

八万 (n) – 80,000
はちまん

九万 (n) – 90,000
きゅうまん

十万 (n) – 100,000
じゅうまん

何万 (inter.) – how many ten-thousands?
なんまん

十一万 (n) – 110,000
じゅういちまん

十二万 (n) – 120,000
じゅうにまん

十三万 (n) – 130,000
じゅうさんまん

十四万 (n) – 140,000
じゅうよんまん

十五万 (n) – 150,000
じゅうごまん

十六万 (n) – 160,000
じゅうろくまん

十七万 (n) – 170,000
じゅうななまん

十八万 (n) – 180,000
じゅうはちまん

十九万 (n) – 190,000
じゅうきゅうまん

二十万 (n) – 200,000
にじゅうまん

二十一万 (n) – 210,000
にじゅういちまん

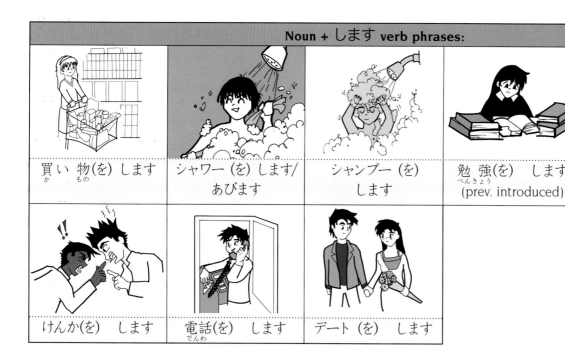

Noun + します verb phrases:

買い物(を)します
か　もの

シャワー(を)します/
あびます

シャンプー(を)
します

勉強(を)します
べんきょう
(prev. introduced)

宿題(を)します
しゅくだい

けんか(を)します

電話(を)します
でんわ

デート(を)します

食事(を)します (v) – to eat/have a meal
しょくじ

ビデオゲーム(を)します (v) – to play video/computer games

バスケット(を)します (v) – to play basketball

旅行(を)します (v) – to travel
りょこう

カラオケ(を)します (v) – to do karaoke

Other words you might like to know:

浮世絵 (n) – traditional Japanese woodblock prints (lit. *visions of the floating world*)
うきよえ
版画 (n) – woodblock prints, art prints
はんが

■ 漢字 Kanji
かんじ

買　売　店　万

買	バイ buy; か(う) – to buy; purchase	`	冖	罒	罒	罒	罒	罒	買
	買います – to buy, purchase; 買(い物) – shopping; か　　　　　　　　　　か　　もの (売)買 – selling and buying ばい　ばい	買	買	買	買				
12 strokes	The bottom of this character is the KANJI for shellfish (貝). In early societies, shells (貝) were used for currency to PURCHASE things. This character looks like an eye (目) with two little legs under it reaching up to some shelves above to BUY something.								

売	バイ; う(る) – to sell	一	十	士	士	声	声	売	
	売ります – to sell; 売(り物) – an item for sale う　　　　　　　　う　　もの								
7 strokes	We see a samurai (士) standing on a primitive table trying TO SELL the table. The problem is, the top of the table has come loose from its two legs (to the point where there is a gap between the legs and the top of the table), so it is difficult to sell.								

店	テン, みせ – store, shop	゛	宀	广	广	庁	店	店	店
	店 – store, shop; (売) 店 – shop								
8 strokes	The first three strokes are an awning with a chimney in the middle to let out all the hot air produced by the fortune teller (占) who claims her business is a perfectly legitimate STORE or SHOP.								

万	マン – ten thousand	一	ヮ	万					
	万 – 10,000								
3 strokes	The first and third strokes form a fancy "T" which stands for ten, and the second and third strokes form a fancy "h" which combined with the "T" gives the "Th" at the beginning of thousand. Combine the ten and thousand to get TEN THOUSAND.								

■ 言葉の探索 Language Detection

1. **(Noun) + (を) します**

   Many verb phrases in Japanese consist of a noun followed by します or をします. Use of the particle を is optional if there is no direct object, but is incorrect when the sentence does have a direct object. In other words, it is OK to say:

   勉強を　します。
   OR:
   日本語を　勉強　します。

   but it is <u>NOT</u> OK to say:
   日本語を　勉強を　します。 The particle を can only appear in a sentence once.

   A) 私は　毎日　買い物 (を)　します。 = I shop every day.
   B) ベン君は　サッカー(を)　しません。 = Ben does not play soccer.
   C) きのう、私は　宿題 (を)　しました。 = I did homework yesterday.
   D) 八時に　食事(を)　しました。 = I had a meal at 8:00.

   Examples that include a direct object:
   A) 私は、昨日　レポートを　タイプしました。 = Yesterday I typed a report.
   B) 日本語と　数学を　勉強しています。 = I am studying Japanese and math.

2. **Quotation marks for a quote within a quote**
   母は、「私は、『宿題を　して　下さい。』と　言いましたよ。」と　言いました。
   Mother said, "I told you, 'Please do the homework.'"

■ 自習 Self Check
じしゅう

1.   (Noun) + (を) します
    Practice saying the following to yourself out loud in Japanese.

    A) I wash my hair every day.
    B) Ben played video games yesterday.
    C) Telephone your mother.
    D) I study science every day.
    E) Every year I travel to Kyushu.

■ 練習の時間 Time for Practice
れんしゅう

1. **Pair Practice**

    Ask your partner how often he or she does the following activities. Use time words such as 毎日 (every day), よく (of-
    まいにち
    ten), or 時々 (sometimes) in your question. Draw the table below on a piece of scrap paper and record your partner's
    ときどき
    answers. Your teacher may ask you to report your results to the class.

    A-さん: 毎日　テレビを　見ますか。
    B-さん: はい、毎日　見ます。
              -OR-　いいえ、全然　見ません。
                        ぜんぜん

    * Remember: For あまり (not very much) and 全然 (not at all) you must use the negative form of the verb.
                                              ぜんぜん

する事	毎日	よく	時々	あまり	ぜんぜん
1. go on a date					
2. play video games					
3. shampoo your hair					
4. go shopping					
5. get into a fight					
6. listen to music					
7. walk with a dog					
8. take a shower					
9. eat cereal (シリアル)					
10. do homework					
11. study Japanese					
12. talk on the phone					
13. play soccer					
14. watch TV					
15. (an activity of your choice)					

2. Whole Class Activity

Using 〜しています。

Charades: Choose a slip of paper from among those your teacher will hand out. Your job is to go to the front of the classroom and act out the activity you selected. Once your classmates call out 「何を　していますか。」 do your best to act out the activity as your classmates try to guess what it is.

■ 文化箱 Culture Chest
ぶん か ばこ

The First Posters of the Stars!

The art of 版画, or woodblock printing, became popular in Japan during the 江戸 period (1603–1867), particularly
a type of 版画 called 浮世絵, which literally means "scenes from the floating world." 浮世絵 included depictions of famous actors and actresses, travel scenes from some of the most beautiful places in Japan, and records of current events.
The word "floating" may be a reference to the "floating" social position and activities of the common people depicted in
浮世絵 as opposed to the rigid social status of the nobility. 浮世絵 can also imply "images of the here and now," a favorite
theme of Japanese art. Because of highly advanced printing techniques, these prints were among the first in the world to
be mass-produced cheaply and purchased by the common people. Prior to this time, it was quite unthinkable for commoners to own artwork. One famous series of woodblock prints is Hiroshige's 53 Stations on the 東海道 (the main road
leading to Edo).

During the early years of the Meiji Restoration (1870s), Japanese ceramics and other artwork, including 浮世絵, poured
out of Japan and into Europe for the first time. These prints, though purchased cheaply in Japan, had a tremendous impact
on the work of many European artists such as Van Gogh, Gauguin, and Toulouse-Lautrec.

Today, artists in Japan still create woodblock prints; their works are known as 新版画 or "new woodblock prints."

■ キアラのジャーナル Kiara's Journal

Read the journal entry below, and then answer these questions.

❶ What was Tokyo called in 1837?
❷ What are ukiyoe?
❸ Kiara mentions artistic techniques that set ukiyoe apart. What are they?
❹ List three of Hokusai's traits that Kiara mentions.
❺ Why do they decide to only go window shopping rather than buying an ukiyoe?

ジャーナルへ

今日、東京へ　帰りました！でも、1837年の　東京　です！それに、東京の　名前は　東京
では　ありません。今、ここの　名前は　江戸です。1837年の　江戸は　とても　面白い
です。有名な　アーティストが　たくさん　います。私は　美術が　大好き　ですから、
よく勉強を　しました。北斎と　広重と　歌麿の　事を　勉強しました。彼らは　江戸時代、
浮世絵というアートを　作りました。その浮世絵は　21c、alloverthewworldで　有名です。ヨー

ロッパの　ゴッホ(Vincent Van Gogh)と　ゴーギャン(Paul Gauguin)と other Impressionist artists も received influence from those 浮世絵。One thing that makes 浮世絵 so interesting is the strong black outlining。それに, the use of space is also very different。

友さんは、「こちらへ　来て下さい。とてもいい　おでんの　屋台 (food cart vendor)が　あります！」と　言いました。ベン君は、「また　食べ物の　事ですか。ちょっと　前に　食べたでしょう！」と、言いました。友さんは、「それは　そう　ですけど、少し　おでんを食べてから　北斎さんの　絵と　広重さんの　絵を　見に　行きましょう。」と、言いました。私は、「友さん、本当に　北斎さんを　知っているんですか。有名な人を　良く　知っていますね。」と、言いました。

友さんは、「この前、北斎さんと　広重さんは　店で　すごい　けんかを　しました。僕は　その二人の　間に　入りました。そして、『ちょっと　やめて下さい。あなた達は　二人とも　素晴らしい　アーティスト(artist)　ですよ！』と、言いました。それから、北斎さんと僕は、一緒に　北斎さんの家に　ご飯を　食べに　行きました。彼はちょっと年を取っています。それからとても laid back artist　です。彼は料理をするのが上手です。」と、言いました。

ベン君は、「そう　ですか。この　辺に　(around here) 浮世絵の　店は　ありますか。母におみやげに　買って　帰ります。母は　日本の　絵が　大好き　です。でも、21c.の東京の店で　買うと、それは　とても　高い　です。」と　言いました。

友さんは、「そう　ですね。でも、時の門に　新しい　物を　持って行くのは　だめです。ここに　持って　来た物　だけ、持って　帰る事ができます。北斎さんの　絵を　持って　帰る事は　出来ません。だから、店で　浮世絵を　ウィンドウショッピング　しましょう。その前に　おでんを　食べましょう！この　店は　江戸で　一番　美味しい　おでんの　店　です。」と、言いました。

■ テクノの時間 Techno Time

Though you've not been introduced to them all yet, type all the vocabulary words from this chapter into your digital dictionary. Be sure to type first the kanji, then hiragana, and then the meaning in English. Remember to use your file labeled "JISHO" (in *romaji*).

■ 会話 Dialogue
かいわ

じゅん ： ごめん下さ～い！

店員 　： は～い。いらっしゃいませ。

ベン 　： この本は、いくら　ですか。

店員 　： はい、一冊　1,025円*　です。
　　　　　　いっさつ

ベン 　： じゃあ、二冊下さい。
　　　　　　にさつ

店員 　： はい、二冊で　2,050円　です。

キアラ： すみません、筆も　三本　下さい。
　　　　　　ふで　　　さんぼん　くだ

店員 　： はい、一本1,500円　ですから、三本で　4,500円　です。全部で　6,550円　です。
　　　　　　いっぽん　　　　　　　　　　　　　　　　　　　　　　　ぜんぶ

友 　　： じゃあ、10,000円から　お願いします。

店員 　： はい、10,000円から　ですね。

　　　　　では、3,450円の　おつり　です。どうも、ありがとう　ございました。

　　　　　また、どうぞ。

* Note: Even though conversations in this chapter use the modern Japanese currency term 円, the Japanese actually did
not start using 円 as their official currency until around 1870 at the beginning of the Meiji Restoration.
　　　　　えん

■ 単語 New Words
たんご

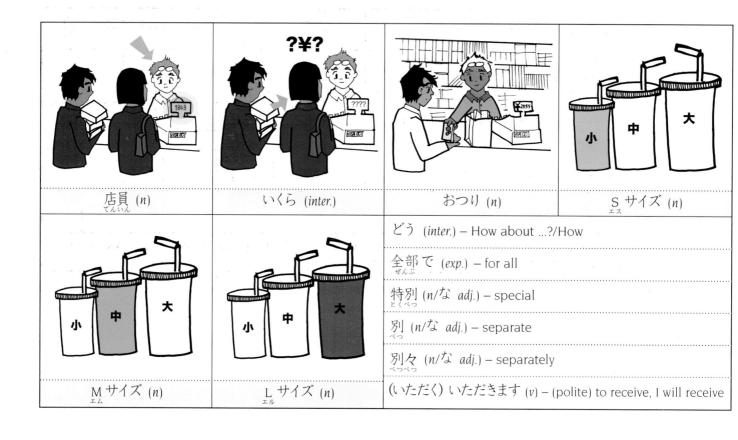

店員 (n) てんいん	いくら (inter.)	おつり (n)	S サイズ (n) エス

M サイズ (n) エム	L サイズ (n) エル	どう (inter.) – How about ...?/How 全部で (exp.) – for all ぜんぶ 特別 (n/な adj.) – special とくべつ 別 (n/な adj.) – separate べつ 別々 (n/な adj.) – separately べつべつ (いただく) いただきます (v) – (polite) to receive, I will receive

Counter for bound objects (books, magazines, notebooks, etc.)		Counter for long cylindrical objects such as pencils, straws, bottles, etc.	
一冊 いっさつ	七冊 ななさつ	一本 いっぽん	七本 ななほん/しちほん
二冊 にさつ	八冊 はっさつ	二本 にほん	八本 はちほん/はっぽん
三冊 さんさつ	九冊 きゅうさつ	三本 さんぼん	九本 きゅうほん
四冊 よんさつ	十冊 じゅっさつ/じっさつ	四本 よんほん	十本 じゅっぽん/じっぽん
五冊 ごさつ	何冊 なんさつ	五本 ごほん	何本 なんぼん
六冊 ろくさつ		六本 ろっぽん	

■ 漢字 Kanji
かんじ

全 1 2 5 6 6 strokes	ゼン – all, entirely	ノ 入 个 全 全 全					
	全(部) – all things, everything; 全(然) – not at all; ぜん ぶ ぜん ぜん 全(国) – the entire country ぜん こく						
	The first 2 strokes look like a roof. The final four strokes are the kanji for king (王). We all like to think we are kings who rule over ALL things under our roof ENTIRELY.						

部 1 11 9 5 10 11 strokes	ブ – section, group of, part	` ` ` ` 立 音 音 音					
	(剣)道(部) – kendo club; けん どう ぶ (全)部 – all things, everything ぜん ぶ	音⁷ 音⁷ 部					
	The left side of this character shows someone standing (立) on a mouth (口), while waving a banner (the last three strokes). You can be sure that you do not want to be a PART of that crazy scene.						

円 1 2 4 3 4 strokes	エン, まる(い) – circle, yen, round	丨 冂 冂 円					
	円 – yen; 円い – round えん まる						
	This kanji has two boxes on top to write in the cost in YEN of each item you are buying, and a space at the bottom to write in the total cost of your order in YEN.						

■ 言葉の探索 Language Detection
こと ば　たん さく

1. Useful shopping expressions

ごめん　下さい！ く だ	= Excuse me! (Said as you enter someone's house or a store.)
いらっしゃいませ！	= Welcome! (Said by the store or restaurant employees as customers enter.)
これは　いくら　ですか。	= How much is this?
五千円　です。 ごせんえん	= It is 5,000 yen.
あの辞書を　下さい。 じしょ　く だ	= I'll take that dictionary/Please give me that dictionary.
このSサイズのシャツを　下さい。 く だ	= I'll take this small shirt/Please give me this small shirt.
10,000円から、お願いします。 ねが	= Here is 10,000 yen. (*lit.* Please take it out of a 10,000 yen [bill].) *Note: This phrase is optional since it is very common for customers to silently hand their money over.
5,000円　の　おつりです。	= Your change is 5,000 yen.

2. Using the particle で to mean for

三つで… For three, it's . . .

The particle で comes after the counter word indicating the quantity of the items in question. This use of で occurs mainly when buying things in stores or restaurants.

二つで	5ドル	= for 2 it is $5
三枚で	300	= for 3 sheets, it is 300 yen
十本で	1,000円	= for 10, it is 1,000 yen

Note: で is not necessary when you are referring to one item.

一つ　1,500円　です。 = One is 1,500 yen.

(カフェテリアで)
A-さん：　このハンバーガーは　一つ　いくら　ですか。 = How much is this hamburger?
B-さん：　200円です。 = ¥200.
A-さん：　じゃあ、四つで、800円ですね。四つ、下さい。 = Well then, for 4, it's ¥800 (right). 4 please.

(店で)
A-さん：　この　黒いシャツは　三枚で　いくら　ですか。
まい = This black shirt, how much for three?
B-さん：　それ　ですか。　それは　三枚で　5000円　です。 = That (one)? That (one) is 3 for ¥5,000.
A-さん：　安い　ですね。　じゃあ、　それを　三枚　下さい。 = That's cheap! Well then, three of those please.

3. Counters

As you learned in Chapter 2, different word endings are used to count people and things in Japanese. For objects, the counter usually depends on the shape. For instance, long cylindrical objects such as pencils, pens, tubes, or bottles use the counter 本.

筆一本 ふで	= 1 brush
えんぴつ二本	= two pencils
ペン三本	= three pens

* Note that the counter FOLLOWS the object that is being counted. For a complete list of counters, see the chart in Appendix 1. If you don't know the exact counter for something, you can usually use the generic counters 一つ、二つ、三つ、etc. However, knowing the correct counter and using it properly makes you a much more fluent speaker of Japanese.

自習 Self Check
じしゅう

1. **Useful shopping expressions**
    Practice saying the following out loud to yourself in Japanese.

    A) How much do those pants near you cost?   C) Here is 7,000 yen.

    B) They are 6,500 yen.   D) Your change is 500 yen.

2. **Practice with counters**
    Practice asking for various numbers of classroom objects using these counters:

    ➲ generic counters (一つ、二つ、・・・・)
    ➲ ~枚
        まい
    ➲ ~人
    ➲ ~本
    ➲ ~冊
        さつ
    ➲ ~ページ

     例   紙を 一枚   下さい。   = Please give me one sheet of paper.
    れい かみ いちまい

3. Review your counting skills. Count from 1,000 to 10,000, by thousands. Then practice asking for these items:

    ➲ 1,000 sheets of paper   ➲ 2,000 sheets of paper
    ➲ 3,000 pencils   ➲ 4,000 pencils
    ➲ 5,000 people   ➲ 6,000 people
    ➲ 7,000 books   ➲ 8,000 books
    ➲ 9,000 trees   ➲ 10,000 trees
    ➲ 11,000 men   ➲ 12,000 women
    ➲ 13,000 (your choice of item)   ➲ 14,000 (your choice of item)
    ➲ 15,000 (your choice of item)   ➲ 20,000 (your choice of item)
    ➲ 30,000 people   ➲ 40,000 people
    ➲ 52,000 people   ➲ 61,000 people
    ➲ 75,000 people   ➲ 88,000 people
    ➲ 93,000 people   ➲ 100,000 people
    ➲ 999,999 people

■ 練習の時間 Time for Practice
れんしゅう

I. **Pair Practice**

Choose three of the stores below and develop a skit by acting out the roles of customer（客）and store employee
（店員）. You must buy at least one thing from each of the three stores. Use the dialogue below as a model. Then switch
てんいん
roles. Your teacher may ask you to present one of your skits to the class.

本　一冊　¥300

花　一本　¥150
はな

折り紙　一枚　¥1
お　がみ

鉛筆　一本　¥55
えんぴつ
ノート　一冊　¥150
消しゴム　一つ　¥57
け

パン　一つ　¥375
カップケーキ　一つ　¥205

Lサイズの赤いタンクトップ　一枚　¥1,225

例　(ケーキ屋で)
れい　や
EXAMPLE
店員　：　いらっしゃいませ。
てんいん
客　：　こんにちは。この　ケーキは　一つ　いくら　ですか。
きゃく　　　　　　　　　　　　　　　　　　　ひと
店員　：　その　ケーキ　ですか。一つ、350円　です。
　　　　　　　　　　　　　　　　　ひと
客　：　じゃ、二つ下さい。
　　　　　　　　ふた
店員　：　はい。二つで　700円　です。1,000円からですね。はい、300円の　おつりです。ありがとうございまし
　　　　た。また、どうぞ。(clerk hands over cakes and the change)
客　：　どうも。

2. Pair Practice

You are the customer and your partner is the waiter/waitress at a new Italian restaurant. Use the menu below to order the following items. The waiter/waitress then tells you how much your meal will cost.

> *One slice of cheese pizza and two bottles of orange juice.*
> Customer: チーズのピザを一枚と　オレンジジュースを2本　ください。
> Waiter/waitress: 全部で　1,400円です。

a. two pepperoni pizzas and one iced coffee
b. one green salad, one vegetarian pizza, and one cola
c. one Caesar salad, one cheese pizza, and one ice cream
d. one pepperoni pizza and one cheese pizza
e. one green salad, two vegetarian pizzas, and two orange juices

---

イタリアンレストラン・ナポリ
メニュー

サラダ		デザート	
グリーンサラダ	300	アイスクリーム	350
シーザーサラダ	400		
		飲み物	
ピザ		コーラ	250
ペパローニ	650	オレンジジュース	400
チーズ	600	アイスコーヒー	300
ベジタリアン	650		

■ 文化箱 Culture Chest

Innovating and Conserving

Japanese have long been creative innovators of technology. Did you know, for instance, that the original Space Invaders スペースインベーダー video game came out in Japan in 1978? Many are equally enthusiastic consumers of new technological products. Stores are often busy with shoppers purchasing the latest new devices. Examples include utensils for the kitchen, televisions and electronics for the living room, and even heated toilet seats for the bathroom! Cell phones and handheld devices for playing games and watching movies are often developed and released in Japan long before they appear in other international markets.

Even though consumerism is alive and well in Japan, the Japanese also lead much of the world in environmentally friendly technology in a number of fields. Many individuals recognize the need to balance economic growth with environmental conservation. Beginning in the late 1990s, purchases in stores that previously had been elaborately wrapped now receive only a small piece of decorative tape, and many consumers bring their own shopping bags.

Recycling in cities is now largely mandated by the Japanese government and strictly enforced. Everyone must carefully sort glass, paper, metals, and other trash before putting it out for garbage pickup. How does your community work toward promoting good environmental standards?

■ キアラのジャーナル Kiara's Journal

Read the journal entry below, and then answer these questions.

❶ Where exactly did they meet Hokusai?
❷ Why did they change their plan from window shopping to real shopping?
❸ What did Kiara and Ben buy? How much did their purchases cost?

ジャーナルへ

　　江戸の　おでんは　とても　おいしかった　です。おでんを、食べた後、買い物を　しました。江戸の　銀座に　たくさんの　kabuki theaterが　あります。北斎さんと、彼の　好きな kabuki theaterの　前で　会いました。そして、一緒に　店に　浮世絵を　見に　行きました。私は　富士山の　絵が　大好き　です。その店に　色々な　富士山の　絵が　ありました。ベン君は　歌舞伎役者(kabuki actor)の絵が　好き　でした。

Even though 友さん had said we could not take anything home (through the 時の門), we decided to buy some things anyway. While we were eating おでん、友さん also mentioned that we may be able to transfer things from our 時の門 trip to the 21st century if we bury a time capsule and then dig it up when we get back to our modern 東京。 友さんは、「まだ、はっきり　分かりませんが・・・ if we really can do it or not.」と、言いました。 We will have to find out the right place and right time to bury the time capsule, but all of us were excited about buying real 浮世絵 at the 店。

　　私は、「すみません、この北斎の　絵は　いくら　ですか。」と　聞きました。

　　店員さんは、「それ　ですか。それは　とてもいい　北斎の　版画　ですよ。特別、安くしますよ。千二百円で　どう　ですか。」と　言いました。

　　北斎さんは、「千二百円！私は　あなたに　三百円で　売りましたよ！　この人達は　僕の　友達　です。安くして下さい。」と　言いました。

　　ベン君は、「じゃあ、これも　買います。二枚で　いくら　ですか。」と　聞きました。

　　店員さんは、「北斎さんの　友達　ですから　二枚で　二千円で　どう　でしょう。」と、言いました。

　　北斎さんは、「いい　でしょう。ベン君の　目は　この絵の　中の　色と　同じ　ですね。」と　言いました。

　　ベン君は、「あ、そう　ですね。では、その絵を　下さい。」と、言いました。

　　店員さんは、「はい、いい　買い物　ですね。」と、言いました。

As we went out the door、友さん bowed to the storekeeper and said 「どうも、すみませんでした。」

　　とても　きれいな　浮世絵を　買って　楽しかった　です。持って　帰れたら　よかった　ですけど。

　　お休み。

2) すみません。スリッパは、
その 大きさだけ です。
大丈夫 ですか。

1) すみません。
もっと 大きい
スリッパは
ありますか。

3) 大丈夫 です。
ありがとう ございます。

4) 私は、
もっと 小さい
スリッパが
いい です。
もっと
小さいのは、
ありますか。

5) すみません。本当に、その サイズ
だけ です。もっと 小さいのも
もっと 大きいのも、ありません。

6) 残念
です。

7) 大丈夫
ですか。

9) さ、部屋に
行って
休みましょう。

10) そう ですね。
僕は、お風呂に 入ります。

8) はい、
大丈夫
です。

■ 会話 Dialogue

ベン	： すみません。もっと 大きい スリッパは ありますか。
旅館の人	： すみません。スリッパは、その 大きさ だけです。大丈夫 ですか。
ベン	： 大丈夫 です。ありがとう ございます。
友	： 私は、もっと 小さい スリッパが いい です。もっと 小さいのは、ありますか。
旅館の人	： すみません。本当に、その サイズ だけ です。もっと 小さいのも もっと 大きいのも ありません。
友	： 残念 です。
旅館の人	： 大丈夫 ですか。
友	： はい、大丈夫 です。
キアラ	： さ、部屋に 行って 休みましょう。
じゅん	： そう ですね。僕は、*お風呂に 入ります。

*お風呂 – a traditional Japanese bath which is deep and usually rectangular

■ 単語 New Words

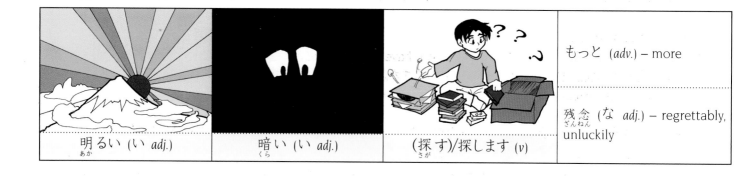

明るい (い adj.) あか	暗い (い adj.) くら	(探す)/探します (v) さが	もっと (adv.) – more
			残念 (な adj.) – regrettably, ざんねん unluckily

■ 漢字 Kanji

暗 2 6 5 1 9 7 8 3 4 10 11 12 13 **13 strokes**	くら(い) – dark, dim	丨	冂	冊	日	日'	日亠	日亠	日ㅜ
	暗い – dark くら	日立	日立	暗	暗	暗			
	Picture the sun (日) going down until there is not a single sound (音) to be heard. Then everything will look and feel very DARK!								

明	メイ – light; あか（るい） – light, bright	丨	冂	月	日	即	明	明	明
8 strokes	明るい – bright; 明（治時代） – reign period from 1868–1912								

Picture the sun (日) about to peek out from behind the moon (月) after an eclipse. Everything will quickly become very BRIGHT!

■ 言葉の探索 Language Detection

1.　もっと　安い　靴は　ありますか。　Do you have any cheaper shoes?
To ask for something cheaper, bigger, smaller, etc., use this pattern:

もっと ADJECTIVE + NOUN は　ありますか。

A)　もっと　静かな　部屋は　ありますか。　= Is there a quieter room?
B)　もっと　小さい自転車は　ありますか。　= Is there a smaller bicycle?
C)　もっと　短かい　靴下は　ありますか。　= Do you have any shorter socks?
D)　もっと　静かな　犬は　いますか。　= Is there a quieter dog?

2.　Using の to replace nouns
　　もっと　大きいの　は　ありますか。　= Do you have a bigger one?
With the "もっと ADJECTIVE + NOUN は　ありますか。" pattern, the NOUN can be dropped and replaced by の if the NOUN is understood by context.

　* Note: For な adjectives, you MUST include な after this type of adjective whether it is followed by a noun or by の.

A)　もっと　美味しいのは　ありますか。　= Is there a more delicious one?
B)　もっと　明るいのは　ありますか。　= Is there a brighter one?
C)　もっと　かわいいのは　ありますか。　= Is there a cuter one?
D)　もっと　きれいなのは　ありますか。　=Is there a prettier one?

■ 自習 Self Check

1.　もっと ADJECTIVE + NOUN は　ありますか。
Practice saying the following in Japanese out loud to yourself.

A)　Do you have any larger shirts?

B)　Do you have any cheaper shoes?

C)　Are there any more delicious restaurants?

D)　Are there any brighter classrooms?

E)　Do you have any darker T-shirts?

F)　Are there any smaller jeans?

G)　Are there any taller buildings? （たてもの）

H)　Is there any more expensive sushi?

2.   もっと ADJECTIVE + のは　ありますか。

Practice saying the following in Japanese out loud to yourself.

A) Are there any more difficult ones?   E) Are there any quieter ones?

B) Are there any scarier ones?   F) Are there any cleaner ones?

C) Are there any wider ones?   G) Do you have any shorter ones?

D) Are there any darker ones?   H) Do you have any blacker ones?

■ 練習の時間 Time for Practice

1. Small Group Practice

Adjective review

Place a complete set of adjective vocabulary cards in a pile in the middle of a desk or the floor, face down. Then make another set of flashcards with four of each of the following: *present*, *past*, *negative*, and *negative past*. Mix this set of cards and place them in a separate pile, face down. The first person turns over one card in each pile and makes a sentence according to the cards. For instance, if the cards are "小さい" and "negative," your sentence would use the negative form of 小さい. It might be something like: その人の　　かばんは　　小さくない　　です。 (*That person's bag is not small.*) Keep going through both piles until everyone has had a chance to make several sentences. Help your group members if they get stuck.

2. Small Group Practice

Make two sets of cards, at least ten cards in each set. One set should have a different noun written (or drawn) on each card, while the other set should have an adjective written on each card. Place each pile face down and take turns turning over the top card in each pile. Once you know the two words, make a comparative sentence. Shuffle the cards and repeat. Some of your sentences might be silly!

 You have the cards 本 and 高い.
もっと　高い本は　ありますか。 = Do you have any more expensive books?

3. Pair practice

Use the menu in section 2 of this chapter. Take turns being the picky customer. This time, when you order, ask for something bigger, smaller, tastier, or in some way different than what is on the menu. Take turns.

4. Pair Practice

You are going clothing shopping in Shinjuku in Tokyo with your friend who is quite picky. Help your friend find something to buy. Here are several items that you both look at. Your friend makes a negative comment about each item, and then asks for a different one. Use the example dialogue below as a model.

 You　　：　この　赤いTシャツは　どう　ですか。
友だち：　小さいです。　もっと　大きい　サイズは　ありませんか。

A) red T-shirt   D) white jacket

B) blue shoes   E) purple socks

C) black pants

■ 文化箱 Culture Chest
ぶん か ばこ

Taking a Bath, Japanese Style

In Japan, bathing is a time-honored social ritual, in part due to the large number of natural hot springs there. Oita Prefecture alone has over 4,000 natural hot springs, and, in the winter, even Japanese monkeys have been known to enjoy a hot dip.

Japanese お風呂 (baths) include natural outdoor 温泉, or hot springs, often found in scenic mountain locations; public baths known as 銭湯; and simple baths at home. Regardless of which sort of bath is being used, the bather first washes with soap and shampoo and then uses the shower or water faucet outside the tub to thoroughly rinse off. The bather then carefully steps into the deep hot water in the tub for a long relaxing soak. Guests staying with a family are often honored with the first bath. Remember not to drain the water when you are done, though, since everyone in the family uses the same hot water. Traditional Japanese inns, or 旅館, have large bathing areas for their guests. Today, these baths are segregated into male baths, 男風呂, and female baths, 女風呂, and are sometimes quite elaborate, including waterfalls and multiple bathing pools of different temperatures.

■ キアラのジャーナル Kiara's Journal

Read the journal entry below, and then answer these questions.

❶ What did Kiara, Ben, and Tomo do after they bought the ukiyoe?
❷ Did the slippers at the inn fit Ben?
❸ Describe the men's bath.
❹ Describe the women's bath.

ジャーナルへ

　浮世絵を　買って　旅館を　探しました。下町に　かわいい　旅館が　ありました。ベン君には　その旅館の　スリッパは　ちょっと　小さかった　です。ベン君は、「もっと大きいのは　ありますか。」と　聞きました。

　旅館の　人は、「ああ、すみません。それだけ　です。もっと大きいのは　ありません。」と　言いました。

　ベン君は、「大丈夫　です。ありがとう　ございます。」と、言いました。その後、部屋へ　行きました。

　私の　部屋は　とてもきれい　でした。後で、お風呂に　入りました。お風呂は　ちょっと　小さかった　ですが、soaking in a hot bathで、とても　リラックス　しました。

　お風呂の　後、旅館で　みんなで　一緒に　晩ご飯を　食べました。ベン君と　じゅん君は　とても　元気に　話しました。ベン君は、「この旅館の　男の人の　お風呂には、四つの　お風呂が　ありました。それに　高い　滝 (waterfall)も　ありました。すばらしかったです。」と　言いました。

私は「嘘 でしょう。女の人の お風呂は もっと小さかった です。熱くて、リラックスしましたが、ちょっと 暗かった です。」と 言いました。

友さんは、「残念 ですが、昔の 日本には、そういう 事が 良く ありました。江戸時代、guests は だいたい 男の人 でした。In the 20th and 21st centuries, of course, this changes。でも 今は、江戸時代 で、侍が いる時代 ですからね。」と 言いました。

じゅん君は、「そう ですね。去年、家族と 一緒に 山へ 行った時に、女風呂 (women's bath)も、男風呂 (men's bath)も、同じくらいの サイズ でした。」と 言いました。

Hotel onsen, Izu Peninsula

私は　ベン君に、おせんべいと　漫画を　あげます。

I will give sembei and a comic book to Ben.

■ 会話 Dialogue

キアラ　：　はい、私は　ベン君に、おせんべいと　漫画を　あげます。

ベン　：　ありがとう！いただきます。

じゅん：　これは、僕達から　友さんに　です。どうぞ。

友　：　富士山の　浮世絵　ですか。すばらしい！ありがとう。

キアラ：　私は、じゅん君に　この筆を　もらいました。じゅん君、ありがとう。

じゅん：　キアラさん、それで、漢字を　練習して下さいね。

友　：　じゃ、僕は、キアラさんに、漢字の　名前を　あげます。

キアラ：　すてき！漢字の　名前を　もらう事は、とても　うれしい　です。ありがとう。

■ 単語 New Words

煎餅 (n) せんべい	ケーキ (n)	プレゼント (n)	(あげる) あげます (v)	(もらう) もらいます (v) – to receive
				とんでもない (exp.) – Don't be ridiculous

■ 言葉の探索 Language Detection

1.　Verbs for giving: やります/あげます/さしあげます
　　All of these verbs mean "to give."

　　a.　やります is very informal and is usually used for giving food to animals or things to people younger than you.

　　b.　あげます is used in most circumstances. It means you are giving something to someone of equal or greater status. There are many people nowadays who use あげます even in situations where it would be OK to use やります.

　　c.　The more polite form, さしあげます, is used among acquaintances quite formally.

Use the particle に after the name of the person who is given something; に indicates the recipient of the action.

A)　私は　あなたに　本を　あげます。　　　　　　　　　= I will give you a book.
B)　じゅん君は　お母さんに　帽子を　あげました。　　= Jun gave his mom a hat.
C)　キアラさんは　先生に　日本の　おみやげを　あげました。　= Kiara gave her teacher a souvenir from Japan.
D)　ベン君は　犬に　水を　やりました。　　　　　　　= Ben gave some water to the dog.
E)　先生、これを　さしあげます。　　　　　　　　　　= Teacher, I will give you this.

2. Verbs of receiving: もらいます/いただきます

もらいます and the more humble いただきます both mean "to receive." いただきます generally implies that something was received from a superior and もらいます is more commonly used between family and friends. Note that the giver can be followed by either particle に or particle から.

A) 私は　愛子さんに　箱を　もらいました。
= I received a box from Aiko.

B) 花子さんは　ともき君から　ネックレスを　もらいます。
= Hanako will receive a necklace from Tomoki.

C) 母の日に、お母さんは　じゅんさんに　ばら　三本を　もらいました。
= On Mother's Day, Jun's mother received three roses from him.

D) 私は　山本先生から　とても　きれいな　絵を　いただきました。
= I received a very pretty painting from Mr. Yamamoto (a teacher).

* Note: Before Japanese begin a meal, everyone says "いただきます," literally "I will receive," as a way of thanking all who have had a hand in preparing the food.

■ 自習 Self Check

1. あげます/さしあげます – to give

Try to say the following out loud to yourself in Japanese.

A) Mr. Suzuki will give juice to the first year students.
B) I gave cookies (クッキー) to the Russian teacher.
C) Mary gave some money to her friend.
D) Ichirou gave rice to the koi (こい [fish]).
E) Jun's mother did not give Ben a birthday present.
F) (compose a sentence of your own)

2. もらいます/いただきます – to receive

A) I got an eraser from the teacher.
B) Please get paper from your friend.
C) Yes, I have received the present.
D) My little brother received a CD from my uncle.
E) Aiko received some chocolates (チョコレート) from Ben.
F) (compose a sentence of your own)

3. Try to say the following in Japanese. Use やります.

A) I gave the cat a new toy. (おもちゃ)
B) The teacher gave the flowers some water.
C) My grandfather gave the dog some milk.
D) Please give the horse some food.
E) I gave my little sister a new dress.
F) (compose a sentence of your own)

■ 練習の時間 Time for Practice
れんしゅう

---

1. **Pair Practice**

This year for their birthdays, the people shown below received presents from each other. Following the pattern in the example, use as many different combinations of people and presents as possible to ask and state who might have received what from whom.

 例 (talking about the people pictured below
れい EXAMPLE are A-さん and B-さん)

A-さん： お兄さんは お父さんから 何を
もらいましたか。

B-さん： お父さんに ネクタイを 一本 もら
いました。

father

uncle

younger sister

older brother

Kiara

mother

---

2. **Pair Practice**

Use Japanese to ask your partner what he/she received from family members on his/her last birthday. Take turns.

例 You ： 誕生日プレゼントに お母さんに 何を もらいましたか。
れい たんじょうび
EXAMPLE B-さん： 母から このブレスレット を もらいました。

---

3. **Pair Practice**

A-さん should ask B-さん in Japanese what kind of presents B-さん will give each of the family members and friends listed here. Use the sample dialogue below to get started.

例 A-さん： お父さんの 誕生日の プレゼントに 何を あげますか。
れい たんじょうび
EXAMPLE B-さん： そうですね。 父に 靴下を あげます。
くつした

➲ father for Father's Day (父の日)　　　　– 3 books
➲ mother for Mother's Day (母の日)　　　 – 2,000円
➲ friend Keiko for her birthday　　　　　 – a blue t-shirt
➲ younger brother for his birthday　　　　– 5 pencils and a notebook
➲ English teacher for birthday　　　　　　– cake
➲ pet hamster (ハムスター)　　　　　　　 – a ball (玉)
➲ the school principal (校長先生)　　　　 – trip souvenir (おみやげ)
➲ your grandfather/grandmother's birthday present

文化箱 Culture Chest

Gift Giving in Japan

Gift-giving practices in Japan are elaborate and complex. It is customary for most people to send beautifully-wrapped presents called お中元 (from the beginning to middle of July) and お歳暮 (around Dec. 20-28) to people with whom they have a relationship: their matchmaker, family doctor, children's teachers, mentors, bosses and so on. Department stores take full economic advantage of these customs with fancy displays of boxed gifts during those seasons, things like perfectly-ripe fruits or nicely-presented gift sets of coffee or tea.

Japanese also give and receive gifts in many other situations. For instance, it is customary to take a gift when you visit someone's house or when you come back from a trip. When in doubt about gift giving in Japan, it is safest to consult with your 先生 or a Japanese person.

キアラのジャーナル Kiara's Journal

Read the journal entry below, and then answer these questions.

❶ What did they decide to do in Asakusa?
❷ What did Kiara give Ben?
❸ What did Kiara receive from Jun?
❹ What did Tomo receive from Jun?
❺ What was Tomo's present to Kiara?
❻ How do the group members feel about each other now, after having travelled together for quite a while?

ジャーナルへ

　　今日　私は　遅くまで　寝ました。とても疲れて　いました。ゆっくり　朝ご飯を　食べてから、皆で　浅草神社へ　行きました。じゅん君の　家は　その神社の　近くなので、江戸時代の　その場所 (place) が　見たかったから　です。それに、そこが、the right place for the time capsule だから　です！
　　浅草神社は　古くて　とても有名　です。そこで　ベン君は、「じゅん君の　家と　同じ (same) 場所を　探しますよ！そして、let's each buy some kind of おみやげ as presents for each

other! それを、タイムカプセルに　入れて、うめて (bury)、僕達の　時代に　帰って、その
タイムカプセルを　開けましょう！」と　言いました。

じゅん君は、「それは　いい　アイディア　ですね。ベン君は　あたまが　いい　です
ね。」と、言いました。I imagined us opening the time capsule in the 21st century in the garden of Jun's house in Tokyo and seeing the ukiyoe and other presents from the Edo era! From there, we split up to go shopping.

昼に、ラーメン屋で　みんなと　会いました。そのラーメン屋は、ちょっと　まずかった
ですが、そこの　おばあさんは　とても　かわいかった　です。食べてから、また　ショッ
ピングを　しました。私は　煎餅と　魚と　お箸を　買って、それから、浴衣と　北斎さん
の　浮世絵も　買いました。

その晩、旅館で　皆に　おみやげを　あげました。私は　ベン君に　美味しい煎餅と
漫画の　本を　あげました。じゅん君は　友さんに　富士山の　浮世絵を　あげました。
私は、じゅん君に　いい筆を　もらいました。本当に　楽しかった　です。

プレゼントを　皆で　exchangeしてから、私は　筆で　漢字を　書く　練習を　始めま
した。友さんは　私の　名前を　漢字で　書きました。「気新」と　書きました。「気」の
意味は　"energy, spirit."「新」の　意味は　"new。" So Tomo said my new name means something like "new/revitalized energy/spirit" in English.

じゅん君は、「かっこいい　ですね！私の　名前は　ひらがな　だけ　ですよ！」と　言
いました。私は、「友さん、すてきな　漢字を、どうも　有り難う　ございます。」と　言
いました。友さんは、「いやいや、どういたしまして (You are welcome)。あなた達と　一緒に
　いるのは　本当に　楽しい　です。ありがとうね。」と、言って、and at that point、友さん
started to tear up! But he managed to say、「皆　いい友達に　なりましたね。有り難う・・・。
じゃ、食べましょう！」

What happened tonight was really sweet. 私は　やっぱり　じゅん君の　家へ　帰りたい (I want to...)・・・　ですが、この　旅行も　楽しい　です。

これは、私の　妹が　くれました。
My younger sister gave me this.

■ 会話 Dialogue
かい わ

ベン　　：　キアラさん、いつも　その　ブレスレットを　していますね。かわいい　ですね。

キアラ　：　あ、これ　ですか。これは、私の　妹が　くれました。誕生日プレゼント　です。
たんじょうび

ベン　　：　へえ、僕も、誕生日に　この　シャツを、兄から　もらいました。
ぼく　たんじょうび

キアラ　：　7月4日は、妹の　誕生日　です。私も　すてきな　プレゼントを　妹に　あげます。
しちがつよっか　　たんじょうび

じゅん　：　何を　あげますか。
なに

キアラ　：　着物と、たくさんの　日本の　お菓子と　漢字の　名前も　あげます！
きもの　　　　　　　　　　　か　し　　　かんじ　　　なまえ

■ 単語 New Words
たん ご

(お)菓子 (n) – Japanese candy/sweets　　　　　　　　　　くれる/くれます (v) – (to) give
か し

■ 言葉の探索 Language Detection
こと ば　たん さく

1.　くれます = something is given to you or to someone else

When くれます is used, the name of the giver is the subject and is followed by が or sometimes は. Just remember that in most cases you can use が (Ga) for the <u>Giver</u>. The recipient is followed by the particle に. You can think of the person receiving something as getting down on "bended <u>knee</u>" to receive something if he/she is extremely grateful.

A)　友達が　私に　この　ブレスレットを　くれました。　= My friend gave me this bracelet.

B)　数学の　先生が　私に　いい本を　くれました。　= The math teacher gave me a good book.
すう

C)　キャシーさんは　私に　新しいCD　二枚を　くれました。 = Kathy gave me two new CDs.

■ 自習 Self Check
じ しゅう

Try to say the following out loud to yourself in Japanese. Use くれます

A) My father gave me money.

B) My friend gave me a purple shirt.

C) My grandfather will give me new clothes.

D) Our mother gave my little brother an expensive backpack.

E) My mother gave me three beautiful pencils.

F) (compose a sentence of your own)

■ 練習の時間 Time for Practice
れんしゅう

1.　Group Practice

Use a piece of scrap paper to draw the certificate below, writing your name on the blank that says 名前. Your teacher will re-distribute the forms to the class. On the new certificate that you receive, draw a picture of a present appropriate to give to the person whose name is at the top (be nice ☺). Sign the paper, and return the form to your teacher. Once you have received your new "present," be prepared to tell the class who gave you what, using the appropriate verb for giving/receiving. Use the sample statement below as a model.

名前：_____

プレゼント：

サイン：_____

1. トム君は　私に　すごい車を　くれました。　　　= Tom gave me a cool car.
   -OR- ぼくは　トム君に　すごい車を　もらいました。　　*or* I received a cool car from Tom.

2. アリシャさんは　私に　赤いドレスを　くれました。　= Alicia gave me a red dress.
   -OR- 私は　アリシャさんに　赤いドレスを　もらいました。　*or* I received a red dress from Alicia.

■ 文化箱 Culture Chest
ぶん　か　ばこ

Celebrations

How do you celebrate your birthday, or a holiday like Independence Day or Thanksgiving? Do you have a party, and get together with your family? Or do you go out to dinner with friends? Because Japanese houses tend to be small, celebrations involving friends or colleagues usually take place outside the home, in restaurants or halls.

Many traditional holidays, such as 雛祭り(Girl's Day, on March 3) or 子供の日(Children's Day, on May 5), are celebrated by decorating the house. Other holidays, such as お正月 (the New Year's holiday), involve getting together with relatives and making visits to the local shrine or temple. During お盆, in August, many people travel back to their hometown, to visit and clean the graves of their ancestors.

■ キアラのジャーナル　Kiara's Journal
き　あ　ら

Read the journal entry below, and then answer these questions.

❶ How does Kiara feel about leaving Edo?
❷ Why do they plan to leave through the gate at the Asakusa Shrine?
❸ Who does Kiara say she wants to travel with again?

ジャーナルへ

江戸は　とても　楽しかった　です。We've had an incredible time: 北斎さんと　会って、買い物をして、お土産を　交換 (exchange)　しました。でも、I miss being able to talk to my　父や母や　友達など。明日は、浅草神社から　私達の　時代に　帰ります。浅草神社は　じゅん君の　家と　近いから　です。あ！ところで、私達は、とうとう(at last)、found the location of Jun's house in the 江戸時代！We put the presents in the time capsule and buried them there. Will the time capsule be able to transfer from Edo to our era? If we go into the 時の門 there, we've got a pretty good chance of getting back into our own time. また、いつか、友さんと　旅行 (to travel)を　したいですね。

おやすみ。

■ テクノの時間　Techno Time

To earn the passport stamp for this chapter, you will need to successfully participate in a text chat with Kiara. She's been trying to send messages back to this time period and is writing to you. To begin, you will need to open a word processing document and title it "TC9" followed by the first three letters of your family name and then the first three letters of your given name (no spaces). You will need to respond appropriately to the messages you receive. Be sure to ask questions of Kiara if appropriate for the conversation.

■ 単語チェックリスト　New Word Checklist

Japanese	Location	English
9-1		
いちまん　一万 (n)	9-1	ten thousand
うきよえ　浮世絵 (n)	9-1	woodblock print (prior to and through the Edo Period)
うる/うります　売る/売ります (売って) (v)	9-1	(to) sell
え　絵 (n)	9-1	painting, drawing
えいが　映画 (n)	9-1	movie
かいもの　買い物 (n)	9-1	shopping
かいもの(を) する/します　買い物(を) する/します (v)	9-1	(to) go shopping
かう/かいます　買う/買います (買って) (v)	9-1	(to) buy
からおけ(を) する/します　カラオケ(を) する/します (v)	9-1	(to) karaoke (to sing)
きゅうせん　九千 (n)	9-1	nine thousand
きゅうまん　九万 (n)	9-1	ninety thousand
けんか(を)する/します (v)	9-1	(to) argue
ごせん　五千 (n)	9-1	five thousand
ごまん　五万 (n)	9-1	fifty thousand
さっかー(を) する/します　サッカー(を) する/します (v)	9-1	(to) play soccer
さんぜん　三千 (n)	9-1	three thousand

Japanese	Location	English
さんまん　三万 (n)	9-1	thirty thousand
しゃわー(を) する/します　シャワー(を) する/します (v)	9-1	(to) take a shower
しゃんぷー(を) する/します　シャンプー(を) する/します (v)	9-1	(to) shampoo
じゅういちまん　十一万 (n)	9-1	one hundred ten thousand
じゅうごまん　十五万 (n)	9-1	one hundred fifty thousand
じゅうさんまん　十三万 (n)	9-1	one hundred thirty thousand
じゅうななまん　十七万 (n)	9-1	one hundred seventy thousand
じゅうにまん　十二万 (n)	9-1	one hundred twenty thousand
じゅうまん　十万 (n)	9-1	one hundred thousand
じゅうよんまん　十四万 (n)	9-1	one hundred forty thousand
じゅうろくまん　十六万 (n)	9-1	one hundred sixty thousand
しゅくだい(を) する/します　宿題(を) する/します (v)	9-1	(to) do homework
しょっくじ(を)する/します　食事(を)する/します (v)	9-1	(to) dine; to have a meal
しろ　城 (n)	9-1	castle
せん　千 (n)	9-1	one thousand
でーと(を) する/します　デート(を) する/します (v)	9-1	(to) go on a date
でんわ(を)する/します　電話(を) する/します (v)	9-1	(to) telephone
なかなおり(を) する/します　仲直り(を) する/します (v)	9-1	(to) make up; to become friends (again)
ななせん　七千 (n)	9-1	seven thousand
ななまん　七万 (n)	9-1	seventy thousand
なんぜん　何千 (inter.)	9-1	how many thousands
にじゅういちまん　二十一万 (n)	9-1	two hundred ten thousand
にじゅうまん　二十万 (n)	9-1	two hundred thousand
にせん　二千 (n)	9-1	two thousand
にまん　二万 (n)	9-1	twenty thousand
ばすけ(を) する/します　バスケ(を) する/します (v)	9-1	(to) play basketball
はちまん　八万 (n)	9-1	eighty thousand
はっせん　八千 (n)	9-1	eight thousand
はんが　版画 (n)	9-1	woodblock print (modern)
びでおげーむ(を) する/します　ビデオゲーム(を) する/します (v)	9-1	(to) play video/computer games
まん　万 (n)	9-1	ten thousand
みせ　店 (n)	9-1	shop; store
よんせん　四千 (n)	9-1	four thousand
よんまん　四万 (n)	9-1	forty thousand
りょこう(を) する/します　旅行(を) する/します (旅行(を) して) (v)	9-1	(to) take a trip; to travel
ろくせん　六千 (n)	9-1	six thousand
ろくまん　六万 (n)	9-1	sixty thousand

9-2

Japanese	Location	English
いくら (inter.)	9-2	how much?
いただく/いただきます (いただいて) (v)	9-2	(to) receive (very polite), lit.: I will receive.
いっさつ　一冊 (n)	9-2	one volume
いっぽん　一本 (n)	9-2	one cylindrical object
えす(S)さいず　Sサイズ (n)	9-2	small (S) size
えむ(M)さいず　Mサイズ (n)	9-2	medium (M) size
える(L)さいず　Lサイズ (n)	9-2	large (L) size
おつり (n)	9-2	change (cash)
きゅうさつ　九冊 (n)	9-2	nine volumes
きゅうほん　九本 (n)	9-2	nine cylindrical objects
ごさつ　五冊 (n)	9-2	five volumes
ごほん　五本 (n)	9-2	five cylindrical objects
さんさつ　三冊 (n)	9-2	three volumes

Japanese	Location	English
さんぼん　　三本 (n)	9-2	three cylindrical objects
じゅっさつ　　十冊 (n)	9-2	ten volumes
じゅっぽん　　十本 (n)	9-2	ten cylindrical objects
ぜんぶで　　全部で (exp.)	9-2	in all; total; all together
てんいん　　店員 (n)	9-2	shopkeeper; clerk
どう　ですか (inter.)	9-2	How about it?
とくべつ　　特別 (n/な adj.)	9-2	special
ななさつ　　七冊 (n)	9-2	seven volumes
ななほん　　七本 (n)	9-2	seven cylindrical objects
なんさつ　　何冊 (inter.)	9-2	how many volumes
なんぼん　　何本 (inter.)	9-2	how many cylindrical objects
にさつ　　二冊 (n)	9-2	two volumes
にほん　　二本 (n)	9-2	two cylindrical objects
はっさつ　　八冊 (n)	9-2	eight volumes
はっぽん　　八本 (n)	9-2	eight cylindrical objects
べつ　　別 (n/な adj.)	9-2	separate
べつべつ　　別々 (n/な adj.)	9-2	separately; individually
よんさつ　　四冊 (n)	9-2	four volumes
よんほん　　四本 (n)	9-2	four cylindrical objects
ろくさつ　　六冊 (n)	9-2	six volumes
ろっぽん　　六本 (n)	9-2	six cylindrical objects

9-3

Japanese	Location	English
あかるい　　明るい (い adj.)	9-3	bright; light
くらい　　暗い (い adj.)	9-3	dark
さがす/さがします　　探す/探します (探して) (v)	9-3	(to) search
ざんねん　　残念 (な adj.)	9-3	regrettably, unluckily
もっと (adv.)	9-3	more

9-4

Japanese	Location	English
あげる/あげます　　上げる/上げます (上げて) (v)	9-4	(to) give
けーき　　ケーキ (n)	9-4	cake
せんべい　　煎餅 (n)	9-4	rice crackers
とんでもない (exp.)	9-4	Don't be ridiculous! Not a chance! My pleasure
ぷれぜんと　　プレゼント (n)	9-4	present; a gift
もらう/もらいます (もらって) (v)	9-4	(to) receive

9-5

Japanese	Location	English
おかし　　(お)菓子 (n)	9-5	Japanese traditional sweets
くれる/くれます (くれて) (v)	9-5	(to) receive
くれる/くれます (v)	9-5	(to) give

Meeting Basho in Kanazawa

Learning Goals

By the end of this chapter you will learn:

A) simple weather forecasts in Japanese

B) how to politely invite someone to do something

C) how to accept or decline invitations

D) how to say that you want or do not want to do things

E) about the famous haiku poet, Matsuo Basho

F) 10 additional kanji

Performance Goals

By the end of this chapter you will be able to:

A) give a weather forecast

B) politely invite people to do things with you

C) accept or decline invitations

D) say that you want or do not want to do things

E) read and write 10 additional kanji

Geta at a temple on Koyasan

明日も　晴れ　でしょう。
Probably tomorrow will also be sunny.

1) 私は、春が 好き です。

2) 僕も、この 季節が 好きです。

3) 僕は、夏が 大好き です。

4) 私は、秋が 好きです。食べ物が、美味しい です から。

5) 春も、夏も、秋も、冬も 皆 きれい です。私は、全部の 季節が 好き です。それが、俳句の 心 です。

6) ほら！お城の 夕焼けが、きれい ですね！

7) そう ですね。明日も、晴れ でしょう。

■ 会話 Dialogue
かいわ

キアラ ： 私は、春が 好き です。
　　　　 はる

じゅん ： 僕も、この 季節が 好き です。
　　　　　　　 きせつ　　 す

ベン　 ： 僕は、夏が 大好き です。
　　　　　　 なつ

友　　 ： 私は、秋が 好き です。食べ物が、美味しい ですから。
　　　　　 あき　　　　　　　　　　　　 おい

芭蕉　 ： 春も、夏も、秋も、冬も、皆 きれい です。私は、全部の季節が 好き です。それ
ばしょう　 はる　 なつ　 あき　 ふゆ　みんな　　　　　　　　　　　 ぜんぶ　 きせつ
　　　　 が、俳句の 心 です。
　　　　　　 はいく

キアラ ： ほら！お城の ＊夕焼けが、きれいですね！
　　　　　　　 しろ　　 ゆうや

芭蕉　 ： そう ですね。明日も、晴れ でしょう。
ばしょう　　　　　　 あした　 は

＊夕焼け – sunset. *Lit.*: burning (sun) of the evening (sky)
　ゆうや

■ 単語 New Words
たんご

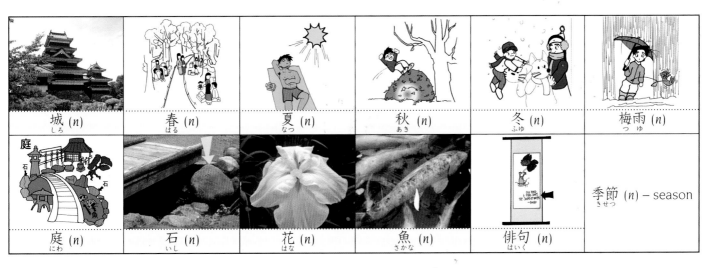

城 (n) しろ	春 (n) はる	夏 (n) なつ	秋 (n) あき	冬 (n) ふゆ	梅雨 (n) つゆ
庭 (n) にわ	石 (n) いし	花 (n) はな	魚 (n) さかな	俳句 (n) はいく	季節 (n) – season きせつ

Weather related words

天気予報 (n) てんきよほう	晴れ (n) は	雨 (n) あめ	雪 (n) ゆき	天気 (n) – weather てんき
				晴れる/晴れます (v) – to become clear は は
				降る/降ります (v) – to precipitate, to fall ふ ふ
雷 (n) かみなり	竜巻 (n) たつまき	台風 (n) たいふう	曇る/曇ります (v) くも くも	大雨 (n) – heavy rain おおあめ
				曇 (n) – cloudy くもり
				地震 (n) – earthquake じしん

一度 — 1 time, 1 degree
いちど
二度 (n) – 2 times, 2 degrees
にど
三度 (n) – 3 times, 3 degrees
さんど
四度 (n) – 4 times, 4 degrees
よんど
五度 (n) – 5 times, 5 degrees
ごど
六度 (n) – 6 times, 6 degrees
ろくど
七度 (n) – 7 times, 7 degrees
ななど
八度 (n) – 8 times, 8 degrees
はちど

*九度 (n) – 9 times, 9 degrees
きゅうど
十度 (n) – 10 times, 10 degrees
じゅうど
何度 (inter.) – How many times/degrees?
なんど

Note: There is a slightly different intonation between the pronunciation of times and degrees. This can be heard in the audio file for this section.

* 9 degrees can alternatively be pronounced as くど, but not 9 times.

■ 漢字 Kanji
かんじ

春 9 strokes	はる – spring	一	二	三	夫	夫	表	春	春	
	春 – spring はる	春								
	SPRING includes two (二) big (大) days (日) for children in Japan, the first day of school in April and Children's Day in May.									
夏 10 strokes	なつ – summer	一	丆	万	百	百	百	夏	夏	
	夏 – summer なつ	夏	夏							
	This shows a thumbtack (丁) that has stuck in an eyeball (目) until a tear comes out of the eye to the left (the 8th stroke). Unfortunately this is happening again (又) and again (又) due to a powerful SUMMER storm that sends thumbtacks flying everywhere.									
秋 9 strokes	あき – autumn, fall	ノ	二	千	手	禾	禾	利	秋	
	秋 – autumn, fall あき	秋								
	The first stroke of this kanji looks like the blade of an axe used to cut up trees (木) to make a fire (火) to keep warm on a cold AUTUMN night.									
冬 5 strokes	ふゆ – winter	ノ	夂	夂	冬	冬				
	冬 – winter ふゆ									
	Now that it is WINTER, the long tear (the first stroke) from the hint for the kanji for summer above, again (又) and again (又) is turning into two pieces of ice (the last two strokes) due to the WINTER cold.									
石 5 strokes	セキ；いし – stone, rock	一	丆	不	石	石				
	石 – stone, rock いし									
	Imagine the final 3 strokes (口) as a STONE so hard that any attempt to drive a nail (丁) into the STONE results in the nail simply being bent to the left.									

■ 言葉の探索 Language Detection

1. 暑い　でしょう。

A. でしょう is derived from です and implies some doubt. It is best translated as meaning "probably." It is used often in Japanese in weather forecasts and in other circumstances where one is assuming something will happen in the future. When asking a question in Japanese, the last syllable has a raised inflection, similar to what happens in English. With statements, the tone is flat or the inflection goes down as in these examples. でしょう can be preceded by nouns, adjectives, or the dictionary forms of verbs.

1. 明日は　雨でしょう。 = Tomorrow it will probably rain.
2. 金曜日は　寒い　でしょう。 = It will probably be cold on Friday.
3. あの自転車は　高い　でしょう。 = That bike is probably expensive.

B. でしょう can also mean "right?" when you are trying to confirm something. As in English, when making a statement, the last syllable has a lowered inflection, however when there is some doubt in the statement or if it is an outright question, the intonation is raised.

1. 高橋さん　でしょう。 = You are Takahashi, right?
2. 日本語が　好き　でしょう。 = You like Japanese, right?
3. お寿司を　食べる　でしょう。 = You eat sushi, right?

2. 天気予報 – Weather forecasts
Below is an example of a typical weather forecast you might hear in Japan. Notice the use of でしょう。

天気予報を　お伝えします。明日の　東京地方は、晴れ、時々　曇り　でしょう。予想最低気温は 12度、予想最高気温は　25度、降水確率は、20%です。

English Translation:
Now for the weather forecast. Tomorrow the Tokyo region will be sunny with periods of clouds. The expected low temperature will be 12 degrees (Celsius) with a high temperature of 25 degrees, and a 20% chance of precipitation.

■ 自習 Self Check

1. でしょう

Can you say the following in Japanese?

A) Russia's winter probably is cold.
B) Kyuushuu's summer probably is hot.
C) It will probably snow tomorrow.
D) It will probably rain the day after tomorrow.

E) Indonesia's trees are probably very big.
F) Kyoto is probably cool in April.
G) It will probably be beautiful in the morning.
H) My father will probably give me money for my birthday.

2.   Weather forecast

Refer to the example weather forecast in the 探索 above to say the following things in Japanese:
たんさく

A) Now for the weather forecast.
B) Tomorrow the Kyoto region will be rainy with periods of clouds.
C) The low temperature should be 15 degrees.
D) The high temperature should be 23 degrees.
E) The chance of precipitation is 80%.

■ 練習の時間 Time for Practice
れんしゅう

1.   Pair Practice

Take out your set of flash cards for weather-related vocabulary from this section. First, flash your cards briefly to your partner. See if she/he can correctly provide the English and/or Japanese. Take turns. Then, lay nine of these cards out on a piece of scrap paper on the table between you (English or picture side up) in a tic-tac-toe format and play tic-tac-toe with your partner. Play paper-rock-scissors to see who goes first. The winner selects a square that they wish to take and says the Japanese word for the English card that's in the square. For example, for *winter* you would say "これは　冬　です。" If you're correct, pick up the card and place either an X or an O on the square. If you're wrong, ふゆ
lay it back down and it's your partner's turn. After three games, switch languages and play by translating from Japanese to English.

2.   Small Group Practice

Use a piece of scrap paper to copy the chart below. Interview two classmates about the seasonal weather in the place they were born. Then report your results to your partner or to the class.

例   You   : どこで　生まれましたか。   = Where were you born?
れい   う
EXAMPLE   B-さん   : (the place you were born)で　生まれました。   = I was born in _____.
       You   : (that same place)の　春の　天気は　どうですか。 = How is _____'s spring weather?
                            はる   てんき
       B-(一)さん ： 春は、少し寒いです。そして、時々　雪が　降ります。 = Spring is a little cold. And further-
            はる   すこ   ときどき ゆき ふ   more, sometimes snow falls.

名前 _____ 場所 (place) ばしょ _____	春の天気	夏の天気	秋の天気	冬の天気

■ 文化箱 Culture Chest

金沢
かなざわ

Medieval 金沢 was ruled by the 前田藩 (clan). In Japan each clan was ruled by a 大名 or regional feudal lord. The kanji 大名 literally means "big name" and if you were the ruler of an area, you would be the most important name in the region.

Between 1185 and 1600, Japan saw the rise of the 侍 or military class and the decline of power of the nobility, the ruling class that had controlled the country up until the end of the 平安時代 (794–1185). By the late 16th century, the 大名 had gained firm political control over their domains and most swore loyalty to the 将軍, Japan's most powerful military leader. By the late 1500s, under the strong hands of successive 将軍, Japan gradually became more and more politically stable.

Incense and offerings, Kyoto

During this more peaceful era, samurai had to justify their privileged existence, since their role as warrior was no longer important. This is when ideals of loyalty and preserving honor on the battlefield became codified for the first time, and when many of the "traditional" Japanese arts, such as the tea ceremony, began to flourish.

By the time Basho traveled the country, the Tokugawa clan had brought a measure of unification and peace to much of Japan. However, bandits and other hardships still made it dangerous for Basho to travel to the northern rural regions. By being able to cover so much ground so quickly without being injured or killed, legends grew that he may have had ninja skills.

■ キアラのジャーナル Kiara's Journal

Read the journal entry below, and then answer these questions.

❶ Where and in what time period are Kiara, Ben, and Jun now?
❷ Had Tomo ever met Matsuo Basho prior to this experience?
❸ Write down what you learned about haiku from this diary entry.

ジャーナルへ

今度は、私達は、石川県の　金沢に　来ました。今は　1690年の　春　です。近くの店の人は、「今、金沢に　松尾芭蕉さんが　来ています。」と、言いました。うれしかったです！芭蕉さんは　俳句で　世界一　有名な人　です。

私は、学校で　英語の　俳句を　作りました。私は　俳句が　好きです。短くて　面白いと　思います。俳句は　5－7－5　のsyllable lines　です。いつも　季語（季節の　言葉）を

入れます。季語を　入れると、もっと面白くなります。For example, 春の　季語は、桜、青い leaves、動物の babies などです。

Here is a poem by 芭蕉 that shows how 季語 can add a deeper meaning to a 俳句。

『さまざまな事	various things
思い出す	remembered
桜かな』	the cherry blossoms

芭蕉さんは、Mie prefectureの　伊賀上野という　ところで、この句を　作くりました。芭蕉さんの　生まれた所です。Seeing the beautiful cherry blossoms in his hometown probably brought back a lot of memories for 芭蕉。

The spring is a time of change in Japan (the new school year starts on April 1st, and many workers are transferred to new jobs in new locations around this time as well) so for the Japanese the image of cherry blossoms could trigger a flood of memories of many of the changes in their life. You put 季語 to something you feel very deeply. The 季語 help you imagine an image of a season, and you can come closer to understanding the author's thoughts. Therefore, Japanese say that 俳句 are very 深い deep、高い high and 広い wide despite being very 短い short poems。

Anyway, back to our time in Kanazawa...私達は、始めに金沢　のお城 (castle) に　行きました。森の池の近くに、年取った　おじいさんが　いました。私は　友さんに、「あの　人は　だれ　ですか。」と　聞きました。

友さんは、「あの人は　松尾芭蕉　です。彼は　いつも　俳句を、森や池など、きれいな所で　作ります。僕は　今まで　芭蕉さんと　まだ　会ったことが　ありませんでした。」と、言いました。He suggested that we go up and introduce ourselves.

ベン君は　芭蕉さんに、「すみません。僕たちは　日本を　旅行しています。今、金沢へ花見に　来ました。ここの　春は　とてもきれいですね。」と、言いました。He did not want to come right out and ask Basho's name, but wanted to make sure that it was him.

芭蕉さんは、「そうですか。僕も　風の　ように　この国を　あちこち回って、ここに花を見に　来ました。この　お城の　桜は　とても　きれい　ですね。」と言いました。

■ テクノの時間　Techno Time

Though you've not been introduced to them all yet, type all the vocabulary words from this chapter into your digital dictionary. Remember to use your file labeled "JISHO" (in *romaji*).

■ 会話 Dialogue
（かいわ）

じゅん　：　芭蕉さんは、本当に　すてきな　人ですね。
　　　　　　（ばしょう）

ベン　　：　芭蕉さんに、「僕達と一緒に、時の　門の　*旅を　しませんか。」と言いませんか。
　　　　　　（ばしょう）　　　　（ぼくたち）（いっしょ）　　　　　（たび）

キアラ　：　そして、「一緒に、たくさんの　俳句を　作りませんか。」と言いましょう。
　　　　　　　　　　　（いっしょ）　　　　　（はいく）（つく）

じゅん　：　彼は、「はい。いいですよ。」と言うでしょう！
　　　　　　（かれ）

友　　　：　残念　ですが　それは　ちょっと・・・・。それが　時の門の　ルールです。だれも、
　　　　　　（ざんねん）
　　　　　　私達と　一緒に　時の門に　入る事は　出来ません。でも、芭蕉さんに、「ここで
　　　　　　（いっしょ）　　　　　　　（はい）　（で）　　　　　　（ばしょう）
　　　　　　一緒に、食事をしませんか。」と、言いましょう！
　　　　　　（いっしょ）（しょくじ）

* 旅 – travel, take a trip
　（たび）

■ 単語 New Words
（たんご）

 (作る)作ります (v) （つく）（つく）	 (使う) 使います (v) （つか）（つか）	だれも (*exp.*) – no one 残念 (な *adj.*) – regrettable, unlucky （ざんねん）

■ 漢字 Kanji
（かんじ）

使　作

使 8 strokes	つかう – to use	ノ	イ	仁	仟	仨	佢	伊	使
	使(う) – to use （つか）								
	People (the radical on the left) like to think there is only one (一) "correct" view of history (史) but the truth is that everyone (一) USES his or her personal bias when trying to understand history. These three radicals USED together make up the character 使 – "to use."								

作 7 strokes	サク, つくる – to make	ノ	イ	イ'	仁	作	作	作	
	作(る) – to make; 作(文) – essay （つく）　　（さく）（ぶん）								
	The person (the radical on the left side) is MAKING a set of bookshelves with three shelves already in place. He's using a hammer (the third stroke) to nail the top corner together.								

■ 言葉の探索 Language Detection

1. 食べませんか。= Won't you eat (with me)?

   This polite form of an invitation in Japanese can be described as a negative invitation or an invitation in the negative. Similar to the English "Won't you please…," in Japanese you can extend a polite invitation by making a negative question. It is implied that you mean "with me." To use this form, take the verb that you want to use, drop the 〜ます ending and add 〜ませんか.

A)	飲みませんか。	= Won't you drink (with me)?
B)	英語で　話しませんか。	= Won't you speak English (with me)?
C)	テレビゲームを　しませんか。	= Won't you play video games?

2. 食べましょう。 = Let's eat.

   To say "Let's do such and such" in Japanese, change the 〜ます ending to 〜ましょう.

A)	庭で　お茶を　飲みましょう。	= Let's drink tea in the garden.
B)	6月に　日本へ　行きましょう。	= Let's go to Japan in June.
C)	散歩を　しましょう。	= Let's go for walk.

3. 食べましょうか。 = Shall we eat?

   Placing a か after ましょう softens the invitation a little. It is a slightly more polite way to offer an invitation by making the invitation more of a question.

A)	海で　泳ぎましょうか。	= Shall we swim in the ocean?
B)	昼寝を　しましょうか。	= Shall we take a nap?
C)	一緒に　日本語を　勉強　しましょうか。	= Shall we study Japanese together?

4. どこも, どこへも and どこにも…

   These three are used similarly to the expressions だれも and 何も, which were introduced in Chapter 5-3. だれも (no one) and 何も (nothing) are used to mean that someone or something does not exist in a place or time. どこも, どこへも, and どこにも are likewise used for negative expressions in which case どこも often translates as "nowhere" and どこへも and どこにも often translate as "not going anywhere." Note that どこも can also mean "everywhere" as in どこも　きれい　ですね。(Everywhere is clean.).

A)	その　生徒の　宿題は　どこにも　ありません。	= That student's homework isn't any place.
B)	この近くに　お寿司屋さんは　どこにも　ありません。	= In this vicinity, there is no sushi restaurant anywhere.
C)	私は　どこも　好き　では　ありません。	= I do not like anywhere.
D)	学校は　どこも　楽しい　です。	= At school, everywhere is fun.

5. ちょっと…

This expression, which you learned earlier, literally means something is "a little…." This expression can also be a very good way to decline a request in Japanese without giving a reason. If you have something else going on but would rather not give a reason, or if you just don't want to accept an invitation, this often works. It would be rude in most cases to ask for a further elaboration of ちょっと if someone turns down your request.

さとし：えみさん、土曜日に映画に　行きませんか。	= Emi, won't you go to a movie (with me) on Saturday?
えみ　：ええと、土曜日は　ちょっと・・・	= Umm, Saturday is a little …
サラ　：まりこさん、あした、ダンスパーティーへ　行きませんか。	= Mariko, won't you go to a dance party with me tomorrow?
まりこ：すみません、ダンスは　ちょっと・・・・	= I'm sorry, dancing is a little …

■ 自習 Self Check

1. …ませんか。 – Polite invitation

Can you say the following, out loud, in Japanese?

A) Won't you come to my house?

B) Would you like to play basketball (with me)?

2. Verb stem + ましょう　（ましょうか）

A) Let's eat at that restaurant over there.

C) Let's drink water.

B) Shall we return (go home)?

D) Shall we sing?

3. どこも、どこにも、どこへも

A) I will not go anywhere tomorrow.

B) It is not cold anywhere.

C) Everywhere is hot.

■ 練習の時間 Time for Practice

1. Pair Practice

Politely invite your partner to do the following activities, using the negative invitation pattern. Your partner will either accept or decline. Switch roles.

You　：	バスケを　しませんか。
友だち：	はい、しましょう。
	-OR- いいえ、バスケは　ちょっと・・・・
	-OR- ちょっと・・・・

A) バスケを　する

B) 宿題を　する

C) 図書館へ　行く

D) お昼ご飯を　食べる

E) 音楽を　聞く

F) 料理を　する

G) メキシコ料理を　食べる

H) 映画を　見る

I) 犬の　散歩を　する

J) 買い物を　する

K) 私の家へ　来る

L) チェスを　する

2.　Pair Practice

You and your partner will each choose two of the activities listed above (or two of your own). Invite your partner to do these activities with you. Set up a time and a place to meet. Use the question words いつ and どこ. Remember to reconfirm the time and date.

A-さん：　一緒に　宿題を　しませんか。
B-さん：　はい、しましょう。いつ　しますか。
A-さん：　あしたの　八時半は　どう　ですか。
B-さん：　いいですね。どこで　しましょうか。
A-さん：　スターバックスで　しましょう。
B-さん：　じゃ、明日の　八時半に　スターバックスで　会いましょう。

3.　Pair Practice

Choose two of the scenarios below and create a short (5–6 line) dialogue for each with your partner. Use the grammar patterns you have been practicing above. After you have rehearsed both dialogues, present one to your class.

A)　Your friend suggests a movie on Tuesday night. You have to study and suggest Saturday instead.
B)　Your mother wants to take you shopping for new shoes with her friends.
C)　Your Japanese pen pal wants you to visit Japan in October.
D)　Your friends are going to go to Mexico for spring break and invite you to go along.
E)　Your friend invites you to meet after school but you have a headache. Your friend suggests you take medicine, but you hate to take medicine.
F)　Your friend invites you to write a 40-page paper (作文) with her.

■ 文化箱 Culture Chest

松尾芭蕉

芭蕉 is the pen name of Matsuo Munefusa (松尾 宗房) (1644–1694). He is one of the most famous Japanese poets and is widely claimed to have popularized the haiku 俳句 (5 – 7 – 5) poetic format. Arriving in Edo in 1672, he was immediately popular and spent much of the rest of his life either at his banana leaf hut "芭蕉庵" near the capital or traveling, seeking inspiration from nature for his poems. In the West, his most famous haiku is about a frog:

Turtles in a pond in Kyoto

古池や	old pond
蛙　とびこむ	a frog jumps
水の　音	the sound of water

■ キアラのジャーナル Kiara's Journal

Read the journal entry below, and then answer these questions.

❶ How does Kiara describe the poet Basho?
❷ Where did Kiara go with Basho?
❸ What sort of place was it?
❹ What did Tomo want to do?
❺ Why couldn't they do what Tomo wanted to do immediately?

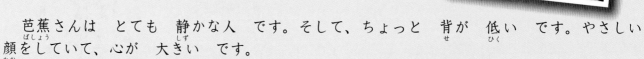

ジャーナルへ

　　芭蕉さんは　とても　静かな人　です。そして、ちょっと　背が　低い　です。やさしい顔をしていて、心が　大きい　です。

　　芭蕉さんは、「兼六園へ　一緒に　行きませんか。あそこは、日本の、one of the three most beautiful gardens。木や　花や　石の　橋や　水などが　すばらしい　です。」と、言いました。

　　兼六園の　名前の　意味は　面白い　です。It literally means the garden that combines the six characteristics that make up an excellent garden according to ancient garden design in China. The six characteristics are that a garden should be spacious and yet intimate, have some man-made elements but still should look natural and not tacky, and finally should have water elements and a nice view. I suppose it is hard to find a garden that can combine all 6 characteristics in a balanced fashion. でも、the cool thing about 兼六園 is that それを　全部　持っています！

　　兼六園の　中を、あちこち　歩きました。とても　静かな所　です。十一時に、友さんは、「じゃ、焼きそばを　食べませんか。近くの　レストランの　焼きそばは　とても美味しいです。」と、言いました。じゅん君は、「おととい　焼きそばを　食べましたよ。ここは　海の　近くですから、お寿司を　食べませんか。」と、言いました。友さんは、「お寿司ですか。それも　いい　ですね。では、今すぐ、行きませんか。」と、言いました。芭蕉さんは　石の　上に　座って、俳句を　作り始めました。友さんは、「芭蕉さんが　俳句を作り終わってから　行きましょう。」と、言いました。

日本語を、もっと　勉強したい　です。

I want to study Japanese more.

■ 会話 Dialogue

キアラ ： 私は、したい事が　たくさん　あります。

ベン　： どんな事ですか。

キアラ ： 日本語を、もっと勉強したいです。時の門の　*旅も　たくさん　したい　です。友達と
　　　　 遊びたい　です。もっと　柔道も　したい　です。買い物も　したい　です。

じゅん： †メールも　したいです。テレビも　映画も　見たい　です。

ベン　： 僕は、芭蕉さんと　俳句を　作りたい！

友　　： 私は、何かを　食べたい　です！

* 旅 – travel, take a trip

† メール – e-mail

■ 単語 New Words

何か – something　　　　　　　　　　　　　　遊ぶ/遊びます (v) – to play

■ 言葉の探索 Language Detection

1. 食べたいです。 = I want to eat.

   To say you want to do something, you drop the 〜ます and add 〜たいです to the verb stem (the part of the verb that comes before the ます). Use this pattern only to express your own desires, not those of someone else.

   NOTE: With the "verb stem + たい　です" pattern, it is OK to change the direct object particle from を to が; it is also permissible to use を in this case as well.

   A) 私は　寿司が　食べたい　です。　　　= I want to eat sushi.
   B) 私は　お茶が　飲みたい　です。　　　= I want to drink green tea.
   C) 私は　7月に　日本へ　行きたい　です。 = I want to go to Japan in July.
   D) 私は　写真を　撮りたい　です。　　　= I want to take photographs.

■ 自習 Self Check

1. Using the 〜たい-form (want to . . .)

   Try to say the following out loud, to yourself, in Japanese.

   A) I want to sell my book.
   B) I want to wake up at 7:00.
   C) I want go on a date with (name someone famous). (デートをします)
   D) I want to dance. (ダンスをします)

2. しりとり

しりとり is a game played in many places under different names. By now, you have been exposed to quite a few vocabulary words and kanji. In Japanese しりとり, you try to see how many words you can string together by using the last syllable of the previous word as the first sound of the next word. For instance, わたし－しち－ちいさい... In this case the first word ends with し, and the next begins with し and then ends with ち. Then ち starts the third word, and so on. Use the kanji and vocabulary that you have been taught. Hint: Try not to use too many words that end in い.

By the way, しり means *bottom/end* and とり is the noun form of とる which means *take*, so a rough direct translation of しりとり could be "taking from the end." Traditionally if you say a word which ends in "ん", you lose the game!

■ 練習の時間 Time for Practice

---

1. Small Group Practice

Put all your "verb" flash cards into one pile. Take turns flipping over a card and creating a sentence in the たい-form. Your group members will help you make sure your grammar is correct.

(*a card is turned over that reads* 勉強する)
You might say: 私は　毎日　日本語を　勉強したいです。 = I want to study Japanese every day.

(*turn over a card that reads* 行きます)
You might say: あのコンサートに　行きたいです。 = I want to go to that concert.

---

2. Pair Practice

Get out a sheet of scrap paper and something to write with. Flip a coin to see who goes first. When the teacher says 始めましょう, Student A begins speaking sentences using the たい-form. Student B writes down what Student A says. Once your teacher says はい、終りです, trade roles. When you are both finished, exchange papers and check for accuracy.

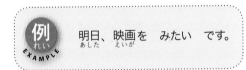
明日、映画を　みたい　です。

■ キアラのジャーナル Kiara's Journal

Read the journal entry below, and then answer these questions.

❶ What sort of restaurant did they enter?
❷ What did Kiara decide to have to drink?
❸ What did Jun decide to eat?
❹ What did Tomo want to eat that he could not get?
❺ What does Kiara want to do someday?

ジャーナルへ

　お寿司屋さんの　人は、「いらっしゃいませ。何名様　ですか。」と、言いました、友さんは、「五人　です。」と、言いました。

　ウェイトレスさんは、「こちらへ　どうぞ。」と、言いました。

　芭蕉さんは、「キアラさんは　何が　いい　ですか。私は　このセットが　食べたいです。」と　言いました。

　私は、「いいですね。私も　それが　食べたい　です。それと、麦茶が　飲みたいです。ベン君は　何を　食べますか。」と　聞きました。

　ベン君は、「そう　ですね。僕は　いなり寿司が　食べたい　です。それと　お水も飲みたい　です。じゅん君は　何を　食べますか。」と、じゅん君に　聞きました。

　じゅん君は、「そう　ですね。僕は、ええと、手巻き寿司が　食べたい　です。それから、ジュースが　飲みたい　です。」と、言いました。

　友さんは、「皆さん、あまり　食べませんね。私は、ちらし寿司と、寿司セットと、いなり寿司が　食べたいです。お茶も　飲みたいですね。あ！それと、私は、狸ですが、狸そばも　食べたいです。」と、言いました。ウェイトレスさんは、「ここは、寿司屋ですから、そばは　ありません。」と言いました。私は、「友さん、狸そばって、何ですか。」と聞きました。狸そばは、狸が　入ったそばではありませんでした。友さんは「東京では、天ぷらのflakeが　入ったそばを、狸そばと言います。」と、言いました。お寿司屋さんに　おそばは　ありませんでしたが、私もsomeday 狸そばが　食べたいです。

まだ　起きたく　ない　です。

I do not want to wake up yet.

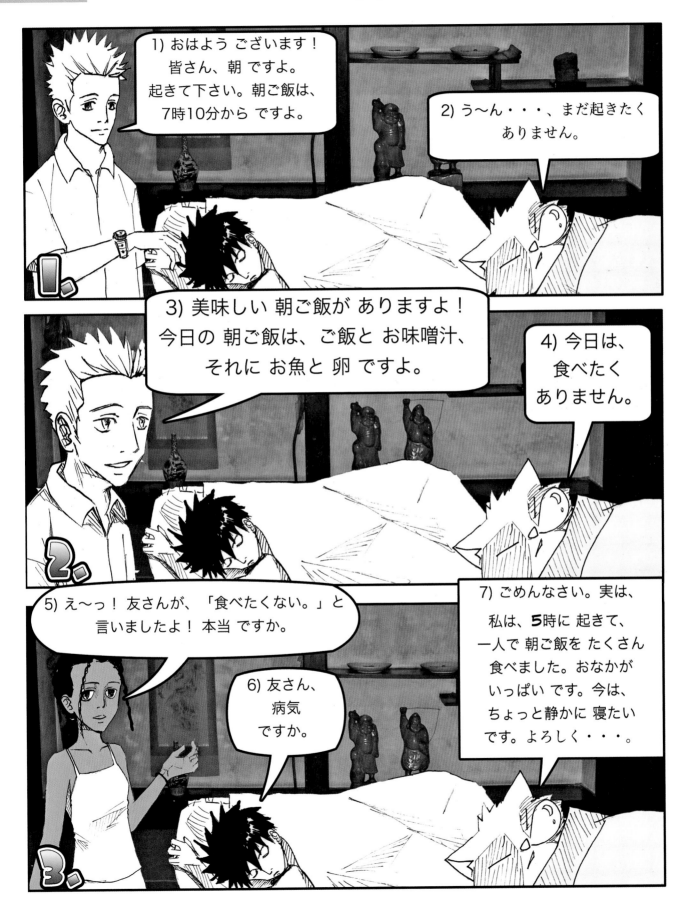

■ 会話 Dialogue
かいわ

ベン　：　おはよう　ございます！　皆さん、朝　ですよ。起きて　下さい。朝ご飯は、7時10分か
みな　　　　　　　　お　　　　　　　　　あさ　はん
　　　　　らですよ。

友　　：　う～ん・・・、まだ　起きたく　ありません。

ベン　：　美味しい　朝ご飯が　ありますよ！今日の　朝ご飯は、ご飯と　おみそ汁、それに
お　い　　あさ　はん　　　　　　　　　　　　あさ　はん　　　　はん　　　　　　　　しる
　　　　　お魚と　卵　ですよ。
さかな　たまご

友　　：　今日は、食べたく　ありません。

キアラ：　え～っ！　友さんが、「食べたくない。」と　言いましたよ！　本当　ですか。
とも　　　　　　　　　　　　　　　　　　　　　　　　　　　ほんとう

じゅん：　友さん、病気　ですか。
びょうき

友　　：　ごめんなさい。実は、私は、5時に　起きて、一人で　朝ご飯を　たくさん　食べまし
じつ　　　　　　　　お　　　　　　　　あさ　はん
　　　　　た。お腹が　いっぱい　です。
なか
　　　　　今は、ちょっと　静かに　寝たい　です。　よろしく・・・。
しず　　ね

■ 単語 New Words
たんご

		うそ (n) – a lie
本当 (n) ほんとう	お腹が　いっぱい (exp.) なか	実は (adv.) – by the way, actually じつ
		一人で (exp.) – by oneself, alone ひとり
		まだ (adv.) – not yet, still
		もう (part.) – already

■ 漢字 Kanji
かんじ

当

当 6 strokes	トウ; あ(たる) – to hit the mark	丨　丷　丷　当　当　当
	当たる – to hit the mark; (本)当 – really, truthfully あ　　　　　　　　　　　　ほん　とう	
	This kanji shows a workbench with a hammer coming down, HITTING THE MARK causing sparks to fly out.	

■ 言葉の探索 Language Detection
ことば　たんさく

1. 食べたく　ありません。 OR 食べたく　ないです。 = I don't want to eat.

   To say that you do NOT want to do something, drop the い from the end of the たい-form of a verb and add 〜くありません. This is the same pattern used to negate an い adjective such as 美味しい (i.e., 美味しくありません, or 美味しくないです). The 〜たい pattern, meaning "want to...," also conjugates like an い adjective for the past tense (〜たかった).

   NOTE: With the negative pattern, it is more common to use を instead of が for the direct object.

A) 私は　カラオケを　したく　ありません。	= I do not want to do karaoke.
B) 私は　散歩を　したく　ありません。	= I do not want to take a walk.
C) 私は　昨日　写真を　撮りたく　ありません　でした。	= I did not want to take pictures yesterday.
D) 去年も　日本語を　勉強　したかった　です。	= I wanted to study Japanese last year too.

2. まだ – not yet or still

   Used with a negative verb, まだ indicates that the action of the verb hasn't happened yet. It is used with です or before the verb (negative form) that it modifies.

A) 友さんは　まだ　食べていませんでした。	= Tomo had not eaten yet.
B) あなたの　家に　まだ　行きたくありません。	= I don't want to go to your house yet.
C) 雨は　まだ　降って　いません。	= It's not raining yet.
D) キアラさん、まだ　宿題を　して　いませんか。	= Kiara, haven't you done your homework yet?
E) あしたの　数学の　テストの　勉強は　もう　しましたか。	= Have you already studied for tomorrow's math test?
いいえ、まだです。	= No, not yet.
F) お姉さんは　まだ　独身 (single)　ですか。	= Is your older sister still single?
はい、まだ　独身　です。	= Yes, she is still single.

3. もう – already

   This adverb もう in conjunction with a verb indicates that the action has already happened.

A) 朝ご飯を　もう　食べました。	= I have already eaten breakfast.
B) 友達と　もう　話しました。	= I have already spoken with my friend.
C) もう　コーラを　飲みました。	= I already drank the cola.

■ 自習 Self Check
じしゅう

1. Say the following, out loud to yourself, in Japanese.

   A) I do not want to drink milk.

   B) I do not want to go surfing.

   C) I wanted to take a shower at 7:00 a.m.

   D) I did not want to sleep.

2. Say the following in Japanese.
   A) I don't want to study yet.
   B) Have you eaten lunch? No, not yet.
   C) Yamamoto-sensei hasn't come here yet.
   D) I haven't watched (name a popular movie) yet.

■ 練習の時間 Time for Practice

1. Pair Practice

Play tic-tac-toe. Do じゃんけんぽん (paper/rock/scissors) to see who goes first. The first player chooses a space and changes that word from the dictionary form to the たい　です form out loud. Play the game again, this time changing each into the たくありません or ～たくない　です form. If you have time, play this game again using the past affirmative (～たかったです) and past negative (～たくなかったです).

手伝う	来る	練習 する
起きる	寝る	勉強 する
買い物する	開ける	聞く

話す	書く	立つ
座る	閉じる	終わる
飲む	料理をする	テニスをする

はじめる	見る	出す
着る	売る	言う
食べる	待つ	入る

2. Whole Class Practice

Your teacher will give you a slip of paper with two activities on it: one that you "want to do" and one that you "will do." Circulate among your classmates, politely inviting them to join you in the activity that you "want to do," until you find someone who "will do" that activity with you. (Note: You must agree to "do" at least one activity that you "will do" and find someone else willing to agree to do what you "want to do", in order to sit down.)

A-さん：　土曜日に (name a film)を　みませんか。
B-さん：　いいえ、その　映画は　みたくありません。
　　　　-OR-　すみません、土曜日は　ちょっと・・・・
　　　　-OR-　はい、いいですよ。私も　その　映画が　みたいです。

3. **Pair Practice**

まだ and もう

Following the example, ask you partner if he or she still has not done the various things below. Your partner should answer honestly.

例

朝ご飯を 食べる
Question： まだ 朝ご飯を 食べて いませんか。
Answer ： はい、まだ 食べて いません。
　　　　 -OR-　いいえ、もう 食べました。

A) 昼ご飯を 食べる
B) 晩ご飯を 食べる
C) 友達と 話す
D) 宿題を する
E) 家に 帰る
F) (Create as many additional questions as you can in the remaining time.)

■ 文化箱 Culture Chest

Cherry Blossoms

Springtime in Japan always makes the television news headlines. Daily weather reports map and track the exact date and location the cherry blossoms will be in full bloom (満開). Coworkers, friends, and families gather in parks for spring parties. Everyone brings food and drinks, and sits on "portable" tatami mats under the blooming trees, eating, drinking, and singing. Cherry petals gently waft to and fro before lightly falling on the visitors below. If you've never seen dozens of cherry trees in full bloom, you might be overwhelmed the first time you visit a Japanese park or garden in spring. During this season, nightly news reports show people enjoying the blossoms around the country, beginning with Kyushu in the south, and, as the weather warms, moving up to Sapporo, in Hokkaido. These news and weather reports demonstrate how the Japanese are fascinated with this display of natural beauty. The fascination is even greater because the 満開 season is so short. Do you know if there are any cherry trees near you?

■ キアラのジャーナル Kiara's Journal

Answer the following questions based upon the diary entry below.

❶ What happened in the garden at 4:50 p.m.?
❷ Was Basho ready to return to the ryokan?
❸ What did Ben suggest doing?
❹ Why did Tomo agree to do what Ben suggested?

ジャーナルへ

　今日は、兼六園に 六時間ぐらい いました。朝から 晩まで よい天気でした。少し 風が ありましたが、それが とてもcomfortableでした。午後 五時十分前に、とつぜん、うるさい 声が 聞こえました。その声は、「みなさん、4時50分です。あと１０分で、お庭が 閉ま

ります。今日は、どうも　有り難うございました。お気をつけて、お帰り下さい。」と　言いました。

　芭蕉さんは　まだ　石の　上に　座っていました。「私は　この庭が　大好きです。旅館へ　帰りたくありません。」と、言いました。

　ベン君は、「僕も　帰りたくないです。どうしましょうか。ビーチで　散歩を　しませんか。」と、言いました。友さんは、「散歩　ですか。いいですね。ビーチに　たこ焼き屋が　ありますね。」と、言いました。

　私は、たこ焼きは　あまり　食べたく　ありませんでしたが、ビーチが　好きですから、いっしょに行きました。私は　ピザと　メキシコの料理と中国の　料理が　食べたかったです。でも、残念ですが、ここに、それは　ありません。

　本当に、きれいな　サンセットで、明日も　晴れると　思いましたが、友さんが、海の風を　よくかいだ(smelled)後、「明日は、大雨になりますよ。」と言いました。

食べ物も、飲み物も、たくさん　持って行きましょう。
Let's take a lot of food and drinks.

■ 会話 Dialogue
かいわ

友　　　： 桜は、来週、一番　きれい　でしょう。
　　　　　さくら　　　　ばん

キアラ： 皆で、お花見を　しませんか！
　　　　　みんな　　はなみ

ベン　： いい　ですね！　しましょう、しましょう！

じゅん： 芭蕉さんも、一緒に　行きません か。
　　　　　ばしょう　　いっしょ

芭蕉　： それは　いい　ですね。

キアラ： 美味しい　物も、食べたい　です。
　　　　　おい

友　　　： もちろん　です！　食べ物も、飲み物も、たくさん　持って行きましょう。でも、カラオ
　　　　　ケは　したくありませんね。

ベン　： 僕は、カラオケを　したい　です。芭蕉さんの　俳句を　ロックンロールで　歌いたい
　　　　　ぼく　　　　　　　　　　　　　　　　　　　はいく
　　　　　です！

キアラ： かっこいい・・・。

■ 単語 New Words
たんご

桜 (n) さくら	花見 (n) はなみ	ロックンロール (n)	持って 行く/行きます (v) も　　い　　い
持って 来る/来ます (v) も　　く　　き	持って 帰る/帰ります (v) も　　かえ　　かえ	連れて 行く/行きます (v) つ　　い　　い	もちろん (exp.) – of course 連れて 来る/来ます (v) – つ　　く　　き to bring (person) 連れて 帰る/帰ります つ　　かえ　　かえ (v) – to take (person) back (home)

■ 漢字 Kanji
かんじ

桜 10 strokes	さくら – cherry blossoms, cherry tree	一	十	才	木	杉	杉	杉	桜
	桜 – cherry blossoms, cherry tree さくら	桜	桜						
	This KANJI is quite easy to remember. There is a large tree (木) on the left with three petals falling on a woman (女) sitting under the CHERRY tree during 花見.								

■ 言葉の探索 Language Detection

1. 持って行く – take (something)

As you learned in Chapter 6, you can combine verb phrases by putting all but the last verb in the TE form.

There are also many cases where two verbs are combined into one phrase with the first verb being in the TE form. A common example is with 持って行く, which combines the verbs "to hold" and "to go." If you hold (something) and go somewhere with it, the new verb you have made becomes *to take* (something).

If the second verb is 来る the phrase becomes *to bring* (持って来る) because you are coming somewhere with something.

If the second verb is 帰る the phrase becomes *to bring back* (持って帰る) because you are returning somewhere with something.

Note that this term is only used for taking or bringing a THING or an OBJECT.

A) 私は　かさを　持って行きます。	= I will take an umbrella.
B) お水を　持って来て　下さい。	= Please bring water.
C) 私は　毎日　家へ　日本語の本を　持って帰ります。	
	= I bring my Japanese book back home every day.

2. 連れて行く – to take somebody somewhere

To talk about taking or bringing people somewhere, use the て -form of the verb 連れる and attach it to a verb of direction.

連れて行きます　　= to take somebody somewhere
連れて来ます　　　= to bring somebody somewhere
連れて帰ります　　= to return somewhere with someone

A) 私は　ゆみさん　と　私の犬を　連れて行きます。	= I will take Yumi and my dog (with me).
B) けんじのお父さんは　けんじを　アメリカへ　連れて来ます。	= Kenji's dad will bring Kenji to the U.S.
C) 妹さんを　パーティーから　連れて帰って下さい。	= Please take your younger sister back home from the party.

■ 自習 Self Check

1. 持って行く、持って来る、持って帰る

Try to say the following in Japanese:

A) I will bring money.

B) Kiara did not take a jacket to school.

C) I returned home with my homework.

2. 連れて行く、連れて来る、連れて帰る

Try to say the following in Japanese:

A) I will take Jun (with me).

B) Ben brought a cute first year student to my house.

C) I did not return home with my younger brother.

D) My teacher brought a friend to the classroom.

■ 練習の時間 Time for Practice
れんしゅう

---

1. **Small Group Practice**

Create a sentence

Your teacher will give you a grid similar to the one below. Put your name (in katakana) in Space #1 and write verbs of your choice (use the dictionary form) in each of the remaining spaces. Take turns rolling the dice.

　The first roll (of two dice) determines which verb you will use in your sentence. For instance, if you roll a "5," move your marker to space 5. Your second roll (with one die) determines what verb form you use in your sentence based on the choices below:

1 = non past (～ます)
2 = negative non past (～ません)
3 = past tense (～ました)
4 = past negative (～ませんでした)
5 = want to ~ (～たい)
6 = do not want to ~ (～たくないです or ～たくありません)

Once you have rolled twice, make a sentence using the indicated form of the verb. If your group agrees that your sentence makes sense, put your name in Space 5 and pass the dice to your neighbor. You may write on your partners' papers (for instance, if you roll another "5"). Continue until all grids are filled. The person whose name is in the most spaces is the winner.

1名前	2	3	4	5	6
7	8	9	10	11	12

---

2. **Small Group Practice**

Plan a flower-viewing party or some other appropriate party of your choice.

Step 1 –　Prepare an invitation in Japanese that includes the reason for the party/picnic, time, place, what to bring, who can come, etc.

Step 2 –　Announce the invitation to your class.

Step 3 –　Make a list in Japanese of all the things that each person will take to the party. Use 持って行きます.

A)　まさ君は　寿司を　持って行きます。　= Masa will take sushi.
B)　友子さんは　飲み物を　持って行きます。= Tomoko will take drinks.

Also, since many people will need rides to the party, make a separate list of who will bring which people to the party. Use 連れて行きます.

A)　私は　健太郎を　連れて行きます。= I'll take Kentarou.
B)　トム君は　ケンくんと　ナオミさんを　連れて行きます。
　　= Tom will take Ken and Naomi.

■ 文化箱 Culture Chest

花よりだんご

花よりだんご is a Japanese proverb which can be translated as "food and drink before flowers." A dango is a somewhat sweet Japanese snack that comes in a wide range of varieties and is a popular treat for 花見 (cherry blossom viewing) picnics and festivals. Although viewing transient cherry blossoms fluttering to the ground and picnicking below them is an ancient tradition in Japan, this expression might insinuate that the real attraction is the food and drink that accompanies the flowers!

The larger meaning of 花よりだんご can be the idea that the here and now concerns of people win out over more high-minded pursuits, or that substance often wins out over style.

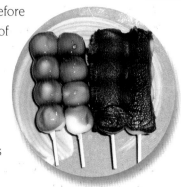

Sakura Song

Sakura Sakura

Arranged by: Ayna and Ryan

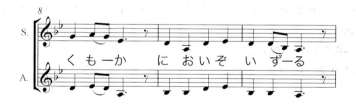

■ キアラのジャーナル Kiara's Journal

Read the journal entry below, and then answer these questions.

❶ Describe three activities Kiara did in the park today.
❷ What did Tomo say after dinner?
❸ What does Basho do in response?
❹ Write down one possible English translation for the poem that Basho wrote.
❺ What is the last thing that Kiara says to Basho?

ジャーナルへ

　　今日、お花見を　しました。兼六園には、桜が　たくさん　あります。その　桜の木の下まで、たくさんの　食べ物と　ジュースを　持って　行きました。桜は　とても　美しくて、おにぎりと　焼きそばと　だんごは　とても　美味しかったです。そして、琴の　音楽も　とても　きれい　でした。

　　じゅん君は、「もう少し、ジュースを　飲みたいです。もっとありますか。焼きそばも下さい。」と、言いました。ベン君は、「ありますよ。どうぞ。友さん、そこの　焼きそばを　取って下さい。」と言いました。そして、「ねえ、この　音楽は　とても　いいですね。」と、言いました。

　　芭蕉さんは、「ええ、そう　ですね。あの　人は　三十年間　琴を　ひいていますから、とても上手　です。僕は　毎年　春に、琴が　聞きたくなります。琴は　春の　声だと　思います。」と　言いました。

　　『琴が　春の　声・・・』、その　言葉は、いつまでも(forever)　私の　心に　あるでしょう。私達は、時の　門の旅から、何も　持って行けないし、誰も　連れて行けません。でも、旅でもらった　すてきな　言葉は、どこへでも　自由に(freely)　持って行くことが　出来ます。それは、一番　すてきな　プレゼント　ですね。

　　友さんは、「このまま　ここに　いたいですが、私達は、行かなくてはなりません。(must go)」と、言いました。芭蕉さんは、「そうですか。」と言って、

　　　『鐘消えて
　　　　花の香は撞く
　　　　夕哉』

という俳句を　詠みました。その意味は：お寺の鐘の音が消えて(As the sound of the temple bell fades)、静かな　春の　夕ぐれ(evening)に、花の　香(scents)が lingers (like the fading tone).

　　本当に　きれいな　俳句だと　思いました。

　　友さんが　静かに、「じゃ、皆さん、行きますよ。芭蕉さん、本当に　ありがとうございました。」と、言いました。そして私は、「芭蕉さん、私は、日本語の　勉強を　もっとがんばります。」と言いました。芭蕉さんは、「*約束ですよ、キアラさん。さようなら。」と言いました。「さようなら、芭蕉さん。あなたを　わすれません。」

*約束 – promise, appointment / 約束する (to promise)

■ テクノ の時間 Techno Time

At this point, you have been traveling through Japan and through time with Ben, Jun, Kiara, and of course Tomo. This Techno Time is your passport activity and chance to write an e-mail in Japanese to Tomo. In your e-mail:

⊃ use an appropriate greeting
⊃ talk about some things you would like to do in Japan (things the characters have done)
⊃ mention two things you would not like to do in Japan
⊃ write about two things you wanted to do this school year
⊃ write about one activity you did, but did not like doing
⊃ ask two questions of Tomo
⊃ use an appropriate ending

When you are finished, send your message to Tomo. His e-mail: tomo@timeforjapanese.com. DON'T FORGET to copy the message to your teacher as well.

■ 単語チェックリスト New Word Checklist

Japanese	Location	English
10-1		
あき　　秋 (n)	10-1	fall/autumn
あめ　　雨 (n)	10-1	rain
いし　　石 (n)	10-1	stone, rock
いちど　　一度 (n)	10-1	one time, one degree (temp.)
おおあめ　　大雨 (n)	10-1	heavy rain
かみなり　　雷 (n)	10-1	lightning
きせつ　　季節 (n)	10-1	season
きゅうど　　九度 (n)	10-1	nine times, nine degrees
くもり　　曇り (n)	10-1	cloudy
くもる/くもります　　曇もる/曇ります (v)	10-1	(to) become cloudy
ごど　　五度 (n)	10-1	five times, five degrees
さかな　　魚 (n)	10-1	fish
さんど　　三度 (n)	10-1	three times, three degrees
じしん　　地震 (n)	10-1	earthquake
じゅうど　　十度 (n)	10-1	ten times, ten degrees
しろ　城 (n)	10-1	castle
たいふう　　台風 (n)	10-1	typhoon
たつまき　　竜巻 (n)	10-1	tornado
つゆ　　梅雨 (n)	10-1	rainy season
てんき　　天気 (n)	10-1	weather
てんきよほう　　天気予報 (n)	10-1	weather report
なつ　　夏 (n)	10-1	summer
ななど　　七度 (n)	10-1	seven times, seven degrees
なんど　　何度 (inter.)	10-1	how many times/degrees

Japanese	Location	English
にど　二度 (n)	10-1	two times, 2 degrees
にわ　庭 (n)	10-1	garden
はいく　俳句 (n)	10-1	haiku (poem)
はちど　八度 (n)	10-1	eight times, eight degrees
はな　花 (n)	10-1	flower
はる　春 (n)	10-1	spring
はれ　晴れ (n)	10-1	clear (skies)
はれる/はれます　晴れる/晴れます (晴れて) (v)	10-1	(to) become clear (weather)
ふゆ　冬 (n)	10-1	winter
ふる/ふります　降る/降ります (降って) (v)	10-1	(to) precipitate
ゆき　雪 (n)	10-1	snow
よんど　四度 (n)	10-1	four times, four degrees
ろくど　六度 (n)	10-1	six times. six degrees

10-2

Japanese	Location	English
だれも (exp.)	10-2	no one
つくる/つくります　作る/作ります (作って) (v)	10-2	(to) make
使う/使います (使って) (v)	10-2	(to) use
ざんねん　残念 (な adj.)	10-2	regrettable, unlucky

10-3

Japanese	Location	English
あそぶ/あそびます　遊ぶ/遊びます (遊んで) (v)	10-3	(to) play
なにか　何か	10-3	something

10-4

Japanese	Location	English
ほんとう　本当 (n)	10-4	truth, reality
おなかが いっぱい　お腹が 一杯 (exp.)	10-4	have a full stomach
うそ (n)	10-4	a lie
じつは　実は (adv.)	10-4	as a matter of fact, by the way, actually
ひとりで　一人で (exp.)	10-4	alone, by oneself
まだ (adv.)	10-4	not yet, still
もう (part.)	10-4	already

10-5

Japanese	Location	English
さくら　桜 (n)	10-5	cherry tree/blossom
はなみ　花見 (n)	10-5	cherry blossom viewing, flower viewing
ろっくんろーる　ロックンロール (n)	10-5	rock and roll (music)
もって いく/いきます　持って 行く/行きます (v)	10-5	take something
もって くる/きます　持って来る/来ます (v)	10-5	bring something
もって かえる/かえります　持って 帰る/帰ります (v)	10-5	return with something
つれて くる/きます　連れて 来る/来ます (v)	10-5	bring someone
もちろん (exp.)	10-5	of course
つれて かえる/かえります　連れて 帰る/帰ります (v)	10-5	(to) return with someone

Kanji List

Kanji	Ch./section	Pronunciation	Meaning	Example usage
木	1-2	モク；き	tree	木曜日 – Thursday
日	1-2	ニ；にち；に；ひ；び	day; sun	日本 – Japan
本	1-2	ホン；もと	book; origin	本当 – really?
東	1-3	トウ；ひがし	east	東北 – northeastern part of Honshu
京	1-3	キョウ	capital	東京 – Tokyo
語	1-3	ゴ	language	日本語 – Japanese language
私	1-4	わたくし；わたし	I, me	私達 – we/us
父	1-4	フ；ちち；(お)とう(さん)	father	祖父 – grandfather
母	1-4	ボ；はは；(お)かあ(さん)	mother	祖母 – grandmother
気	1-5	き	spirit; energy	元気 – healthy, energetic
元	1-5	ゲン；もと	an ancient currency; origin	地元 – hometown
人	1-5	ジン；ニン；ひと	person	日本人 – Japanese person
休	1-5	やす(む)	to rest, take a break, a vacation	春休み – spring break
何	2-1	なに；なん	what	何人 – how many people?, what nationality?
家	2-1	カ；いえ；うち	home	家族 – family
兄	2-1	キョウ；あに；(お)にい(さん)	older brother	従兄 – older male cousin
姉	2-1	あね；(お)ねえ(さん)	older sister	従姉 – older female cousin
弟	2-1	ダイ；おとうと	younger brother	兄弟 – siblings
妹	2-1	いもうと	younger sister	妹さん – someone else's younger sister
一	2-2	イチ；ひと(つ)	one	一つ – one (thing)
二	2-2	ニ；ふた(つ)	two	二枚 – two sheets
三	2-2	サン；みっ(つ)	three	三本 – 3 cylindrical objects
四	2-2	シ；よん；よっ(つ)	four	四人 – four people
五	2-2	ゴ；いつ(つ)	five	五枚 – five flat objects
六	2-2	ロク；むっ(つ)	six	六ページ – page 6
七	2-2	シチ；なな；なな(つ)	seven	七月 – July
八	2-2	ハチ；やっ(つ)	eight	八つ – eight things
九	2-2	キュウ；く；ここの(つ)	nine	九時 – nine o'clock
十	2-2	ジュウ；とう	ten	十分 – ten minutes
百	2-2	ヒャク	hundred	三百 – three hundred
犬	2-3	いぬ	dog	子犬 – a small dog
高	3-1	コウ；たか(い)	tall, expensive	高校 – high school
小	3-1	ショウ；ちい(さい)	small	小学校 – elementary school
中	3-1	チュウ；なか	middle	中学校 – middle school
大	3-1	ダイ；おお(きい)	big; large	大学 – college/university
学	3-1	ガク	to learn	学生 – student
校	3-1	コウ	school	高校 – high school
年	3-1	ネン；とし	year	五年間 – five years (period)
先	3-1	セイ；う(まれる)	earlier, future	先生 – teacher
生	3-1	セイ；う(まれる)	to be born	生徒 – student
山	3-1	サン；やま	mountain	富士山 – Mt. Fuji
英	3-2	エイ	gifted, talented	英語 – English
国	3-2	コク；ゴク；くに	country, nation	中国 – China
音	3-2	オン；おと	sound	音楽 – music
楽	3-2	ガク；たの(しい)	fun, enjoyable	文楽 – puppet theater
今	3-2	コン；いま	now	今月 – this month
分	3-2	ブン；フン；プン；わ(かる)	minute, portion; to understand	六分 – six minutes
書	3-3	ショ；か(く)	write	図書館 – library
寺	3-3	ジ；てら	temple	東大寺 – Todaiji Temple
時	3-3	ジ；とき	time	一時 – one o'clock
門	3-3	モン	gate	寺の門 – temple's gate
間	3-3	カン；あいだ	interval, space	時間 – time, hour, interval of time

Kanji	Ch./section	Pronunciation	Meaning	Example usage
下	3-3	カ；した；くだ(る)	below, descend, give, under	下さい – please
暑	3-4	あつ(い)	hot (weather/temp.)	暑い – is hot
寒	3-4	さむ(い)	cold (weather/temp.)	寒い – is cold
神	3-4	シン；ジン；かみ	God/god, spirits	神様 – God, gods
社	3-4	シャ；ジャ	company, association	社会 – social studies
風	3-5	フウ；かぜ	wind	台風 – typhoon
友	3-5	ユウ；とも	friend	友達 – friend
言	4-1	ゲン；い(う)	to speak	言語 – language
外	4-1	ガイ；そと	outside	外国人 – foreign person
話	4-2	ワ；はなし；はな(す)	to speak, conversation	昔話 – folk tales
食	4-3	ショク；た(べる)	food, eat	食べ物 – foods
飲	4-3	の(む)	drink	飲み物 – drinks
物	4-3	ブツ；もの	tangible thing, object	買い物 – shopping (purchases)
行	4-4	い(く)；こう	go	旅行 – travel, a trip
来	4-4	ライ；く(る)	next, coming, to come	来週 – next week
帰	4-4	かえ(る)	return (home)	帰ります – to return
見	4-5	み(る)；み(える)	to see, visible, can be seen	花見 – flower viewing
聞	4-5	ブン；き(く)；き(こえる)	to listen, to ask	聞きます – to listen
午	5-1	ゴ	noon	午前 – morning, a.m.
後	5-1	ゴ；あと	after, afterward	午後 – afternoon, p.m.
良	5-1	よ(い)；い(い)	good	良い – good, excellent
月	5-1	ゲツ；がつ；つき	month, moon	先月 – last month
火	5-1	カ；ひ	fire	火曜日 – Tuesday
水	5-1	スイ；みず	water	水曜日 – Wednesday
金	5-1	キン；かね	gold, money	金持ち – rich man
土	5-1	ド；つち	soil, ground	土曜日 – Saturday
曜	5-1	ヨウ	day of the week	何曜日 – what day of the week?
千	5-2	セン	thousand	千円 – 1,000 yen
末	5-2	マツ	end	週末 – weekend
毎	5-2	マイ	every	毎日 – every day
週	5-2	シュウ	week	先週 – last week
電	5-4	デン	electricity	電気 – electricity
達	5-4	タチ(たち)；たち；だち	to reach or arrive at; pluralizes some words	私達 – us, we
体	6-1	タイ；からだ	body	体育館 – gymnasium
目	6-1	モク；め	eye	二つ目 – one after next, second
口	6-1	くち；ぐち	mouth	入り口 – entrance
耳	6-1	みみ	ear	耳 – ear
手	6-1	シュ；た；て	hand	下手 – unskillful
足	6-1	ソク；あし た(りる)	foot, leg; to be enough, sufficient	足首 – ankle
心	6-1	シン；こころ	heart, spirit, soul	安心 – relief, peace of mine
持	6-1	も(つ)	to hold, to have	持って来る – to bring
待	6-1	ま(つ)	to wait	待つ – to wait
強	6-1	キョウ；つよ(い)	to be strong	強い – strong
平	6-2	ヘイ	even, flat	平和 – peace
和	6-2	ワ	peace and harmony; ancient name for Japan	和食 – Japanese style meal
低	6-2	ひく(い)	short, low	低い – is short (stature)
太	6-2	タイ；ふと(い) ふと(る)	plump, thick	太っています – is fat
医	6-3	イ	related to medicine/medical field	医者 – doctor
者	6-3	シャ；もの	person	学者 – scholar
薬	6-3	くすり	medicine	薬屋 – pharmacy
着	6-4	き(る)	to wear	着物 – traditional Japanese clothing
花	7-1	はな	flower	花火 – fireworks
池	7-1	チ；いけ	pond	電池 – battery
趣	7-1	シュ	gist, tend (to), become	趣味 – hobby
味	7-1	ミ；あじ；あじ(わう)	taste, flavor, to appreciate	味見 – sampling, tasting

Kanji	Ch./section	Pronunciation	Meaning	Example usage
事	7-1	ジ; こと	thing	仕事 – work, job
好	7-2	す(き)	like	好き – to like
上	7-3	ジョウ; うえ; かみ; あ(がる)	above, upper; climb; go up (a hill)	上手 – skillful
色	7-4	いろ	color	色々 – various
白	7-4	ハク; しろ; しろ(い)	white	白い – white
黒	7-4	コク; くろ; くろ(い)	black	黒板 – blackboard
赤	7-4	セキ; あか; あか(い)	red, crimson, scarlet	赤ちゃん – baby
青	7-4	セイ; あお; あお(い)	blue, green; young	青葉 – spring leaves
歌	7-5	カ; うた; うた(う)	song, sing	歌舞伎 – kabuki theater
思	7-5	シ; おも(う)	to think, believe	思います – to think
美	8-1	ビ; うつく(しい)	beautiful	美人 – beautiful person
長	8-1	チョウ; なが(い)	head, chief; long (in length)	校長 – school principal
短	8-1	みじか(い)	short (length)	短い – is short (length)
海	8-1	カイ; うみ	ocean, sea	日本海 – Sea of Japan
安	8-2	アン; やす(い)	safe; cheap	安全 – safe
悪	8-2	わる(い)	bad	悪い – is bad, evil
面	8-2	メン; おも	face, mask	面 – mask
天	8-2	テン; あま	heaven	天ぷら – deep fried fish and vegetables
立	8-2	た(つ)	to stand	立ちます – to stand
昔	8-2	むかし	long ago	昔々 – long long ago
々	8-2	(reduplicating mark)		人々 – people
有	8-3	ユウ; あ(る)	to exist, to be	有名 – famous
広	8-3	ひろ(い)	wide, spacious	広島 – city name
島	8-3	トウ; しま	island	大島 – large island, family name
買	9-1	バイ; か(う)	to buy, purchase	買います – to buy
売	9-1	バイ; う(る)	to sell	売ります – to sell
店	9-1	テン; みせ	store, shop	本店 – head office
万	9-1	マン	ten thousand	一万 – 10,000
全	9-2	ゼン	all, entirely	全国 – the entire country
部	9-2	ブ	section, group of	部活 – club activities
円	9-2	エン; まる (い)	yen, round	百円 – 100 yen
暗	9-3	くら(い)	dark, dim	暗い – dark
明	9-3	メイ; あか(るい)	light, bright	明るい – bright
春	10-1	はる	spring	春 – spring
夏	10-1	なつ	summer	夏休み – summer vacation
秋	10-1	あき	autumn, fall	秋田 – city/prefecture in northern Japan
冬	10-1	ふゆ	winter	冬 – winter
石	10-1	セキ ; いし	stone, rock	石山 – family name
使	10-2	つか(う)	to use	使う – to use
作	10-2	つく(る)	to make	作る – to make
当	10-4	トウ; あ(たる)	really, truthfully	本当 – really?
桜	10-5	さくら	cherry blossoms/tree; to be correct	桜んぼう – (edible) cherry

Appendix 1
Grammar References

Verb Conjugation Summary

Type 1 Verbs

non-past (〜ます)	non-past negative (〜ません)	〜て-form	past (〜ました)	past negative (〜ませんでした)	dictionary (infinitive) form	English meaning
あります	ありません	あって	ありました	ありませんでした	ある	to exist (inanimate)
言います	言いません	言って	言いました	言いませんでした	言う	to say
読みます	読みません	読んで	読みました	読みませんでした	読む	to read
書きます	書きません	書いて	書きました	書きませんでした	書く	to write

Type 2 Verbs

non-past (〜ます)	non-past negative (〜ません)	〜て-form	past (〜ました)	past negative (〜ませんでした)	dictionary (infinitive) form	English meaning
開けます	開けません	開けて	開けました	開けませんでした	開ける	to open (books)
食べます	食べません	食べて	食べました	食べませんでした	食べる	to eat
見ます	見ません	見て	見ました	見ませんでした	見る	to look

Irregular Verbs

non-past (〜ます)	non-past negative (〜ません)	〜て-form	past (〜ました)	past negative (〜ませんでした)	dictionary (infinitive) form	English meaning
来ます	来ません	来て	来ました	来ませんでした	来る	to come
します	しません	して	しました	しませんでした	する	to do

Verbs by Chapter

ある/あります	2-1	to exist (inanimate things)
いる/います	2-1	to exist (animate beings)
言う/言います	4-1	to say
行く/行きます	4-4	to go
帰る/帰ります	4-4	to return
来る/来ます	4-4	to come
撮る/撮ります	4-2	to take (a photo)
知る/知ります	4-2	to know something/someone
食べる/食べます	4-3	to eat
手伝う/手伝います	4-1	to help, to assist
飲む/飲みます	4-3	to drink
生まれる/生まれます	5-2	to be born
起きる/起きます	5-1	to wake (up)
終わる/終わります	5-2	to finish, to end
散歩(を)する/散歩(を)します	5-4	to take a walk
寝る/寝ます	5-1	to sleep
始める/始めます	5-2	to begin
勉強(を)する/勉強(を)します	5-2	to study
入れる/入れます	6-1	to put into
生まれる/生まれます	6-1	to be born
かける/かけます	6-4	to wear glasses or sunglasses
風邪をひく/風邪をひきます	6-3	to catch a cold
被る/被ります	6-4	to wear on your head
呼ぶ/呼びます	6-3	to call out (to), to call
きる/きます 着る/着ます	6-4	to wear (above waist; dresses)
(薬を)飲む/(薬を)飲みます	6-3	to take medicine
怪我(を)する/怪我(を)します	6-3	to get wounded
心配(を)する/心配(を)します	6-3	to worry
住む/住みます (v)	6-4	to live/reside
する/します	6-4	to wear (accessories); to do
出る/出ます	6-1	go out, leave, get out
習う/習います	6-5	to learn
入る/入ります	6-1	come in, go in, enter
履く/履きます	6-4	to wear below the waist
昼寝(を)する/昼寝(を)します	6-3	to nap
太っている/太っています	6-2	to be fat
太る/太ります	6-2	to get fat
待つ/待ちます	6-1	to wait
持つ/持ちます	6-1	to have, hold, carry
やせている/やせています	6-2	to be skinny
歌う/歌います	7-1	to sing
思う/思います	7-2	to think
泳ぐ/泳ぎます	7-1	to swim

頑張る/頑張ります	7-3	to do one's best	
寝る/寝ます	7-1	to sleep	
弾く/弾きます	7-1	to play (a stringed instrument)	
やってみる/やってみます	7-3	to try (to do something)	
やる/やります	7-3	to do	
やめる/やめます	8-2	to stop	
上げる/上げます	9-4	to give	
売る/売ります	9-1	to sell	
買い物(を)する/買い物(を)します	9-1	to go shopping	
買う/買います	9-1	to buy	
カラオケ(を)する/カラオケ(を)します	9-1	to (sing) karaoke	
くれる/くれます	9-5	to give	
けんか(を)する/けんか(を)します	9-1	to argue	
探す/探します	9-3	to search	
散歩(を)する/散歩(を)します	9-1	to take a walk	
シャワー(を)する/シャワー(を)します	9-1	to take a shower	
シャンプー(を)する/シャンプー(を)します	9-1	to shampoo	
宿題(を)する/宿題(を)します	9-1	to do homework	

食事を)する/食事(を)します	9-1	to have a meal
デート(を)する/デート(を)します	9-1	to go on a date
電話(を)する/電話(を)します	9-1	to telephone
仲直り(を)する/仲直り(を)します	9-1	to make up; to become friends (again)
もらう/もらいます	9-4	to receive
旅行(を)する/旅行(を)します	9-1	to take a trip; to travel
遊ぶ/遊びます	10-3	to play; amuse; hang out
曇る/曇ります	10-1	to be cloudy
使う/使います	10-2	to use
作る/作ります	10-2	to make
連れて行く/連れて行きます	10-5	to take someone
連れて帰る/連れて帰ります	10-5	to return with someone
連れて来る/連れて来ます	10-5	to bring someone
晴れる/晴れます	10-1	to be clear (skies)
降る/降ります	10-1	to precipitate
持って行く/持って行きます	10-3	to take something
持って帰る/持って帰ります	10-5	to take back or to return something
持って来る/持って来ます	10-5	to bring something

Counters

People (2-1) (人)		Generic counters (2-4)		Grades (3-1) (年生)	
1	一人 ひとり	1	一つ ひとつ	1	一年生 いちねんせい
2	二人 ふたり	2	二つ ふたつ	2	二年生 にねんせい
3	三人 さんにん	3	三つ みっつ	3	三年生 さんねんせい
4	四人 よにん	4	四つ よっつ	4	四年生 よねんせい
5	五人 ごにん	5	五つ いつつ	5	五年生 ごねんせい
6	六人 ろくにん	6	六つ むっつ	6	六年生 ろくねんせい
7	七人/七人 しちにん/ななにん	7	七つ ななつ	7	中学一年生 ちゅうがくいちねんせい
8	八人 はちにん	8	八つ やっつ	8	中学二年生 ちゅうがくにねんせい
9	九人 きゅうにん	9	九つ ここのつ	9	中学三年生 ちゅうがくさんねんせい
10	十人 じゅうにん	10	十 とお	10	高校一年生 こうこういちねんせい
11	十一人 じゅういちにん	11	十一 じゅういち	11	高校二年生 こうこうにねんせい
12	十二人 じゅうににん	12	十二 じゅうに	12	高校三年生 こうこうさんねんせい
?	何人 なんにん	?	いくつ	?	何年生 なんねんせい

Months (5-2) (月) つき	Days of the month (5-3) (日々/ひにち) にちにち	Thousands and ten thousands (9-1)
1	一月 いちがつ	千 せん
2	二月 にがつ	二千 にせん
3	三月 さんがつ	三千 さんぜん
4	四月 しがつ	四千 よんせん
5	五月 ごがつ	五千 ごせん
6	六月 ろくがつ	六千 ろくせん
7	七月 しちがつ	七千 ななせん
8	八月 はちがつ	八千 はっせん
9	九月 くがつ	九千 きゅうせん
10	十月 じゅうがつ	一万 10,000 いちまん
11	十一月 じゅういちがつ	一万千 いちまんせん
12	十二月 じゅうにがつ	一万二千 いちまんにせん
14		一万四千 14,000 いちまんよんせん
18		一万八千 18,000 いちまんはっせん
19		一万九千 いちまんきゅうせん
20		二万 20,000 にまん
30		三万 30,000 さんまん
31		三万一千 31,000 さんまんいっせん
?	何月 なんがつ	何千 なんせん 何万 なんまん

	Days of the month (5-3)	
1	一日 ついたち	
2	二日 ふつか	
3	三日 みっか	
4	四日 よっか	
5	五日 いつか	
6	六日 むいか	
7	七日 なのか	
8	八日 ようか	
9	九日 ここのか	
10	十日 とおか	
11	十一日 じゅういちにち	
12	十二日 じゅうににち	
14	十四日 じゅうよっか	
18	十八日 じゅうはちにち	
19	十九日 じゅうくにち	
20	二十日 はつか	
30	三十日 さんじゅうにち	
31	三十一日 さんじゅういちにち	
?	何日 なんにち	

Hours (o'clock) (3-2) (時) じ	Minutes (3-2) (分) ふん、ぶん	Class periods (3-3) (時間目) じかんめ
1	一時 いちじ	一分 いっぷん	一時間目 いちじかんめ
2	二時 にじ	二分 にふん	二時間目 にじかんめ
3	三時 さんじ	三分 さんぷん	三時間目 さんじかんめ
4	四時 よじ	四分 よんぷん	四時間目 よじかんめ
5	五時 ごじ	五分 ごふん	五時間目 ごじかんめ
6	六時 ろくじ	六分 ろっぷん	六時間目 ろくじかんめ
7	七時/七時 しちじ ななじ	七分/七分 ななふん しちふん	七時間目 or ななじかんめ 七時間目 しちじかんめ
8	八時 はちじ	八分 はっぷん	
9	九時 くじ	九分 きゅうふん	
10	十時 じゅうじ	十分/十分 じゅっぷん じっぷん	
11	十一時 じゅういちじ	十一分 じゅういっぷん	
12	十二時 じゅうにじ	十二分 じゅうにふん	
15		十五分 じゅうごふん	
20		二十分/二十分 にじゅっぷん にじっぷん	
25		二十五分 にじゅうごふん	
30		三十分/三十分 さんじゅっぷん さんじっぷん	
?	何時 なんじ	何分 なんぷん	何時間目 なんじかんめ

Flat objects (4-2)	Page numbers (4-2)	Days of the week (5-1)
1	一枚 いちまい	一ページ いちぺーじ	月曜日 げつようび
2	二枚 にまい	二ページ にぺーじ	火曜日 かようび
3	三枚 さんまい	三ページ さんぺーじ	水曜日 すいようび
4	四枚 よんまい	四ページ よんぺーじ	木曜日 もくようび
5	五枚 ごまい	五ページ ごぺーじ	金曜日 きんようび
6	六枚 ろくまい	六ページ ろくぺーじ	土曜日 どようび
7	七枚/七枚 ななまい しちまい	七ページ ななぺーじ	日曜日 にちようび
8	八枚 はちまい	八ページ はちぺーじ	
9	九枚 きゅうまい	九ページ きゅうぺーじ	
10	十枚 じゅうまい	十ページ じゅうぺーじ	
?	何枚 なんまい	何ページ なんぺーじ	何曜日 なんようび

Cylindrical objects (9-2) (本) ほん、ぽん、ぼん	Bound objects (9-2) (冊) さつ	Degrees (temp.) (10-1) (度) ど
1	一本 いっぽん	一冊 いっさつ	一度 いちど
2	二本 にほん	二冊 にさつ	二度 にど
3	三本 さんぼん	三冊 さんさつ	三度 さんど
4	四本 よんほん	四冊 よんさつ	四度 よんど
5	五本 ごほん	五冊 ごさつ	五度 ごど
6	六本 ろっぽん	六冊 ろくさつ	六度 ろくど
7	七本 ななほん	七冊 ななさつ	七度 ななど
8	八本 はっぽん	八冊 はっさつ	八度 はちど
9	九本 きゅうほん	九冊 きゅうさつ	九度/九度 きゅうど くど
10	十本 じゅっぽん	十冊 じゅっさつ	十度 じゅうど
15	十五本 じゅうごほん	十五冊 じゅうごさつ	十五度 じゅうごど
20	二十本 にじゅっぽん	二十冊 にじゅっさつ	二十度 にじゅうど
?	何本 なんぼん	何冊 なんさつ	何度 なんど

Question Words

いくつ	2-4	how many (things)?	何月 なんがつ	5-2	what month?
どこ	2-4	where?	何日 なんにち	5-3	what day (of the month)?
どう	3-5	how	何年 なんねん	5-4	what year?
どんな	6-2	what kind?	何色 なにいろ	7-4	what color
いくら	9-2	how much?	何千 なんぜん	9-1	how many thousands?
何時 なんじ	3-2	what time?	何冊 なんさつ	9-2	how many volumes?
何分 なんぷん	3-2	how many minutes?	何本 なんぼん	9-2	how many cylindrical objects?
何曜日 なんようび	5-1	what day (of the week)?	何度 なんど	10-1	how many degrees (temp.)/times?

い Adjectives & な Adjectives

い adjectives

大きい (い adj.) おお	3-1	big, large
楽しい (い adj.) たの	3-2	fun, enjoyable
暑い (い adj.) あつ	3-4	hot (weather)
寒い (い adj.) さむ	3-4	cold (weather)
涼しい (い adj.) すず	3-4	cool (weather)
蒸し暑い (い adj.) む あつ	3-4	humid (weather)
忙しい (い adj.) いそが	5-4	busy
低い (い adj.) ひく	6-1	low, short
弱い (い adj.) よわ	6-1	weak
悲しい (い adj.) かな	6-1	sad
高い (い adj.) たか	6-1	high, tall, expensive
強い (い adj.) つよ	6-1	strong
遠い (い adj.) とお	6-1	far, distant
長い (い adj.) なが	6-1	long
渋い (い adj.) しぶ	6-2	astringent, tasteful, low-key
痛い (い adj.) いた	6-3	painful
素晴らしい (い adj.) すば	6-5	wonderful
かっこいい (い adj.)	7-5	cool
嬉しい (い adj.) うれ	8-1	glad; happy
美味しい (い adj.) おい	8-1	delicious
美しい (い adj.) うつく	8-1	beautiful
うるさい (い adj.)	8-1	noisy, loud
危ない (い adj.) あぶ	8-1	dangerous
かしこい (い adj.)	8-1	wise; bright
かわいい (い adj.)	8-1	cute
きたない (い adj.)	8-1	dirty, messy
きびしい (い adj.)	8-1	strict
こわい (い adj.)	8-1	scary
じれったい (い adj.)	8-1	irritating
ずるい (い adj.)	8-1	cunning
小さい (い adj.) ちい	8-1	small
つまらない (い adj.)	8-1	boring
ばかばかしい (い adj.)	8-1	foolish; silly
ひどい (い adj.)	8-1	terrible
短い (い adj.) みじか	8-1	short
みにくい (い adj.)	8-1	ugly
青い (い adj.) あお	8-2	blue-colored
赤い (い adj.) あか	8-2	red-colored
面白い (い adj.) おもしろ	8-2	interesting
黄色い (い adj.) きいろ	8-2	yellow-colored
黒い (い adj.) くろ	8-2	black-colored
白い (い adj.) しろ	8-2	white-colored
安い (い adj.) やす	8-2	cheap
広い (い adj.) ひろ	8-3	wide, spacious
まずい (い adj.)	8-3	not tasty
狭い (い adj.) せま	8-3	narrow
明るい (い adj.) あか	9-3	bright; light

な adjectives

大事 (な adj.) だいじ	5-1	important
静か (な adj.) しず	6-1	quiet
有名 (な adj.) ゆうめい	6-1	famous
おしゃれ (な adj.)	6-2	fashionable
上手 (な adj.) じょうず	6-2	skillful
スマート (な adj.) すまーと	6-2	slim, stylish
大丈夫 (な adj.) だいじょうぶ	6-3	all right
無理 (な adj.) むり	6-3	difficult
シンプル (な adj.)	6-4	simple
素敵 (な adj.) すてき	6-4	wonderful, nice
ハンサム (な adj.) はんさむ	6-4	handsome, good-looking
嫌い (な adj.) きら	7-2	dislike
好き (な adj.) す	7-2	like
大嫌い (な adj.) だいきら	7-2	hate
大好き (な adj.) だいす	7-2	love
得意 (な adj.) とくい	7-3	skilled at
苦手 (な adj.) にがて	7-3	unskilled at
下手 (な adj.) へた	7-3	not good at
色々 (な adj.) いろいろ	7-4	various, various colors
きれい (な adj.)	8-1	pretty; clean
ふしぎ (な adj.)	8-1	mysterious
おだやか (な adj.)	8-4	calm, peaceful
ひま (な adj.)	8-4	free (time)
特別 (な adj.) とくべつ	9-2	special
残念 (な adj.) ざんねん	10-2	regrettable, unlucky

Adjective Conjugation Summary

い adjectives	Non-past tense ～いです	Past tense ～かったです	Negative ～くありません ～くないです	Negative past ～くありませんでした ～くなかったです	英語
まずい	まずいです	まずかったです	まずくありません まずくないです	まずくありませんでした まずくなかったです	tastes disgusting
ひどい	ひどいです	ひどかったです	ひどくありません ひどくないです	ひどくありませんでした ひどくなかったです	terrible
忙しい	忙しいです	忙しかったです	忙しくありません 忙しくないです	忙しくありませんでした 忙しくなかったです	busy

な adjectives	～です	～でした	～ではありません ～ではないです (or じゃ in place of では)	～ではありませんでした ～ではなかったです (or じゃ in place of では)	
暇	暇です	暇でした	暇ではありません 暇ではないです	暇ではありませんでした 暇ではなかったです	free time
おだやか	おだやかです	おだやかでした	おだやかではありません おだやかではないです	おだやかではありませんでした おだやかではなかったです	calm, peaceful

Irregular adjective					
いい or 良い	いいです or 良いです	良かったです	良くありません 良くないです	良くありませんでした 良くなかったです	good

Adverbs & Time Words

朝	2-5	morning	ちょっと	3-2	a little, somewhat	先月	5-4	last month
とても	3-1	very	次	3-3	next	いつも	6-1	always
少し	3-1	a little, not much	後で	3-3	afterwards	まあまあ	6-2	so so, not bad, moderate
明日	3-2	tomorrow	放課後	3-3	time after school	たいてい	7-2	usually
今	3-2	now	速く	3-5	quickly	あまり	7-4	not very
時々	3-2	sometimes	まだ	4-3	not yet	全然	7-4	not at all
昨日	3-2	yesterday	来週	5-4	next week	まったく	8-4	really, indeed, truly
今日	3-2	today	今年	5-4	this year	もっと	9-3	more

Note: This list offers a sampling of time words. More may be found in the Glossary, where they are listed as nouns, since many function as both adverbs and as nouns.

Particles

は	1-3	denotes the sentence topic
か	1-4	signifies a question
に	1-5	in or at, denotes location or place
に	3-2	at or on, used with specific time words
に	9-4	to indicate recipient of an action or object
の	2-1	indicates possession
の	9-3	to replace a noun
が	2-1	denotes the sentence subject, used with あります/います
が	7-1	new information marker
が	7-3	but, conjunction meaning "but," to combine two sentences
が	9-5	to indicate the giver of an action or object
と	2-2	and (to connect more than one noun)
と	4-1	quotation particle
を	2-3	indicates the direct object
も	2-4	too, also, replaces particles は、が、and を
でも	3-4	but, however, used to link two sentences
で	3-4; 6-3	by means of, to use X as a tool
から	4-1	from
で	4-3; 6-3	place of action (with an action verb)
で	9-2	for, used when shopping or ordering food
へ/に	4-4	used with verbs of movement
から	5-3	from, used with specific locations or specific times
まで	5-3	until, used with specific locations or specific times
もう	10-4	already
まだ	10-4	not yet (with negative verb)

Noun Categories

People

家族 かぞく	(my) family
ご家族 かぞく	someone else's family
おじさん	uncle or older man
おばさん	aunt or older woman
兄弟 きょうだい	siblings
先生 せんせい	teacher
友達 ともだち	friend
人 ひと	person
生徒 せいと	student
大学生 だいがくせい	college/university student
子供達 こどもたち	children

Activities

空手 からて	karate (martial art)
相撲 すもう	sumo wrestling
柔道 じゅうどう	judo
卓球 たっきゅう	Ping-Pong
歌舞伎 かぶき	kabuki drama
空手 からて	karate
茶道 / 茶道 さどう ちゃどう	tea ceremony
趣味 しゅみ	hobby
乗馬 じょうば	horseback riding
ジョギング じょぎんぐ	jogging

水泳 すいえい	swimming
スキー すきー	skiing
スポーツ すぽーつ	sports
寝る事 ねること	sleeping
能 のう	Noh drama theater
映画 えいが	movie
漫画 まんが	manga; comics
料理 りょうり	cooking
旅行 りょこう	a trip; travel

Objects/Things

(お)箸 はし	chopsticks
Tシャツ てぃーしゃつ	T-shirt
写真 しゃしん	photograph
ぼうし	hat/cap
漫画 まんが	Japanese comics
絵 え	painting, drawing
浮世絵	woodblock print
映画	movie
プレゼント	present

Places

海 うみ	ocean; sea
島 しま	island

ビーチ びーち	beach
城 しろ	castle
庭 にわ	garden
病院 びょういん	hospital
店 みせ	shop; store
神社 じんじゃ	shrine
寺 てら	temple
家 / 家 いえ うち	house/home
本屋 ほんや	bookstore
パン屋 ぱんや	bakery
日本 にほん	Japan
東京 とうきょう	capital of Japan
長崎 ながさき	(City of) Nagasaki
天橋立 あまのはしだて	(City of) Amanohashidate
平泉 ひらいずみ	(City of) Hiraizumi
金沢 かなざわ	(City of) Kanazawa
江戸 えど	(City of) Edo (now Tokyo)
平安京 へいあんきょう	(ancient City of) Heian-kyou (now Kyoto)
中学校 ちゅうがっこう	junior high school
高校 こうこう	high school
大学 だいがく	college/university

Appendix 2
Japanese Names

Girls' Names

花子 はなこ	友子 ゆうこ	明子 あきこ	えみ	さゆり	妙子 たえこ	まゆみ	恵美子 えみこ	操 みさお	素子 もとこ	かおり	美也子 みやこ	真澄 ますみ	絵里子 えりこ	浜子 はまこ

Boys' Names

健一 けんいち	道夫 みちお	一郎 いちろう	良和 よしかず	じゅん	友弘 ともひろ	友和 ともかず	ケン	けんじ	豊 ゆたか	友和 ともかず	明 あきら	潤吉 じゅんきち	友保 ともやす	秋宏 あきひろ	雅広 まさひろ

Family Names

石田 いしだ	石口 いしぐち	山口 やまぐち	山本 やまもと	山崎 やまさき	鈴木 すずき	高橋 たかはし	佐々木 ささき	松田 まつだ	上田 うえだ	木村 きむら	高村 たかむら	佐藤 さとう	田中 たなか	渡辺 わたなべ	吉田 よしだ
加藤 かとう	松本 まつもと	井上 いのうえ	斉藤 さいどう	池田 いけだ	本田 ほんだ	前田 まえだ	藤田 ふじた								

Appendix 3
Food and Drinks (食べ物と 飲み物)
たべもの のみもの

Fruits (果物)
くだもの

フルーツ ふるーつ	fruit
イチゴ いちご	strawberry
オレンジ おれんじ	orange
バナナ ばなな	banana
なし	Asian pear
メロン めろん	melon
りんご	apple
トマト とまと	tomato

Meals

朝ご飯 あさ はん	breakfast
昼ご飯 ひる はん	lunch
晩ご飯 ばん はん	dinner, evening meal
おやつ	snack

Condiments

砂糖 さとう	sugar
塩 しお	salt

醤油 しょうゆ	soy sauce
わさび	wasabi (Japanese horseradish)

Main Dishes and Side Dishes

ご飯 はん	cooked rice, a meal
いか	squid
うどん	thick, white noodles
おこのみ焼き や	savory Japanese lunch or dinner pancake

かに	crab
魚 さかな	fish
寿司 す し	food made with vinegared rice
のり	seaweed
ステーキ すてーき	steak
たこ	octopus
タコス たこす	Mexican tacos
たこ焼き や	breaded octopus balls
すきやき	sukiyaki; thinly-sliced meat and vegetables in hot broth
そば	thin buckwheat noodles
てり焼き や	teriyaki; grilled meat with sauce
豆腐 とうふ	bean curd (tofu)
ハンバーガー は ん ば ー が ー	hamburger
ホットケーキ ほ っ と け ー き	pancake; hotcake
巻き寿司 ま ず し	rolled sushi
ラーメン ら ー め ん	ramen noodles
漬け物 つ もの	pickled vegetables

| 卵
たまご | egg |
| パン
ぱ ん | bread |

Sweets and Snacks (甘い物とつまみ)
あま もの

アイス・クリーム あ い す・く り ー む	ice cream
飴 あめ	candy
(お)菓子 か し	Japanese traditional sweets
カップケーキ か っ ぷ け ー き	cupcake
クッキー く っ き ー	cookie
ケーキ け ー き	cake
煎餅 せんべい	rice crackers
だんご	round sticky rice balls on a stick
チョコレート ち ょ こ れ ー と	chocolate
餅 もち	sticky rice cake

Drinks (飲み物)
の もの

| (お)水
みず | water |

アイス・コーヒー あ い す・こ ー ひ ー	iced coffee
アイス・ティー あ い す・て ぃ ー	iced tea
お茶 ちゃ	green tea
牛乳 ぎゅうにゅう	milk
コーヒー こ ー ひ ー	coffee
コーラ こ ー ら	cola
ジュース じ ゅ ー す	juice
牛乳 / ミルク ぎゅうにゅう み る く	milk
ミルク・セーキ み る く・せ ー き	milkshake
レモネード れ も ね ー ど	lemonade

Vegetables (野菜)
やさい

人参 にんじん	carrot
大根 だいこん	daikon; white radish
キャベツ き ゃ べ つ	cabbage
ほうれんそう	spinach

Appendix 4
Classroom Objects

漢字	Romaji	英語
椅子 い す	*isu*	chair
鉛筆 えんぴつ	*enpitsu*	pencil
かばん	*kaban*	satchel, bag
紙 かみ	*kami*	paper
ガム	*gamu*	gum
教科書 きょうかしょ	*kyoukasho*	textbook
教室 きょうしつ	*kyoushitsu*	classroom
消しゴム け ご む	*keshigomu*	eraser
黒板 こくばん	*kokuban*	blackboard
黒板消し こくばんけ	*kokuban keshi*	blackboard eraser
コンピューター	*konpyu-ta-*	computer
作文 さくぶん	*sakubun*	essay
宿題 しゅくだい	*shukudai*	homework
辞書 じしょ	*jisho*	dictionary
下敷き したじ	*shitajiki*	hard plastic sheet for writing on
生徒 せいと	*seito*	student
先生 せんせい	*sensei*	teacher
地図 ち ず	*chizu*	map
チョーク	*cho-ku*	chalk
机 つくえ	*tsukue*	desk
ティッシュ	*tisshu*	tissue
テーブル	*te-buru*	table

漢字	Romaji	英語
テープ	*te-pu*	tape
電気 でんき	*denki*	lights
電話 でんわ	*denwa*	phone
ドア	*doa*	door
時計 とけい	*tokei*	clock
ノート	*no-to*	notebook
ホワイトボード ほ わ い ー と ぼ ー ど	*howai-tobo-do*	whiteboard
はさみ	*hasami*	scissors
旗 はた	*hata*	flag
バッグ	*baggu*	bag
プランナー	*puranna-*	planner, handbook
筆箱 ふでばこ	*fudebako*	pencil box
ホッチキス	*hotchikisu*	stapler
ボールペン	*bo-rupen*	ballpoint pen
本 ほん	*hon*	book
本棚 ほんだな	*hondana*	bookshelves
マジック ま じ っ く	*majikku*	marker
窓 まど	*mado*	window
めがね	*megane*	glasses
定規 じょうぎ	*jougi*	ruler

Japanese-English Glossary

This glossary has simplified abbreviations to make it easier to use. The following abbreviations are used for parts of speech:

い *adj.*	い adjective
な *adj.*	な adjective
adv.	adverb
conj.	conjunction
exp.	expression
inter.	interrogative
interj.	interjection
n	noun
part.	particle
pron.	pronoun
v	verb

The numbering system for location of vocabulary words in the chapters is made up of the volume number (the first digit; 1 is this volume, *Beginning Japanese*); a two-digit chapter number; followed by the section number. For example:

1025

Vol. 1   Chapter 2   section 5

Japanese	Location	English
あ		
ああ (*exp.*)	1025	Ah! Oh!
あお　青 (*n*)	1074	blue
あおい　青い (い *adj.*)	1082	blue-colored
あか　赤 (*n*)	1074	red
あかい　赤い (い *adj.*)	1082	red-colored
あかるい　明るい (い *adj.*)	1093	bright; light
あき　秋 (*n*)	1101	fall/autumn
あくしゅ (*n*)	1042	handshake
あける/あけます　開ける/開けます (開けて) (*v*)		
	1034	(to) open (door/window)
あげる/あげます　上げる/上げます (上げて) (*v*)		
	1094	(to) give
あさ　朝 (*n*)	1025	morning
あさごはん　朝ご飯 (*n*)	1025	breakfast
あし　足 (*n*)	1061	leg, foot
あした　明日 (*n*)	1032	tomorrow
あそこ (*pron.*)	1024	over there
あそぶ/あそびます　遊ぶ/遊びます (遊んで) (*v*)		
	1103	(to) play
あたま　頭 (*n*)	1061	head
あつい　暑い (い *adj.*)	1034	hot (weather)
あと　後 (*n*)	1033	after
あとで　後で (*n*)	1033	afterwards
あに　兄 (*n*)	1021	older brother (my)
あね　姉 (*n*)	1021	older sister (my)
あの	1023	that (thing) over there
あぶない　危ない (い *adj.*)	1081	dangerous
あまのはしだて　天橋立 (*n*)	1082	Amanohashidate (city)
あまり (*adv.*)	1074	not very
あめ　雨 (*n*)	1101	rain
あめ (*n*)	1023	candy, rain
あめふと　アメフト (*n*)	1071	American football
あめりか　アメリカ (*n*)	1041	United States of America
あめりかし　アメリカ史 (*n*)	1032	American history
あめりかじん　アメリカ人 (*n*)	1041	American
ありがとう (*exp.*)	1023	thanks
ありがとうございます (*exp.*)	1023	thank you
ある/あります (*v*)	1021	(to) exist (inanimate things)
あれ (*pron.*)	1015	that (over there)
いいえ (*interj.*)	1014	no
いう/いいます　言う/言います (言って) (*v*)		
	1041	(to) say
いえ/うち　家 (*n*)	1022	house, home
いきましょう　行きましょう (*v*)	1035	let's go
いぎりす　イギリス (*n*)	1041	England
いぎりすけい　イギリス系 (*n*)	1041	English descent
いぎりすじん　イギリス人 (*n*)	1041	English (person)
いく/いきます　行く/行きます (行って) (*v*)		
	1044	(to) go
いくつ (*inter.*)	1024	how many (things)?
いくら (*inter.*)	1092	how much?
いけばな　生け花 (*n*)	1071	flower arranging
いし　石 (*n*)	1101	stone, rock
いしゃ　医者 (*n*)	1063	doctor
いそがしい　忙しい (い *adj.*)	1054	busy
いたい　痛い (い *adj.*)	1063	painful
いただく/いただきます (いただいて) (*v*)		
	1092	(to) receive (very polite), lit.: I will receive.
いたりあ　イタリア (*n*)	1041	Italy
いたりあご　イタリア語 (*n*)	1042	Italian language
いたりあじん　イタリア人 (*n*)	1041	Italian (person)
いち　一 (*n*)	1021	one
いちがつ　一月 (*n*)	1052	January
いちじ　一時 (*n*)	1032	one o'clock
いちじかんめ　一時間目 (*n*)	1033	first period
いちど　一度 (*n*)	1101	one time

Japanese	Location	English
いちねんせい　一年生 (n)	1031	first year student
いちばんしたのあに/あね　一番上の　兄/姉 (n)	1021	my oldest brother/sister
いちばんしたのおとうと/いもうと　一番下の　弟/妹 (n)	1021	my youngest brother/sister
いちぺーじ/いっぺーじ　一ページ (n)	1042	one page/page one
いちまい　一枚 (n)	1042	one sheet/piece
いちまん　一万 (n)	1091	ten thousand
いつ (inter.)	1052	when?
いつか　五日 (n)	1053	fifth (day of the month)
いっさつ　一冊 (n)	1092	one volume
いつつ　五つ (n)	1024	five (things)
いっぷん　一分 (n)	1032	one minute
いっぽん　一本 (n)	1092	one cylindrical object
いつも (n/adv.)	1061	always
いぬ　犬 (n)	1021	dog
いま　今 (n/adv.)	1032	now
いもうと　妹 (n)	1021	younger sister (my)
いもうとさん　妹さん (n)	1022	younger sister (someone else's)
いやりんぐ　イヤリング (n)	1064	earring
いらっしゃいませ (exp.)	1043	welcome (usually used at a place of business)
いる/います (v)	1021	(to) exist (animate beings)
いれる/いれます　入れる/入れます (入れて) (v)	1061	put into
いろ　色 (n)	1074	color
いろいろ　色々 (な adj.)	1074	various, various colors
いんどねしあ　インドネシア (n)	1041	Indonesia
いんどねしあご　インドネシア語 (n)	1042	Indonesian (language)
いんどねしあじん　インドネシア人 (n)	1041	Indonesian (person)
うきよえ　浮世絵 (n)	1091	woodblock print (prior to and through the Edo Period)
うた　歌 (n)	1071	song
うたう/うたいます　歌う/歌います (歌って) (v)	1071	(to) sing
うたうこと　歌う事 (n)	1071	singing
うつくしい　美しい (い adj.)	1081	beautiful
うで (n)	1061	arm
うま　馬 (n)	1082	horse
うまれる/うまれます　生まれる/生まれます (生まれて) (v)	1052	(to) be born
うみ　海 (n)	1081	ocean; sea
うる/うります　売る/売ります (売って) (v)	1091	(to) sell
うるさい (い adj.)	1081	noisy, loud
うれしい　嬉しい (い adj.)	1081	glad; happy
え　絵 (n)	1091	painting, drawing
えあこん　エアコン (n)	1035	air conditioner
えいが　映画 (n)	1091	movie
えいご　英語 (n)	1032	English language
えす(S)さいず　Sサイズ (n)	1092	small (S) size
えむ(M)さいず　Mサイズ (n)	1092	medium (M) size
えむぴーすりー　ぷれーやー　MP3 プレーヤー (n)	1031	MP3 player
える(L)さいず　Lサイズ (n)	1092	large (L) size
えんぴつ　鉛筆 (n)	1024	pencil
おいしい　美味しい (い adj.)	1081	delicious
おおあめ　大雨 (n)	1101	heavy rain
おおきい　大きい (い adj.)	1031	big, large
おーすとらりあ　オーストラリア (n)	1041	Australia

Japanese	Location	English
おーすとらりあじん　オーストラリア人 (n)	1041	Australian
おかあさん　お母さん (n)	1022	mother (someone else's)
おかえりなさい　お帰りなさい (exp.)	1015	welcome home
おかし　(お)菓子 (n)	1095	Japanese traditional sweets
おきる/おきます　起きる/起きます (起きて) (v)	1051	(to) wake (up)
おくる/おくります　送る/送ります (送って) (v)	1051	(to) send
おじいさん (n)	1022	grandfather (someone else's)
おじさん (n)	1022	uncle or man quite a bit older than you
おしゃれ (な adj.)	1062	fashionable
おだやか (な adj.)	1084	calm, peaceful
おつり (n)	1092	change (cash)
おとうさん　お父さん (n)	1022	father (someone else's)
おとうと　弟 (n)	1021	younger brother (my)
おとうとさん　弟さん (n)	1022	younger brother (someone else's)
おとこ　男 (n)	1064	man, male
おとこのこ　男の子 (n)	1064	boy
おどり　踊り (n)	1071	dancing
おっと (interj.)	1083	oops, uh-oh, sorry
おなか (n)	1061	stomach
おなかが　いっぱい　お腹が　一杯 (exp.)	1104	have a full stomach
おにいさん　お兄さん (n)	1022	older brother (someone else's)
おねえさん　お姉さん (n)	1022	older sister (someone else's)
おばあさん (n)	1022	grandmother (someone else's)
おばさん (n)	1022	aunt or woman quite a bit older than you
おはし　お箸 (n)	1015	chopsticks
おはよう (exp.)	1015	good morning (informal)
おはようございます (exp.)	1015	good morning (formal)
おもう/おもいます　思う/思います (思って) (v)	1072	(to) think
おもしろい　面白い (い adj.)	1082	interesting
おやすみ　お休み (exp.)	1015	good night (informal)
おやすみ　なさい　お休み　なさい (exp.)	1015	good night (formal)
およぐ/およぎます　泳ぐ/泳ぎます (泳いで) (v)	1071	(to) swim
およぐこと　泳ぐ事 (n)	1071	swimming
おらんだ　オランダ (n)	1041	Holland
おらんだご　オランダ語 (n)	1042	Dutch language
おらんだじん　オランダ人 (n)	1041	Dutch person
おれんじ　オレンジ (n)	1082	orange (colored)
おれんじ　オレンジ (n)	1074	orange
おわる/おわります　終わる/終わります (終わって) (v)	1052	(to) finish
おんがく　音楽 (n)	1032	music
おんな　女 (n)	1064	woman, female
おんなのこ　女の子 (n)	1064	girl

か

Japanese	Location	English
か (part.)	1014	particle signifying a question
がいこく　外国 (n)	1041	foreign country
がいこくじん　外国人 (n)	1041	foreigner
かいもの　買い物 (n)	1091	shopping
かいもの(を)　する/します　買い物(を)　する/します (v)	1091	(to) go shopping
かう/かいます　買う/買います (買って) (v)	1091	(to) buy

Japanese	Location	English
かえる　蛙 (n)	1072	frog
かえる/かえります　帰る/帰ります (帰って)(v)	1044	(to) return
かお　顔 (n)	1061	face
かがく　科学 (n)	1032	science
ががく　雅楽 (n)	1075	gagaku, ancient Japanese court music
かく/かきます　書く/書きます(書いて)(v)	1013	(to) write
がくせい　学生 (n)	1031	student
かける/かけます (かけて)(v)	1064	(to) wear glasses or sunglasses
かしこい (い adj.)	1081	wise; bright
かぜ　風 (n)	1035	wind
かぜ　風邪 (n)	1063	(a) cold
かぜ(を) ひく/ひきます　風邪(を) ひく/ひきます (v)	1063	(to) catch a cold
かぞく　家族 (n)	1021	family (my)
かた　肩 (n)	1061	shoulder
かっこいい (い adj.)	1075	cool
かっこう　格好 (n)	1062	appearance
がっこう　学校 (n)	1031	school
がっしょう　合唱 (n)	1033	chorus; choir
かていか　家庭科 (n)	1032	family consumer science
かなしい　悲しい (い adj.)	1061	sad
かなだ　カナダ (n)	1041	Canada
かなだじん　カナダ人 (n)	1041	Canadian
かに (n)	1083	crab
かのじょ　彼女 (pron.)	1074	she; girlfriend
かばん　鞄 (n)	1024	bag, satchel
かぶき　歌舞伎 (n)	1075	kabuki theater
かぶる/かぶります　被る/被ります (v)	1064	wear something on your head
かみ　紙 (n)	1024	paper
かみ(のけ)　髪(の毛)(n)	1061	hair
かみなり　雷 (n)	1101	lightning
かめ　亀 (n)	1082	turtle
かもく　科目 (n)	1032	school subject
かようび　火曜日 (n)	1051	Tuesday
から (part.)	1032	from
からおけ(を) する/します　カラオケ(を) する/します (v)	1091	(to) karaoke (to sing)
からて　空手 (n)	1011	karate (martial art)
かれ　彼 (pron.)	1074	he; boyfriend
かれら　彼ら (pron.)	1082	they, them
かわいい (い adj.)	1081	cute
かんこく　韓国 (n)	1041	South Korea
かんこくけい　韓国系 (n)	1041	Korean descent
かんこくご　韓国語 (n)	1042	Korean language
かんこくじん　韓国人 (n)	1041	Korean (person)
かんごふ　看護婦 (n)	1063	nurse
がんばる/がんばります　頑張る/頑張ります (頑張って)(v)	1073	(to) do one's best
きいろ　黄色 (n)	1074	yellow
きいろい　黄色い (い adj.)	1082	yellow-colored
きく/ききます　聞く/聞きます(聞いて)(v)	1013	(to) listen
きせつ　季節 (n)	1101	season
ぎたー　ギター (n)	1071	guitar
ぎたー(を) ひく／ひきます　ギター(を) 弾く/弾きます (v)	1071	(to) play guitar
きたない (い adj.)	1081	dirty, messy
きのう　昨日 (adv./n)	1032	yesterday
きびしい (い adj.)	1081	strict

Japanese	Location	English
きもの　着物 (n)	1064	kimono (Japanese traditional clothing)
きゅうきゅうしゃ(を) よんで　救急車(を) 呼んで (exp.)	1063	Call an ambulance!
きゅうさつ　九冊 (n)	1092	nine volumes
きゅうじゅう　九十 (n)	1022	ninety
きゅうせん　九千 (n)	1091	nine thousand
きゅうど　九度 (n)	1101	nine times
きゅうにん　九人 (n)	1021	nine people
きゅうふん　九分 (n)	1032	nine minutes
きゅうぺーじ　九ページ (n)	1042	nine pages, page nine
きゅうほん　九本 (n)	1092	nine cylindrical objects
きゅうまい　九枚 (n)	1042	nine sheets
きゅうまん　九万 (n)	1091	ninety thousand
きょう　今日 (n)	1032	today
きょうしつ　教室 (n)	1032	classroom
きょうだい　兄弟 (n)	1021	siblings
きょねん　去年 (n)	1054	last year
きらい　嫌い (な adj.)	1072	dislike
ぎりの〜	1021	step-
きる/きます　着る/着ます (v)	1064	(to) wear (for things above the waist or dresses)
きれい (な adj.)	1081	pretty; clean
きんいろ　金色 (n)	1074	gold
ぎんいろ　銀色 (n)	1074	silver
きんにく　筋肉 (n)	1061	muscle
きんぱつ　金髪 (n)	1074	blond (hair)
きんようび　金曜日 (n)	1051	Friday
く/きゅう　九 (n)	1021	nine
ぐあいが わるい　具合が 悪い (exp.)	1063	sick, feel bad
くがつ　九月 (n)	1052	September
くじ　九時 (n)	1032	nine o'clock
くすり　薬 (n)	1063	medicine
くすり(を) のむ/のみます　薬(を) 飲む/飲みます (v)	1063	(to) take medicine
くち　口 (n)	1061	mouth
くつ　靴 (n)	1064	shoes
くつした　靴下 (n)	1064	socks
くび　首 (n)	1061	neck
くもり　曇り (n)	1101	cloudy
くもる/くもります　曇もる/曇ります (v)	1101	(to) become cloudy
くらい　暗い (い adj.)	1093	dark
くらす　クラス (n)	1032	class
くる/きます　来る/来ます (来て)(v)	1044	(to) come
くるま　車 (n)	1043	car, vehicle
ぐれい　グレイ (n)	1074	gray
くれる/くれます (くれて)(v)	1095	(to) give
くろ　黒 (n)	1074	black
くろい　黒い (い adj.)	1082	black-colored
〜くん　君	1013	used immediately AFTER a boy's name
けいけん　経験 (n)	1065	experience
けいざいがく　経済学 (n)	1032	economics
けいたい (でんわ)　けいたい (電話)(n)	1031	cellular phone
けーき　ケーキ (n)	1094	cake
けが(を) する/します　怪我(を) する/します (v)	1063	(to) be hurt, get wounded
けしごむ　消しゴム (n)	1024	eraser
げつようび　月曜日 (n)	1051	Monday
けんか(を)する/します (v)	1091	(to) argue
げんき　元気 (n/な adj.)	1015	healthy, energetic
けんこう　健康 (n)	1063	health
けんこうに いい です　健康に いい です (exp.)	1063	good for your health

Japanese	Location	English
けんどう　剣道 (n)	1033	kendo
けんどうぶ　剣道部 (n)	1033	kendo club
ご　五 (n)	1021	five
こうこう　高校 (n)	1031	high school
こうこういちねんせい　高校一年生 (n)	1031	tenth grader
こうこうさんねんせい　高校三年生 (n)	1031	twelfth grader
こうこうせい　高校生 (n)	1031	high school student
こうこうにねんせい　高校二年生 (n)	1031	eleventh grader
こえ　声 (n)	1061	voice
ごかぞく　ご家族 (n)	1021	someone else's family
ごがつ　五月 (n)	1052	May
こくご　国語 (n)	1032	national language (Japanese language)
こくばん　黒板 (n)	1024	blackboard
ごご　午後 (n)	1032	p.m.
ここ (pron.)	1024	here
ここのか　九日 (n)	1053	ninth (day of the month)
ここのつ　九つ (n)	1024	nine (things)
こころ　心 (n)	1061	heart (not one's physical heart); soul
ごさつ　五冊 (n)	1092	five volumes
ごじ　五時 (n)	1032	five o'clock
ごじかんめ　五時間目 (n)	1033	fifth period
ごじゅう　五十 (n)	1022	fifty
ごせん　五千 (n)	1091	five thousand
ごぜん　午前 (n)	1032	a.m.
こちら (pron.)	1014	this person (polite)
ごど　五度 (n)	1101	five times, five degrees (temp.)
ことし　今年 (n)	1054	this year
こどもたち　子供達 (n)	1082	children
ごにん　五人 (n)	1021	five people
この	1023	this (thing)
ごはん　ご飯 (n)	1015	cooked rice, a meal
ごふん　五分 (n)	1032	five minutes
ごぺーじ　五ページ (n)	1042	page five
ごほん　五本 (n)	1092	five cylindrical objects
ごまい　五枚 (n)	1042	five sheets, five pages
ごまん　五万 (n)	1091	fifty thousand
ごるふ　ゴルフ (n)	1071	golf
これ (pron.)	1015	this (one)
～ごろ	1032	about
こわい (い adj.)	1081	scary
こんげつ　今月 (n)	1054	this month
こんしゅう　今週 (n)	1054	this week
こんにちは　今日は (exp.)	1015	hello
こんばんは　今晩は (exp.)	1015	good evening
こんぴゅーたーらぼ　コンピューターラボ (n)	1033	computer lab

さ

Japanese	Location	English
さあ (interj.)	1035	well...
さいん　サイン (n)	1042	signature
さがす/さがします　探す/探します (探して) (v)	1093	(to) search
さかな　魚 (n)	1101	fish
さくぶん　作文 (n)	1032	essay
さくら　桜 (n)	1105	cherry tree/blossom
さっかー(を) する/します　サッカー(を) する/します (v)	1091	(to) play soccer
さどう/ちゃどう　茶道 (n)	1071	tea ceremony
さむい　寒い (い adj.)	1034	cold (weather)
さむらい　侍 (n)	1061	samurai
さようなら (exp.)	1015	goodbye
さん　三 (n)	1021	three

Japanese	Location	English
～さん	1013	used immediately AFTER a name
さんがつ　三月 (n)	1052	March
さんさつ　三冊 (n)	1092	three volumes
さんじ　三時 (n)	1032	three o'clock
さんじかんめ　三時間目 (n)	1033	third period
さんじゅう　三十 (n)	1022	thirty
さんじゅういちにち　三十一日 (n)	1053	thirty-first (day of the month)
さんじゅうにち　三十日 (n)	1053	thirtieth (day of the month)
さんぜん　三千 (n)	1091	three thousand
さんど　三度 (n)	1101	three times, three degrees
さんにん　三人 (n)	1021	three people
ざんねん　残念(な) (な adj.)	1093	regrettably, unluckily
さんねんせい　三年生 (n)	1031	third year student
さんぷん　三分 (n)	1032	three minutes
さんぺーじ　三ページ (n)	1042	three pages, page three
さんぽ　散歩 (n)	1054	walk
さんぽ(を) する/します　散歩(を) する/します (v)	1054	(to) take a walk
さんぼん　三本 (n)	1092	three cylindrical objects
さんまい　三枚 (n)	1042	three sheets
さんまん　三万 (n)	1091	thirty thousand
じーんず　ジーンズ (n)	1064	jeans
しがつ　四月 (n)	1052	April
しけん　試験 (n)	1032	test, exam
じしん　地震 (n)	1101	earthquake
しずか　静か(な) (な adj.)	1061	quiet
したぎ　下着 (n)	1064	underwear
したじき　下敷き (n)	1024	writing pad, mat
しち/なな　七 (n)	1021	seven
しちがつ/なながつ　七月 (n)	1052	July
しちじ/ななじ　七時 (n)	1032	seven o'clock
しちにん/ななにん　七人 (n)	1021	seven people
じつは　実は (adv.)	1104	as a matter of fact
しぶい　渋い (い adj.)	1062	tasteful, subtle
しま　島 (n)	1083	island
しめる/しめます　閉める/閉めます (閉めて) (v)	1034	(to) close (doors/windows)
じゃあ また (exp.)	1015	see you later (informal)
じゃけっと　ジャケット (n)	1064	jacket
しゃしん　写真 (n)	1021	photograph
しゃしん(を) とる/とります　写真(を) 撮る/撮ります (撮って) (v)	1042	(to) take a photo
しゃつ　シャツ (n)	1064	shirt
しゃわー(を) する/します　シャワー(を) する/します (v)	1091	(to) take a shower
しゃんぷー(を) する/します　シャンプー(を) する/します (v)	1091	(to) shampoo
じゅう　十 (n)	1021	ten
じゅういち　十一 (n)	1022	eleven
じゅういちがつ　十一月 (n)	1052	November
じゅういちじ　十一時 (n)	1032	eleven o'clock
じゅういちにち　十一日 (n)	1053	eleventh (day of the month)
じゅういちまん　十一万 (n)	1091	one hundred ten thousand
じゅうがつ　十月 (n)	1052	October
じゅうきゅうまん　十九万 (n)	1052	one hundred ninety thousand
じゅうく/じゅうきゅう　十九 (n)	1022	nineteen
じゅうくにち　十九日 (n)	1053	nineteenth (day of the month)
じゅうご　十五 (n)	1022	fifteen
じゅうごにち　十五日 (n)	1053	fifteenth (day of the month)
じゅうごまん　十五万 (n)	1091	one hundred fifty thousand
じゅうさん　十三 (n)	1022	thirteen

Japanese	Location	English
じゅうさんにち　十三日 (n)	1053	thirteenth (day of the month)
じゅうさんまん　十三万 (n)	1091	one hundred thirty thousand
じゅうじ　十時 (n)	1032	ten o'clock
じゅうしちにち　十七日 (n)	1053	seventeenth (day of the month)
じゅーす　ジュース (n)	1063	juice
じゅうど　十度 (n)	1101	ten times, ten degrees (temp.)
じゅうどう　柔道 (n)	1033	judo
じゅうなな/じゅうしち　十七 (n)	1022	seventeen
じゅうななまん　十七万 (n)	1091	one hundred seventy thousand
じゅうに　十二 (n)	1022	twelve
じゅうにがつ　十二月 (n)	1052	December
じゅうにじ　十二時 (n)	1032	twelve o'clock
じゅうににち　十二日 (n)	1053	twelfth (day of the month)
じゅうにまん　十二万 (n)	1091	one hundred twenty thousand
じゅうにん　十人 (n)	1021	ten people
じゅうはち　十八 (n)	1022	eighteen
じゅうはちにち　十八日 (n)	1053	eighteenth (day of the month)
じゅっぺーじ　十ページ (n)	1042	ten pages, page ten
じゅうまい　十枚 (n)	1042	ten sheets
じゅうまん　十万 (n)	1091	one hundred thousand
じゅうよっか　十四日 (n)	1053	fourteenth (day of the month)
じゅうよん/じゅうし　十四 (n)	1022	fourteen
じゅうよんまん　十四万 (n)	1091	one hundred forty thousand
じゅうろく　十六 (n)	1022	sixteen
じゅうろくにち　十六日 (n)	1053	sixteenth (day of the month)
じゅうろくまん　十六万 (n)	1091	one hundred sixty thousand
じゅぎょう　授業 (n)	1032	class
しゅくだい　宿題 (n)	1032	homework
しゅくだい(を) する/します　宿題(を) する/します (v)	1091	(to) do homework
じゅっさつ　十冊 (n)	1092	ten volumes
じゅっぷん/じっぷん　十分 (n)	1032	ten minutes
じゅっぽん　十本 (n)	1092	ten cylindrical objects
しゅみ　趣味 (n)	1071	hobby
しょうがくせい　小学生 (n)	1031	elementary school student
しょうがっこう　小学校 (n)	1031	elementary school
じょうず　上手 (な adj.)	1062	skillful
じょうだん　冗談 (n)	1072	joke
しょうてすと　小テスト (n)	1032	small test, quiz
じょうば　乗馬 (n)	1071	horseback riding
しょうゆ　醤油 (n)	1015	soy sauce
じょぎんぐ　ジョギング (n)	1071	jogging
しょくじ(を)する/します　食事(を)する/します (v)	1091	(to) dine; to have a meal
しる/しります　知る/知ります (知って) (v)	1042	(to) know something/ someone
じれったい (い adj.)	1081	irritating
しろ　城 (n)	1101	castle
しろ　白 (n)	1074	white
しろい　白い (い adj.)	1082	white-colored
じんじゃ　神社 (n)	1033	shrine
しんぱい(を) する/します　心配(を) する/します (v)	1063	(to) worry

Japanese	Location	English
しんぷる　シンプル (な adj.)	1064	simple
しんりがく　心理学 (n)	1032	psychology
すいえい　水泳 (n)	1071	swimming
すいようび　水曜日 (n)	1051	Wednesday
すうがく　数学 (n)	1032	math
すーつ　スーツ (n)	1064	suit
すかーと　スカート (n)	1064	skirt
すき　好き (な adj.)	1072	like
〜すぎ	1032	past, after, (too) much
すきー　スキー (n)	1071	skiing
すぐしたの おとうと/いもうと　すぐ下の 弟/妹 (n)	1021	my next youngest brother/ sister
すけぼー(を) する　スケボー(を) する (v)	1071	(to) skateboard
すけじゅーる　スケジュール (n)	1032	schedule
すこし　少し (adv.)	1031	little
すし　寿司 (n)	1011	anything made with vinegared rice including vegetables, spices, fish, or other foods
すずしい　涼しい (い adj.)	1034	cool (weather)
すてき　素敵 (な adj.)	1064	wonderful, nice
すばらしい　素晴らしい (い adj.)	1065	wonderful
すぺいん　スペイン (n)	1041	Spain
すぺいんご　スペイン語 (n)	1042	Spanish
すぺいんじん　スペイン人 (n)	1041	Spaniard
すぽーつ　スポーツ (n)	1071	sports
ずぼん　ズボン (n)	1064	pants, trousers
すまーと　スマート (な adj.)	1062	slim, stylish
すむ/すみます　住む/住みます (住んで) (v)	1064	(to) live/reside
すもう　相撲 (n)	1011	Japanese sumo wrestling
する/します (v)	1051	(to) do
する/します (して) (v)	1044/1064	(to) do; (to) wear
ずるい (い adj.)	1081	cunning
すわる/すわります　座る/座ります(座って) (v)	1013	(to) sit
せ/せい　背 (n)	1061	stature, height
せいせき　成績 (n)	1033	score, grade
せいと　生徒 (n)	1031	student
せいぶつがく　生物学 (n)	1032	biology
せかいし　世界史 (n)	1032	world history
せまい　狭い (い adj.)	1083	narrow
せん　千 (n)	1091	one thousand
せんげつ　先月 (n)	1054	last month
せんしゅう　先週 (n)	1054	last week
せんせい　先生 (n)	1011	teacher
せんせい　〜先生	1013	used immediately AFTER a teacher's, lawyer's, or doctor's name
ぜんぜん　全然 (adv.)	1074	not at all
ぜんぶ　全部 (n/adv.)	1083	all, everything
ぜんぶで　全部で (exp.)	1092	in all; total; all together
せんべい　煎餅 (n)	1094	rice crackers
そこ (pron.)	1024	there
そして (conj.)	1071	then; and then
その	1023	that (thing)
そふ　祖父 (n)	1021	grandfather (my)
そぼ　祖母 (n)	1021	grandmother (my)
それ (pron.)	1015	that (one)
それから (conj.)	1071	then; and then
それに (conj.)	1071	moreover; furthermore

た

Japanese	Location	English
たいいく　体育 (n)	1032	physical education
たいいくかん　体育館 (n)	1033	gymnasium

Japanese	Location	English
だいがく　大学 (n)	1031	college/university
だいがくせい　大学生 (n)	1031	college/university student
だいきらい　大嫌い (な adj.)	1072	dislike a lot, hate
だいじ　大事 (な adj.)	1051	important
だいじょうぶ　大丈夫 (な adj.)	1063	all right
だいすき　大好き (な adj.)	1072	love
だいだいいろ　橙色 (n)	1074	orange (colored)
たいてい (adv.)	1072	usually
たいふう　台風 (n)	1101	typhoon
たいわん　台湾 (n)	1041	Taiwan
たいわんじん　台湾人 (n)	1041	Taiwanese (person)
たかい　高い (い adj.)	1061	high, tall, expensive
だから (conj.)	1044	because of that
たくさん (n)	1031	many, a lot
たこ (n)	1025	octopus
たこす　タコス (n)	1025	Mexican taco(s)
だす/だします　出す/出します (出して) (v)	1013	(to) take (it) out
ただいま (exp.)	1015	I'm home
たつ/たちます　立つ/立ちます (立って) (v)	1013	(to) stand
たっきゅうぶ　たっきゅう部 (n)	1033	Ping-Pong club
たつまき　竜巻 (n)	1101	tornado
たのしい　楽しい (い adj.)	1032	fun, enjoyable
たべもの　食べ物 (n)	1043	food(s)
たべる/たべます　食べる/食べます (食べて) (v)	1043	(to) eat
たべること　食べる事 (n)	1071	eating
たまご　卵 (n)	1015	egg
だめ (な adj.)	1034	is bad
だれ (inter.)	1021	who
だれも (exp.)	1102	no one
たろう　太郎 (n)	1014	Taro (male name)
たんじょうび　誕生日 (n)	1052	birthday
ちいさい　小さい (い adj.)	1031	small
ちがう/ちがいます　違う/違います (違って) (v)	1014	is not right, incorrect
ちち　父 (n)	1014	father, dad
ちゃぱつ　茶髪 (n)	1074	brown (hair)
ちゅうがくいちねんせい　中学一年生 (n)	1031	seventh grader
ちゅうがくさんねんせい　中学三年生 (n)	1031	ninth grader
ちゅうがくせい　中学生 (n)	1031	middle school student
ちゅうがくにねんせい　中学二年生 (n)	1031	eighth grader
ちゅうがっこう　中学校 (n)	1031	middle school
ちゅうごく　中国 (n)	1041	China
ちゅうごくけい　中国系 (n)	1041	of Chinese descent
ちゅうごくじん　中国人 (n)	1041	Chinese (person)
ちゅごくご　中国語 (n)	1042	Chinese
ちょーく　チョーク (n)	1024	chalk
ちょっと (adv.)	1032	little, somewhat
(___は、)ちょっと・・・ (exp.)	1043	little …(something is)
ついたち　一日 (n)	1053	first (day of the month)
つかう/つかいます　使う/使います (使って) (v)	1102	(to) use
つぎ　次 (n/adv.)	1033	next
つくる/つくります　作る/作ります (作って) (v)	1102	(to) make
つけもの　漬け物 (n)	1083	pickled vegetables
つなみ　津波 (n)	1011	tidal wave
つまらない (い adj.)	1081	boring
つゆ　梅雨 (n)	1101	rainy season
つよい　強い (い adj.)	1061	strong

Japanese	Location	English
つれて　かえる/かえります　連れて　帰る/帰ります (v)	1101	(to) return with someone
つれて　くる/きます　連れて　来る/来ます (v)	1105	(to) bring someone
て　手 (n)	1061	hand
てぃーしゃつ　Tシャツ (n)	1023	T-shirt
でーと(を) する/します　デート(を) する/します (v)	1091	(to) go on a date
です (copula)	1013	helping verb/linking verb used similarly to "is" or "am"
てすと　テスト (n)	1032	test
てつだう/てつだいます　手伝う/手伝います (手伝って) (v)	1041	(to) help, to assist
では　また (exp.)	1015	see you later (formal)
でも (part./conj.)	1034	but
てら　寺 (n)	1033	temple
でる/でます　出る/出ます (出て) (v)	1061	(to) go out, leave, get out
てんいん　店員 (n)	1092	shopkeeper; clerk
てんき　天気 (n)	1101	weather
てんきよほう　天気予報 (n)	1101	weather report
でんしめーる　電子メール (n)	1051	e-mail
でんわ　電話 (n)	1021	telephone
でんわ(を)する/します　電話(を) する/します (v)	1091	(to) telephone
と (part.)	1022	and
どいつ　ドイツ (n)	1041	Germany
どいつご　ドイツ語 (n)	1042	German
どいつじん　ドイツ人 (n)	1041	German (person)
どう (inter.)	1035	how
どう　でしたか。(inter.)	1065	How was it?
どう　ですか (inter.)	1092	How about it?
どういたしまして (exp.)	1023	you're welcome
とうきょう　東京 (n)	1011	capital of Japan
どうぞ　よろしく (exp.)	1013	best regards, please treat me favorably
どうぞ　よろしく　おねがいします　どうぞ　よろしく　お願いします (exp.)	1013	polite for よろしく　お願いします
とうふ　豆腐 (n)	1011	bean curd (tofu)
どうぶつ　動物 (n)	1072	animals
どうも　ありがとう (exp.)	1023	thank you
どうもありがとうございます (exp.)	1023	thank you
とお　十 (n)	1024	ten (things)
とおい　遠い (い adj.)	1061	far, distant
とおか　十日 (n)	1053	tenth (day of the month)
ときどき　時々 (n/adv.)	1032	sometimes
とくい　得意 (な adj.)	1073	skilled at
どくしょ　読書 (n)	1071	reading
とくべつ　特別 (n/な adj.)	1092	special
どこ (inter.)	1024	where?
ところで (exp./conj.)	1041	by the way
とじる/とじます　閉じる/閉じます (閉じて) (v)	1013	(to) close; shut
としょかん　図書館 (n)	1033	library
とても (adv.)	1031	very
どの	1023	which (thing)
ともだち　友達 (n)	1022	friend
どようび　土曜日 (n)	1051	Saturday
とらんぷ　トランプ (n)	1071	playing cards; card game
とりい　鳥居 (n)	1035	Shinto shrine gate
どれ (inter.)	1015	which (one)
どれす　ドレス (n)	1064	dress (a)
とんでもない (exp.)	1094	Don't be ridiculous! Not a chance! My pleasure

Japanese	Location	English
どんな	1062	what/which kind of

な

Japanese	Location	English
ながい　長い (い adj.)	1061	long
ながさき　長崎 (n)	1041	Nagasaki (city name)
なかなおり(を) する/します　仲直り(を) する/します (v)	1091	(to) make up; to become friends (again)
なつ　夏 (n)	1101	summer
ななさつ　七冊 (n)	1092	seven volumes
ななじゅう　七十 (n)	1022	seventy
ななせん　七千 (n)	1091	seven thousand
ななつ　七つ (n)	1024	seven (things)
ななど　七度 (n)	1101	seven times
ななふん　七分 (n)	1032	seven minutes
ななページ/しちページ　七ページ (n)	1042	seven pages, page seven
ななほん　七本 (n)	1092	seven cylindrical objects
ななまい/しちまい　七枚 (n)	1042	seven sheets
ななまん　七万 (n)	1091	seventy thousand
なにか　何か	1103	something
なにいろ　何色 (inter.)	1074	what color
なにけい　何系 (inter.)	1041	what ethnicity or heritage
なにじん　何人 (inter.)	1041	what nationality
なのか　七日 (n)	1053	seventh (day of the month)
なまえ　名前 (n)	1013	name
ならう/ならいます　習う/習います (習って) (v)	1065	(to) learn
なん/なに　何 (inter.)	1021	what
なんがつ　何月 (inter.)	1052	what month
なんさつ　何冊 (inter.)	1092	how many volumes
なんじ　何時 (inter.)	1032	what time
なんじかんめ　何時間目 (inter.)	1033	what period
なんぜん　何千 (inter.)	1091	how many thousands
なんど　何度 (inter.)	1101	how many times
なんにち　何日 (inter.)	1053	what day of the month
なんにん　何人 (inter.)	1021	how many people
なんねん　何年 (inter.)	1054	what year
なんねんせい　何年生 (inter.)	1031	what grade/year
なんぷん　何分 (inter.)	1032	how many minutes
なんページ　何ページ (inter.)	1042	how many pages, what page
なんぼん　何本 (inter.)	1092	how many cylindrical objects
なんまい　何枚 (inter.)	1042	how many sheets
なんようび　何曜日 (inter.)	1051	what day of the week
に　二 (n)	1021	two
に (part.)	1015	used after a location or time word
に よろしく (exp.)	1065	Say hello to ...
にがつ　二月 (n)	1052	February
にがて　苦手 (な adj.)	1073	unskilled at
にさつ　二冊 (n)	1092	two volumes
にじ　二時 (n)	1032	two o'clock
にじかんめ　二時間目 (n)	1033	second period
にじゅう　二十 (n)	1022	twenty
にじゅういち　二十一 (n)	1022	twenty-one
にじゅういちにち　二十一日 (n)	1053	twenty-first (day of the month)
にじゅういちまん　二十一万 (n)	1091	two hundred ten thousand
にじゅうくにち　二十九日 (n)	1053	twenty-ninth (day of the month)
にじゅうごにち　二十五日 (n)	1053	twenty-fifth (day of the month)
にじゅうさんにち　二十三日 (n)	1053	twenty-third (day of the month)

Japanese	Location	English
にじゅうしちにち　二十七日 (n)	1053	twenty-seventh (day of the month)
にじゅうににち　二十二日 (n)	1053	twenty-second (day of the month)
にじゅうはちにち　二十八日 (n)	1053	twenty-eighth (day of the month)
にじゅうまん　二十万 (n)	1091	two hundred thousand
にじゅうよっか　二十四日 (n)	1053	twenty-fourth (day of the month)
にじゅうろくにち　二十六日 (n)	1053	twenty-sixth (day of the month)
にじゅっぷん　二十分 (n)	1032	twenty minutes
にせん　二千 (n)	1091	two thousand
にちようび　日曜日 (n)	1051	Sunday
にっけいじん　日系人 (n)	1041	Japanese descent
にど　二度 (n)	1101	two times
にねんせい　二年生 (n)	1031	second year student
にばんめの あに/あね　二番目の 兄/姉 (n)	1021	my second oldest brother/ sister
にふん　二分 (n)	1032	two minutes
にページ　ニページ (n)	1042	two pages, page two
にほん　二本 (n)	1092	two cylindrical objects
にほん　日本 (n)	1011	Japan
にほんご　日本語 (n)	1011	Japanese language
にほんし　日本史 (n)	1032	Japanese history
にほんじん　日本人 (n)	1041	Japanese person
にまい　二枚 (n)	1042	two sheets
にまん　二万 (n)	1091	twenty thousand
にゅーじーらんど　ニュージーランド (n)	1041	New Zealand
にゅーじーらんどじん　ニュージーランド人 (n)	1041	New Zealander
にわ　庭 (n)	1101	garden
ねくたい　ネクタイ (n)	1064	necktie
ねこ　猫 (n)	1021	cat
ねずみ (n)	1072	rat, mouse
ねずみいろ　鼠色 (n)	1074	gray (mouse-colored)
ねつ　熱 (n)	1063	fever
ねる/ねます　寝る/寝ます (寝て) (v)	1051	(to) sleep
ねること　寝る事 (n)	1071	sleeping
のう　能 (n)	1075	Noh (a type of theater)
のーと　ノート (n)	1024	notebook
のど　咽喉 (n)	1061	throat
のみもの　飲み物 (n)	1043	drink(s)
のむ/のみます　飲む/飲みます (飲んで) (v)	1043	(to) drink

は

Japanese	Location	English
は (part.)	1013	particle that denotes the sentence topic
はい	1014	yes, here (roll call)
はいいろ　灰色 (n)	1074	gray, ash-colored
はいく　俳句 (n)	1101	haiku (poem)
ばいばい　バイバイ (exp.)	1015	bye-bye
はいる/はいります　入る/入ります (入って) (v)	1061	(to) come in, go in, enter
ばかばかしい (い adj.)	1081	foolish; silly
はく/はきます　履く/履きます (履いて) (v)	1064	(to) wear (items below the waist)
はこ (n)	1081	box
はじめまして　初めまして (exp.)	1013	How do you do?
はじめましょう　始めましょう (exp.)	1011	Let's begin.
はじめる/はじめます　始める/始めます (v)	1052	(to) begin

Japanese	Location	English
ばすけ(を) する/します　バスケ(を) する/します (v)		
	1091	(to) play basketball
はすけぶ　バスケ部 (n)	1033	basketball team
はち　八 (n)	1021	eight
はちがつ　八月 (n)	1052	August
はちじ　八時 (n)	1032	eight o'clock
はちじゅう　八十 (n)	1022	eighty
はちど　八度 (n)	1101	eight times, eight degrees
はちにん　八人 (n)	1021	eight people
はちぺーじ/はっぺーじ　ハページ (n)	1042	eight pages, page eight
はちまい　八枚 (n)	1042	eight sheets
はちまん　八万 (n)	1091	eighty thousand
はつか　二十日 (n)	1053	twentieth (day of the month)
ばっくぱっく　バックパック (n)	1024	backpack
はっさつ　八冊 (n)	1092	eight volumes
はっせん　八千 (n)	1091	eight thousand
はっぷん/はちふん　八分 (n)	1032	eight minutes
はっぽん/はちほん　八本 (n)	1092	eight cylindrical objects
はな　花 (n)	1101	flower
はな　鼻 (n)	1061	nose
はなす/はなします　話す/話します (話して) (v)		
	1042	(to) speak
はなみ　花見 (n)	1105	cherry blossom viewing, flower viewing
はは　母 (n)	1014	mother, mom
はやく　速く (adv.)	1035	quickly
はる　春 (n)	1101	spring
はれ　晴れ (n)	1101	clear (skies)
ばれーぼーるぶ　バレーボール部 (n)	1033	volleyball club (team)
はれる/はれます　晴れる/晴れます (晴れて) (v)		
	1101	(to) become clear (weather)
ぱん　パン (n)	1043	bread
はん　半 (n)	1032	half (hour)
ばん　晩 (n)	1025	evening
はんが　版画 (n)	1091	woodblock print (modern)
ばんごはん　晩ご飯 (n)	1025	dinner, evening meal
はんさむ　ハンサム (な adj.)	1064	handsome, good-looking
ぱんつ　パンツ (n)	1064	underwear
ぱんやさん　パン屋さん (n)	1043	bakery
ぴあの　ピアノ (n)	1071	piano
びーち　ビーチ (n)	1081	beach
ひく/ひきます　弾く/弾きます (弾いて) (v)		
	1071	(to) play (a stringed instrument)
ひくい　低い (い adj.)	1061	low, short (height)
ひげ (n)	1061	moustache, beard
ひざ　膝 (n)	1061	knee
びじゅつ　美術 (n)	1032	art
びでおげーむ　ビデオゲーム (n)	1071	video games
びでおげーむ(を) する/します　ビデオゲーム(を) する/します (v)		
	1091	(to) play video games
ひと　人 (n)	1022	person
ひどい　(い adj.)	1081	terrible
ひとつ　一つ (n)	1024	one (thing)
ひとり　一人 (n)	1021	one person
ひとりで　一人で (exp.)	1104	alone, by oneself
ひま　(な adj.)	1084	free (time)
ひみつ　秘密 (n)	1061	secret
ひゃく　百 (n)	1022	one hundred
びょういん　病院 (n)	1063	hospital
びょうき　病気 (n)	1063	illness, sickness
ひらく/ひらきます　開く/開きます (開いて) (v)		
	1013	(to) open (a book)
ひる　昼 (n)	1025	daytime, noon
ひるごはん　昼ご飯 (n)	1025	lunch

Japanese	Location	English
ひるね　昼寝 (n)	1063	nap
ひるね(を) する/します　昼寝(を) する/します (v)		
	1063	(to) nap
ひるやすみ　昼休み (n)	1032	lunch break
ひろい　広い (い adj.)	1083	wide, spacious
ぴんく　ピンク (n)	1074	pink
ぶかつ　部活 (n)	1033	club activity
ふく　服 (n)	1064	clothes
ふしぎ　(な adj.)	1081	mysterious
ふたつ　二つ (n)	1024	two (things)
ふたり　二人 (n)	1021	two people
ふつう　普通 (な adj./adv.)	1064	usual, normal
ふつか　二日 (n)	1053	second (day of the month)
ぶつりがく　物理学 (n)	1032	physics
ふとっています　太っています (v)	1062	(to) be fat
ふとる/ふとります　太る/太ります (太って) (v)		
	1062	(to) get fat
ふとん　布団 (n)	1063	futon
ふゆ　冬 (n)	1101	winter
ぶらすばんど　ブラスバンド (n)	1033	brass band
ふらんす　フランス (n)	1041	France
ふらんすご　フランス語 (n)	1042	French language
ふらんすじん　フランス人 (n)	1041	French person
ふる/ふります　降る/降ります (降って) (v)		
	1101	(to) precipitate
ぷれぜんと　プレゼント (n)	1094	present; a gift
ぶんか　文化 (n)	1065	culture
ぺこぺこ	1025	mimetic expression for hunger
へた　下手 (な adj.)	1073	not good at
べつ　別 (n/な adj.)	1092	separate
べつべつ　別々 (n/な adj.)	1092	separately; individually
へや　部屋 (n)	1015	room (a)
ぺん　ペン (n)	1024	pen
べんきょう(を) する/します　勉強する/勉強(を) します (v)		
	1052	(to) study
べんけい　弁慶 (proper name)	1061	Benkei (famous samurai name)
ほいくえん　保育園 (n)	1031	kindergarten
ほうかご　放課後 (n/adv.)	1033	time after school
ぼうし　(n)	1023	hat/cap
ほーむるーむ　ホームルーム (n)	1032	homeroom
ぼーるぺん　ボールペン (n)	1024	(ballpoint) pen
ぼく　僕 (pron.)	1011	I, me (used by males only)
ほけんたいいく　保健体育 (n)	1032	health (class)
ぽるとがる　ポルトガル (n)	1041	Portugal
ぽるとがるご　ポルトガル語 (n)	1042	Portuguese
ほんとう　本当 (n)	1104	truth, reality
ほんや　本屋 (n)	1043	bookstore

ま

Japanese	Location	English
まあまあ (adv.)	1062	so so, not bad, moderate
まいしゅう　毎週 (n)	1054	every week
まいつき　毎月 (n)	1054	every month
まいにち　毎日 (n)	1032	every day
まいねん/まいとし　毎年 (n)	1054	every year
まえ　前 (n/adv.)	1051	front, in front, before
まずい　(い adj.)	1083	not tasty, not good
まだ　(adv.)	1043	not yet
まつ/まちます　待つ/待ちます (待って) (v)		
	1061	(to) wait
まつり　祭り (n)	1051	festival
まったく　全く (adv.)	1084	really, indeed, truly
まで　(part.)	1053	until
まん　万 (n)	1091	ten thousand

Japanese	Location	English
まんが　漫画 (n)	1024	Japanese comics
みじかい　短い (い adj.)	1081	short (length)
みず　水 (n)	1024	water
みせ　店 (n)	1091	shop; store
みっか　三日 (n)	1053	third (day of the month)
みっつ　三つ (n)	1024	three (things)
みどり　緑 (n)	1074	green
みなさん　皆さん (n)	1031	everyone (polite)
みにくい (い adj.)	1081	ugly
みみ　耳 (n)	1061	ear
みる/みます　見る/見ます (見て) (v)	1013	(to) look/see
みんな　皆 (n)	1031	everyone, all
むいか　六日 (n)	1053	sixth (day of the month)
むかし　昔 (n)	1082	long ago
むかしむかし　昔々 (n)	1082	long long ago
むしあつい　蒸し暑い (い adj.)	1034	humid (weather)
むずかしい　難しい (い adj.)	1032	difficult
むっつ　六つ (n)	1024	six (things)
むらさき　紫 (n)	1074	purple
むり　無理 (な adj.)	1063	impossible, unreasonable
むりしないで ください　無理しないで 下さい (exp.)	1063	Don't overexert.
め　目 (n)	1061	eye
めいく　メイク (n)	1064	makeup
めがね　眼鏡 (n)	1064	eyeglasses
めきしこ　メキシコ (n)	1041	Mexico
めきしこけい　メキシコ系 (n)	1041	Mexican descent (person of)
めきしこじん　メキシコ人 (n)	1041	Mexican (person)
もくようび　木曜日 (n)	1051	Thursday
もち　餅 (n)	1064	sticky rice cake
もちろん (exp.)	1105	of course
もつ/もちます　持つ/持ちます (持って) (v)	1061	(to) have, hold, carry
もって いく/いきます　持って 行く/行きます (v)	1105	(to) take something
もって かえる/かえります　持って 帰る/帰ります (v)	1105	(to) return with something
もって くる/きます　持って 来る/来ます (v)	1105	(to) bring something
もっと (adv.)	1093	more
もの　物 (n)	1043	thing
もらう/もらいます (もらって) (v)	1094	(to) receive

や

Japanese	Location	English
やきゅう　野球 (n)	1071	baseball
やきゅうぶ　野球部 (n)	1033	baseball team
やせて いる/やせて います (v)	1062	(to) be/is skinny
やっつ　八つ (n)	1024	eight (things)
やってみる/やってみます (やってみて) (v)	1073	(to) see if you can do (something); (to) try to do (something)
やま　山 (n)	1031	mountain
やまもと　山本 (n)	1031	Yamamoto (family name)
やめる/やめます (やめて) (v)	1082	(to) stop
やる/やります (やって) (v)	1073	(to) do
ゆうめい　有名 (な adj.)	1061	famous
ゆき　雪 (n)	1101	snow
ゆび　指 (n)	1061	finger(s)
ようか　八日 (n)	1053	eighth (day of the month)

Japanese	Location	English
ようこそ (exp.)	1014	Welcome!, Nice to see you.
ようちえん　幼稚園 (n)	1031	nursery school
ようふく　洋服 (n)	1064	clothes, Western clothes
よじ　四時 (n)	1032	four o'clock
よじかんめ　四時間目 (n)	1033	fourth period
よっか　四日 (n)	1053	fourth (day of the month)
よっつ　四つ (n)	1024	four (things)
よにん　四人 (n)	1021	four people
よむ/よみます　読む/読みます (読んで) (v)	1013	(to) read
よろしく おねがいします　よろしく お願いします (exp.)	1013	best regards, please treat me favorably (polite)
よわい　弱い (い adj.)	1061	weak
よん/し　四 (n)	1021	four
よんさつ　四冊 (n)	1092	four volumes
よんじゅう　四十 (n)	1022	forty
よんせん　四千 (n)	1091	four thousand
よんど　四度 (n)	1101	four times
よんぷん　四分 (n)	1032	four minutes
よんぺーじ　四ページ (n)	1042	four pages, page four
よんほん　四本 (n)	1092	four cylindrical objects
よんまい　四枚 (n)	1042	four sheets
よんまん　四万 (n)	1091	forty thousand

ら

Japanese	Location	English
らいげつ　来月 (n)	1054	next month
らいしゅう　来週 (n)	1054	next week
らいねん　来年 (n)	1054	next year
りくじょうぶ　陸上部 (n)	1033	track and field club
りょうり　料理 (n)	1071	cooking
りょこう　旅行 (n)	1071	trip; travel
りょこう(を) する/します　旅行(を) する/します (旅行(を) して) (v)	1091	(to) take a trip; to travel
れきし　歴史 (n)	1032	history
ろく　六 (n)	1021	six
ろくがつ　六月 (n)	1052	June
ろくさつ　六冊 (n)	1092	six volumes
ろくじ　六時 (n)	1032	six o'clock
ろくじかんめ　六時間目 (n)	1033	sixth period
ろくじゅう　六十 (n)	1022	sixty
ろくせん　六千 (n)	1091	six thousand
ろくど　六度 (n)	1101	six times
ろくにん　六人 (n)	1021	six people
ろくぺーじ　六ページ (n)	1042	six pages, page six
ろくまい　六枚 (n)	1042	six sheets
ろくまん　六万 (n)	1091	sixty thousand
ろしあ　ロシア (n)	1041	Russia
ろしあご　ロシア語 (n)	1042	Russian (language)
ろっくんろーる　ロックンロール (n)	1105	rock and roll (music)
ろっぷん　六分 (n)	1032	six minutes
ろっぽん　六本 (n)	1092	six cylindrical objects

わ

Japanese	Location	English
わがまま (な adj.)	1081	selfish
わさび (n)	1015	wasabi, Japanese horse-radish
わたし　私 (pron.)	1013	I, me
わたしたち　私達 (pron.)	1013	we, us
わっ! (interj.)	1035	similar to "wow!"
わるい　悪い (い adj.)	1082	bad

English-Japanese Glossary

This glossary has simplified abbreviations to make it easier to use. The following abbreviations are used for parts of speech:

い *adj.*	い adjective	*interj.*	interjection
な *adj.*	な adjective	*n*	noun
adv.	adverb	*part.*	particle
conj.	conjunction	*pron.*	pronoun
exp.	expression	*v*	verb
inter.	interrogative		

The numbering system for location of vocabulary words in the chapters is made up of the chapter number, followed by the section number. For example:

"3-2" = Chapter 3, section 2

English	Location	Japanese
A		
a.m.	3-2	ごぜん　午前 (n)
about	3-2	～ごろ
after	3-3	あと　後, すぎ
afterwards	3-3	あとで　後で
Ah! Oh!	2-5	ああ (exp.)
air conditioner	3-5	えあこん　エアコン (n)
all right	6-3	だいじょうぶ　大丈夫 (な adj.)
all, everything	8-3	ぜんぶ　全部 (n/adv.)
alone, by oneself	10-4	ひとりで　一人で (exp.)
always	6-1	いつも (n/adv.)
Amanohashidate (city)	8-2	あまのはしだて　天橋立 (n)
American	4-1	あめりかじん　アメリカ人 (n)
American football	7-1	あめふと　アメフト (n)
American history	3-2	あめりかし　アメリカ史 (n)
and	2-2	と (part.)
animals	7-2	どうぶつ　動物 (n)
appearance	6-2	かっこう　格好 (n)
April	5-2	しがつ　四月 (n)
(to) argue	9-1	けんか(を)する/します (v)
arm	6-1	うで (n)
art	3-2	びじゅつ　美術 (n)
as a matter of fact	10-4	じつは　実は (adv.)
August	5-2	はちがつ　八月 (n)
aunt or woman quite a bit older than you		
	2-2	おばさん (n)
Australia	4-1	おーすとらりあ　オーストラリア (n)
Australian	4-1	おーすとらりあじん　オーストラリア人 (n)
B		
backpack	2-4	ばっくばっく　バックパック (n)
bad	8-2	わるい　悪い (い adj.)
bag, satchel	2-4	かばん　鞄 (n)
bakery	4-3	ぱんやさん　パン屋さん (n)
(ballpoint) pen	2-4	ぼーるぺん　ボールペン (n)
breakfast	2-5	あさごはん　朝ご飯 (n)
baseball	7-1	やきゅう　野球 (n)
baseball team	3-3	やきゅうぶ　野球部 (n)
basketball team	3-3	ばすけぶ　バスケ部 (n)
(to) be born	5-2	うまれる/うまれます　生まれる/生まれます(生まれて) (v)
(to) be fat	6-2	ふとっています　太っています (v)
before, front, in front	5-1	まえ　前 (adv.)
(to) be hurt, get wounded	6-3	けが(を) する/します　怪我 (を)する/します (v)
(to) be skinny	6-2	やせて います　痩せて います (v)
beach	8-1	びーち　ビーチ (n)
bean curd (tofu)	1-1	とうふ　豆腐 (n)

English	Location	Japanese
beautiful	8-1	うつくしい　美しい (い adj.)
because of that	4-4	だから (conj.)
become clear (weather)	10-1	はれる/はれます　晴れる/晴れます (v)
become cloudy	10-1	くもる/くもります　曇もる/曇ります (v)
(Let's) begin./ (to) begin	1-1	はじめましょう。始めましょう。(exp.)
(to) begin	5-2	はじめる/はじめます　始める/始めます (始めまして) (v)
Benkei (famous samurai name)	6-1	べんけい　弁慶 (proper name)
best regards, please treat me favorably		
	1-3	どうぞ　よろしく (exp.)
best regards, please treat me favorably (polite)		
	1-3	よろしく　おねがいします　よろしくお願いします (exp.)
big, large	3-1	おおきい　大きい (adj.)
biology	3-2	せいぶつがく　生物学 (n)
birthday	5-2	たんじょうび　誕生日 (n)
black	7-4	くろ　黒 (n)
blackboard	2-4	こくばん　黒板 (n)
black-colored	8-2	くろい　黒い (い adj.)
blond (hair)	7-4	きんぱつ　金髪 (n)
blue	7-4	あお　青 (n)
blue-colored	8-2	あおい　青い (い adj.)
bookstore	4-3	ほんやさん　本屋さん (n)
boring	8-1	つまらない (い adj.)
box	8-1	はこ (n)
boy	6-4	おとこのこ　男の子 (n)
brass band	3-3	ぶらすばんど　ブラスバンド (n)
bread	4-3	ぱん　パン (n)
bright; light	9-3	あかるい　明るい (い adj.)
(to) bring someone	10-5	つれて　くる/きます　連れて来る/来ます (v)
(to) bring something	10-5	もって　くる/きます　持って来る/来ます (v)
brown (hair)	7-4	ちゃぱつ　茶髪 (n)
busy	5-4	いそがしい　忙しい (い adj.)
but	3-4	でも (part./conj.)
(to) buy	9-1	かう/かいます　買う/買います(買って) (v)
by the way	4-1	ところで (exp./conj.)
bye-bye	1-5	ばいばい　バイバイ (exp.)
C		
cake	9-4	けーき　ケーキ (n)
Call an ambulance!	6-3	きゅうきゅうしゃを　よんで　救急車を呼んで (exp.)
calm, peaceful	8-4	おだやか (な adj.)
Canada	4-1	かなだ　カナダ (n)
Canadian	4-1	かなだじん　カナダ人 (n)
candy, rain	2-3	あめ (n)
capital of Japan	1-1	とうきょう　東京 (n)

English	Location	Japanese
car, vehicle	4-3	くるま　車 (n)
castle	10-1	しろ　城 (n)
cat	2-1	ねこ　猫 (n)
catch a cold	6-3	かぜ(を) ひく/ひきます　風邪(を) ひく/ひきます (v)
cellular phone	3-1	けいたい (でんわ)　けいたい(電話) (n)
chalk	2-4	ちょーく　チョーク (n)
change (cash)	9-2	おつり (n)
cherry blossom viewing, flower viewing	10-5	はなみ　花見 (n)
cherry tree/blossom	10-5	さくら　桜 (n)
children	8-2	こどもたち　子供達 (n)
China	4-1	ちゅうごく　中国 (n)
Chinese	4-2	ちゅごくご　中国語 (n)
Chinese (person)	4-1	ちゅうごくじん　中国人 (n)
chopsticks	1-5	おはし　お箸 (n)
chorus; choir	3-3	がっしょう　合唱 (n)
class	3-2	くらす　クラス (n)
class	3-2	じゅぎょう　授業 (n)
classroom	3-2	きょうしつ　教室 (n)
clean	8-1	きれい (な adj.)
clear (skies)	10-1	はれ　晴れ (n)
Close/Shut (it) please.	1-3	とじてください。閉じて下さい。(exp.)
(to) close; shut (doors/windows)	3-4	しめる/しめます　閉める/閉めます (閉めて) (v)
(to) close; shut (bound paper objects)	1-3	とじて/とじます　閉じる/閉じます (閉じて) (v)
clothes	6-4	ふく　服 (n)
clothes, Western clothes	6-4	ようふく　洋服 (n)
cloudy	10-1	くもり　曇り (n)
club activity	3-3	ぶかつ　部活 (n)
cold (a)	6-3	かぜ　風邪 (n)
cold (weather)	3-4	さむい　寒い (い adj.)
college/university student	3-1	だいがくせい　大学生 (n)
college/university	3-1	だいがく　大学 (n)
color	7-4	いろ　色 (n)
(to) come in, go in, enter	6-1	はいる/はいります　入る/入ります (入って) (v)
(to) come	4-4	くる/きます　来る/来ます (来て) (v)
computer lab	3-3	こんぴゅーたーらぼ　コンピューターラボ (n)
cooked rice, a meal	1-5	ごはん　ご飯 (n)
cooking	7-1	りょうり　料理 (n)
cool	7-5	かっこいい (い adj.)
cool (weather)	3-4	すずしい　涼しい (い adj.)
crab	8-3	かに (n)
culture	6-5	ぶんか　文化 (n)
cunning	8-1	ずるい (い adj.)
cute	8-1	かわいい (い adj.)

D

English	Location	Japanese
dancing	7-1	おどり　踊り (n)
dangerous	8-1	あぶない　危ない (い adj.)
dark	9-3	くらい　暗い (い adj.)
daytime, noon	2-5	ひる　昼 (n)
December	5-2	じゅうにがつ　十二月 (n)
delicious	8-1	おいしい　美味しい (い adj.)
difficult	3-2	むずかしい　難しい (い adj.)
(to) dine; (to) have a meal	9-1	しょくじ(を) する/します食事(を) する/します (v)
dinner, evening meal	2-5	ばんごはん　晩ご飯 (n)
dirty, messy	8-1	きたない　汚い (い adj.)
dislike a lot, hate	7-2	だいきらい　大嫌い (な adj.)
dislike	7-2	きらい　嫌い (な adj.)
(to) do	5-1	する/します (して) (v)
(to) do	7-3	やる/やります (やって) (v)
(to) do homework	9-1	しゅくだい(を)　する/します　宿題(を) する/します (v)
(to) do one's best	7-3	がんばる/がんばります　頑張る/頑張ります (頑張って) (v)

English	Location	Japanese
doctor	6-3	いしゃ　医者 (n)
dog	2-1	いぬ　犬 (n)
Don't be ridiculous! Not a chance! My pleasure	9-4	とんでもない (exp.)
Don't overexert.	6-3	むりしないで　ください　無理しないで 下さい (exp.)
dress (a)	6-4	どれす　ドレス (n)
(to) drink	4-3	のむ/のみます　飲む/飲みます (飲んで) (v)
drink(s)	4-3	のみもの　飲み物 (n)
Dutch language	4-2	おらんだご　オランダ語 (n)
Dutch person	4-1	おらんだじん　オランダ人 (n)

E

English	Location	Japanese
ear	6-1	みみ　耳 (n)
earring	6-4	いやりんぐ　イヤリング (n)
earthquake	10-1	じしん　地震 (n)
(to) eat	4-3	たべる/たべます　食べる/食べます (食べて) (v)
eating	7-1	たべること　食べる事 (n)
economics	3-3	けいざい　経済 (n)
egg	1-5	たまご　卵 (n)
eight	2-1	はち　八 (n)
eight (things)	2-4	やっつ　八つ (n)
eight cylindrical objects	9-2	はちほん/はっぽん　八本 (n)
eight minutes	3-2	はちふん/はっぷん　八分 (n)
eight o'clock	3-2	はちじ　八時 (n)
eight pages, page eight	4-2	はちぺーじ/はっぺーじ　ハページ (n)
eight people	2-1	はちにん　八人 (n)
eight sheets	4-2	はちまい　八枚 (n)
eight thousand	9-1	はっせん　八千 (n)
eight times, eight degrees	10-1	はちど　八度 (n)
eight volumes	9-2	はっさつ　八冊 (n)
eighteen	2-2	じゅうはち　十八 (n)
eighteenth (day of the month)	5-3	じゅうはちにち　十八日 (n)
eighth (day of the month)	5-3	ようか　八日 (n)
eighth grader	3-1	ちゅうがくにねんせい　中学二年生 (n)
eighty	2-2	はちじゅう　八十 (n)
eighty thousand	9-1	はちまん　八万 (n)
elementary school	3-1	しょうがっこう　小学校 (n)
elementary school student	3-1	しょうがくせい　小学生 (n)
eleven	2-2	じゅういち　十一 (n)
eleven o'clock	3-2	じゅういちじ　十一時 (n)
eleventh (day of the month)	5-3	じゅういちにち　十一日 (n)
eleventh grader	3-1	こうこうにねんせい　高校二年生 (n)
e-mail	5-1	でんしめーる　電子メール (n)
England	4-1	いぎりす　イギリス (n)
English (person)	4-1	いぎりすじん　イギリス人 (n)
English descent	4-1	いぎりすけい　イギリス系 (n)
English language	3-2	えいご　英語 (n)
eraser	2-4	けしごむ　消しゴム (n)
essay	3-2	さくぶん　作文 (n)
evening	2-5	ばん　晩 (n)
every day	3-2	まいにち　毎日 (n)
every month	5-4	まいつき　毎月 (n)
every week	5-4	まいしゅう　毎週 (n)
every year	5-4	まいねん/まいとし　毎年 (n)
everyone (polite)	3-1	みなさん　皆さん (n)
everyone, all	3-1	みんな　皆 (pron.)
(to) exist (animate beings)	2-1	いる/います (v)
(to) exist (inanimate things)	2-1	ある/あります (v)
experience	6-5	けいけん　経験 (n)
eye	6-1	め　目 (n)
eyeglasses	6-4	めがね　眼鏡 (n)

F

English	Location	Japanese
face	6-1	かお　顔 (n)
fall/autumn	10-1	あき　秋 (n)
family (my)	2-1	かぞく　家族 (n)
family consumer science	3-2	かていか　家庭科 (n)
famous	6-1	ゆうめい　有名 (な adj.)
far, distant	6-1	とおい　遠い (い adj.)

English	Location	Japanese
fashionable	6-2	おしゃれ (な adj.)
father (someone else's)	2-2	おとうさん　お父さん (n)
father, dad	1-4	ちち　父 (n)
February	5-2	にがつ　二月 (n)
festival	5-1	まつり　祭り (n)
fever	6-3	ねつ　熱 (n)
fifteen	2-2	じゅうご　十五 (n)
fifteenth (day of the month)	5-3	じゅうごにち　十五日 (n)
fifth (day of the month)	5-3	いつか　五日 (n)
fifth period	3-3	ごじかんめ　五時間目 (n)
fifty	2-2	ごじゅう　五十 (n)
fifty thousand	9-1	ごまん　五万 (n)
finger(s)	6-1	ゆび　指 (n)
(to) finish	5-2	おわる/おわります　終わる/終わります (終わって) (v)
first (day of the month)	5-3	ついたち　一日 (n)
first period	3-3	いちじかんめ　一時間目 (n)
first year student	3-1	いちねんせい　一年生 (n)
fish	10-1	さかな　魚 (n)
five	2-1	ご　五 (n)
five (things)	2-4	いつつ　五つ (n)
five cylindrical objects	9-2	ごほん　五本 (n)
five minutes	3-2	ごふん　五分 (n)
five o'clock	3-2	ごじ　五時 (n)
five people	2-1	ごにん　五人 (n)
five sheets, five pages	4-2	ごまい　五枚 (n)
five thousand	9-1	ごせん　五千 (n)
five times, five degrees (temp.)	10-1	ごど　五度 (n)
five volumes	9-2	ごさつ　五冊 (n)
Flower	10-1	はな　花 (n)
flower arranging	7-1	いけばな　生け花 (n)
food(s)	4-3	たべもの　食べ物 (n)
foolish; silly	8-1	ばかばかしい (い adj.)
foreign country	4-1	がいこく　外国 (n)
foreigner	4-1	がいこくじん　外国人 (n)
forty	2-2	よんじゅう　四十 (n)
forty thousand	9-1	よんまん　四万 (n)
four	2-1	よん/し　四 (n)
four (things)	2-4	よっつ　四つ (n)
four cylindrical objects	9-2	よんほん　四本 (n)
four minutes	3-2	よんぷん　四分 (n)
four o'clock	3-2	よじ　四時 (n)
four pages, page four	4-2	よんぺーじ　四ページ (n)
four people	2-1	よにん　四人 (n)
four sheets	4-2	よんまい　四枚 (n)
four thousand	9-1	よんせん　四千 (n)
four times	10-1	よんど　四度 (n)
four volumes	9-2	よんさつ　四冊 (n)
fourteen	2-2	じゅうよん/じゅうし　十四 (n)
fourteenth (day of the month)	5-3	じゅうよっか　十四日 (n)
fourth (day of the month)	5-3	よっか　四日 (n)
fourth period	3-3	よじかんめ　四時間目 (n)
France	4-1	ふらんす　フランス (n)
free (time)	8-4	ひま (な adj.)
French language	4-2	ふらんすご　フランス語 (n)
Frenchman	4-1	ふらんすじん　フランス人 (n)
Friday	5-1	きんようび　金曜日 (n)
friend	2-2	ともだち　友達 (n)
frog	7-2	かえる　蛙 (n)
from		から (part.)
front, in front, before	5-1	まえ　前 (adv.)
fun, enjoyable	3-2	たのしい　楽しい (い adj.)
futon	6-3	ふとん　布団 (n)

G

English	Location	Japanese
gagaku, ancient Japanese court music	7-5	ががく　雅楽 (n)
garden	10-1	にわ　庭 (n)
German (language)	4-2	どいつご　ドイツ語 (n)
German (person)	4-1	どいつじん　ドイツ人 (n)
Germany	4-1	どいつ　ドイツ (n)

English	Location	Japanese
(to) get fat	6-2	ふとる/ふとります　太る/太ります (太って) (v)
girl	6-4	おんなのこ　女の子 (n)
(to) give	9-4	あげる/あげます　上げる/上げます (上げて) (v)
(to) give	9-5	くれる/くれます (くれて) (v)
glad; happy	8-1	うれしい　嬉しい (い adj.)
go	4-4	いく/いきます　行く/行きます (行って) (v)
(to) go on a date	9-1	でーと(を) する/します　デート(を) する/します (v)
(to) go out, leave, get out	6-1	でる/でます　出る/出ます (出て) (v)
(to) go shopping	9-1	かいもの(を) する/します　買い物(を) する/します (v)
gold	7-4	きんいろ　金色 (n)
golf	7-1	ごるふ　ゴルフ (n)
goodbye	1-5	さようなら (exp.)
good evening	1-5	こんばんは　今晩は (exp.)
good for your health	6-3	けんこうに いい です　健康に いい です (exp.)
good morning (formal)	1-5	おはようございます (exp.)
good morning (informal)	1-5	おはよう (exp.)
good night (formal)	1-5	おやすみ なさい　お休み なさい (exp.)
good night (informal)	1-5	おやすみ　お休み (exp.)
grandfather (my)	2-1	そふ　祖父 (n)
grandfather (someone else's)	2-2	おじいさん (n)
grandmother (my)	2-1	そぼ　祖母 (n)
grandmother (someone else's)	2-2	おばあさん (n)
green	7-4	みどり　緑 (n)
gray	7-4	ぐれい　グレイ (n)
gray, ash-colored	7-4	はいいろ　灰色 (n)
gray (mouse colored)	7-4	ねずみいろ　鼠色 (n)
guitar	7-1	ぎたー　ギター (n)
gymnasium	3-3	たいいくかん　体育館 (n)

H

English	Location	Japanese
haiku (poem)	10-1	はいく　俳句 (n)
hair	6-1	かみ(のけ)　髪(の毛) (n)
half hour	3-2	はん　半 (n)
hand	6-1	て　手 (n)
handshake	4-2	あくしゅ (n)
handsome, good-looking	6-4	はんさむ　ハンサム (な adj.)
hat/cap	2-3	ぼうし (n)
have a full stomach	10-4	おなかが いっぱい　お腹が一杯 (exp.)
(to) have, hold, carry	6-1	もつ/もちます　持つ/持ちます (持って) (v)
he; boyfriend	7-4	かれ　彼 (pron.)
head	6-1	あたま　頭 (n)
health (class)	3-2	ほけんたいいく　保健体育 (n)
health	6-3	けんこう　健康 (n)
healthy, energetic	1-5	げんき　元気 (n/な adj.)
heart (not one's physical heart); soul	6-1	こころ　心 (n)
heavy rain	10-1	おおあめ　大雨 (n)
height, stature	6-1	せ/せい　背 (n)
hello	1-5	こんにちは　今日は (exp.)
(to) help, to assist	4-1	てつだう/てつだいます　手伝う/手伝います (手伝って) (v)
helping verb/linking verb used similarly to "is" or "am"	1-3	です (copula)
here	2-4	ここ (pron.)
high school student	3-1	こうこうせい　高校生 (n)
high school	3-1	こうこう　高校 (n)
high, tall, expensive	6-1	たかい　高い (い adj.)
history	3-2	れきし　歴史 (n)
hobby	7-1	しゅみ　趣味 (n)
Holland	4-1	おらんだ　オランダ (n)
homeroom	3-2	ほーむるーむ　ホームルーム (n)
homework	3-2	しゅくだい　宿題 (n)
horse	8-2	うま　馬 (n)
horseback riding	7-1	じょうば　乗馬 (n)
hospital	6-3	びょういん　病院 (n)
hot (weather)	3-4	あつい　暑い (い adj.)

English	Location	Japanese
house, home	2-2	いえ/うち　家 (n)
how about it?	9-2	どう　ですか (exp.)
How do you do?	1-3	はじめまして　初めまして (exp.)
how many (things)?	2-4	いくつ (inter.)
how many cylindrical objects	9-2	なんぼん　何本 (inter.)
how many minutes	3-2	なんぷん　何分 (inter.)
how many pages, what page	4-2	なんぺーじ　何ページ (inter.)
how many people	2-1	なんにん　何人 (inter.)
how many sheets	4-2	なんまい　何枚 (inter.)
how many thousands	9-1	なんぜん　何千 (inter.)
how many times	10-1	なんど　何度 (inter.)
how many volumes	9-2	なんさつ　何冊 (inter.)
how much?	9-2	いくら (inter.)
How was it?	6-5	どう　でしたか。(exp.)
how	3-5	どう (inter.)
hunger, mimetic expression for	2-5	ペコペコ
humid (weather)	3-4	むしあつい　蒸し暑い (い adj.)

I

English	Location	Japanese
I, me (used by males only)	1-1	ぼく　僕 (pron.)
I, me	1-3	わたし　私 (pron.)
I'm home	1-5	ただいま (exp.)
illness, sickness	6-3	びょうき　病気 (n)
important	5-1	だいじ　大事 (な adj.)
in all; total; all together	9-2	ぜんぶで　全部で (exp.)
Indonesia	4-1	いんどねしあ　インドネシア (n)
Indonesian (language)	4-2	いんどねしあご　インドネシア語 (n)
Indonesian (person)	4-1	いんどねしあじん　インドネシア人 (n)
interesting	8-2	おもしろい　面白い (い adj.)
irritating	8-1	じれったい (い adj.)
is bad	3-4	だめ (な adj.)
is not right, incorrect	1-4	ちがう/ちがいます　違う/違います (違って) (v)
island	8-3	しま　島 (n)
Italian (person)	4-1	いたりあじん　イタリア人 (n)
Italian language	4-2	いたりあご　イタリア語 (n)
Italy	4-1	いたりあ　イタリア (n)

J

English	Location	Japanese
jacket	6-4	じゃけっと　ジャケット (n)
January	5-2	いちがつ　一月 (n)
Japan	1-1	にほん　日本 (n)
Japanese comics	2-4	まんが　漫画 (n)
Japanese descent	4-1	にっけいじん　日系人 (n)
Japanese history	3-2	にほんし　日本史 (n)
Japanese language	1-1	にほんご　日本語 (n)
Japanese person	4-1	にほんじん　日本人 (n)
Japanese sumo wrestling	1-1	すもう　相撲 (n)
Japanese traditional sweets	9-5	おかし　(お)菓子 (n)
jeans	6-4	じーんず　ジーンズ (n)
jogging	7-1	じょぎんぐ　ジョギング (n)
joke	7-2	じょうだん　冗談 (n)
judo	3-3	じゅうどう　柔道 (n)
juice	6-3	じゅーす　ジュース (n)
July	5-2	しちがつ/なながつ　七月 (n)
June	5-2	ろくがつ　六月 (n)

K

English	Location	Japanese
kabuki theater	7-5	かぶき　歌舞伎 (n)
(to) karaoke (to sing)	9-1	からおけ(を)　する/しますカラオケ(を)する/します (v)
karate (martial art)	1-1	からて　空手 (n)
kendo club	3-3	けんどうぶ　剣道部 (n)
kendo	3-3	けんどう　剣道 (n)
kimono (Japanese traditional clothing)	6-4	きもの　着物 (n)
kindergarten	3-1	ほいくえん　保育園 (n)
knee	6-1	ひざ　膝 (n)
(to) know something/someone	4-2	しる/しります　知る/知ります(知って) (v)
Korean (person)	4-1	かんこくじん　韓国人 (n)
(of) Korean descent	4-1	かんこくけい　韓国系 (n)
Korean language	4-2	かんこくご　韓国語 (n)

L

English	Location	Japanese
large (L) size	9-2	える(L)さいず　Lサイズ (n)
last month	5-4	せんげつ　先月 (n)
last week	5-4	せんしゅう　先週 (n)
last year	5-4	きょねん　去年 (n)
(to) learn	6-5	ならう/ならいます　習う/習います (習って) (v)
leg, foot	6-1	あし　足 (n)
Let's begin.	1-1	はじめましょう　始めましょう (exp.)
Let's go	3-5	いきましょう　行きましょう (v)
library	3-3	としょかん　図書館 (n)
lightning	10-1	かみなり　雷 (n)
like	7-2	すき　好き (な adj.)
(to) listen	1-3	きく/ききます　聞く/聞きます (聞いて) (v)
(to) listen	1-3	きいて　聞いて (v)
little	3-1	すこし　少し (adv.)
little, somewhat	3-2	ちょっと (adv.)
little ... (something is)	4-3	(＿＿は、)ちょっと・・・ (exp.)
(to) live/reside	6-4	すむ/すみます　住む/住みます (住んで) (v)
long	26-1	ながい　長い (い adj.)
long ago	8-2	むかし　昔 (n)
long long ago	8-2	むかしむかし　昔々 (n)
(to) look/see	1-3	みる/みます　見る/見ます (見て) (v)
Look/Watch please.	1-3	みてください　見て下さい。(exp.)
love	7-2	だいすき　大好き (な adj.)
low, short (height)	6-1	ひくい　低い (い adj.)
lunch	2-5	ひるごはん　昼ご飯 (n)
lunch break	3-2	ひるやすみ　昼休み (n)

M

English	Location	Japanese
MP3 player	3-1	えむぴーすりー　ぷれーやー　MP3 プレーヤー (n)
make up	6-4	めいく　メイク (n)
(to) make up; to become friends (again)	9-1	なかなおり(を)　する/します　仲直り(を)する/します (v)
(to) make	10-2	つくる/つくります　作る/作ります(作って) (v)
man, male	6-4	おとこ　男 (n)
many, a lot	3-1	たくさん (n)
March	5-2	さんがつ　三月 (n)
math	3-2	すうがく　数学 (n)
May	5-2	ごがつ　五月 (n)
(to have a) meal	9-1	しょくじ(を)　する/します　食事(を)する/します (v)
medicine	6-3	くすり　薬 (n)
medium (M) size	9-2	えむ(M)さいず　Mサイズ (n)
Mexican descent	4-1	めきしこけい　メキシコ系 (n)
Mexican person	4-1	めきしこじん　メキシコ人 (n)
Mexican tacos	2-5	たこす　タコス (n)
Mexico	4-1	めきしこ　メキシコ (n)
middle school	3-2	ちゅうがっこう　中学校 (n)
middle school student	3-1	ちゅうがくせい　中学生 (n)
Monday	5-1	げつようび　月曜日 (n)
more	9-3	もっと (adv.)
moreover; furthermore	7-1	それに (conj.)
morning	2-5	あさ　朝 (n)
mother (someone else's)	2-2	おかあさん　お母さん (n)
mother, mom	1-4	はは　母 (n)
mountain	3-1	やま　山 (n)
mouth	6-1	くち　口 (n)
movie	9-1	えいが　映画 (n)
muscle	6-1	きんにく　筋肉 (n)
music	3-2	おんがく　音楽 (n)
mustache, beard	6-1	ひげ (n)
(my) next youngest brother/sister	2-1	すぐしたの　おとうと/いもうと　すぐ下の　弟/妹 (n)
(my) oldest brother/sister	2-1	いちばんしたの　あに/あね　一番上の　兄/姉 (n)

English	Location	Japanese
(my) second oldest brother/sister		
	2-1	にばんめの　あに/あね　二番目の兄/姉 (n)
(my) youngest brother/sister	2-1	いちばんしたの　おとうと/いもうと　一番下の　弟/妹 (n)
mysterious	8-1	ふしぎ (な adj.)
N		
Nagasaki (city of)	4-1	ながさき　長崎 (n)
name	1-3	なまえ　名前 (n)
nap	6-3	ひるね　昼寝 (n)
(to) nap	6-3	ひるね(を) する/します　昼寝(を) する/します (v)
narrow	8-3	せまい　狭い (い adj.)
national language (Japanese language)		
	3-2	こくご　国語 (n)
neck	6-1	くび　首 (n)
necktie	6-4	ねくたい　ネクタイ (n)
New Zealand	4-1	にゅーじーらんど　ニュージーランド (n)
New Zealander	4-1	にゅーじーらんどじん　ニュージーランド人 (n)
next month	5-4	らいげつ　来月 (n)
next week	5-4	らいしゅう　来週 (n)
next year	5-4	らいねん　来年 (n)
next	3-3	つぎ　次 (n/adv.)
nine	2-1	く/きゅう　九 (n)
nine (things)	2-4	ここのつ　九つ (n)
nine cylindrical objects	9-2	きゅうほん　九本 (n)
nine minutes	3-2	きゅうふん　九分 (n)
nine o'clock	3-2	くじ　九時 (n)
nine pages, page nine	4-2	きゅうぺーじ　九ページ (n)
nine people	2-1	きゅうにん　九人 (n)
nine sheets	4-2	きゅうまい　九枚 (n)
nine thousand	9-1	きゅうせん　九千 (n)
nine times	10-1	きゅうど　九度 (n)
nine volumes	9-2	きゅうさつ　九冊 (n)
nineteen	2-2	じゅうく/じゅうきゅう　十九 (n)
ninth (day of the month)	5-3	ここのか　九日 (n)
ninth grader	3-1	ちゅうがくさんねんせい　中学三年生 (n)
ninety	2-2	きゅうじゅう　九十 (n)
ninety thousand	9-1	きゅうまん　九万 (n)
nineteenth (day of the month)	5-3	じゅうくにち　十九日 (n)
no one	10-2	だれも (exp.)
no	1-4	いいえ
Noh (a type of theater)	7-5	のう　能 (n)
noisy, loud	8-1	うるさい (い adj.)
noon, daytime	2-5	ひる　昼 (n)
nose	6-1	はな　鼻 (n)
not at all	7-4	ぜんぜん　全然 (adv.)
not good at	7-3	へた　下手 (な adj.)
not tasty, not good	8-3	まずい (い adj.)
not very	7-4	あまり (adv.)
not yet	4-3	まだ (adv.)
notebook	2-4	のーと　ノート (n)
November	5-2	じゅういちがつ　十一月 (n)
now	3-2	いま　今 (n/adv.)
nurse	6-3	かんごふ　看護婦 (n)
nursery school	3-1	ようちえん　幼稚園 (n)
O		
ocean; sea	8-1	うみ　海 (n)
October	5-2	じゅうがつ　十月 (n)
octopus	2-5	たこ (n)
of Chinese descent	4-1	ちゅうごくけい　中国系 (n)
of course	10-5	もちろん (exp.)
older brother (my)	2-1	あに　兄 (n)
older brother (someone else's)	2-2	おにいさん　お兄さん (n)
older sister (my)	2-1	あね　姉 (n)
older sister (someone else's)	2-2	おねえさん　お姉さん (n)
one	2-1	いち　一 (n)
one (thing)	2-4	ひとつ　一つ (n)
one cylindrical object	9-2	いっぽん　一本 (n)

English	Location	Japanese
one hundred thousand	9-1	じゅうまん　十万 (n)
one hundred	2-2	ひゃく　百 (n)
one hundred fifty thousand	9-1	じゅうごまん　十五万 (n)
one hundred forty thousand	9-1	じゅうよんまん　十四万 (n)
one hundred ninety thousand	5-2	じゅうきゅうまん　十九万 (n)
one hundred seventy thousand	9-1	じゅうななまん　十七万 (n)
one hundred sixty thousand	9-1	じゅうろくまん　十六万 (n)
one hundred ten thousand	9-1	じゅういちまん　十一万 (n)
one hundred thirty thousand	9-1	じゅうさんまん　十三万 (n)
one hundred twenty thousand	9-1	じゅうにまん　十二万 (n)
one minute	3-2	いっぷん　一分 (n)
one o'clock	3-2	いちじ　一時 (n)
one page/page one	4-2	いちぺーじ/いっぺーじ　一ページ (n)
one person	2-1	ひとり　一人 (n)
one sheet/piece	4-2	いちまい　一枚 (n)
one thousand	9-1	せん　千 (n)
one time	10-1	いちど　一度 (n)
one volume	9-2	いっさつ　一冊 (n)
oops, sorry	8-3	おっと (interj.)
(to) open (book/bound object)	1-3	ひらく/ひらきます　開く/開きます (開いて) (v)
(to) open (door/window)	3-4	あける/あけます　開ける/開けます (開けて) (v)
orange	7-4	おれんじ　オレンジ (n)
orange (colored)	7-4	だいだいいろ　橙色 (n)
orange (colored)	8-2	おれんじ　オレンジ (n)
over there	2-4	あそこ (pron.)
P		
p.m.	3-2	ごご　午後 (n)
page five	4-2	ごぺーじ　五ページ (n)
painful	6-3	いたい　痛い (い adj.)
painting, drawing	9-1	え　絵 (n)
pants, trousers	6-4	ずぼん　ズボン (n)
paper	2-4	かみ　紙 (n)
particle signifying a question	1-4	か (part.)
particle that denotes the sentence topic		
	1-3	は (part.)
particle used after a location or time word		
	1-5	に (part.)
past, after	3-2	～すぎ
pen	2-4	ぺん　ペン (n)
pencil	2-4	えんぴつ　鉛筆 (n)
person	2-2	ひと　人 (n)
photograph	2-1	しゃしん　写真 (n)
physical education	3-2	たいいく　体育 (n)
physics	3-2	ぶつりがく　物理学 (n)
piano	7-1	ぴあの　ピアノ (n)
pickled vegetables	8-3	つけもの　漬け物 (n)
Ping-Pong club	3-3	たっきゅうぶ　たっきゅう部 (n)
pink	7-4	ぴんく　ピンク (n)
(to) play	10-3	あそぶ/あそびます　遊ぶ/遊びます (遊んで) (v)
(to) play (a stringed instrument)	7-1	ひく/ひきます　弾く/弾きます (弾いて) (v)
(to) play basketball	9-1	ばすけ(を) する/します　バスケ(を) する/します (v)
(to) play guitar	7-1	ぎたー(を)　ひく/ひきます　ギター(を)　弾く/弾きます (v)
(to) play soccer	9-1	さっかー(を)　する/します　サッカー(を)　する/します (v)
(to) play video games	9-1	びでおげーむ(を)　する/しますビデオゲーム(を)　する/します (v)
playing cards; card game	7-1	とらんぷ　トランプ (n)
polite for よろしく　お願いします		
	1-3	どうぞ よろしく おねがいします　どうぞ よろしく お願いします (exp.)
Portugal	4-1	ぽるとがる　ポルトガル (n)
Portuguese (language)	4-2	ぽるとがるご　ポルトガル語 (n)
Portuguese (person)	4-1	ぽるとがるじん　ポルトガル人 (n)
(to) precipitate	10-1	ふる/ふります　降る/降ります (降って) (v)

English	Location	Japanese
present; a gift	9-4	ぷれぜんと　プレゼント (n)
pretty	8-1	きれい　(な adj.)
psychology	3-2	しんりがく　心理学 (n)
purple	7-4	むらさき　紫 (n)
(to) put into	6-1	いれる/いれます　入れる/入れます（入れて）(v)

Q

English	Location	Japanese
quickly	3-5	はやく　速く (adv.)
quiet	6-1	しずか　静か (な adj.)

R

English	Location	Japanese
rain	10-1	あめ　雨 (n)
rainy season	10-1	つゆ　梅雨 (n)
rat, mouse	7-2	ねずみ (n)
(to) read	1-3	よむ/よみます　読む/読みます（読んで）(v)
reading	7-1	どくしょ　読書 (n)
really, indeed, truly	8-4	まったく　全く (adv.)
(to) receive	9-4	もらう/もらいます（もらって）(v)
(to) receive (very polite, lit.: I will receive.)	9-2	いただく/いただきます（いただいて）(v)
red	7-4	あか　赤 (n)
red-colored	8-2	あかい　赤い (い adj.)
regrettably, unluckliy	9-3	ざんねん　残念(な)(n/な adj.)
(to) return with someone	10-5	つれて　かえる/かえります　連れて　帰る/帰ります (v)
(to) return with something	10-5	もって　かえる/かえります　持って　帰る/帰ります (v)
(to) return	4-4	かえる/かえります　帰る/帰ります（帰って）(v)
rice crackers	9-4	せんべい　煎餅 (n)
rock and roll (music)	10-5	ろっくんろーる　ロックンロール (n)
room (a)	1-5	へや　部屋 (n)
Russia	4-1	ろしあ　ロシア (n)
Russian (language)	4-2	ろしあご　ロシア語 (n)

S

English	Location	Japanese
sad	6-1	かなしい　悲しい (い adj.)
samurai	6-1	さむらい　侍 (n)
Saturday	5-1	どようび　土曜日 (n)
Say hello to . . .	6-5	に　よろしく (exp.)
(to) say	4-1	いう/いいます　言う/言います（言って）(v)
scary	8-1	こわい (い adj.)
schedule	3-2	すけじゅーる　スケジュール (n)
school	3-1	がっこう　学校 (n)
school subject	3-2	かもく　科目 (n)
science	3-2	かがく　科学 (n)
score, grade	3-3	せいせき　成績 (n)
(to) search	9-3	さがす/さがします　探す/探します（探して）(v)
season	10-1	きせつ　季節 (n)
second (day of the month)	5-3	ふつか　二日 (n)
second period	3-3	にじかんめ　二時間目 (n)
second year student	3-1	にねんせい　二年生 (n)
secret	6-1	ひみつ　秘密 (n)
(to) see if you can do (something); to try to do (something)	7-3	やってみる/やってみます（やってみて）(v)
see you later (formal)	1-5	では　また (exp.)
see you later (informal)	1-5	じゃあ　また (exp.)
selfish	8-1	わがまま (な adj.)
(to) sell	9-1	うる/うります　売る/売ります（売って）(v)
(to) send	5-1	おくる/おくります　送る/送ります（送って）(v)
separate	9-2	べつ　別 (n/な adj.)
separately; individually	9-2	べつべつ　別々 (n/な adj.)
September	5-2	くがつ　九月 (n)
seven	2-1	しち/なな　七 (n)
seven (things)	2-4	ななつ　七つ (n)
seven cylindrical objects	9-2	ななほん　七本 (n)
seven minutes	3-2	ななふん　七分 (n)
seven o'clock	3-2	しちじ/ななじ　七時 (n)

English	Location	Japanese
seven pages, page seven	4-2	ななぺーじ/しちぺーじ　七ページ (n)
seven people	2-1	しちにん/なKにK　七人 (n)
seven sheets	4-2	ななまい/しちまい　七枚 (n)
seven thousand	9-1	ななせん　七千 (n)
seven times	10-1	ななど　七度 (n)
seven volumes	9-2	ななさつ　七冊 (n)
seventeen	2-2	じゅうなな/じゅうしち　十七 (n)
seventeenth (day of the month)	5-3	じゅうしちにち　十七日 (n)
seventh (day of the month)	5-3	なのか　七日 (n)
seventh grader	3-1	ちゅうがくいちねんせい　中学一年生 (n)
seventy	2-2	ななじゅう　七十 (n)
seventy thousand	9-1	ななまん　七万 (n)
(to) shampoo	9-1	しゃんぷー(を)　する/します　シャンプー(を)　する/します (v)
she; girlfriend	7-4	かのじょ　彼女 (pron.)
Shinto shrine gate	3-5	とりい　鳥居 (n)
shirt	6-4	しゃつ　シャツ (n)
shoes	6-4	くつ　靴 (n)
shop; store	9-1	みせ　店 (n)
shopkeeper; clerk	9-2	てんいん　店員 (n)
shopping	9-1	かいもの　買い物 (n)
short (length)	8-1	みじかい　短い (い adj.)
shoulder	6-1	かた　肩 (n)
shrine	3-3	じんじゃ　神社 (n)
siblings	2-1	きょうだい　兄弟 (n)
sick, feel bad	6-3	ぐあいが　わるい　具合が　悪い (exp.)
signature	4-2	さいん　サイン (n)
silver	7-4	ぎんいろ　銀色 (n)
simple	6-4	しんぷる　シンプル (な adj.)
(to) sing	7-1	うたう/うたいます　歌う/歌います（歌って）(v)
singing	7-1	うたうこと　歌う事 (n)
(to) sit	1-3	すわる/すわります　座る/座ります（座って）(v)
six	2-1	ろく　六 (n)
six (things)	2-4	むっつ　六つ (n)
six cylindrical objects	9-2	ろっぽん　六本 (n)
six minutes	3-2	ろっぷん　六分 (n)
six o'clock	3-2	ろくじ　六時 (n)
six pages, page six	4-2	ろくぺーじ　六ページ (n)
six people	2-1	ろくにん　六人 (n)
six sheets	4-2	ろくまい　六枚 (n)
six thousand	9-1	ろくせん　六千 (n)
six times	10-1	ろくど　六度 (n)
six volumes	9-2	ろくさつ　六冊 (n)
sixteen	2-2	じゅうろく　十六 (n)
sixteenth (day of the month)	5-3	じゅうろくにち　十六日 (n)
sixth (day of the month)	5-3	むいか　六日 (n)
sixth period	3-3	ろくじかんめ　六時間目 (n)
sixty	2-2	ろくじゅう　六十 (n)
sixty thousand	9-1	ろくまん　六万 (n)
(to) skateboard	7-1	すけぼー(を)　する　スケボー(を)　する (v)
skiing	7-1	すきー　スキー (n)
skilled at	7-3	とくい　得意 (な adj.)
skillful	7-3	じょうず　上手 (な adj.)
skirt	6-4	すかーと　スカート (n)
(to) sleep	5-1	ねる/ねます　寝る/寝ます（寝て）(v)
sleeping	7-1	ねること　寝る事 (n)
slim, stylish	6-2	すまーと　スマート (な adj.)
small (S) size	9-2	えす(S)さいず　Sサイズ (n)
small test, quiz	3-2	しょうてすと　小テスト (n)
small	3-1	ちいさい　小さい (い adj.)
snow	10-1	ゆき　雪 (n)
so so, not bad, moderate	6-2	まあまあ (adv.)
socks	6-4	くつした　靴下 (n)
someone else's family		ごかぞく　ご家族 (n)
something	10-3	なにか　何か
sometimes	3-2	ときどき　時々 (n/adv.)
song	7-1	うた　歌 (n)
South Korea	4-1	かんこく　韓国 (n)
soy sauce	1-5	しょうゆ　醤油 (n)
Spain	4-1	すぺいん　スペイン (n)

English	Location	Japanese
Spaniard	4-1	すぺいんじん　スペイン人 (n)
Spanish	4-2	すぺいんご　スペイン語 (n)
(to) speak	4-2	はなす/はなします　話す/話します (話して) (v)
special	9-2	とくべつ　特別 (n/な adj.)
sports	7-1	すぽーつ　スポーツ (n)
spring	10-1	はる　春 (n)
Stand please.	1-3	たってください　立って下さい。(exp.)
(to) stand	1-3	たつ/たちます　立つ/立ちます (立って) (v)
step-	2-1	ぎりの〜
sticky rice cake	6-4	もち　餅 (n)
stomach	6-1	おなか (n)
stone, rock	10-1	いし　石 (n)
(to) stop	8-2	やめる/やめます (やめて) (v)
strict	8-1	きびしい (い adj.)
strong	6-1	つよい　強い (い adj.)
student	3-1	がくせい　学生, せいと　生徒 (n)
(to) study	5-2	べんきょう(を) する/します　勉強する/勉強(を) します (v)
suit	6-4	すーつ　スーツ (n)
summer	10-1	なつ　夏 (n)
Sunday	5-1	にちようび　日曜日 (n)
sushi	1-1	すし　寿司 (n)
(to) swim	7-1	およぐ/およぎます　泳ぐ/泳ぎます (泳いで) (v)
swimming	7-1	およぐこと　泳ぐ事 (n)
swimming	7-1	すいえい　水泳 (n)
T		
Taiwan	4-1	たいわん　台湾 (n)
Taiwanese (person)	4-1	たいわんじん　台湾人 (n)
(to) take (it) out	1-3	だす/だします　出す/出します (出して) (v)
(to) take a photo	4-2	しゃしん(を) とる/とります 写真(を) 撮る/撮ります (撮って) (v)
(to) take a shower	9-1	しゃわー(を)　する/します シャワー(を)　する/します (v)
(to) take a trip; (to) travel	9-1	りょこう(を)する/します　旅行(を) する/します (旅行(を) して) (v)
(to) take a walk	5-4	さんぽ(を) する/します　散歩(を) する/します (v)
(to) take medicine	6-3	くすり(を) のむ/のみます　薬(を) 飲む/飲みます (v)
(to) take someone	10-5	つれて いく/いきます　連れて 行く/行きます (v)
(to) take something	10-5	もって いく/いきます　持って 行く/行きます (v)
Taro (male name)	1-4	たろう　太郎 (n)
tasteful, subtle	6-2	しぶい　渋い (い adj.)
tea ceremony	7-1	さどう/ちゃどう　茶道 (n)
teacher	1-1	せんせい　先生 (n)
telephone	2-1	でんわ　電話 (n)
(to) telephone	9-1	でんわ(を) する/します　電話(を) する/します (v)
temple	3-3	てら　寺 (n)
ten	2-1	じゅう　十 (n)
ten (things)	2-4	とお　十 (n)
ten cylindrical objects	9-2	じゅっぽん　十本 (n)
ten minutes	3-2	じゅっぷん/じっぷん　十分 (n)
ten o'clock	3-2	じゅうじ　十時 (n)
ten pages, page ten	4-2	じゅっぺーじ　十ページ (n)
ten people	2-1	じゅうにん　十人 (n)
ten sheets	4-2	じゅうまい　十枚 (n)
ten thousand	9-1	いちまん　一万 (n)
ten thousand	9-1	まん　万 (n)
ten times, ten degrees (temp.)	10-1	じゅうど　十度 (n)
ten volumes	9-2	じゅっさつ　十冊 (n)
tenth (day of the month)	5-3	とおか　十日 (n)
tenth grader	3-1	こうこういちねんせい　高校一年生 (n)
terrible	8-1	ひどい (い adj.)
test	3-2	てすと　テスト (n)
test, exam	3-2	しけん　試験 (n)

English	Location	Japanese
thanks	2-3	ありがとう (exp.)
thank you	2-3	どうもありがとう (exp.)
that (one)	1-5	それ (pron.)
that (over there)	1-5	あれ (adj.)
that (thing)	2-3	その
that (thing) over there	2-3	あの
they, them	8-2	かれら　彼ら (pron.)
then; and then	7-1	そして (conj.)
then; and then	7-1	それから (conj.)
there	2-4	そこ (pron.)
thing	4-3	もの　物 (n)
(to) think	7-2	おもう/おもいます　思う/思います (思って) (v)
third (day of the month)	5-3	みっか　三日 (n)
third period	3-3	さんじかんめ　三間目 (n)
third year student	3-1	さんねんせい　三年生 (n)
thirteen	2-2	じゅうさん　十三 (n)
thirteenth (day of the month)	5-3	じゅうさんにち　十三日 (n)
thirtieth (day of the month)	5-3	さんじゅうにち　三十日 (n)
thirty	2-2	さんじゅう　三十 (n)
thirty thousand	9-1	さんまん　三万 (n)
thirty-first (day of the month)	5-3	さんじゅういちにち　三十一日 (n)
this (one)	1-5	これ (pron.)
this (thing)	2-3	この
this month	5-4	こんげつ　今月 (n)
this person (polite)	1-4	こちら (pron.)
this week	5-4	こんしゅう　今週 (n)
this year	5-4	ことし　今年 (n)
three	2-1	さん　三 (n)
three (things)	2-4	みっつ　三つ (n)
three cylindrical objects	9-2	さんぼん　三本 (n)
three minutes	3-2	さんぷん　三分 (n)
three o'clock	3-2	さんじ　三時 (n)
three pages, page three	4-2	さんぺーじ　三ページ (n)
three people	2-1	さんにん　三人 (n)
three sheets	4-2	さんまい　三枚 (n)
three thousand	9-1	さんぜん　三千 (n)
three times, three degrees	10-1	さんど　三度 (n)
three volumes	9-2	さんさつ　三冊 (n)
throat	6-1	のど　咽喉 (n)
Thursday	5-1	もくようび　木曜日 (n)
tidal wave	1-1	つなみ　津波 (n)
time after school	3-3	ほうかご　放課後 (n/adv.)
today	3-2	きょう　今日 (n)
tomorrow	3-2	あした　明日 (n)
tornado	10-1	たつまき　竜巻 (n)
track and field club	3-3	りくじょうぶ　陸上部 (n)
trip; travel	7-1	りょこう　旅行 (n)
truth, reality	10-4	ほんとう　本当 (n)
T-shirt	2-3	てぃーしゃつ　Tシャツ (n)
Tuesday	5-1	かようび　火曜日 (n)
turtle	8-2	かめ　亀 (n)
twelfth (day of the month)	5-3	じゅうににち　十二日 (n)
twelfth grader	3-1	こうこうさんねんせい　高校三年生 (n)
twelve o'clock	3-2	じゅうにじ　十二時 (n)
twelve	2-2	じゅうに　十二 (n)
twentieth (day of the month)	5-3	はつか　二十日 (n)
twenty	2-2	にじゅう　二十 (n)
twenty minutes	3-2	にじゅっぷん　二十分 (n)
twenty-eighth (day of the month)	5-3	にじゅうはちにち　二十八日 (n)
twenty-fifth (day of the month)	5-3	にじゅうごにち　二十五日 (n)
twenty-first (day of the month)	5-3	にじゅういちにち　二十一日 (n)
twenty-fourth (day of the month)	5-3	にじゅうよっか　二十四日 (n)
twenty-ninth (of the month)	5-3	にじゅうくにち　二十九日 (n)
twenty-second (day of the month)	5-3	にじゅうににち　二十二日 (n)
twenty-seventh (day of the month)	5-3	にじゅうしちにち　二十七日 (n)
twenty-sixth (day of the month)	5-3	にじゅうろくにち　二十六日 (n)
twenty-third (day of the month)	5-3	にじゅうさんにち　二十三日 (n)

English	Location	Japanese
twenty thousand	9-1	にまん　二万 (n)
twenty-one	2-2	にじゅういち　二十一 (n)
two	2-1	に　二 (n)
two (things)	2-4	ふたつ　二つ (n)
two cylindrical objects	9-2	にほん　二本 (n)
two hundred ten thousand	9-1	にじゅういちまん　二十一万 (n)
two hundred thousand	9-1	にじゅうまん　二十万 (n)
two minutes	3-2	にふん　二分 (n)
two o'clock	3-2	にじ　二時 (n)
two pages, page two	4-2	にぺーじ　二ページ (n)
two people	2-1	ふたり　二人 (n)
two sheets	4-2	にまい　二枚 (n)
two thousand	9-1	にせん　二千 (n)
two times	10-1	にど　二度 (n)
two volumes	9-2	にさつ　二冊 (n)
typhoon	10-1	たいふう　台風 (n)

U

English	Location	Japanese
ugly	8-1	みにくい (い adj.)
uh-oh, oops	8-3	おっと (interj.)
uncle or man quite a bit older than you	2-2	おじさん (n)
underwear	6-4	したぎ　下着 (n)、ぱんつパンツ (n)
United States of America	4-1	あめりか　アメリカ (n)
unskilled at	7-3	にがて　苦手 (な adj.)
until	5-3	まで (part.)
(to) use	10-2	つかう/つかいます　使う/使います (使って) (v)
used immediately AFTER a boy's name	1-3	～くん　君
used immediately AFTER a name	1-3	～さん
used immediately AFTER a teacher's, lawyer's, or doctor's name	1-3	せんせい　～先生
usual, normal	6-4	ふつう　普通 (adj./adv.)
usually	7-2	たいてい (adv.)

V

English	Location	Japanese
various, various colors	7-4	いろいろ　色々 (な adj.)
very	3-1	とても (adv.)
video games	7-1	びでおげーむ　ビデオゲーム (n)
voice	6-1	こえ　声 (n)
volleyball club (team)	3-3	ばれーぼーるぶ　バレーボール部 (n)

W

English	Location	Japanese
wake (up)	5-1	おきる/おきます　起きる/起きます (起きて) (v)
(to) wait	6-1	まつ/まちます　待つ/待ちます (待って) (v)
walk	5-4	さんぽ　散歩 (n)
wasabi, Japanese horseradish	1-5	わさび (n)
water	2-4	みず　水 (n)
we, us	1-3	わたしたち　私達 (pron.)
weak	6-1	よわい　弱い (い adj.)
(to) wear (for things above the waist or dresses)	6-4	きる/きます　着る/着ます (v)
(to) wear (items below the waist)	6-4	はく/はきます　履く/履きます (履いて) (v)
(to) wear glasses or sunglasses	6-4	かける/かけます (かけて) (v)
(to) wear something on your head	6-4	かぶる/かぶります　被る/被ります (v)

English	Location	Japanese
(to) do; (to) wear	4-4/6-4	する/します (v)
weather	10-1	てんき　天気 (n)
weather report	10-1	てんきよほう　天気予報 (n)
Wednesday	5-1	すいようび　水曜日 (n)
welcome (usually used at a place of business)	4-3	いらっしゃいませ (exp.)
welcome home	1-5	おかえりなさい　お帰りなさい (exp.)
Welcome!, Nice to see you.	1-4	ようこそ (exp.)
well...	3-5	さあ (interj.)
what	2-1	なん/なに　何 (inter.)
what color	7-4	なにいろ　何色 (inter.)
what day of the month	5-3	なんにち　何日 (inter.)
what day of the week	5-1	なんようび　何曜日 (inter.)
what ethnicity or heritage	4-1	なにけい　何系 (inter.)
what grade/year	3-1	なんねんせい　何年生 (inter.)
what/which kind of	6-2	どんな
what month	5-2	なんがつ　何月 (inter.)
what nationality	4-1	なにじん　何人 (inter.)
what period	3-3	なんじかんめ　何時間目 (inter.)
what time	3-2	なんじ　何時 (inter.)
what year	5-4	なんねん　何年 (inter.)
when?	5-2	いつ (inter.)
where?	2-4	どこ (inter.)
which (one)	1-5	どれ (inter.)
which (thing)	2-3	どの
which/what kind of	6-2	どんな (inter.)
white	7-4	しろ　白 (n)
white-colored	8-2	しろい　白い (い adj.)
who	2-1	だれ (inter.)
wide, spacious	8-3	ひろい　広い (い adj.)
wind	3-5	かぜ　風 (n)
winter	10-1	ふゆ　冬 (n)
wise; bright	8-1	かしこい　賢い (い adj.)
woman, female	6-4	おんな　女 (n)
wonderful	6-5	すばらしい　素晴らしい (い adj.)
wonderful, nice	6-4	すてき　素敵 (な adj.)
woodblock print (modern)	9-1	しんはんが　新版画 (n)
woodblock print (prior to and through the Edo Period)	9-1	はんが　版画 (n)
woodblock print (prior to and through the Edo Period)	9-1	うきよえ　浮世絵 (n)
world history	3-2	せかいし　世界史 (n)
(to) worry	6-3	しんぱい(を)　する/します心配(を) する/します (v)
similar to "wow!"	3-5	わっ! (interj.)
(to) write	1-3	かく/かきます　書く/書きます(書いて) (v)
writing pad, mat	2-4	したじき　下敷き (n)

Y

English	Location	Japanese
Yamamoto (family name)	3-1	やまもと　山本 (n)
yellow	7-4	きいろ　黄色 (n)
yellow-colored	8-2	きいろい　黄色い (い adj.)
yes, here (roll call)	1-4	はい
yesterday	3-2	きのう　昨日 (adv./n)
younger brother (my)	2-1	おとうと　弟 (n)
younger brother (someone else's)	2-2	おとうとさん　弟さん (n)
younger sister (my)	2-1	いもうと　妹 (n)
younger sister (someone else's)	2-2	いもうとさん　妹さん (n)
you're welcome	2-3	どういたしまして (exp.)